My Monster, My Hero

By

S. L. Freeman

My Monster, My Hero

ISBN 978-0-9953617-1-3

Here's proof

AUTHOR'S NOTE

Where indicated, the names and identifying characteristics of all people mentioned in this book have been changed in order to protect their privacy. Although certain dates and locations have also been changed, dialogue has been recreated to my best recollection.

'My Monster, My Hero' is a true story... *my* story.

PROLOGUE

My bedroom is quiet and dark, pitch black except for the fluorescent glow emitted from the alarm clock on Jake's bedside table; 2:15am. I listen to the A/C, softly humming as it fights to cool the air on yet another hot and humid night.

Once again, I'm denied sleep by the evil living inside me. Devoid of mercy or compassion and possessing me for more than half my life, it's a monster… *my* monster, and it is absolutely relentless in its quest to take over my body. Tonight, like so many others, it has again succeeded in delivering its message… pain!

I lie awake and attempt to divert my attention from the searing pain in my feet, hips, and hands; praying the prescription meds will work for a change. I know they won't erase the pain entirely, but just enough to let me close my eyes and escape for a few hours would be a god send. Unfortunately, I've been in this situation countless times before. I know relief will not be coming my way, not unless I do something about it.

There is only one thing stronger than the *monster* living inside me, one thing which can prevent it from plaguing me with another night of suffering and torment. My escape doesn't come in the form of medicine or prayer, no, my salvation lays beside me; peacefully still. There he rests in the deepest sleep; seemingly dead to the world. The sound of his slow, deep breaths are hypnotic, and each time he exhales I'm reminded of the *power* he possesses.

I hold out for as long as I can, trying desperately to fight back against the relentless attack on my own; a futile struggle. I'm all but defeated; I can take no more. If I'm to have any hope of victory tonight I will need the strength, love and passion that only the man beside me can deliver. And so it begins.

I reach over, turn on the bedside lamp then prop myself up on one elbow; hovering unsteadily above my sleeping saviour. I stare at Jake's face, studying his features while patiently waiting for him to wake as a result of me turning on the lamp. The light has no effect though, and he remains fast asleep. Softly, I kiss him on the forehead and then again on his barely parted lips; he doesn't move. I kiss him again, this time lingering a little longer so as to steal the air from his next breath. His eyes flash open and a surprised expression is swiftly replaced with a warm smile, which disappears just as fast once he realises my reason for disturbing him.

"Bad night Baby?"

I nod, fighting to keep my tears at bay. This isn't the first time I've woken my lover from his peaceful slumber to rescue me from my pain induced insomnia.

As he reaches up and gently strokes my cheek with the back of his hand, I see the concern in his eyes; the sympathy.

"Is there anything I can do to help?" Instinctively, he already knows what I need from him.

I run my hand slowly down his naked chest and across his stomach, before pausing at the waistband of his boxers. Keeping my eyes fixed firmly on his, I gradually slide my hand inside his underwear and wrap my fingers around *him.* With each passing second he grows thicker and harder, causing my heart to race as a sensual ache builds deep inside me. The warmth between my thighs is more than welcome, and immediately my *monster* begins to lose his grip.

I roll on top, straddling him with my knees either side of his waist. He holds me firmly by the hips as I lean back and slide his boxers down, just enough to release his erection. I quickly grasp it again. He's so hard that I can feel his pulse beating between my fingers. I waste no time pulling my underwear to one side; the crisp night air feels cool and fresh as it meets my wetness. Leaning forward, I kiss him passionately as I gently guide my husband into me, slowly at first. Nineteen years of passion… still slowly at first; then deeply.

My *monster* fades to a distant memory as I begin to roll my hips, riding my lover. He feels like a powerful stallion between my legs, and as I embrace the welcome feeling of fullness, my entire body is consumed with pain erasing pleasure.

As always, I'm quick to find my first release. I let out an instinctive, yet controlled moan as the muscles deep within my belly contract hard, before gradually relaxing; flooding me with orgasm induced ecstasy. I steady myself and wait for my breath to return before resuming a perfect rhythm of pleasure. It isn't long before the familiar feeling of light headedness and euphoria starts to build again. I grab Jake by the wrists and pin his hands to the mattress. Having total control of such a powerful being pushes me to the brink again. Jake is quick to sense this and drives his pelvis upwards; impaling me until I let go once more. This time I bury my head into the pillow beside him to muffle my screams.

I lie with my head against his neck; panting breathlessly. He puts his mouth to my ear and whispers softly; "Are you ready Baby?"

I nod, pushing myself up with what strength I have left. With my hands on his chest, I slowly begin to rave on top of my man; my *saviour*. I feel his shaft throb inside me, so quicken my pace in response. I dig my fingers into his skin as he squeezes my hips and thrusts into me with precision. We're now breathing as one, moving as one… making love as one.

I feel him throb again and I know he can't hold on much longer; neither can I. My body arches involuntarily and I throw my head back as I feel him surge, firing his warm release inside me. My entire body, my soul, feels as though it's been brought to life, and as I let my final orgasm escape I'm rewarded with a glorious flash of heaven, freedom from the evil inside; a taste of the world without pain.

I collapse on his chest, exhausted and out of breath. Our hot, sweaty bodies moulded together; motionless except for the rise and fall of breathless lungs.

"My pleasure," he smiles; kissing me softly on the forehead.

I close my eyes and cherish his embrace, revelling in the freedom he has provided, and as I lay there clutching my lover, I pray that my *monster* takes a little longer to return this time.

Seconds after experiencing such incomparable pleasure, my thoughts of passion are quickly replaced with a familiar loathing for the searing pain rapidly returning to my body. Again I ask myself, *'When will this stop?'* A rhetorical question; pointless for sure. I know full well that once he sinks those teeth into me, there's no chance of him letting go.

This night, I will eventually find sleep. But as always, it would never have been granted were it not for the physical, and intangible pleasure, passion and love that I share with Jake… my soul mate.

CHAPTER ONE

AT FIRST SIGHT

It was a scorching hot summer's day, a week or so after new year's. We were in the middle of a heat wave, and even though it was only week four of the Christmas holidays, the inevitable boredom of such a long break from high school had already started to take hold.

I was watching television at home on the farm, a three-hundred-acre property which was about four hours' drive from Melbourne; the nearest major city. I lived with my mother and father, Lynn and David, and although I had two older brothers, they'd already moved off the farm to work in a nearby town called Sunbury. I missed Shaun and Dylan, and as the only child still living at home I often found myself feeling quite lonely.

The peace and quiet of the farm, as beautiful and appealing as it is to me now, was drowning me. Fourteen-year-old girls aren't really into chickens, sheep and cows. This, coupled with a feeling of unexplained nausea, had rendered the day a complete write-off.

Usually the piercing tone of the phone ringing would have me bouncing to my feet, eager to answer it, but not today. I sluggishly dragged myself off the couch and picked up the receiver.

"Hello, Sophie speaking."

"Hi Soph. You need to meet me down at the lake, I've got a surprise for you!" beamed Kylie, one of my best friends from school. "My cousin Jake is staying at my place for the weekend and we're going to the lake for a swim. You should come and meet him. I've been telling him all about you."

When I think back to this phone call, as much as a few hours at the lake would've broken the monotony of the day, I distinctly remember not wanting to go. I was lethargic and out of sorts, so I guess at the time I just didn't feel particularly social.

"I would, but I'm feeling a bit off Kylie. I might give it a miss."

"No way! Trust me you should come down, even just to say hi. You don't have to swim, just say a quick hello and give him a chance to meet you."

I paused for a moment, giving my friends suggestion a little more thought, when *something* came over me and urged me to go. I can't really describe it, other than to say it was a weird, internal feeling which persuaded me to make the effort to go and meet this boy.

"Ok, I'll come down. When are you guys going?"

"Awesome! I'm so excited!" replied the matchmaker in a high pitch girly voice; brimming with delight. "We'll be there within the next half hour. Tom's coming as well."

Tom was her older brother.

"Ok, I'll meet you guys down there. See you soon."

"Cool. Bye," said Kylie before hanging up.

I could tell by the sound of her voice that she was smiling, and I've got to say it made me a little nervous. *What have I got myself into?*

Little did I know, going to the lake that summer's afternoon would change my life… or more like *start* it! It was a decision which to this day, feels like it was made for me by a higher power; a guardian angel maybe. Sounds cliché I know, but that's the only way to describe it.

The lake was about a five-minute drive from our house, so on my way to the bathroom, I asked Mum if she would take me. "Mum would you mind driving me to the lake? Kylie's going for a swim with Tom and her cousin." I deliberately omitted the fact her cousin was a boy.

"Sure."

"Great. Thanks Mum," I replied appreciatively.

"When do you want to leave?"

"In about twenty minutes or so? I just need to freshen up." I wondered whether she would question me, as to why I'd bother freshening up just to go for a swim, but she didn't.

Driving to the lake, a song on the radio muffles the sound of tyres on gravel. Subconsciously, I admit to not having very high expectations. I suppose I'm the kind of person who doesn't get her hopes up; it saves a lot of disappointment.

We arrived at the lake and almost immediately I spot Kylie and her older brother. They were about a hundred meters away; standing on the edge of the water. There was no sign of Jake though.

"What time do you want me to pick you up Soph?"

"Would it be ok if you come and get me in a couple of hours?"

Mum looks at her watch. "Make it five-thirty then."

"That'd be good," I agree.

"Have fun, and be careful around the water."

"I will… promise. Thanks for the lift Mum."

I lean across and kiss her on the cheek before climbing out of the car. I didn't tell her I'd been invited down to the lake to meet a boy. Being her only daughter, I figured I could dodge the 'twenty questions' if I kept that information to myself.

As I walked through the gate which granted access to the lake, I looked out over the water and spotted who I assumed was Jake.

"Hey Soph, you made it!" Kylie smiled, as I walked towards her and Tom.

"Hi Sophie," said Tom, who was about three years older than us.

A few months earlier, Kylie mentioned that her brother had a bit of a thing for me, but as nice as Tom was, he just wasn't my type. Not that I knew what my *type* was at fourteen!

"Hey Jake, come and meet Sophie!" Kylie yelled out from the edge of the water.

I looked out towards Jake, who was now swimming to the bank. As he reached the shallows, he stood up and began walking in the waist deep water towards me.

Holy shit!...

I have no doubt there will be times throughout my story where you will question the legitimacy of some of the descriptions and feelings I portray, simply because they seem so far-fetched and unbelievable. I completely understand, and if I hadn't of *lived* through it, I probably wouldn't believe some of the things I'm going to tell you either! Trust me though, every word is as real as it gets.

Oh my god... that body!

I felt my knees weaken as he emerged from the lake; the water streaming from his body. The sun glistened off every water drop beading from his muscles; more of his form becoming visible as he walked towards me. His physique displayed clear evidence that he did some form of training. I'd later discover he regularly practiced Martial Arts, which explained his development. Once I was able to peel my eyes from his stomach and chest, I noticed that his hair; light brown, messy and wet, fell to a height just above his shoulders. I was actually surprised he had long hair, since all the 'country' boys from school had short back and sides. You think long hair on a guy would look feminine, but let me assure you, there was *nothing* feminine about him.

As he closed in to me, I realized I'd been holding my breath the whole time.

Breathe Sophie... breathe! I force myself to take a breath, which ends up more like a faint gasp, as he extends his right hand towards me.

"Hi Sophie. I'm Jake."

I was immediately taken by the way he looked directly into my eyes as he spoke. There was a deep intensity in the way he focused on me which made me feel as though his bright blue eyes weren't simply looking *at* me… but *into* me. It was as if he could see what I was thinking; a prospect which made me blush instantly. As cool as I tried to be, never had I felt so exposed and vulnerable.

"Hi," I said timidly; placing my hand in his. He gripped gently, yet firm enough that I could feel his strength. There was no doubt, this was no ordinary teenager.

It's been more than nineteen years now, but when I reflect on the first time I met Jake, I still feel the same buzz of excitement race through my veins; my entire body consumed by the same warmth and electric-like charge. To this day I've never felt anything like it, anything so special; so magical.

"I'm Kylie's cousin. She's told me a lot about you."

I gaze at him, accidently staring at his face; studying him. If I didn't know what my type was two minutes ago, I sure as hell knew now!

I quickly snap myself out of my stunned state. "I hope she's only told you good things," I reply; a slight rattle in my voice.

His mouth curls into a cheeky closed lip grin. "Mostly good," he smiles.

Although my nausea from earlier in the day had all but vanished, it had now been replaced by a barrage of nerves unlike anything I'd ever experienced. *Get a hold of yourself Sophie*.

You hear people talk about experiencing 'love at first sight' and finding their 'soul mate'. Well with my hand on my heart, I can honestly say on that hot summer's day back in January 1997, that's *exactly* what I found in Jake.

That afternoon it was as though somebody had a remote control to the universe and hit the fast forward button. Time felt like it passed at the speed of light.

I hadn't planned on swimming, but I must confess that after meeting Jake I didn't need much coaxing to get into the water. For the next two hours, the four of us talked, laughed and swam. It was great fun and our time together elapsed in what felt like an instant.

Jake and I joked and flirted with each other so innocently, yet with such purpose. I warmed to his sense of humour immediately and I distinctly remember laughing out loud time and time again. As strong as my reaction to his physical appearance had been, his relaxed and happy personality made an equally powerful impression. Right from the start, he made me laugh… he made me happy.

How I wanted to hold his hand, embrace him, even kiss him. Courage eluded me on that day, but I'm still grateful for the way it played out. Even if I could, I definitely wouldn't have changed a thing. It was one of the sweetest and most unforgettable experiences of my life.

At one point we were sitting on a submerged tree branch, side by side, the bare skin of our thighs touching ever so lightly under the surface of the lake. We could both feel it, the instant attraction and sexual desire pulling us towards each other. I was half expecting steam to rise from the surrounding water; boiling from the intensely sensual energy that flowed between us. Neither Jake nor I wanted to move, savouring every second of contact with one and other. The whole situation felt unreal, as though it'd been staged.

Memories of that afternoon resemble beautiful scenes from a flawlessly crafted love story. It was as incredible as it was unbelievable. My first encounter with Jake had been ridiculously perfect.

5:30pm arrived all too soon. I saw Mum pull up at the gate before sounding the car horn to let me know it was time to go.

"Looks like your ride's here Sophie," Jake says. The tone of his voice making it clearly evident that he's disappointed at the prospect of having to say goodbye.

"I can't believe how fast this afternoon went," I exclaim. "I wish I didn't have to go yet."

He looks deep into my eyes. "Me neither."

I blush for the umpteenth time.

"Well it was really nice to meet you," he smiles warmly, extending his right hand towards me.

I reach out to him and he grasps my hand. This time, instead of shaking it as he did when we were introduced, he holds my hand still and gently squeezes. His unspoken gesture is a clear signal; a signal I feel *everywhere*. It melts me.

"It was nice… nice meeting you too," I fumble; his continued grasp on my hand throwing me into a spin.

"Next time I come out to visit Kylie and Tom, maybe I'll see you again?" he says, looking directly into my eyes as he lets go.

"Yeah that'd be great," I reply enthusiastically, finding the courage to meet his gaze directly.

All the while Kylie and Tom were standing off to the side, more than likely with smirks on their faces. I wouldn't know because I couldn't take my eyes off Jake.

Eventually I turn to them. "Bye Kylie. See you later Tom."

"Bye Soph," waves Tom.

"Thanks for coming down. I hope you had fun," grins Kylie suggestively.

"Of course I did. I always have fun with my best friend," I giggle sarcastically.

"Yeah right," she laughs, well aware of the *real* reason I had such an amazing time. "I'll call you later?"

"Sure thing."

I turn back towards Jake. "Bye," I smile warmly.

"Bye Sophie." He shoots me a wink that almost buckles me at the knees.

How does he do that!

As I walk towards the car a strange feeling rapidly grows inside me. A feeling similar to the one you get when saying goodbye to someone at the airport. I hadn't even got to the car and I already missed him.

What is this?

I can't help myself. Just as I reach the gate I turn to see him one more time.

He waves then yells out to me, "See you soon Sophie!"

I wave back; laughing. As I savour one final look at Jake, I have what can only be describe as a *revelation*; a vivid realisation as to the importance of the feelings and emotions I just experienced. I'm suddenly aware of the significance this amazing new person *will* have on the rest of my life. I'm certain of it.

I open the door and get in the car. After surveying the unfamiliar teenage boy in the distance, Mum looks at me with a raised eyebrow.

I close the door and look back towards Jake. “I’m going to marry him,” I declare; the exact words. I’ve never forgotten them and neither has Mum.

“Ok then. If you say so.” she says; unconvinced. “So what’s his name then?”

“Jake… his name is Jake,” I repeat, just so I can hear it again.

She starts the engine.

“And I *am* going to marry him.” I add, whispering under my breath.

As the car pulls away, I’m totally convinced… the direction of my life just changed forever.

CHAPTER TWO

PICK UP THE PHONE

For the rest of the summer holidays, *all* I could think about was Jake. I swear, not a minute went by without his name floating through my thoughts; as if those four letters had been burnt into my mind. I'd often catch myself daydreaming about him, visualising every detail of his face and how he'd look deep into my eyes when we spoke; the way his gaze would cause me to blush instantly. If not his face, then I'd be fantasising about his body, and what it would feel like to run my hands over every sculptured muscle.

What has he done to me? I'd only just met this boy and I felt infected by him. Every night was a struggle to sleep, and when I would eventually drift off, I found myself dreaming of our first encounter. They were so vivid, I'd be woken by the sensation of butterflies in my belly, similar to the ones I felt when I first met him. Then there were the *other* dreams, the ones which I'd wake from to find myself hot and flustered, breathing heavily and aching in my most intimate place. This happened time and time again, more nights than I could count. For a girl who'd never experienced such powerful and thought consuming feelings about another person, I was utterly convinced I'd met someone special.

Now that I think back on those nights, and decipher my thoughts, dreams and *feelings*, the explanation is crystal clear… I wanted him.

The summer holidays ended and the 1997 school year began. I was now fifteen, after having a birthday the week prior to the start of term.

On the first day back I had but one goal, to quiz Kylie on everything she knew about her cousin. I would've done this sooner but I didn't want to come across too eager to learn more about him. I guess I knew she would've been all too happy to give me some friendly banter about having a crush on Jake, so I waited.

I walked through the gates of Crystal Creek Secondary College, a high school of about six hundred pupils, most of whom were from farms similar to mine. It was a friendly school with a laid back country town atmosphere. I wasn't a huge fan though, mainly because everyone knew too much about each other, which is probably why I never wanted to date anyone from school; we were all just too close.

On reflection, the fact that Jake was from Sunbury, a large town about forty minutes' drive from Crystal Creek, made him even more appealing. He was someone new; unknown to me and my friends.

At my first available opportunity, I sat down with Kylie and bombarded her with questions about the boy who'd filled my thoughts and dreams for the past few weeks. I wasn't surprised to learn he was the eldest of four, with three younger sisters. It explained why he felt so comfortable talking to me when we first met. In the short time I spent with Jake, I sensed he had a very kind and gentle nature, one he didn't feel the need to cover with the usual teenage boy ego and bravado. I'm sure this was attributed to his role as an older brother to three sisters. I'd talked with boys at school plenty of times before, but Jake's personality and the way he listened and spoke to me, set him apart from any boy I'd ever met before. He was different; sensitive.

Kylie described his parents and sisters to me. She also gave me a few other details about where he went to school and his interest in Karate, a traditional form of Martial Arts. There was however one detail which had me completely intrigued, even excited. Jake had spent four years as a competitive ballroom dancer.

"You're kidding me… a dancer?"

"No, I'm dead serious Soph. He used to dance with his sister, Alice. They competed in Melbourne all the time and were really into it. I'm pretty sure they won quite a few competitions too because I've seen their trophies and medals."

Kylie was well aware that my absolute favourite movie of all time was *'Dirty Dancing'*, I must have seen it at least twenty times, and she knew telling me that Jake was a competitive ballroom dancer would only throw fuel on the fire.

I couldn't believe it. I'd never met a boy who could dance before, and given that Sara, one of my other friends, had invited me as a guest to the Debutante Ball in a few weeks' time, my mind began to race.

Kylie would be making her debut as well. Her and Sara were both a year older than me, so I planned on making mine after turning sixteen the following year. Little did I know, in twelve months' time, doing my deb would be the *last* thing on my mind.

"Tell me he's coming to the deb!" I demanded excitedly.

"Why? Do you want me to ask him?" Kylie replied with a cheeky smirk on her face; knowing the answer already.

"Would you invite him for me?" I cringed at the eagerness in my voice.

My excitement caused Kylie to laugh out loud. "You like him, don't you?"

"Well he was really nice the other day at the lake. I'd like to get to know him a little better… that's all," I said calmly, trying to remain cool and not give away the fact I'd thought of nothing but Jake for weeks.

"Ok, I'll give him a buzz and see if he wants to come to the deb. Just for *you*," she emphasised; a huge grin stretching from ear to ear. "And I'll give you his number too, so you can call him yourself since you love him *soooo* much," she teased unashamedly.

"Shut up Kylie!" I snapped defensively. "I will take his number though." I laughed.

Kylie giggled; finding great amusement in my inability to cover up the obvious.

"I knew you'd like Jake… and I'm pretty sure he liked you too."

"You think so?" A warm feeling flooded through me at the possibility that her observations might be true.

God I hope he likes me!

"Yeah. I know him pretty well Soph and I'm fairly certain he's into you. You really should give him a call, see where it goes."

"I will. Thanks for his number Kylie."

"Well that's what friends are for," she smiled as she scribbled down Jake's number.

I immediately began to feel nervous at the thought of calling Jake and hearing his voice again. *What would I say? What would we talk about? Does he even like me?* So many thoughts raced through my mind. I'd already conjured visions of us dancing together at the Debutante Ball, just like a scene from my favourite movie. Feelings began to stir deep within me, feelings which always seemed to appear whenever I would think of Jake. My mind was in overdrive and it wasn't slowing down.

As Kylie handed me the number, I felt a shiver run through me. As much as I was looking forward to talking with him, I was already scared senseless at the prospect of picking up the phone and dialling his number.

I decided to wait until Kylie had asked him to her deb before ringing him. That way I would at least have a plausible reason for calling, as well as something to talk about. Phoning just to hear the sound of his voice, as accurate as that was, probably would've made me appear a touch on the creepy side.

So a few days passed when Kylie finally got back to me with Jake's answer. He had accepted her invitation to the Ball. I was so excited and couldn't wait to get home from school to call him. Though as eager as I was to talk to Jake again, I was shitting myself.

I took the phone into my room, sat on my bed and dialled his number. But before the phone could connect, I hung up. I re-dialled the number, then hung up again. I couldn't tell you exactly how many times I did this, but it must have been close to double figures.

"Just do it Sophie. It's only a boy!" I said to myself, frustrated at my lack of courage.

I dialled the number again; it started to ring.

"Shit! Shit! Shit!" I said under my breath. The anticipation of somebody answering was almost unbearable.

Then, just as I was about to hang up *again*, a young girl's voice answered. "Hello." It must have been one of Jake's sisters.

"Hi. I was just… I was wondering… um… if I could speak to Jake," I stammered, completely forgetting to give my name.

"Jake! There's a girl on the phone!" the young girl yelled, holding the phone away from her mouth. "She wants to talk to you!"

I heard the phone being placed down on what sounded like a bench top. My already racing heart, thumped even faster and my mouth started to dry up. I was absolutely terrified. *There's no backing out now Soph!*

I heard Jake clear his throat, then pick up the phone.

"Hello, this is Jake."

My mouth was so dry. I felt like I'd just eaten a handful of sand, and when I tried to answer nothing came out.

"Hello?" he repeated, after a brief but awkward silence.

I swallowed and eventually found my voice.

"Hi Jake, it's Sophie; Kylie's friend. We met at the lake a few weeks ago," my words spilling out at a nervously fast pace.

"Hi Sophie. Kylie told me she gave you my number. I'm glad you called." He must have sensed I was nervous because he took control of the conversation immediately. "So, I'm going to Kylie's Deb Ball in a few weeks. Tell me you're going too?"

"Yeah… I'm going," is all I can get out; my mouth still not functioning properly.

"Well it should be a lot of fun. I'm really looking forward to seeing you again," he replied confidently. "I had a great time with you at the lake in the holiday's."

I was again surprised by how easily he spoke to me, and how willingly he said what he felt.

"Me too," the brevity of my response making me cringe.

"Do you like to dance?"

"Actually I do. Dirty Dancing is my favourite movie," I reply, impressed I've managed to string together more than two words in one sentence, then instantly mortified that I just referred to *dirty* dancing.

"Really! Well if that's the case, then I'd better make sure I ask you for a dance at some stage," he chuckled.

I giggled nervously. *Holy crap!* I didn't know what to say. He'd reduced me to a mute in one swift sentence and I could feel the blushing warmth flood into my cheeks. I was speechless and now starting to feel like an idiot. I couldn't think let alone talk. I had to end this phone call fast, before I embarrassed myself even further.

"You there Sophie?"

"Yeah." Another one-word response. I just couldn't get anything else out.

There was no doubt Jake could tell I'd fallen to bits after his suggestion of dancing together. Rather than prolonging the awkwardness, he gave me an out. "Well I'll let you go Sophie. I look forward to seeing you at the Ball; and I'm serious about that dance too."

"Ok sure," I muttered nervously.

"Alright then, I'll see you in a few weeks. Thanks for calling and I'll talk to you soon."

"Ok. Bye Jake."

"Bye Sophie," he said cheerfully before hanging up.

I looked down at the phone in my hand. "Fuck!" I hissed loudly.

What an absolute disaster. Way to go Sophie. My initial thoughts on the call was that it resembled something similar to a slow motion train crash; a complete wreck. I guess nerves just got the better of me.

There's no doubt it was awkward but deep down I was still glad I called him that afternoon, and I was equally appreciative of Jake for rescuing me from a conversation of two word sentences. Little did I know, it wouldn't be the last time he would *rescue* me.

If I was having trouble getting him out of my mind after our meeting at the lake, then there was absolutely no chance now! Hearing his voice again completely melted me, confirming what I'd felt weeks earlier; and listening to his suggestions about dancing together had already caused me to invoke images of him and I, wrapped firmly in each other's arms on a crowded dance floor.

Having the exact date of our next meeting was as exciting as it was torturous. The countdown had now begun, and as always, when you're really looking forward to something, time has a tendency to drag.

The Crystal Creek Debutante Ball couldn't arrive fast enough. It was going to be a long four weeks but as it turned out, would definitely be worth the wait.

CHAPTER THREE

WOULD YOU LIKE TO DANCE?

The Debutante Ball was being held at the Crystal Creek Town Hall. I was so nervous I couldn't see straight, so I thought I'd use the twenty-minute journey to get myself together. It was a scenic drive and I tried to calm myself by looking at the farmhouses scattered across the countryside, but it was having little to no effect on my shattered nerves. To be honest, I'd been anxious for the last week and the realisation I was going to see Jake in a matter of minutes was almost too much for me.

"You're awfully quiet, are you ok?"

"Yeah Mum, I'm fine. I just hope I look alright," I replied, subtly searching for reassurance that I'd chosen the right outfit.

"Awe Sophie, you look beautiful. You always do love."

"Thanks," I smiled appreciatively, before returning my gaze to the passing scenery.

I had spent the whole afternoon second guessing the outfit I'd chosen. I was a bit of a 'Tomboy' and wasn't keen on dresses, but I knew if Jake asked me to dance, which I prayed he did, then a dress would be the best choice. So I decided on a long flowing black skirt, and a fitted satin shirt in dark purple. I wore my hair out so it fell loosely over my shoulders and down my back, it was dark brown and quite wavy. I had a touch of make-up on, as well as some soft perfume.

As much as I tried to relax and convince myself that I was confident about seeing Jake again, for the life of me I couldn't get control of the feeling in my stomach. There must have been over a thousand butterflies fluttering wildly around in my belly.

It was close to 6:30pm when the car pulled up outside the hall. There weren't many people out the front as most of the guests were inside, ready for the start of the Ball.

"Here we are."

"Thanks for the lift Mum." I leaned over and kissed her on the cheek.

"I'll come back about eleven to pick you up. I'll be parked here." She cuddled me with a firm 'look-after-yourself' embrace. "You look beautiful Soph. I'm sure Jake will be impressed!" she grinned.

I hadn't mentioned it to her, but she'd obviously put two and two together and figured out that the boy I'd met in the holidays would be here.

"Mum!" I exclaimed; blushing.

"He's here isn't he?" she probed, doing a very poor job at keeping a straight face.

"I'm not sure, I think Kylie might have invited him," I replied casually, attempting to play it down.

"Well have a great time… but don't leave the hall," she cautioned protectively.

"I won't." I climbed out of the car. "See you at eleven," I said before closing the door.

I waved goodbye then walked towards the hall as Mum drove away. As I opened the glass door to the foyer, the sounds of guests talking and laughing from inside the main auditorium filled the air. There were a few people in the foyer greeting each other and admiring dresses and outfits. I said a quick 'hello' to some friends from school before making my way over to the seating plan; pinned on a notice board in the centre of the foyer.

I wasn't on Kylie's table as she had a heap of family members coming to see her, Jake included. I scanned the seating plan for Sara's table and found my name. I also had a quick look to see where Kylie's table was, so I knew exactly where Jake would be. As soon as I saw his name on the seating plan I felt my whole body tremble with an overwhelming combination of excitement, anticipation and fear.

Oh my god he's really here!

He would be directly across the dance floor from me.

"Ladies and gentleman please take your seats," commanded a voice over the microphone. I hurried into the main auditorium towards my table. No sign of Jake yet.

"Hi Sophie, you're sitting next to me," said Rebecca in a welcoming voice. She was Sara's little sister, and even though she was a few years younger than me, we were good friends.

"Hi Bec, you look beautiful," I replied. She was wearing a pale pink dress and had her hair tied in a half up-half down style.

"Thanks. You look really pretty too Sophie."

"Awe, thanks Bec," I smiled fondly, her compliment giving my confidence a small yet much needed lift.

The auditorium was still buzzing with conversation as guests busily moved around the room searching for their seats. I sat down and took a few deep breaths to calm my nerves. I hadn't seen Jake yet, and I needed a second to steady myself before looking around the room to find him.

Keep calm Soph. Just take a look around... casually! I was desperate not to look too obvious.

Whilst everyone at my table chatted away, I slowly turned towards the direction of Kylie's table, where I knew Jake would be seated. As I slowly scanned the room of smiling and excited faces, the growing beat of my heart began to drown out every other sound. I knew any second I would see him and I held my breath in anticipation.

I don't know how long he'd been looking at me, but when I finally found Jake amongst the crowd, he was staring *directly* at me. The thumping in my chest disappeared, as if his eyes on me caused my heart to stop beating altogether! The noise of the crowd completely vanished and time stood still. I kept his gaze for what felt like an eternity. I didn't turn away; I couldn't if I wanted too. I'd waited so long to see him again that I was completely awestruck… frozen. The cute smile on his lips coupled with the way he looked into my eyes was mesmerising. Every feeling I'd been missing since saying goodbye to him at the lake filled my body, like an ocean wave crashing onto the sand. I was breathing deeply and the hairs on my arms stood on end, no doubt courtesy of the pure shot of adrenaline that was now running through my veins.

So I'm guessing you may be thinking I'm slightly over exaggerating. How can a girl who's only fifteen years old have such powerful feelings and emotions running through her, with just a single look from a boy she's only met once! The way he gazed at me, so intense and unwavering, solidified *every* feeling from our first meeting; confirming the seriousness of my initial impressions. Believe me when I tell you, there *is* such a thing as love at first sight!

It was over nineteen years ago now, but that moment when our eyes met at the Ball, it changed not only my heart but my entire life… forever. It sounds dramatic, but as you continue to read my story, you will learn and appreciate that Jake was not your ordinary boy. The way I felt then is the same as I do now. He was put on this Earth for me, and I for him.

Jake lifted his hand and waved casually. "Hi Sophie," he mouthed silently from across the room.

I returned the greeting and gesture, "Hi Jake." I so desperately wanted to hear his voice.

I was so relieved he was actually here, but that relief rapidly morphed into a concoction of excitement and trepidation, once I realised the dance I promised him was fast approaching.

"Attention ladies and gentleman!" The MC's voice booming through the sound system snapped me back to reality.

Jake winked at me and I smiled back, before diverting our attention to the main stage.

"I would like to begin by thanking you all for coming to the 1997 Crystal Creek Debutante Ball. Everyone looks fantastic and I'm sure you're all eager to see the girls making their debut tonight. I've just been back stage and I can assure you they all look amazing. Their partners haven't scrubbed up too bad either," he joked. "There are sixteen girls to be presented with their partners, and we will begin shortly. Just a few housekeeping issues before we get started." The MC went on to list a number of rules regarding underage drinking, smoking areas and the like.

I took the opportunity to sneak another glance at Jake. He was looking at the MC and seemed to be listening intently. I was thankful because it gave me a quick opportunity to covertly study him.

He looked so different from when I seen him emerge from the lake. His hair was now neatly tied back in a tight pony tail; shiny under the lights of the auditorium. He wore a crisp white shirt, unbuttoned at the top with the sleeves neatly rolled up to his forearms, a black satin vest and a silver watch. He looked sharp and fresh; polished.

I may have lingered a little too long because he turned suddenly and caught me staring at him. *Busted Sophie, nice one!*

I wasn't fast enough to turn away without him noticing, so I flashed him an embarrassed grin instead. He smiled back.

Some months later, I asked Jake if he knew I was looking at him while the MC was talking. He didn't directly confirm or deny it but I could tell by the way he grinned, he knew. *Cheeky, right from the start.*

The official proceedings began. The debutante's and their partners were called out one couple at a time. Each excited pair would appear from behind the back curtain, arm in arm, then walk to the front of the stage as the crowd applauded and cheered loudly. A professional photographer would snap a few photos, then they would exit the stage via some stairs before slowly walking a lap of the dance floor; parading for the guests. They would then take up their position in front of the main stage, beside the other couples who had already been presented. It was very well rehearsed and was quite beautiful to watch.

Everyone looked so happy and proud. The girls were dressed in big white gowns made of satin and tulle, decorated with sequins and sparkling diamanté stones. The boys wore formal black suits with red vests and matching bow ties. I knew most of the debutantes and their partners from school, and was surprised by how well they all scrubbed up. I was amazed by how grown up Kylie and Sara looked in their gowns; make-up and hair done so elegantly. They looked so beautiful and happy, and as delighted as I was for both of them, I couldn't help but wish I was up their making my debut as well... Jake by my side of course.

After the last couple walked their lap of honour, the MC announced the debutante's would now be led by their partners in two traditional dances; the 'Evening Three Step' and the 'Waltz'.

When the music started and the couples began to dance, I couldn't help but look across the room towards Jake. He watched intently as they danced around the floor, and I could tell by the smile on his face, he was obviously enjoying the display.

I was mesmerised by him; watching his every move and expression intently. *How could he make sipping a drink look so hot!*

He glanced over at me and smiled; catching me by surprise... *again*!

Discretely he pointed at me and mouthed a single word; '*You*'. Then he pointed at himself; '*Me'*. To finish his message, he pointed towards the dancing couples and nodded his head slowly, before firing me a cheeky grin.

Oh my god! My heart raced and a hot flush washed over me, kind of like the one you get just before you faint. I was definitely relieved to be sitting down.

When the dancing finished, all the couples lined up in front of the stage a final time so the audience could give them one last round of applause. Everyone rose to their feet; whistling and cheering.

I was well aware I'd been busted twice already, but I couldn't help myself; stealing another glance at Jake. He too was standing, which gave me my first full view of him; head to toe. His shoes were polished, and he wore tailored black pants which matched his shirt and vest perfectly. My eyes widened at the sight. *Damn! He looks so good!*

Now I don't mean to sound unappreciative, because it was a lovely night, but the next hour and a half felt like a day and a half! All the couples took their seats with their friends and families then we worked our way through a three course meal.

I didn't look at Jake much during dinner as the table was full of conversation and laughter. I was having fun and a good time for sure, but I couldn't wait for it to end, only because I felt like the night was rapidly disappearing and I hadn't even got to *talk* to him yet. I was getting anxious and must have checked the clock above the stage at least twenty times.

After dessert, the MC led the room in a number of toasts to the debutant's, their partners and the special guests. As I raised my glass, I wondered how much longer I would have to wait. Finally, he made an announcement that was literally music to my ears.

"Ladies and gentleman, that concludes tonight's formalities. Congratulations to all our young couples, and I would personally like to thank all the family and friends for your attendance tonight. As you finish dessert please feel free to make your way to the dance floor. I trust you have had a fantastic night and I hope you enjoy the rest of your evening. Thank you."

Everybody clapped and there were a few whistles and cheers. As the room filled with music prompting people to gather on the dance floor, I was bursting with expectation. *Finally!* The moment I'd waited for had arrived.

My eyes darted to find Jake amongst the crowd of people who were making their way to the middle of the room. Within seconds, the floor was alive with people dancing to the beat of the music. I couldn't see him at first, as the crowded dance floor made it hard to find him. Then I spotted Jake; my eyes locking onto him like a hawk zeroing in on a field mouse. He was already dancing with Kylie's mum, his aunty Lynda. They were smiling and laughing, and I watched him intently.

Wow! He could dance, and he made it look easy! He moved effortlessly, leading Lynda with control and grace. She was laughing and having a great time, and Jake looked like he was in his element; so confident and happy.

I watched them for a few minutes while I danced in a small group with some friends from school. Then the unthinkable happened... Brooke!

She was a year above me at school, tall, attractive, and already had a reputation after dating a few of the guys at Crystal Creek Secondary College. She was nice, but *really* liked the boys, and they seemed to *like* her too! That worried me.

She walked up to Jake and Lynda, then casually leaned in and said something to them. They stopped dancing, then Kylie's mum smiled and let go of Jake. Brooke grabbed hold of him immediately.

Fuck! Fuck! Fuck! I screamed loudly in my head. *He's mine!* My heart sank as the worst case scenario started to play out in my mind… Brooke stealing Jake from me!

I continued to dance with my friends, doing the best I could to look like I was still having fun, but through the crowd I watched their every move. It's a wonder my death stare didn't burn a hole straight through her head.

Jake was a gentleman, so politely he danced with her. It looked like both of them were having fun. Brooke was smiling and gazing back at him; *directly* at him. There was no mistaking her intentions; her flirtatious expression was like an open invite!

This is bad! I was absolutely seething and couldn't help but feel like I'd missed out. I felt defeated, and as the music faded out at the end of the song, Brooke wrapped her arms around Jake. There was no question she planned on keeping a firm hold of him until the next song started, so as to continue the fun they were both having.

I felt physically ill at the thought of missing my chance; my stomach twisting itself into a knot. Then I noticed Jake lean forward and whisper something in her ear. He smiled at Brooke sincerely and she smiled back. It didn't look good, but just when I thought it was all over, I saw her nod understandingly as a look of disappointment appeared on her face. She let him go, and instantly my spirits lifted. Jake turned from her and began scanning the room, searching for someone… for *me*.

The next song started. I can't remember what it was; I didn't care. Aside from gently swaying to the music, I stood relatively still so as to make it easy for him to find me. Seconds later, our eyes met and he began walking towards me. I gasped sharply and felt every muscle in my body tighten, making it almost impossible to move, let alone keep in time with the song!

As Jake made his way through the crowd, edging closer to me with each step, I felt my breath quicken. My mouth was dry, my hands were trembling and my knees were getting weaker by the second. Finally, after weeks of waiting anxiously to see him again, he was standing right in front of me.

"Hello stranger," he smiled broadly as he extended his hand towards me.

"Hi Jake," I blushed, placing my hand in his.

As he wrapped his fingers around mine and shook my hand gently, the electricity I'd felt at the lake returned instantly, only this time it was like a bolt of lightning straight through me! Honestly, I'd never felt like this before; I was absolutely buzzing.

He leaned in a little closer so I could hear his voice over the sound of the music. "You look amazing Sophie. I've been waiting all night to talk to you."

He stood close and looked directly into my eyes; still holding my hand. His scent was amazing, like nothing I'd ever smelt before; so fresh and masculine. This boy was no boy at all… he was a *man*!

"Me too. I was worried the night was nearly over," I replied, looking away shyly. His piercing blue eyes were making me feel flushed, so much so I could feel the warmth flooding my cheeks. I turned back to see him smiling with amusement. *God his lips look good.*

He let go of my hand. "So… about that dance then?" he hinted with an accompanying grin. "But only if you want to?" he added sincerely, giving me the opportunity to back out.

"I'm not very good."

"I promise I'll look after you; nothing fancy," he said reassuringly.

"Ok."

I'd dreamt about this moment, but as much as I wanted to dance with Jake, now that I was about to I was literally a ball of nerves.

He clasped my right hand with his left and lifted our arms out to the side. "Now put your other hand on my shoulder," he instructed, as his right hand found its way to my waist.

My insides clenched tightly as he grasped me softly, just above my hip. As directed, I put my left hand on his shoulder and he gently pulled me closer to him. We were now in a traditional, all be it relaxed ballroom dancing hold.

I still don't know what song was playing, but it must have been perfect because we started moving and were effortlessly staying with the beat of the music. Considering I'd never danced like this before, I think I was actually doing alright. Every so often he would let go of my hip and spin me away from him, before spinning me back to our original hold. Each time he did, my skirt would flair out as I spun, like a breeze had blown through the room. Not only did it remind me that I'd chosen the right outfit for the Ball but it made me feel so special; beautiful. I also knew Jake appreciated the occasional glimpse of bare skin as my skirt gently lifted, revealing my legs as I spun.

It was everything I could've imagined. As the song played and we danced together, I couldn't help but feel like I was in a scene from my favourite movie. As our bodies moved in synchronisation, I found myself falling further for him.

Dancing with Jake at the Ball that night was one of the most beautiful experiences of my life, and I will never forget how he made me feel. It was as though there wasn't another person in the room, or on the planet for that matter. He didn't take his eyes off me, not once, and the smile never left his face. All my feelings of anxiety and shyness had completely vanished. I found myself looking into his eyes, unable to hide the emotions that were bursting from my heart. I was in love with Jake, no doubt, but I still couldn't keep up with just how fast and deep I was falling for him. It was out of control; crazy, but I guess that's why people say their 'madly' in love, because there really isn't any other rational explanation for it. It's like the power of love completely takes over, and all you can do is give in!

We must have danced to five or six songs in a row, and as time passed I grew a little more confident in the way I moved. I revelled in the feeling of his hand on my hip, and I rocked and swayed them side to side in appreciative response. We were both having a great time. It was ridiculously perfect.

"Did you want to have a break Sophie? I'll get you a drink," he offered between songs.

"Sure, that'd be great. I'm pretty thirsty actually."

Jake held my hand and we walked over to the bar area.

"I'll just have a water please," I said as he turned to me; guessing the answer to his next question.

"So you're a mind reader then!" he joked before turning his attention to the barman.

If only! I would've given anything to know what he was thinking. The thought making me smile to myself.

"What can I get you?" asked the barman.

"Two waters thanks," replied Jake politely.

"Sure thing."

"So are you having fun Sophie?"

"You can call me Soph, and yes I'm having a great time," I smiled affectionately.

"Good. Me too," he grinned, squeezing my hand.

"You're such a good dancer!" My voice was brimming with excitement; the thrill of dancing still fresh in my system.

"Thanks *Soph*," he smiled, emphasising my shortened name. "My younger sister, Alice, and I used to have lessons and partner each other in competitions. It's a lot of fun isn't it?"

"Yeah I love it. My favourite movie's actually Dirty Dancing." Instantly I remembered that I'd already told him on the phone.

"Oh yeah, I love that movie too. I must have seen it at least ten times!"

"Seriously?" I questioned; slightly surprised.

"Yeah seriously! It's one of Mum's favourites as well, so every time she put the video on I ended up watching it."

I couldn't believe it. No fifteen-year-old boy I knew would've even admitted to watching *'Dirty Dancing'*, let alone confess to loving it! I suppose I didn't know any other boys who did ballroom dancing as a sport either! Jake was so different to any guy I'd ever met. He was clearly soft and quite gentle on the inside, a stark contrast to his appearance. His tall, well-built frame which was developed beyond his years, and the way he held himself screamed strength and masculinity. He gave off the most unique blend of energies, one of sincere tenderness; the other, an unmistakable feeling of security and protection. Everything about him swept me away.

While we had our drinks, I pointed out some of my friends from school and we chatted about the evening so far. I felt so comfortable with him and the conversation flowed effortlessly. Thankfully my two word sentences, which were so embarrassing when I called him weeks ago, were gone. We talked for about ten minutes without an awkward silence in sight. I felt as though I'd redeemed myself from my previous efforts over the phone, and was relieved that finding things to chat about was easy. The chemistry between us was undeniable, and I knew he could feel it too.

He finished his drink and put the glass on the bar. "Would you like to have another dance?"

"Yeah definitely!" I beamed excitedly, in a tone way too eager for my liking.

He led me by the hand through the chairs and tables. As soon as we were back on the dance floor we picked up where we left off, only this time there was a very different vibe to the way we moved.

The traditional ballroom dancing hold was gone. Jake had both hands on my hips and I rested mine on his arms. Now we were moving much slower and with an undeniable purpose. His hands on my hips felt amazing, and every so often he would give a gentle squeeze. Each time, I would grip his arms and close my eyes momentarily; letting him know I liked it. The energy between us was building by the second. It was sensual, magical, and totally unstoppable!

It wasn't long before I was overcome with a strong and relatively new feeling which began to invade my body. I think my overcharged adolescent hormones combined with the excitement and fun of dancing with him, had started to react with each other. I was now trying to control a potent internal force which wasn't subsiding any time soon. As my focus darted between his eyes and lips, I realised what I needed to extinguish this fire inside me, and I needed to act now… before time ran out.

As much as I didn't want it to, this night *was* going to end. It was inevitable, and before Jake left to go back to Sunbury, I was desperate to make sure he knew how I felt. Words simply weren't going to cut it, I needed to *show* him. There was only one thing to do but the question was, did I have the courage to do it.

CHAPTER FOUR

FRESH AIR

As I write these words I still have absolutely no idea where I found such bravery. Maybe cupid shot his arrow directly into the part of my brain which controls impulse, or perhaps I had it in me all along; I just needed someone like Jake to bring it out.

I gazed into his eyes as we danced, utterly captivated, and before I had a chance to filter what I was saying, the words were rolling off the tip of my tongue. "Do you want to go outside for some air?"

Oh my god Sophie! Did you honestly just say that! I was shocked by my own audacity. I couldn't believe I actually asked him to come outside with me; I still can't.

Slightly embarrassed, I blushed and began to worry that maybe I was too forward. My concern didn't last long though because, judging by the cheeky smile Jake returned, he was amused by my boldness.

"Yeah, that sounds good. It's getting a bit stuffy in here isn't it?" he grinned, tactfully coming up with an excuse to go outside.

"It is a bit," I agreed; playing along.

"Well lead the way Soph."

I smiled suggestively then turned and proceeded to make my way towards the foyer. As much as I wanted to I didn't hold Jake's hand as I led him through the crowd, so as not to draw any attention to us. I knew he was close behind me though. My heart raced with expectation and the overwhelming feeling of being followed outside... by Jake.

Just as I entered the foyer, a voice shouted, "Hey Soph! Where do you two think you're going?"

I didn't have to look to see who it was; I knew that voice.

I turned around to see Kylie standing there; eyebrows raised and an assuming grin on her face. She was with her debutante partner, Ben, who was also smiling.

"Hey guys. Having fun? You look absolutely amazing Kylie," I said, in a desperate bid to divert her attention away from the obvious.

"Yeah you certainly do," added Jake.

"We're not having as much fun as you two!" she teased. "Going outside to *cool off* are we?"

I glared at her. I know there was no malice in what she was saying, we were best friends after all, but that didn't stop her from enjoying my embarrassment.

"Yeah it was getting warm on the dance floor, so I thought we'd go outside for some fresh air," I replied quickly, trying my best to make it sound innocent but failing miserably.

"You two look like you're getting along well," she smirked, once again provoking us with a condescending tone.

"Yeah Soph's quite the dancer. We're having a great time actually. Thank you for asking," said Jake; equally condescending. I appreciated him rescuing me from Kylie's harmless banter.

"Well enjoy your *fresh air*," she emphasised, obviously doubting our motive for going outside. "Don't get lost out there will you!" She was relentless.

"We won't. Oh by the way, sorry for interrupting. It looked like you were just about to make your move Kylie," I grinned, giving her a taste of her own medicine before turning sharply and continuing towards the door.

Jake laughed. "Bye guys."

"Have fun!" Kylie called out as we neared the foyer door, stealing her last opportunity to joke around. She was enjoying it, and truth be told so was I. We often paid each other out, it was just the type of friendship we had.

I opened the door and instantly felt invigorated as the cool night air hit the warmth of my face. I held the door for Jake; greedily taking another whiff of his intoxicating scent as he walked past me.

He smelt so good that I had to consciously refrain from biting my bottom lip in response to his delicious aroma.

"Why thank you," he smiled, holding his hand out to me. I grasped it immediately.

As we walked outside I could hear Kylie and Ben chuckling together. I couldn't help but smile.

About thirty meters from the entrance to the hall was a small stone wall. It functioned as a boundary to the front garden, stood about two feet high and was dimly lit by an overhead street light.

"Over there looks like a good place to sit?" Jake suggested.

For the first time I could hear a faint hint of nerves in his voice.

"Sure." I replied, deliberately keeping my response as short as possible. It was my best chance at keeping my own nerves under wraps.

The feelings which ran through my body while I danced with Jake were all still there, but now a good dose of nervous anticipation had been added to the mix. Not to mention a touch of guilt for disobeying my mother's orders to not leave the hall. *Sorry Mum.* As anxious and excited as I was, I felt completely safe with Jake; protected. My mind was in a spin from such a paradox of emotions.

The sound coming from the hall softened as we walked further from the entrance. He led me by the hand over to the wall and we sat down, side by side. I couldn't believe we were finally alone together. My heart was pounding so loud I thought Jake would be able to hear it.

"You're a lot of fun Soph."

"Thanks, you too."

He squeezed my hand a little tighter. "I'm *really* glad I met you at the lake that day." I could hear the sincerity in his voice and see it in his eyes; the streetlight dimly illuminating his face.

Oh my god... he wants me too! I could feel it.

"Thanks for dancing with me tonight, I absolutely loved it. I've never danced with someone like that before. It's such good fun," I spoke fast; the nervousness in my voice clearly amplified.

Jake reached his other hand out and I took it. We were now sitting close, facing each other and holding hands firmly. I could sense he wanted to kiss me, but was hesitating.

"You're not too cold are you?" he asked, causing a momentary diversion from the inevitable. Understandably, he was clearly proceeding with caution.

"No I'm just right. *Perfect* actually," I hinted, my tone smooth and inviting; an intentional green light.

Then, for the first time that night, there was silence.

We sat there, eyes locked, neither of us saying a word. This was no ordinary silence between teenagers; there was no awkwardness or searching for something to say. It was a beautiful peacefulness, filled with craving and desire. As we savoured the moment, I wasn't sure if it was Jake's heart or mine that I could hear thumping rapidly.

He took a deep breath. "Sophie?"

"Yes," I replied softly.

He hesitated, before speaking tentatively. "Can I… can I kiss you?"

I smiled and gave permission with a subtle nod.

He gradually leaned in closer. I closed my eyes, and just as I inhaled he kissed me ever so lightly on the lips; lingering for a few seconds before pulling back slowly. I exhaled blissfully before opening my eyes.

"Are you ok with this?"

"Definitely," I smiled, immediately closing my eyes; inviting him to continue.

For the second time I felt Jakes warm lips on mine. This time he kissed me a little longer and with more pressure; our mouths still closed. I started to feel a tightening of muscles, the ones *deep* down in my belly. I was also graced with a deliciously warm sensation that rushed around my body.

He pulled back again and I opened my eyes.

"Still ok?" he smiled.

I nodded, returned his appreciative grin and closed my eyes again.

More Jake. Keep going.

I felt him let go of one of my hands before grasping me behind the neck, under my hair. He gently pulled my head towards him and then kissed me… I mean *really* kissed me!

I opened my mouth, Jake followed, and our tongues gently danced together for the first time. It was utterly mind blowing. The warm sensation which was already shooting through my veins, localised in one *very* intimate place. It was like nothing I'd ever felt before and I didn't want him to stop. The mixture of adrenaline and desire on a scale I'd never experienced before had ignited something inside me; beautiful, magical and instantly addictive. In that moment I willingly surrendered to him. I was his, and he knew it.

The way he kissed me with such passion and intensity, opened the flood gates to a river of sensuality; raw and powerful. It felt *so* good I was having a hard time believing it was ok, that it wasn't wrong or forbidden; even wicked on some level. Right or wrong, I didn't care. No amount of self-control could have stopped me. The taste of his mouth, the feel of his lips on mine… I loved every second of it!

We didn't realise at the time, but with that first kiss Jake and I had begun our life together. Instantly the strength of our connection was clear, and in that moment we forged an eternal bond which would go on to carry me through the toughest and most painful chapters of my life. In my heart I knew… I would love him forever.

I don't know exactly how long we were out there, lost in our own world; a million miles away, but as guests began to spill out of the hall we knew it was time to return.

Our lips parted and we sat there gazing into each other's eyes. I felt all hot and flustered and I knew why. There's no other way to say it… I was aroused… *really* aroused! So much so that I could *feel* it. A sensation that left me blushing.

"That was amazing Sophie. Thank you."

I let out an excited giggle and waited to compose myself before replying. "Yes… it was."

"I've been thinking about kissing you since the lake," Jake confessed.

"Me too. I'm so glad you feel the same way."

"Are you kidding! You're absolutely incredible Sophie. I've never met anyone like you."

"And I've never met anyone like you either," I echoed. "Where did you come from? You're so… perfect."

Jake laughed out loud. "I'm not perfect… not by a long shot! And I'm from Sunbury remember?" he joked.

He turned to look at the crowd of people filing out the front doors of the hall. "I guess the Ball is over." His tone was sombre; the disappointment in his voice clearly evident.

As I watched his expression sadden, it was obvious he didn't want our time alone to end; neither did I.

I gently placed my hand on his cheek and turned his face back towards me. "Thank you Jake. Thank you for *everything*." I emphasised, with a suggestive grin that ensured he clearly understood the part of the evening for which I was most appreciative.

"My pleasure," he smiled; shooting me a seductive wink which made me want him even more.

"I don't want to go," I pleaded, wrapping my arms around him and burying my head under his chin; pressing my cheek firmly against his chest.

"Me neither. But it's ok. Do you know why?"

"Why?" I questioned; confused as to how saying goodbye could ever be ok.

"Because… this is only the beginning." He put his hand on the back of my head and held me against him; melting me with the exact words I wanted to hear.

"I can't believe it's after eleven already!" Jake said after glancing at his watch.

"I know. Tonight has gone *way* too fast. My mum will be here any minute."

With my arms still wrapped around him, I looked into his eyes. "Jake?"

"Yeah."

"Before I go… please kiss me again." I begged.

He put his hand under my chin and gently tilted my head back. I closed my eyes as he leaned in and kissed me softly; tenderly, for what would be the last time that night. I savoured the taste of his lips, as well as the glorious electric-like surge which raced through me. I knew as soon as we stopped there was no way of knowing when I'd feel it again.

Our lips separated and we embraced. I inhaled deeply, greedily taking in as much of his sweet, masculine scent as I could. We stood up and walked towards the hall. There was a crowd of people gathered out the front. I was well aware that a heap of friends from school had seen me with Jake, and that I would surely have some answering to do at school on Monday, but I couldn't have cared less.

I heard the sound of a car horn and saw Mum slowly driving up the street. I waved to her as she parked across the road. "My mum's here. I might make a quick getaway; save twenty questions from Kylie and Sara."

"That's probably not a bad idea. No doubt Kylie's going to grill me on the way home. I had an amazing night Soph. I'll never forget it."

"Me too. It feels like a dream."

"It is," he smiled.

"Can I call you?"

"Of course you can… anytime. I'll look forward to it."

"I'd better not keep Mum waiting, I should go." I felt a tightening in my chest as our departure grew closer.

"Ok. I'll miss you." Jake lifted my hand and kissed it softly. As much as I wanted to feel his lips on mine again, I knew he was considering the possibility that my mother's eyes were on us. The thing is, as amazing as a hot and steamy kiss would've been, his words and the way he kissed my hand, almost caused me to melt into a puddle on the footpath. It was the most romantic experience of my life so far; genuinely beautiful.

"Bye Jake."

"Bye Sophie."

Our eyes, expressions and body language told exactly the same story; we didn't want to go.

I took a deep breath and reluctantly let go of his hand. As I turned and walked across the street, the strange tightness in my chest instantly became recognisable. It was pain, and it wasn't in my chest at all… it was in my heart.

I got in the car and closed the door.

"Hi Soph."

"Hey Mum."

I think Mum must have sensed I was a little torn-up, because she didn't ask me about the night straight away; or about Jake.

As she reversed out and drove away, Jake stood on the other side of the road; a street light illuminating the gentle smile on his face. He raised one hand and waved. I knew how he was feeling and it was hard to bear. After such a beautiful night together, the anguish of saying goodbye was another new emotion for me, the polar opposite of all the others I'd experienced over the last few hours.

I kept his gaze until we'd driven out of sight, then I exhaled slowly, relaxing back into my seat as the emotional ups and downs of the evening had finally come to an end.

"So… how was your night Sophie?"

"It was fun," I replied casually; turning to look out the window to hide a smile which would've given *everything* away.

CHAPTER FIVE

DISTANCE

It was almost twenty years ago now, but I still rate the Crystal Creek Debutante Ball of 1997 as one of the most amazing nights of my life. I'm well aware of how cliché it sounds, but it really was what dreams are made of. I know I said it before, but it was such a surreal experience that I honestly felt like I was in a movie; a beautiful love story fit for the big screen. It's no wonder I had a hard time believing it actually happened to me!

For weeks after the Ball I had reoccurring dreams about him; looking into his eyes while we danced, his hands on my hips, the feel of his soft lips on mine when we kissed, and the moment our tongues touched ever so gently for the first time. I'd wake up in the dead of night, breathing heavily and feeling as though I'd been submerged from the waist down. Jake had invaded my thoughts during the day, and my dreams at night. All I could do was pray that I had the same effect on him.

It's surprising how far away Jake felt. It was a mere forty-minute car trip but not being old enough to drive, it might as well have been four hours away! The only contact I had with him was by telephone and good old fashioned letters. Remember it was back in a time when every teenager didn't have their own cell phone. We talked three or four times a week and we'd send each other a letter every couple of weeks or so. I remember whenever I'd hear the phone ring I would stop whatever I was doing instantly; my ears pricking up as I listened and waited anxiously. I must've looked like a puppy when it hears another dog barking in the distance, my head tilted to one side; listening intently for those magic words. 'Sophie, it's Jake!' Mum would yell. I couldn't get to the phone fast enough to hear his voice.

I'd become so much more relaxed in conversation with him that it wasn't uncommon for us to talk for two hours or more. Now I think about it, I can't recall ever ending a conversation with him voluntarily. It would be either his parents or mine barking at us to get off the phone. 'Sophie, it's been two and a half hours! Wind it up!' Mum or Dad would say. Or I'd hear his mother or father calling out to him, 'What could you two possibly talk about for three hours Jake? Let the girl go!'

Whenever we talked, time would speed away on us; especially on the weekends. I remember one such Saturday afternoon call. We were casually chatting away, when mid-sentence Jake exclaimed, 'Holy shit Soph! We've been on the phone for six and a half hours! That's like a whole day of school!' We both burst out laughing. Thank god we lived close enough that the calls were charged at a standard rate, because if they were long distance our parents would've killed us.

Of all the calls between us, there was one in particular which has been burnt into my memory. Jake and I got onto the subject of our amazing night at the Ball. It wasn't the first discussion we'd had about it; after all it was one of our favourite subjects. As I sat in my room listening to him describe how he felt when our bodies were pressed against each other while we danced, I closed my eyes and cast myself back to that night. It was so vivid in my memory, I felt like I was there again; melting in his arms. I didn't realise I was doing it straight away, but as I listened to his voice describe every detail, I found myself drawing small circles on my leg with the tip of my finger. The way he spoke about holding me close, how our bodies moved as one; it was driving me wild! The circles I traced softly on my leg grew larger; now including the inside of my thigh.

"Keep talking Jake. Tell me what happened when we went outside," I demanded.

As he continued his step by step account, my hand gradually travelled further up my leg, deliberately brushing past my most *intimate* place which was absolutely aching for attention. I ran my hand under my shirt and lightly stroked the soft skin of my stomach, before gradually sliding it into the top of my pants. With each word I moved further and further down until I felt the wetness he'd created; slippery, warm and begging for my caress.

Giving in to temptation, I began to pleasure myself. Gently, I slid my index finger between my *lips* before concentrating all attention on my magic button; swollen and sensitive. I touched myself in such a way that I couldn't help but collapse onto my back and surrender to the moment; my eyes rolling to the back of my head with pleasure. Over and over again, I stoked my *fire*, taking great care not to breathe too deeply into the phone. I would've died of embarrassment if Jake realised what I was doing.

In no time at all I felt myself edging closer to letting go, and as our story unfolded in my ears, a sensation of intense pressure rapidly developed inside me; my pelvic floor muscles contracting in preparation. I couldn't hold off any longer. All it took was Jake's description of our tongues curling together for the first time to push me over the edge. I bit down hard on my lip as my orgasm erupted; blissful pleasure flowing through my body like a tidal wave. I deliberately kept my teeth firmly clamped down on my bottom lip, and exhaled lightly through my nostrils; an attempt to mute any noise escaping which might have given away my mischievous actions. It certainly wasn't easy silencing such an explosion, but somehow I succeeded.

"Soph? You still there?"

"Yeah, I'm here," my voice slightly shaken as my body tingled with the most splendid combination of pleasure and relaxation; every ounce of tension and pressure completely vaporised.

"You haven't said anything for a while."

"I'm just lost in our story. I could listen to you forever."

"Yeah, it sure was one hell of a night wasn't it?"

"It was so amazing Jake. I still can't believe it happened."

"Well I'm sure there are going to be plenty more like it," he said reassuringly.

"I certainly hope so." The sly smile on my face and post climax glow in my cheeks, evidence that he'd just given me *another* unforgettable experience, without even realising it! Jake was utterly oblivious to the fact that his smooth voice and tender words had just made my usual session of masturbation so much more sensual and potent. It was as though he was right there beside me, holding me; *touching* me. How I longed for the day when he would be.

As for the letters, well I could *tell* you how amazing they were, especially the ones he wrote to me; so full of emotion and truth at such a young age, but you would probably find it hard to believe a teenage boy could write with such feeling. So instead I've decided to include one of his letters exactly as he wrote it, that way you can see for yourself. Reading one of his letters will also give you some idea of his sensitivity and ability to lay his feelings out in the open; completely bare. It's one of the things I found so endearing about him… and still do.

So here is one of Jake's letters to me. I must have read it twenty or thirty times, and it still floods my heart with warmth even now, so many years later. Keep in mind, he was only fifteen when he wrote this.

To my dearest Sophie,

It's ten at night and I am unable to sleep. I'm finding it impossible to get you out of my mind. Not that I am at all complaining. Because of this, I have decided to write a letter to share my inner-most feelings with you.

You, Sophie Taylor, are the first thing to enter my mind each morning, after I have been dreaming about you all night, and the last thing as I drift off to sleep.

I know we live apart, but each day I keep you with me, in my thoughts and in my heart. I have never felt this way before about anything or anyone.

In my mind you fill me with happiness, in my heart you fill me with love. When I feel your tender touch, I melt. When your body presses to mine, I'm in a state of bliss. It's truly unexplainable, but I know I hunger for it when we are apart.

As I live from day to day, my only wish is that you keep safe, happy, and that you are living each day without any worries. But if ever something is bothering you, I want you to tell me. I will do everything in my power to help you out, and that's a promise.

I think I'm starting to drift off now, so I guess I will get going.

With eternal love,

Jake.

P.S. Your kisses are so tender. Your lips feel like silk.

It is such a beautiful letter, but one interesting aspect is the part where he mentioned how my safety and happiness was his only wish. For him to declare this after only a few weeks into our relationship, with the promise to do everything in his power to ensure I remained so, totally blew me away. For a boy so young, it was such a selfless and honourable thing to say. Nobody had ever said something so profound to me before, and I've often questioned whether finding Jake was actually fate. I can't help but feel like there was something more to us meeting, like maybe he was sent from a higher power. A gift, a heavenly offering that only God knew I would need so desperately in the not too distant future, and ultimately for the rest of my life.

In one paragraph of a simple letter, written at the age of fifteen, Jake had defined his role as my protector. As you read the rest of my story you will fully appreciate and understand the significance of his words, written so long ago. Since writing that letter, not only has Jake fulfilled his promise as my protector, but on more than one occasion he has also been my saviour… my *hero*.

Opening one of his letters was always exciting; I never knew what to expect. The following poem was one such example. His words swept me off my feet.

To Sophie,

I don't see you very much,
but when I feel your touch,
it makes me warm inside for ages.

When I hold you near,
with your breath upon my ear,
then I realise how much I miss you.

You're on my mind each night,
hoping that one day we might,
be with each other forever.

When I held you close to dance,
I knew it was romance,
moving as one to the music.

As your tender lips met mine,
for that first perfect time,
my heart bursts into flames with pleasure.

Jake

So that was how the weeks past and our relationship developed; via phone and letters. We had only seen each other *twice* but had talked for countless hours. We knew everything there was to know about one and other. We'd built a level of trust between us which I'd never experienced with anyone before. I told him my deepest secrets and he told me his. We shared our aspirations and dreams for the future and discussed the most private subjects. As a teenage girl, to find someone so understanding and sincere at that stage of my life meant everything to me. I had no insecurities with Jake and knew I could tell him anything, without fear of judgment or criticism. I guess that's why our first official date, which was actually my first *ever*, could only be described as extraordinary. We didn't have to go through the entire 'getting to know each other' process, because we felt like we'd been in a relationship for a couple of months already.

If I thought the whole experience at the Debutante Ball was amazing, then nothing could have prepared me for a night at the movies with Jake. My self-control would be put to the ultimate test.

CHAPTER SIX

FIRST DATE

At least eight weeks had passed, and as wonderful as it was to hear Jake's voice over the phone and to read his heart felt letters, I was absolutely desperate to see him. I longed to hold his hand again and wrap my arms around him; to stare into his eyes and kiss his lips.

I once heard someone say 'absence makes the heart grow fonder'. Well after spending those few months away from Jake, I experienced first-hand just how accurate that was. It was though every time we spoke, my feelings for him multiplied ten-fold; and when I wasn't talking to Jake, I was thinking about him… every minute of the day. I struggled to concentrate on anything at school or home. I know it sounds as though I was bordering on obsession, but I couldn't help it. It was as if in that first kiss he'd given me a part of himself, and now I could feel him in my heart constantly. If I *was* obsessed, then I didn't care because it felt wonderful.

We couldn't wait any longer to see each other, so after some heavy negotiation with our parents we arranged to go on our first official date. Since we were still only fifteen, our parents included a few conditions; one of which was that we had to go in a group with a few friends. This didn't bother me at all. I didn't care what restrictions or conditions our parents put on us. Even if they said we could only go out for five minutes, it would still be worth it. Honestly, I would've agreed to anything as long as I got to hold him in my arms again.

So the arrangement was for us all to meet at the movies on the upcoming Friday night. Jake was going to bring two of his friends from school and I would be taking Kylie and Sara with me. Kylie's mum offered to drop us off at the movies in Sunbury, then pick us up about an hour after it finished.

It seemed like the week dragged on forever but eventually Friday arrived, and I have to say I wasn't the only one who was excited. The fact that Kylie and Sara were going to meet two of Jake's friends had them both in a spin. At school that day I have absolutely no doubt the three of us didn't learn a thing. When we weren't looking at the clock, we would be giggling excitedly at each other in class. Then when our recess and lunch time breaks came around, all we could talk about was how much fun we were going to have and how cool it was that we were all going on our first official date together with three other boys. I loved that my two best friends were as happy and excited as me.

That afternoon, when the bus dropped me off at my farm gate, I ran all the way home as fast as my legs would carry me. It was about eight hundred meters of dirt track, and by the time I reached the house I was completely breathless.

"In a bit of a hurry are we?" said Mum, knowing full well I was busting to go out that night.

"Hi Mum… Have to… Get ready." I was puffing so much that I could only manage two word sentences.

"What time's Kylie's mum picking you up?"

"Five… Movie starts… At six," I panted.

"What are you going to see?"

"It's called Daylight." My breathing began to return to normal. "I think it's an action movie… with Sylvester Stallone."

"Sounds good."

"Yeah Jake said the preview looked great."

"So who are his friends that are going with you girls to the movies?"

"They're friends of his from school. I think their names are Chris and Michael. Jake said they're nice."

"Nice guys hey… just like Jake then," Mum grinned.

"Yep, just like Jake," I blushed before giggling happily.

"Sophie?"

"Yeah Mum. What is it?"

"It sounds like you really care about him."

"I do… I care about him a lot."

"And he probably feels the same way about you?"

"Yes. Well he said he does. What are you trying to say?"

"I just hope you know that teenage boys can be a little bit all over the place sometimes."

"What do you mean?"

"Well one minute they might say they love you, then in the next they might be interested in something or someone else. I just don't want you to get hurt, that's all."

"Mum, Jake's not like other boys. I trust him. I know he'd never hurt me."

"I hope not Soph. I also want you to make sure he doesn't put any pressure on you; you know… pressure to do anything you don't want to."

I didn't dare tell her I was prepared to do *everything* with him already, deciding that information was best kept to myself. My insides contracted at the thought.

"He'd never do that. I know you care about me Mum but you don't have to worry. Believe me, Jake isn't like that. Anyway I promise I'll be careful," I replied, trying to be as reassuring as I could.

"Well that's all I needed to hear. I just want you to be safe and realise there's no need to rush these sorts of things."

"I won't."

"Okay then. Now go and get ready," she smiled. "You don't want to be late."

"Thanks Mum."

I ran down the hall to my bedroom. I had a lot of work to do.

Before long I was plucked, polished, perfumed and ready for my first date with Jake.

There was a knock at the door. "Come in Kylie," invited Mum.

"Hi Lynn. Is Sophie ready to go?" I could hear the excitement in her voice from my bedroom.

"She should be just about ready. You look nice Kylie," commented Mum.

"Thanks."

"Sophie… Kylie's here!" Mum yelled down the hallway.

I sprayed one more hit of perfume on my neck and walked out into the kitchen. "Hey Kylie."

"Hey Soph, you ready to go?"

"Sure am. Have you already picked up Sara?"

"Yep she's in the car."

"Ok Mum, I'll be home later. The movie finishes about eight."

"We'll bring Soph home around nine-thirtyish if that's ok?" explained Kylie.

"That'll be fine. Ok girls, have fun and be careful."

"We will." Both of us answered in unison causing us to laugh.

I gave Mum a hug then we walked out to the car where Kylie's mum and Sara were waiting.

The whole way into Sunbury we chatted and laughed about Jake and what his friends were going to be like. We were all buzzing with excitement, which made the forty-minute trip pass in the blink of an eye.

"I'll meet you girls here at eight-thirty sharp," directed Kylie's mum.

We all said goodbye before climbing out of the car onto the side walk; directly in front of the cinema entrance.

As I looked up and down the main street and into the glass doors of the Cinema in search of Jake, the familiar 'butterflies in my belly' sensation returned in force.

Two or three minutes passed and although I could hear Kylie and Sara talking, I wasn't listening to a word. I was on high alert.

"Hey Sophie… turn around," prompted Sara.

I paused momentarily. I knew she must've spotted Jake and his friends walking down the street. My whole body flooded with adrenaline. I hadn't even thought of what to say, or whether he was going to kiss me straight away. I didn't know what to expect and felt completely underprepared.

Breathe Sophie. Relax and breathe.

I turned around and instantly spotted Jake walking towards us with two other guys. He was about fifty or so meters away which gave me just enough time to compose myself. Jake waved and I could see he was smiling. He was wearing jeans and a white t-shirt; considerably more casual than the Ball but still looked fantastic. My heart thumped hard in my chest as he edged closer and closer, then all of a sudden he started walking faster; leaving his friends trailing behind him.

Once he got within a few meters, he looked towards my friends. "Kylie… Sara," he said, greeting them both with a smile before turning back to me. Then he took a few more steps and stopped directly in front of me. All the feelings, emotions, and the anticipation of seeing him bombarded me all at once; rendering me completely stunned and motionless. I could hardly breathe and I couldn't move. I was frozen.

Unlike our first two meetings, this time there was no welcoming handshake. Instead, Jake reached up and placed his hands softly on each of my cheeks. He looked directly into my eyes then leant forward and kissed me lightly on the lips, before wrapping his arms around me.

He put his mouth to my ear. "God I missed you Sophie… I missed you so much," he whispered. His greeting so warm and sensual it turned my body to jelly; weakening my knees to the point where I honestly thought I was going to drop to the ground right there on the footpath.

I closed my eyes and hugged him tightly. "I missed you too Jake. I can't believe you're here!"

All the letters we'd sent and the hours spent talking on the phone had completely changed us. It felt like we'd been together for months already, only not in the physical sense. We were *finally* together, face to face, and it was just as amazing as I'd dreamt countless nights over.

"Get a room you two," beamed Kylie, prompting laughter from the others.

I'd briefly forgotten we weren't alone and her comment took me by surprise.

"Sophie… Kylie… Sara, these are my friends; Chris and Michael." Jake gestured with his hand towards each of us as he spoke, so everyone was properly introduced and knew who was who. They all looked so nervous, and now that I think about it, Jake and I were the only two who didn't look completely petrified.

Chris was a little bit shorter than Jake. He also had long hair pulled back in a ponytail. I remembered Jake telling me they'd both decided to grow their hair together. Chris had a nice smile and was really friendly. He and Jake had been friends since grade two.

Michael and Jake became friends at the beginning of high school, four years earlier. He was about the same height as Jake, maybe a little taller, and had a slender build with blonde hair. He shook each of our hands during our introduction, and for some reason I got the vibe that he was a bit of a 'ladies' man'. He still seemed nice enough though.

I knew Kylie and Sara would have definitely been relieved after finally meeting Chris and Michael. We'd joked at school about how funny it would be if Jake's friends turned out to be a couple of weirdos. Turns out we needn't have worried because they were both friendly, and easy on the eye too which I'm sure my friends appreciated.

"We'd better go in and get our tickets sorted," suggested Chris.

"Good idea," agreed Jake, as he walked over to the door and held it open for all of us. I waited 'til last, then grabbed his hand as we walked into the building and up the stair case to the box office. It felt so nice to be able to hold his hand again; I never wanted to let it go.

As Kylie, Sara, Chris and Michael all bought their tickets, Jake turned to me. "Do you mind if I buy your ticket?"

"Oh, you don't have to Jake. Mum gave me some money."

"You didn't offer to buy *my* ticket you cheap bastard!" joked Chris.

"Well if you'd kissed me when I picked you up, then maybe I would have!" Jake replied sharply.

Everyone laughed, even the girl at the ticket counter.

"So you don't mind Soph... if I get your ticket?"

"Of course not," I smiled appreciatively.

"Great. I really want to." He turned to the girl at the counter, "Two tickets to Daylight please."

Jake had told me about his part time job as a trolley pusher at one of the local supermarkets, so I knew it would be *his* money that he was spending on me; not his parents. I also knew it was hard earned too. He'd mentioned how he would do nine hours straight on a Saturday and Sunday, collecting trollies from the shopping centre car park in the blistering summer heat. Even though it was only a movie ticket, Jake's chivalry instantly reminded me of a promise he'd made in one of his letters; to look after and protect me. It made me feel valued and special; definitely respected.

We all walked to the candy bar area and the boys bought some popcorn, lollies and six frozen *Cokes*. I think Jake's offer to buy my ticket gave Chris and Michael the idea to shout my friends the food and drink. It was sweet and the girls appreciated it, as did I.

While the boys waited in line at the candy bar, the girls and I discussed the seating arrangements once inside the theatre.

"I'll sit next to Michael, if that's ok with you Sara?" said Kylie.

"No worries. Chris is really funny; I'll sit next to him."

"Well me and Jake are going to sit the row behind you four," I smirked suggestively.

"You would Soph! You two aren't even going to *watch* the movie… are you?" Kylie accused.

I couldn't help but giggle. She knew me all too well. "I bet you're both relieved that Chris and Michael aren't a couple of weirdos?"

"Shit yeah!" exclaimed Sara. "I was so worried we weren't going to like them."

We started to laugh, remembering some of the conversations we had at school during the week. I was so glad it wasn't going to be an awkward night for my friends. We were still chuckling when the boys returned and suggested we make our way into the theatre to get good seats.

As we walked into the dimly lit theatre, Kylie explained the seating arrangements. "And apparently you two *love birds* are sitting behind us," she added.

"Oh really?" said Jake, faking a surprised expression. "And who's idea was that?"

"Mine," I grinned smugly.

"I like the way you think," he winked before smiling with approval.

We all found our seats towards the rear of the theatre. It was a fairly new addition to the cinema complex so the red velvet seats were beautiful and clean. Inside smelt like a combination of fresh popcorn and that distinctive new car scent.

As planned, Jake and I sat behind our friends which put the two of us at the very back of the theatre. He put his left arm around my shoulders and held onto my hand with his right. While our friends chatted, the two of us sat staring at each other; utterly appreciating the moment and revelling in the magic of being together again.

"I've been waiting so long for this. I've missed you like *crazy*," he said quietly.

"Me too. It's so good to see you again… to hold you. I wish I didn't live so far away from Sunbury." I couldn't hide the despair in my voice.

"I know it makes things hard, but look at the bright side… how good does it feel now we're together again?" Jake's cheerful and happy tone immediately warmed my heart.

I smiled before closing my eyes; inviting him to kiss me again. Then after savouring his flavour I melted into his arms; burying my head under his chin. I tilted my head back and nuzzled against his neck so each time I inhaled my nostrils were filled with his delicious scent. *Mmm... he smells soooo good!*

The lights dimmed; plunging the theatre into complete darkness before the screen flashed to life with commercials and previews. Our four friends quietened down and settled into their seats; ready for the start of the movie.

Okay, it wasn't like Jake and I didn't see *any* of the movie. I did get the general idea that some people got stuck in an underground tunnel and *Sylvester Stallone* was trying to get them all out alive. What I will say though, is years later we hired *'Daylight'* on video because we couldn't remember much else about it. There's no doubt we missed more of the movie than we realised.

I may not have been able to remember much of the film, but what I *do* remember from that night, was losing myself with Jake in the darkness of the theatre. We held each other constantly and kissed like the world was going to end. I think the only time we actually stopped kissing and whispering sexy sweet nothing's in each other's ear, was to have a sip of frozen *Coke* and a quick glance at the movie. We only had a limited amount of time together so we made the most of every single minute. *'Daylight'* was definitely the best movie I *never* saw.

I don't know if it was my head, my heart or my hormones, but I couldn't stop myself from wanting more from him. The feeling of our tongues touching over and over again, combined with him kissing and softly biting my neck was driving me insane. It wasn't long until I began to feel my insides twist and tighten. Familiar sensations like those which I experienced alone in bed at night, the ones which demanded *attention* and would continue to intensify until I did something to alleviate the pressure. I knew exactly what I wanted Jake to do but I resisted the impulses with all my might. Well… sort of resisted.

The movie had probably been going for about an hour. Jake had worked me into a state of sexual arousal which I'd only ever experienced on my own, with one exception. I'll get to Belinda shortly.

I grabbed his hand and placed it high on my leg. I was wearing shorts, so Jake's hand on my bare thigh felt unmistakably forbidden, yet incredibly hot.

He stopped kissing me and pulled his head back slowly. He looked at me in the eyes, our noses almost touching. "What are you doing Sophie?" he whispered.

"Nothing," I replied innocently; the light from the screen illuminating my mischievous smile.

He began to run his hand softly up and down my thigh; gently caressing my skin. So many nights over the last few weeks I'd dreamt of Jake's hands all over my body, but those dreams paled in comparison to the actual feeling of his fingertips on my bare skin. It was electric.

I leant over and put my mouth to his ear. "I love your hands on me," I breathed. "It feels so good."

"Your skin… it's so smooth… so soft. You feel amazing."

With every slow and deliberate stroke of my thigh, I could feel *myself* moisten. His hands and the way he touched me provoked a natural response… intense sexual preparation! I desperately wanted him to touch me *there,* more than I've ever wanted anything! I *needed* him too, and not just for my own gratification but because I yearned for him to know the effect he was having on me.

Don't even think about it Sophie! Control yourself! You don't want to come across too eager... it's only the first date! My conscience; frantically trying to induce as much restraint and self-control as possible

I'm not even going to try and deny it. If Jake had of traced his hand to the top of my thigh and gently slid his fingers under the seam of my shorts, then I wouldn't have had the will power, or the desire, to stop him from feeling the slippery situation he'd created. I also can't deny the fact that I was sending him a barrage of subliminal messages, encouraging such actions. *Do it... Do it Jake... Touch me... Touch me now!*

As it turns out he had far more restraint than me, and was an absolute gentleman. He continued to stroke my bare skin and kiss me passionately, without once venturing beyond the seam of my shorts, even though I knew he wanted to.

Weeks later I questioned him about that night. He said it was driving him absolutely crazy and that he had to use every single ounce of self-control not to take it further. *'Oh my God Soph, it was torture! I wanted to touch you so bad. The hardest part was that I knew you wanted me to.'* It made me laugh. I was glad it was as difficult for him to resist as it was for me.

By the time the movie ended and the credits started to roll, Jake had me at boiling point. A situation which I rectified soon after climbing into bed that night!

As the lights in the theatre slowly grew brighter, our four friends turned around in their seats to face us. Jake and I smiled suggestively at each other as though we'd been up to no good. We were *very* close to it.

"So what'd you think of the movie Soph?" said Kylie sarcastically. The other three chuckled to themselves, knowing full well we didn't see much of it at all.

"It was one of the best movies she's ever seen!" replied Jake; equally sarcastic. Everyone laughed, me included, although I could feel myself blushing.

"So where to now?" said Chris.

"Well we've got twenty minutes or so until Kylie's mum picks us up from out the front," explained Sara.

"Then we should go to the video game arcade next door until it's time to go?" suggested Kylie.

We all agreed and headed out of the theatre towards the arcade which adjoined the cinema complex.

While the others played a few games of air hockey, Jake and I sat at a table in the cafeteria section. We only had twenty minutes left together, and as fun as air hockey is, we weren't about to waste precious time playing a game.

We sat down next to each other in one of the booths. We were holding hands and sitting as close as possible; I might as well have been sitting on his lap.

"How far is it to your farm from Sunbury again?"

He'd asked me this before but for some reason wanted to clarify the distance.

"It's about a forty-minute drive, so maybe fifty kilometres or more. Why?"

"Because I can't wait another five or six weeks to see you again. I'm going to ride my bike out to see you, either next weekend or the one after."

"You'd seriously ride all the way out to see me. That'll take you ages!" I exclaimed, already feeling excited about the possibility of him coming to my house… to my *bedroom*!

"Sophie, the way I feel about you now I'd ride to the other side of the country just to kiss you again. I've never felt this way about anyone before. I want to see you all the time; you're all I ever think about."

"Me too."

"I love talking to you on the phone obviously. But every time I have to hang up, I can't help but feel sad. I literally miss you from the second I say goodbye."

The feelings he described and the sincerity in his voice was overwhelming. I completely understood his pain because I felt *exactly* the same way. Knowing I was about to say goodbye to him again was too much to bear. I could feel myself losing control and I started to well up. With all my might I tried not to cry but was unable to stop a couple of persistent tears from rolling down my cheeks.

Once I felt the tears fall I quickly buried my head against his chest. It wasn't like I was trying to hide because I wasn't the least embarrassed. I just wanted to hold him close and for him to hold me back. I needed him.

Jake put one arm around my shoulders and held the back of my head with his other hand. "It's ok. Don't cry. I'm not going anywhere Soph. I'm yours… I'll always be yours."

Hearing his words definitely made me feel better. I was still upset that I had to say goodbye but I believed every word he said. I took great comfort in knowing he was mine.

I pulled myself together just as Kylie and the others arrived at our table. "We'd better go and wait out the front Sophie; Mum will be here soon."

"Ok. Can you give us a minute? Jake and I will meet you out the front." I wanted to give him a proper goodbye and I needed some privacy.

"Sure thing. Don't be too long though." Kylie was no longer poking fun at me. I think she could see by the redness in my eyes that I was finding it hard to say goodbye to Jake.

Our four friends walked outside, leaving us alone.

"I don't want to say goodbye… it's too hard!" I whispered in despair; knowing I had to.

"Then don't say anything… just kiss me instead." Jake placed his hands on my cheeks, just as he did when I first saw him earlier that night. He moved his face closer to mine and looked deep into my eyes. "I love you Sophie Taylor."

I inhaled sharply; slightly stunned by his revelation, not to mention the *way* he said it. Never had I heard words spoken with such sincerity and candour. Fresh tears broke free and my heart pounded in my chest. My whole body felt warm and alive. I closed my eyes and he placed his lips on mine with the equivalent passion and emotion of our very first kiss. It was beautiful. Once again, Jake had brought my world to a standstill. It was a moment in time, so special that time itself ceased to exist.

Our mouths parted and he wrapped his arms around me.

"I love you too Jake… I love you too!" I whispered in his ear; squeezing him tightly in my arms. It felt so good to say the words. It was as though I'd been holding onto a deep secret and was finally allowed to set it free.

"Well that's a relief," he smiled.

"Trust me… there was never any doubt."

"We'd better get going. I guess I'll see you soon Baby." It was the first time Jake ever called me by that nickname, and to this day he still calls me 'Baby'.

"I can't wait. I already miss you. I'll call and write you some more letters."

"Sounds like a plan," he replied with his trademark cheeky smile.

We held each other close and kissed again before making our way out of the arcade, hand in hand… *lovers.*

Kylie's mum had already arrived and our friends were standing on the sidewalk next to her car; still chatting and laughing as they had been for most of the night. It was obvious they'd all had a great time. We walked over to meet them and the six of us said goodbye to one and other. Chris and Michael moved away from the car as Kylie and Sara climbed in.

Jake and I embraced one last time. "Take care Baby."

"You too. I'll call you tomorrow," I said; squeezing him firmly.

He let me go and I got in the back of the car with Sara. There was no final kiss as we were in full view of Kylie's mother. I felt a heavy sinking feeling in my chest. My heart began to ache already and I knew it would stay that way until I was with Jake again. I prayed it wouldn't be too far away.

As I sat in the back seat, my stomach felt as though it was trying to twist itself into a knot. I could feel my eyes burning and fought hard to hold the tears back. I kept my focus firmly on Jake as the car reversed out onto the street and began to drive towards home. He stood on the sidewalk; one hand waving slowly. The forced smile on his face clearly indicated the hurt he was feeling too.

Once again, I had to watch as he faded into the distance. I *hated* it. I knew I'd see him again but it didn't stop me feeling like my heart had been ripped from my chest. I felt incomplete… broken.

As Kylie talked to her mum about Chris, Michael and the movie, Sara reached across and held my hand. She knew I was upset. "It's ok Sophie, just breathe. You'll be alright."

"Thanks Sara," I said quietly. She was a great friend and I appreciated her comforting gesture.

For the rest of the trip I looked out the window as the car sped past the moonlit countryside. Kylie and Sara talked flat out about the boys but I hardly spoke a word; I couldn't. I just wanted to get home, climb into bed, close my eyes and relive every second of the last few hours.

My first date had passed in the blink of an eye. It was as amazing as it was unforgettable. After the Ball, and now the movie, I wondered whether it was always going to be like this; like a dream.

That night was pivotal in our relationship. We had taken such a big step forward, with Jake openly declaring his love for me, and I for him. Also, our self-control had been put to the ultimate test. Though I was under no illusion that next time I would not let the opportunity pass.

CHAPTER SEVEN

THE BEGINNING OF PLEASURE

Before I continue with my story, it's important you understand how an earlier chapter in my life shaped the person I am today, and how it subsequently affected my relationship with Jake in the future. Since this is a tale of love, passion and pleasure, among other things, I thought it relevant to highlight the events which culminated in the *beginning* of pleasure for me.

As I write this, I'm mindful of the fact the information I'm about to share could be viewed by some as inappropriate, objectionable; even morally unacceptable. If you do happen to feel this way, I apologise, but would hope that you consider my reasons for divulging such a personal experience.

I haven't written this chapter or any part of my story to persuade your views and opinions. I have included it because of its significance to the rest of my life.

I was only eleven-years-old; a student in a small primary school in the country, which was about fifteen-minutes' drive from the farm. To say it was small is a slight understatement considering it comprised of only twenty-five students and two teachers. I was in grade six along with five other students, all of whom were from farms like me. The six of us were close friends, though none were closer than Belinda and I.

Belinda was also eleven and had blonde hair, blue eyes and a few light freckles across her nose. She had a beautifully soft and gentle nature to match her pretty face, and she really was quite girly; a stark contrast to my own 'Tomboy' nature. We were the best of friends and basically inseparable. She lived within walking distance from the school, so occasionally I'd walk home with her on a Friday afternoon and stay at her house for the weekend; before returning to school with her on Monday.

Belinda had two older brothers who had already moved out of home, and her father regularly worked away. Her mother, Jane, was quite religious and would often attend bible study groups on the weekends. It wasn't uncommon for the two of us to be left at home for a couple of hours at a time to entertain ourselves. Don't be alarmed that Jane left two eleven-year-olds at home alone. Remember, we lived out in the country; it was a safe and relaxed community.

Like most kids our age our favourite thing to do was role play different scenarios such as; teachers and students, doctors and nurses, mums and dads etc. Each time we played we'd switch roles, so one day I might pretend to be a sick patient and Belinda would be the doctor; wrapping my make-believe broken leg in a bandage. On other occasions, she would play a well behaved student and I would act as the teacher; rewarding her with a gold star on her work or an '*Excellent*' ink stamp on her hand. All our games were great fun and the time passed by quickly. For hours upon hours, we'd be lost in our make believe hospitals and schools.

With each weekend sleep over, the bond between Belinda and I continued to develop. I always looked forward to spending time with her and sometimes I'd find myself thinking about her even when we weren't together. I thought nothing of it other than the fact that we were best friends, so it felt quite natural to me that I would be thinking about her a lot.

Things changed one summer's afternoon when Belinda and I were playing our regular 'Mums and Dads' role play game. I was the mother, at home cooking dinner, and Belinda acted as the father who was just getting home from work. The house was empty so we were using the actual kitchen to play out the scene.

I was standing at the stove pretending to cook dinner, I think I was stirring a pot with a wooden spoon. I had Belinda's mother's apron on and a pair of her high heels as well. Belinda was wearing one of her father's old ties and had just walked into the kitchen as if arriving home from work.

We'd played this scenario out before, but this time instead of the usual '*Honey I'm home!*', Belinda walked into the kitchen and stood right in front of me; unusually close.

"I've been thinking. Don't mums and dads usually kiss when he gets home from work?" she said; looking straight at me.

"Yeah… I suppose so," I replied.

Belinda paused for a moment. "Well… do you want to try it?" she asked nervously.

"Um… I don't know. I've never kissed anybody before."

"Me neither," she confessed.

We both already knew that neither of us had experienced our first kiss, as we'd discussed the topic before.

"Ok then, only if you want to?" I agreed, never once giving thought to the fact my first kiss was going to be with my best friend; more specifically… a girl!

Belinda smiled. "Ok. Stand still."

I did as she instructed.

"I think you're supposed to close your eyes Sophie?" she suggested.

"Oh… right… yeah sure." I closed them.

I sensed her leaning closer, to the point where I could feel her faint breath on my face. I didn't move. Then I felt her lips press against mine; touching for maybe two or three seconds before pulling back. I opened my eyes and we both giggled.

"That felt nice," I smiled.

"Do you want me to do it again?"

"If you want to?" I replied; hoping she would.

"Close your eyes then."

Again I complied and Belinda kissed me briefly on the lips for a second time.

Since I'd been spending so much time with her, and because I didn't have a great deal of contact with many other children my age, it didn't seem like we were doing anything wrong at all. I liked Belinda, so it felt quite natural for me and her to be each other's first kiss. At the time I didn't have a real grasp on homosexuality, so as far as we were concerned we were just kids playing a game; acting out what our mothers and fathers did when he'd arrive home from work.

After the kiss, we continued to play out our make believe scenario for a while. Belinda detailed how her day at work was and I talked about how our three make believe kids went at school. We played until Jane arrived home and asked for our help with cooking dinner for real.

At school the following week we didn't talk about kissing, and we certainly didn't tell anyone about it either. In hindsight I think we must've felt a little bit weird about the whole situation. I don't think it was guilt because I certainly didn't feel guilty when I was around her; more like nervous. I do know I was thinking about it a lot though, and I couldn't help but feel like I wanted to kiss her again. After all I liked Belinda, she was my best friend, and kissing her felt nice. I'm pretty sure she felt the same way too.

It was probably a fortnight or so until my next sleep over at her house. I distinctly remember how I couldn't wait for the school day to end, full of hope that Jane would be going out for a few hours to give Belinda and I a chance to role play again.

I remember asking Belinda if we were going to be left alone at all over the next two days. Although her father was away with work, it turned out there was no bible study group on for the weekend, so Jane would be home the whole time. I recall feeling disappointed that Belinda and I weren't going to get the opportunity to kiss again. It wasn't until it was time for bed that I realised we'd have all the time alone we needed, since we always slept in the same bed. We'd done so ever since I started staying at her house; well over eighteen months prior.

We had dinner, washed up and were just finishing a movie on T.V.

"Righto girls, time for bed. Go and brush your teeth," directed Jane.

Since we had a swim in their pool before dinner, we didn't need to shower. So after getting into our pyjamas and cleaning our teeth we climbed into bed. Jane came into the room shortly after to give Belinda a kiss goodnight.

"Goodnight girls. Don't stay up talking too late."

"We won't Mum."

"Goodnight Mrs. Davies," I added.

"Night Sophie," said Jane as she left the room. Belinda and I would often stay up talking late into the night, so she closed the door behind her to muffle the sound of our voices.

The bedside lamp was still on, dimly lighting the room. We both lay on our backs beside each other; looking up at the ceiling fan swirling above our heads. A minute or so passed with neither of us speaking. We'd slept together countless times before, but this time something felt slightly different. I certainly hadn't forgotten about our kiss, and the awkward silence was a clear indicator that Belinda hadn't either.

She was first to break the silence. "I was hoping Mum was going to be away for a few hours this weekend."

I turned on my side to face her. "Me too. I wanted to play in the kitchen again. That was fun."

"Did you want to play Mum's and Dads…" she lowered her voice, "so we could kiss again?"

I paused momentarily; slightly embarrassed. "Yeah… it felt nice."

Belinda's lips curled up into a mischievous grin.

"What are you smiling about?" I asked, guessing she must have had an idea; hoping it was the same as mine.

"I was just thinking… we could kiss now if you want?"

"Right now?" I giggled.

"Uh huh."

"Ok, only if you want to?"

Belinda nodded and shuffled a little closer to me. I looked over to check the bedroom door was fully closed. I didn't want her mother to walk in on us. Jane was very religious, and in hindsight I can only imagine how she would've reacted to her daughter kissing another girl.

I put my head back down on the pillow and smiled warmly at her.

Belinda edged even closer. "Aren't you going to close your eyes?"

"Oh… sorry," I grinned as I closed them.

Almost immediately she kissed me softly on the lips. A few seconds passed but unlike the first time, she didn't pull away. She was still kissing me when I opened my eyes to find her looking back at me. It was strange to be looking at someone so close, but nice at the same time, and as we stared at each other an unusual feeling began to develop in my belly; shortly followed by a tingling sensation even lower. This kiss made me feel *vastly* different from the first.

We stopped and I quickly checked the door again.

"I like that a lot," Belinda confessed; smiling broadly.

"Me too. It makes me…" I paused, considering whether to tell her what I felt.

"What?" she prompted.

"It makes me feel… *funny*," I blushed.

"Yeah I know what you mean!" She was noticeably excited that I'd raised the issue. "What does it feel like for you?"

"Well kind of warm I guess. And I sort of get tingles… you know…" I gestured south with my eyes, "…down there."

"I do too! It feels weird… but nice," she elaborated. "Want to try it again?"

I checked the door then leant in once more. This time we kissed for longer but instead of just letting our closed lips touch, we opened our mouths slightly. It was the first time our kiss felt damp and it caused those new and unusual feelings to magnify instantly.

The disappearance of the dull noise coming from the television in the lounge room prompted us to stop and quickly move apart.

Moments later I heard the bedroom door handle turn. I looked up to see Jane peeking her head into the room. Sometimes she would come in to check on us again before going to bed, so it wasn't out of the ordinary.

"Lights off Belinda, I'm going to bed now. Goodnight girls."

"Goodnight," echoed Belinda.

Jane left; leaving the bedroom door open.

I let out a sigh of relief that we'd stopped at the right moment.

Belinda leaned over and switched off the light. The room was pitch black until my eyes adjusted. I could just make out her face, she was still looking straight at me.

Now the door was open we knew kissing again would be far too risky, so instead we just lay there; quietly discussing the new and exciting sensations we'd discovered together. Eventually sleep beckoned and we both drifted off.

The next day Belinda and I played around the house as usual. Although we didn't discuss the activities of the night before, we would occasionally glance at each other before immediately breaking out into girlish laughter.

As the day passed, I grew increasingly eager for night time to arrive so I could lie beside her again. I could tell she looked forward to it as well.

Eventually dusk approached and Jane called us in from outside. "Dinner time girls! Come in and wash up!"

We went inside, showered and got into our pyjamas before sitting down for dinner.

The night played out similar to the previous. After dinner we watched some TV before going to bed at about 10:00pm. The only difference was that Jane decided to go to bed at the same time as us.

We brushed our teeth, climbed into bed and waited for her mum to come in and say goodnight. As soon as she entered the room Belinda wasted no time in asking if we could stay up later.

"Hey Mum, since its Saturday can Soph and I stay up a bit longer; so we can read through some magazines and talk for a while?"

Jane glanced at her watch.

"We promise we'll be quiet, and we won't stay up too late," Belinda added, trying to sweeten the deal.

I knew what she was up to. Her ulterior motives were the same as mine.

"Well I'm going to bed girls. You can stay up until eleven, then it's lights out and time for sleep."

"Thanks Mum."

"Alright. Goodnight girls."

"Goodnight Mrs. Davies," I said as calmly as I could.

"Remember… eleven ok?"

"Sure Mum. Night."

As Jane walked out of the room, she switched the bedroom light off and closed the door behind her so we wouldn't keep her up with our chatting and laughing. Belinda turned on her bedside lamp. I jumped out of bed to grab some magazines off the shelf then climbed back in beside her.

We flicked through some magazines and talked for a while. Then without warning, Belinda turned towards me and put her head on my pillow. "Do you want to kiss again?" she asked with unexpected candour.

I dropped my magazine beside the bed, checked that the door was completely closed then rolled over to face her. "Yes," I replied quietly.

I'd barely answered, when suddenly Belinda closed in and kissed me. The sensations from the night before flooded back almost immediately. I felt her wriggle under the sheets slightly and assumed she too was dealing with similar feelings.

As we continued to kiss, Belinda gently placed her hand on my hip. It was an advance which triggered our experimentation to progress from kissing to something far more intimate.

Given our age at the time I don't think it's necessary, or appropriate, to give a detailed description of what transpired next.

However, I will paint you a general picture so you get an understanding of the level of intimacy we experienced.

With a delicate touch Belinda started with my arms, followed by my legs; before moving to *other* areas. At first I remember feeling naughty, but I didn't want her to stop. I'd never even touched myself like that before so it was a completely new sensation; one that I liked immediately.

I remember feeling a build-up of pressure, which gradually intensified to the point where I had to hold my breath and wait for it to subside; leaving me slightly breathless and tingling all over. At the time I didn't even know what an orgasm was, but I'm pretty sure that was my first one. It's hard to believe it was even possible at that age.

I understand that eleven is extremely young to be participating in the kinds of activities we did, but it happened. Something inside me had been awakened… and it *never* went back to sleep.

As an adult, I attribute my high sex drive and adventurous sexual nature to my time with Belinda and having my first orgasm at such a young age. I often wonder if other women who consider themselves to be overly sexual had similar experiences early on.

Over the course of the next year, Belinda and I were together in a similar manner as I've just described on maybe four or five separate occasions. It was always at her house, always consensual, and definitely private. Regardless of the opinion of others, I will always view our time together as innocent; we were just kids after all. I am thankful though that our parents never found out. I know they would never have let me stay at my friend's house again, and Belinda's parents, due to their strong religious beliefs would've probably moved her to another school.

Towards the end of the year, with the beginning of high school just around the corner, I found myself drifting away from Belinda. Growing a little older and learning more about sexuality opened my eyes to the reality of what we were doing. I started to worry that somebody would find out and I developed a real fear of starting high school with the label of 'gay' or 'lesbian', which would have been an absolute nightmare. It was the early nineties and there was still a fair bit of prejudice against same sex relationships back then, so I made the decision to suppress my attraction to girls; pushing my feelings so far down inside I was certain I'd eventually just 'grow out of it'. It wasn't until I was in my early twenties that I realised, simply ignoring my feelings didn't mean they weren't there.

After Primary school ended, Belinda's family moved away. She ended up going to another high school and I never saw or heard from her again.

CHAPTER EIGHT

A WALK IN THE WOODS

Four or five days had passed since our first date. I wanted to see Jake more than anything, but instead had to rely on phone calls to get my fix. It had been a whole day since we'd spoken and already I longed to hear his voice again.

"Hello, Sophie Taylor speaking."

"Hey Baby it's me. Just a quick call to find out what you're wearing?"

Cheeky.

"My school uniform if you must know," I giggle; blushing slightly.

"Well shit, that wasn't the answer I was after. You could've at least made something up!"

"Ok then. In that case I'm wearing a white cotton singlet with matching panties… and nothing else. How's that sound?"

"Much better. I'm visualising it already."

The thought of Jake on the other end of the phone, eyes closed and picturing me half naked, immediately turns me on. I'm surprised by how fast he awakens such strong sexual feelings within me.

"So you want the good news or the bad Soph."

I pause, and my heart sinks at the thought of hearing any bad news from Jake. "Give me the bad first."

I hold my breath.

"The thing is, I'm not riding my bike out to see you next weekend." His voice sounds cheerful, which confuses me considering the news.

"Why… too far for you is it?" I tease playfully, even though I'm bitterly disappointed.

"Of course not!" he scoffs. "I told you I'd ride across the country to see you again. I wasn't joking either… I seriously would."

The thought comforts me.

"You're right, not coming to see me *is* bad news. Now give me the good news to cheer me up."

"The good news is that my family's driving out to Kylie's place next Saturday for a barbeque with my auntie and uncle. So guess what I'm organising with my parents, and hopefully yours too?"

"Tell me you asked them if I can come over to see you?"

"Not exactly. Have another guess."

"Just tell me Jake, you're killing me!"

"Alright. I've asked Mum and Dad if one of them could drop me off at your place for the day, then pick me up in the afternoon on their way home. That's only if it's ok with your parents of course?"

"That would be so good!" I beam, unable to control the torrent of excitement rushing through me. "I'll go and ask Dad right now"

I put the phone down and run into the lounge room where my father's watching TV. I was a little nervous, as I'd never asked if a boy could come to the house before.

"Hey Dad." I wait to get his attention. "Jake and his family are going to Kylie's next weekend for a barbeque. His parents said, if it's ok with you, they'll drop him off here and pick him up in the afternoon so he can spend the day with me. Please… please… please can he come over?" I blurt out at speed; most of my words blending together.

"Slow down Sophie. What day was that?"

"Next Saturday. So can he come over?"

"If it's ok with his parents, then I'm fine with it. It will give me a chance to meet this boy you're always talking with on the phone."

"Thanks Dad. You're really going to like him."

I kiss my father on the cheek and run back to the phone; my heart racing.

"Yeah you can come over. Dad said it'll be fine."

"Sweet! I can't wait."

"Me neither," I reply excitedly.

"I had the best time with you at the movies, but the whole night just flew by so fast. I felt like I blinked and it was over. I can't wait to spend a whole day with you Soph; especially just the two of us."

"Me too, I'm so excited. I get you all to myself for a whole day!"

My mind had already begun to fill with visions of Jake and I, holding each other in the privacy of my bedroom. I know this sounds a little too eager, even tarty, but I couldn't help but think about finishing what we started in the movie theatre. I was buzzing and couldn't wait for the weekend.

The day Jake was due to arrive, I woke up at about 5:00am. I remember lying there staring at the ceiling; daydreaming for at least twenty minutes before getting up. I felt like I hadn't even been to sleep, probably because I'd been awake most of the night imagining how the following day was going to turn out.

I drag myself out to the kitchen and put some bread in the toaster.

"You're up early," says Mum; walking into the kitchen whilst tying a knot in her dressing gown.

"Yeah I know. To tell you the truth I don't think I slept a wink."

"Too excited about Jake coming over?"

"Probably. I can't wait to see him again," I confess.

"Now just so you know. Your father and I would appreciate it if you didn't close your bedroom door while you and Jake are in there together, ok?"

"Sure Mum. I'll make sure the door stays open."

Fuck! A weeks' worth of fantasies had completely exploded in a split second, and it wasn't even five-thirty in the morning! *Great start!*

"Good. We just want to make sure you take it slow with Jake, that's all. Besides you're only fifteen," she explained in her usual 'we're-only-looking-out-for-you' tone.

"Sure. Door stays open… got it."

I ate my toast and some cereal then crawled back into bed. Jake wasn't due to arrive until 11:00am so I thought I'd try and get a little more sleep before getting ready.

Again, sleep proved utterly impossible. I had my eyes closed and probably looked like I was in a restful slumber, but my thoughts were running wild. Images of us holding each other, kissing, and more filled my head. I wanted him, and even though it was only a few hours before I'd have him in my arms again, the minutes couldn't tick by fast enough.

As I lay there the visions in my head began to intensify. They'd progressed from innocent kissing and holding hands, to far more explicit undertakings. I straightened my legs, crossed one foot over the other and squeezed my thighs together as hard as I could. It was all I could do to prevent my legs from gradually edging further apart; allowing me the access I needed to *take care* of myself.

Not now Sophie. He'll be here soon. Have some control!

After spending at least forty minutes fighting the potent urges rapidly growing inside me, I decided to ditch the idea of sleep and start getting ready. It was a great plan which seemed fool proof, that was until I reached the shower.

The combination of warm water on my body, and the way my hands effortlessly slid across my soapy skin, mixed with an overpowering dose of teenage hormones eventually forced my surrender. I couldn't take it any longer. Let's just say I ended up spending and extra ten minutes in the shower that morning. I really only needed two, but I can be a little greedy sometimes.

It was just after eleven when I heard Dusty bark. He was a light brown kelpie cross who would help Dad round up the sheep. He always barked when an unfamiliar car rolled up the drive way, to let us know somebody was here.

I inhaled sharply because, unlike Dusty the farm dog, I knew exactly who was here. My heart thumped in my chest and my belly once again filled with butterflies. I was actually getting quite used to them now. I ran to the bathroom to give myself one last check over, then made my way out to the drive way so I could welcome Jake. My mother came out as well; Dad was already outside, working on a tractor over in the shed.

I could already see Jake smiling from the passenger seat; his father was driving. I assumed the rest of the family had already been dropped off at Kylie's place. As soon as it stopped, Jake jumped out of the car and for a brief moment I was worried he was going to greet me like he did at the movies. As much as I would've loved a warm embrace and passionate kiss, I don't think our current audience would have approved. Instead, he calmly walked over and wrapped his arms around my shoulders. At least I got the warm embrace! I hugged him back; pulling him close.

"Hey Baby. I've missed you like crazy!" he whispered in my ear before letting go.

"Hi Jake. I'm so glad you're here." I could feel myself blushing.

"Sophie, this is my father; Greg."

"Hello Sophie. I believe we've spoken on the phone a few times," Greg joked, no doubt because over the last few months I'd called his house more times than I could count. Quite often he would answer when I rang.

By now Dad had made his way over to the car and was standing there with Mum, so I introduced them both together. "Hello Mr. Freeman. These are my parents; Lynn and David."

"Please to meet you Greg," said Dad as they shook hands.

"Likewise David. Hello Lynn," Greg replied, turning to shake my mother's hand as well.

"And this is Jake," I beamed excitedly, pointing both my hands towards him as though I was a model showcasing a prize on *'The Price Is Right'*.

"Hello Mr. and Mrs. Taylor. Pleased to meet you," said Jake politely; stepping forward and shaking their hands in turn.

I could tell my parents were impressed, and relieved, that he had some manners.

Jake and I listened as our parents made small talk for five minutes or so about what each other did to make a living. Dad worked in the local dairy factory and Greg was a builder.

"Well nice meeting you all. Be good Jake and I'll see you at five-thirty," said Greg.

"No worries Dad. Have fun at the barbeque."

My mother and father said goodbye as he got back in the car.

"So Jake, I understand you like talking on the telephone?" teased Dad in good humour as we watched Greg drive out the front gate.

"Well I do if it's with Sophie." Jake smiled at me as he replied.

"I almost need a second job to pay the phone bill."

"Stop it Dad," I pleaded; embarrassed.

Jake laughed, seeing the funny side. "Sorry about that Mr. Taylor, but it's a good thing it's not long distance."

"You got that right," agreed my father.

Mum chimed in. "Well, I'm glad we finally got to meet you Jake. Soph's told us all about you. In fact, she talks about you non-stop!" she emphasised.

"Give it a rest," I demanded.

"What? You talk about him all the time!" she laughed.

"Mum!" I snapped.

I looked over a Jake who was grinning. We'd already discussed the possibility that our parents might poke a little fun at the two of us upon introduction.

"Well my family's probably sick of me talking about Sophie all the time too!" declared Jake. I couldn't help blushing.

Mum looked over at Dad; Jake's admission making both of them smile. They liked him… I knew they would.

"Well I've got some more work to do on the tractor before lunch," said Dad as he turned and walked towards the shed.

"Lunch will be in an hour or so David," explained Mum. "Soph, why don't you give Jake a tour of the farm and I'll call you when lunch is ready."

"Good idea."

Before going inside, I gave Jake a quick tour as Mum suggested. I pointed out a few land marks up in the hills to give him an idea of the size of the property, then we went inside and I showed him around the house. It was wonderful to have him at home with me and I was really excited to show him where I lived. Our final stop was my room.

I walked in first. “So this is my bedroom.”

“Very nice. Who’s your favourite?” he asked, referring to the collage of posters plastered over my walls of young male actors and singers; the usual ‘heartthrobs’ of the nineties.

“My favourite? Well actually none of them are my favourite anymore,” I smiled; grabbing hold of his hand and lifting it up to my lips before placing a soft kiss on his knuckles.

“I see,” he grinned. “Just so happens that you’re my favourite too. Wow your beds massive, mine’s only a single.”

“Yeah it’s a queen size; pretty big for one person.”

“That’s the size *I* need! My bloody feet hang over the end of my bed.”

I laughed, picturing Jake’s bare feet poking out from under the covers. “Well you’ll have to see if you fit in mine?” I suggested, giving absolutely no thought to how that sounded.

“Now there’s an offer I can’t refuse,” he grinned.

Immediately I realised what I’d just said and I burst out laughing.

“We’re still talking about your bed aren’t we?” he added, making me laugh even harder.

“I so didn’t mean for it to come out that way!” I blushed; slightly embarrassed.

“Hey no complaints here Baby.” He looked directly into my eyes. “I’d be more than happy to see if I *fit* in yours sometime,” he emphasised.

My body temperature instantly rose twenty degrees, leaving me hot and flustered.

“After all, there’s nothing worse than cold feet!” he winked.

Discussing my bed with him was both amusing and suggestive. It was blatantly obvious what message was between the lines. Vivid images of the fantasies which plagued my thoughts quickly flooded into my head.

Jake sat on my bed and I immediately sat beside him. I desperately wanted him to kiss me.

"I have to leave the door open… parent's orders," I explained; visibly disappointed.

"No probs, I understand. What did they think we were going to do anyway?" he said with a cheeky smirk.

"I have absolutely no idea," I replied sarcastically.

"Yeah right," he chuckled.

I edged closer and he put his arm around me; pulling me to him. I rested my head on his shoulder for a few seconds then looked up at him; his clear blue eyes stared back at me.

"Kiss me," I whispered before closing my eyes and slowly tilting my head back in complete surrender.

I felt him move slightly and could sense his face directly in front of mine. I inhaled a shallow breath in anticipation, then he kissed me. *Finally,* his lips were on mine. Oh how I missed that feeling. It was like my heart continually ached when we were apart and now that we were together again, everything felt better. Jake's lips were like medicine for my heart.

We kissed, lips closed, for about ten seconds before slowly opening our mouths to let our tongues get reacquainted. It felt absolutely amazing, and the wetness of our kiss instantly triggered a similar sensation in another part of my body. I was boiling.

After a few moments we stopped; the open door a constant reminder that we weren't alone. We sat on the bed holding hands while we discussed the past week and how much we missed each other. It was incredible to have Jake with me again. I felt complete, like the missing piece of my heart was back where it should be.

"I don't want to sound too forward, since you only just got here."

"It's ok Soph, say whatever you want."

"It's just that since we live so far away from each other, all we ever get to do is talk on the phone. *Obviously* I love talking to you, but when I'm finally with you in person I feel like I don't want to waste time talking. Do you know what I mean?"

"I know exactly what you're saying Baby. I'm always saying how much I love you over the phone. When we're actually together I want to *show* you," he agreed.

"I feel the same Jake. Maybe after lunch we could go for a walk up in the hills around the property. I can show you a few of my favourite places."

"Are any of these favourite places…" He paused for a second and looked towards the door before lowering his voice. "…a little more private by any chance?"

"Yeah. I know a nice quiet place. I'm sure you'll like it."

"Cool. Sounds like a plan," he replied with a playful grin.

We remained in the relative privacy of my bedroom until Mum called us for lunch. I showed Jake some of my CD's and school photos. Mid conversation we would occasionally stop to steal a quick kiss. It was so sexy, and I loved being able to kiss him whenever I felt the urge; which was pretty much constantly. He was *here*… with *me*… in *my* bedroom, and I never wanted him to leave.

Lunch time involved a roast lamb and a hundred or so questions fired at Jake from my parents. It was like the 'Spanish Inquisition', but he handled them all perfectly. He was a confident person and held conversation with my parents easily; I was even impressed. He talked about his family, school and his sporting interests. I think the only time my father looked a little concerned was when Jake mentioned he didn't play football. He had come from a family of well-known footballers, many of his uncles and cousins were skilled in the sport and I think Dad assumed Jake was too. Also his athletic appearance suggested he'd be good at it, so Dad was definitely surprised that he didn't play the game. Anyway Jake made it through lunch unscathed, and as far as first impressions go, I think he did well.

"I want to show Jake around the rest of the farm so we're going for a walk after lunch," I announced.

"That's a good idea. Make sure you take him up to see the lookout," suggested Dad.

"Yeah I'll take him up to the far hill near the edge of the property."

"You can almost see all the way to Sunbury from up at the lookout," explained Mum.

"Sounds like it's going to be a bit of a hike?" queried Jake.

"It's pretty steep. I think it's about a half hour walk to the top."

"So we'll get a bit of a workout then?"

"You'll be fine Jake. You look fit enough," I smiled. I didn't dare hint at the type of *workout* I was referring to.

We helped Mum clear the table and wash the dishes, then headed out the door on our afternoon adventure.

Hand in hand, Jake and I strolled through the serene bushland; the autumn sunshine and cool breeze creating the perfect weather for a hike. There wasn't another person for miles and it felt like we were the last two people on earth. It was brilliant; enchanting. I had him all to myself and I knew exactly what I wanted to do with him.

"So would you like to see my hideout?" I asked; squeezing his hand encouragingly.

He raised both eyebrows with obvious intrigue. "Hideout? Sure. How far away is it?"

"Just over the next hill. It's this really cool tree which has leafy branches hanging down, almost to the ground. It's kind of like a secret hideaway."

"Lead the way Soph!"

His eagerness made me smile.

Our pace quickened until we reached the location of the 'hideout'. I led Jake in under the branches; closer to the trunk. It was considerably darker as the leaves blocked some of the daylight, and was far more private than I remembered. The perfect place to take the next *step*.

I'm nervous, actually… I'm *very* nervous. I turn to face him. We embrace immediately and our lips lock; tongues frantically exploring each other's mouths with unbridled passion. Occasionally he pulls back and clamps his mouth on the side of my neck; biting down lightly. The sensation of his teeth on my skin sends a delightful shiver right through me. It's so incredibly hot. Compared to our previous encounters, this one's already shaping up to be far more salacious.

We're both breathing heavily and I'm instantly aroused. I can sense Jake is too. I deliberately moan softly in his mouth, sending an unmistakable signal that I want more. He slowly moves his hands from the side of my thighs, upwards; tentatively sliding them under my t-shirt against my bare skin. Gently, but with deliberate firmness, he grasps me by the waist just above my hips; a feeling which almost brings me undone.

All the emotion and sensuality from our date last Friday has returned in force, only this is not the cinema, and now we are very much alone!

With our lips still locked, I grip one of his wrists and gradually move his hand up to my breast. He gently squeezes on the outside of my bra; feeling the shape.

"Touch them," I command.

"You sure Baby?"

I nod approvingly then kiss him again.

He lets go of my waist, and with eager hands slides the cups of my bra up; exposing my chest to his delicate caress. I moan quietly as he touches my bare breasts for the first time.

"Oh my god they're so soft and beautiful," he whispers; gently kneading them under my t-shirt.

I can feel my nipples increase in sensitivity and gradually become erect.

"Can I see them?"

I nod again.

He lifts my t–shirt up over my head. I reach around and unclip my bra, taking it off completely before hanging it over a branch. Jake gasps at the sight of my perky breasts and hard pink nipples. He places his hands back on me, delicately stroking and squeezing;

ensuring his touch is gentle and unhurried. It's incredible, and I'm instantly hooked to the feeling of his hands on me.

"Kiss them," I order; surprised by my own direction. The control is empowering.

I close my eyes as he kisses the side of my neck before working his way down the front of my throat, then further; slowly down the centre of my chest. I watch his eyes widen as he gently cups my breasts with his hands, then ravenously licks and sucks my nipples; giving equal attention to both. Holding the back of his head, I moan quietly and my knees weaken as the slippery feeling between my legs erupts into a torrent of sexual moisture. His lips and tongue on my breasts and nipples already has me close to climax; I'm positively *aching*.

I grab Jake by the wrist and pull his hand down between my legs; grasping it tightly with both thighs. He looks up at me with blazing eyes; one of my nipples still between his lips as he sucks firmly. *Oh my god!* It's the sexiest thing I've ever seen in my life!

His mouth releases me. "You move fast," he grins; applying pressure to my groin.

I bite my lip and nod for the third time.

"Sure you're ok with this?"

Then the fourth.

He kisses me hard on the lips, then pulling his hand free from between my legs, he places his palm on my bare stomach; fingers pointing south. Jake moves his hand lower, gently pushing against my tummy to create a gap at the waistband of my denim shorts. Slowly, he slides his hand down the front of my pants. I inhale sharply as he touches *me* on the outside of my saturated underwear. I close my eyes and hold my breath as he brushes over my clitoris with his fingertips; forcing me to moan as I exhale. Realising he's found *the* spot, Jake begins to move one finger in small circles and I immediately feel a strong tingling sensation building deep inside. I moan again… and again, as he keeps his circular massage slow and methodical.

I pull his head close so we're cheek to cheek; my mouth beside his ear. I want him to hear the effect he's having on me; my breathing now fast and heavy. "That's it Jake… that's it… keep going," I whisper; my voice brimming with pleasure.

He increases his pressure, rubbing my clit a little harder until I can hold off no longer. I bite my lip and let out a hushed squeal in Jakes ear as I climax. The rush of pleasure causes my hips to spasm; twitching back and forward uncontrollably. As my orgasm subsides, my legs feel weak and unsteady and I have to concentrate on standing so I don't drop to the ground.

"Fuck! That was awesome Baby!" he says, displaying an astonished expression as though he can hardly believe what just happened. "That's easily the hottest thing I've ever seen!"

"Oh Jake… that felt amazing," I reply; breathless.

I kiss him softly on the lips, and immediately he drops down and takes one of my nipples in his mouth; sucking hard which causes the fire inside me to reignite. His hand manoeuvres quickly and he pushes against my tummy again, this time creating space at the waistline of my next layer of clothing… my *panties*.

Swiftly his hand slides down further and disappears into my underwear. I feel his fingers against my soft, wet lips; skin on skin. I bite my lip and moan again as Jake moves his vacuum of a mouth to my other nipple.

He looks up at me, clearly awestruck as he gently explores my wetness for the first time. "You're dripping!"

His astonished expression makes me giggle, but I'm immediately distracted as he promptly returns his mouth to my breast.

The familiar feeling of an impending orgasm build again; rapidly. I know I'm close.

I feel him part my *lips* with two fingers, before slowly inserting one inside me. It feels incredible, and I can't help but push against it with my hips. He carefully moves in and out of me and I meet his rhythm with small sharp thrusts from my pelvis. I emit sounds of pure bliss; deliberate signals to reassure him that he's doing everything right.

He releases my nipple from his mouth then quickly grabs me by the back of the neck; kissing me intensely. Our tongues twist together and I groan into Jake's mouth as he continues to pleasure me.

He touches me with increased depth and rhythm, and the internal pressure builds in response; pushing me to the brink.

"Yes! Yes! That's it!" I push my mouth against the side of Jake's neck; an attempt to muffle the uncontrolled squeal which escapes as I erupt. My orgasm, far more intense than the first, drowns his fingers. With my head buried into the side of his neck, I twitch and shake as a wave of ecstasy envelopes me; savouring every second of addictive pleasure before it gradually disperses.

Once again I'm left out of breath and feeling like my legs are made of rubber bands. I cling to him to hold myself up.

I look into his eyes and giggle; blushing at my inability to mute the sounds of pleasure that so freely escaped. I place my hands and head on his chest as Jake slowly takes his hand out of my underwear before embracing me.

"Jake…" I whisper in his ear, "…I don't know what to say."

He kisses me on the forehead then pulls me close. "You don't have to say anything!"

We face each other and interlock our fingers. I lean in; pressing my body against him as we kiss softly on the lips.

"Are you ok? I hope that felt nice Baby?" asks Jake, searching for reassurance that I'm fine with taking things to such an intimate level.

"Did I look like I enjoyed it?"

"Uh huh," he blushes. The reality that he just watched his girlfriend come, sinking in all of a sudden. "You certainly did."

"I'm better than ok Jake. It felt amazing. Trust me. I loved every second of it."

"Good… so did I. I can't believe you let me do that."

"I love you Jake, and I trust you. I wanted you to touch me," I reply sincerely.

"Anytime Baby. I can't wait to do it again."

"Oh you will… no fear of that!" I laugh.

"Glad to hear it. We probably should be getting back?"

"Yeah good idea," I respond; my voice a little shaken. I'm so relaxed that even my speech is docile.

Jake helps me with my bra and t-shirt.

"Probably a good idea if we jog back, then they won't ask any questions as to why you look a little flustered."

We both laugh.

"Good idea. You're a thinker," I reply, unsure as to how I'm going to jog but relieved that his plan will actually make perfect sense when I arrive home looking dishevelled.

"That felt sooo good!" I reiterate as I tidy myself up.

"My pleasure," he grins; clearly proud of his efforts.

"No, I can assure you… it was *my* pleasure," I emphasise.

"Anytime Baby."

"Don't tempt me Jake."

He laughs, assuming that I'm joking. I wasn't. I could've quite easily stayed up there for hours… maybe forever!

We leave our 'hideout' and jog all the way back to the farm house. I have to admit though, running down the hill and through the fields, I was a little wobbly on my feet.

We arrived home and headed into the kitchen for some water. Mum and Dad were already at the dinner table having a cup of tea so we talked with them about the lookout and some of the animals we seen on the property. They had a good laugh about us running all the way home. Jake smiled at me as he took a sip of water and I returned a sly grin. They were none the wiser about our intimate activities over the last half an hour. His plan worked.

The rest of the afternoon was spent lying beside one and other on my bed, listening to music and talking; enjoying our last moments together. It was heaven, and I *never* wanted it to end.

"Thanks for an amazing day Baby. It was the best."

"No, thank *you*," I replied with sincere gratitude; smiling to myself as I recalled the beautiful orgasms he'd given me with such passion and affection.

"I'm absolutely in love with you Sophie. I want to be yours forever." His words and intense gaze completely melted me.

With my chin on his chest and our bodies intertwined, I looked deep into his eyes. "I love you too Jake. Forever… I'm yours forever."

When he left that afternoon, it was the first time we'd said goodbye that I didn't feel upset. I was excited, happy and satisfied… in *every* way possible. It was the perfect day, and now more than ever I was convinced… he was the one.

CHAPTER NINE

BUGS

Even though we were apart most of the time, my relationship with Jake was progressing at the speed of light; I could literally feel the connection between us growing stronger. We were madly in love, to the point where all I could think about was taking the next step with him. The feelings he'd awoken in me were beautiful, exciting and most certainly welcome. I was living a dream.

Now before I continue with the fairy tale romance rapidly unfolding between the two of us, it was around this time that I began to fall ill. Actually, I should say I began to fall *prey* because that's what it felt like… falling prey to an evil and savage entity; a monster for sure.

The illness which attacked me was not your everyday, run of the mill kind of sickness. It was strong as hell and absolutely merciless; efficiently invading my body and methodically destroying my entire life as I knew it. It devoured my sleep, education, sport, friends and almost my life. It seemed as though the only thing strong enough to withstand the ravaging onslaught from my *monster* was Jake.

From this point of the story onwards I want you to understand these symptoms and struggles took place over the next year or so, but all the while Jake and I continued to build our relationship, even in spite of my rapidly deteriorating health.

My *monster* was as ruthless and callous as it was persistent. With all my heart I prayed the love Jake and I shared for each other would be strong enough to withstand the unrelenting battle for survival I found myself in.

I can remember the first time I felt them as though it was yesterday. Even writing this chapter makes me squirm in my seat uncomfortably, like they're under my skin again… eating me alive!

I was lying in bed trying to get some sleep but it was proving to be impossible. My legs kept twitching under the covers and I couldn't stop scratching at them with my fingernails. It felt like there was something crawling on me. I got up, turned on the bedside lamp then pulled all the covers and sheets off my bed, certain I'd discover my bed full of ants, because that's what it felt like… lying on an ants nest!

On initial inspection I couldn't see any of the little black insects I'd suspected to be responsible, so I turned on the main bedroom light and gave my bed and sheets a thorough examination. I thought maybe fleas or mites were to blame for the skin crawling sensation, but I didn't find any of them either.

I remade my bed, turned off the light and jumped back in. Instantly the skin crawling returned to my legs.

"Fucking hell!" I remember cursing out loud in utter frustration.

I got up, turned on the light and repeated the entire process. But just as before, I found nothing.

Whilst I remade my bed for the second time, I realised my legs still felt like they were covered in bugs, even though I wasn't in bed. I went into the kitchen where the fluorescent lights were much brighter and closely inspected both legs. They looked fine, nothing unusual, no red dots or bite marks; perfectly clear. I hadn't found any creepy insects and no evidence there even were any. I was getting frustrated.

The sensation persisted so I decided a hot shower might do the trick. I went into the bathroom and undressed. While I waited for the shower to heat up I inspected the rest of my body in search of any dots or marks, but found nothing unusual.

As soon as the hot water hit my skin the crawling sensation on, or rather *in* my legs vanished. *Finally*, I thought to myself as I closed my eyes; relieved I'd found the solution. I stayed in the shower for about ten minutes, enjoying the therapeutic effect of the warm water.

I turned the shower off, grabbed a towel and dried myself. To my absolute frustration, within minutes of towelling the water from my legs the crawling sensation returned. It wasn't an itch like a mosquito bite or the result of a bee sting, it literally felt like I had bugs crawling *under* my skin. It was a horrible feeling and was made worse through the inability to escape it, no matter what I tried.

From when the crawling started, it would be close to a year of doctors' visits, medications and creams before a diagnosis was eventually discovered. But until that day, the 'bugs' under my skin almost sent me crazy.

I got to a point where I'd wake up, after eventually falling to sleep in the early hours of the morning through sheer exhaustion, and find my fingernails caked with skin and my legs raw and bloodied like I'd been skinned alive. I was literally clawing my legs, and eventually arms, while I slept; leaving my body and sheets bloodied and stained. This incessant scratching left my limbs covered in small cuts, scabs and scars which, as a fifteen-year-old girl, knocked my self-confidence hard.

The insomnia that accompanied the 'bugs' was also taking its toll on me. Some nights after I'd drained the entire hot water tank from a thirty-minute shower, I'd sit up in bed, wide awake in the dark trying desperately not to scratch my legs and arms to the bone. Sleep was almost non-existent, and without it so many other aspects of my life began to unravel.

I started to lose weight even though I was eating my regular intake of food, and days without sleep had left me with dark circles around my eyes. Since I had no energy, I stopped any form of exercise and subsequently missed out on adequate doses of sunshine. This caused my skin to lose its healthy olive glow and slowly fade to a pale, sickly white colour.

Now bear in mind while all this was happening, while I slowly deteriorated, my parents were constantly taking me to doctors for tests and assessments. Every diagnosis ended up being incorrect which subsequently meant every prescribed treatment failed as well.

In total, I think I saw eight or nine doctors over the course of a year in an attempt to find out what was wrong with me. There seemed to be no definitive answer to my illness; my *monster* was undetectable.

The first victim to fall prey to the beast within me was my education. More often than not I would stay home from school, lying in bed trying desperately to sleep. One particular term I only attended for a total of three days! Mum would come in some days and demand that I get up and go to school. I think because the doctors couldn't find the answers, my parents thought I'd created an elaborate illness just to get out of going. The truth was I loved school, but constant fatigue and discomfort made the task of simply getting out of bed difficult, so *learning* anything at school… impossible!

On the days when I'd give in to my mother's demands, I would get ready as slow as I could in the hope that I'd miss the bus anyway. This meant Mum would have to drive me all the way in to Crystal Creek High. More often than not she wouldn't bother which allowed me to return to bed where I'd spend the rest of the day. It was a routine I practiced many times.

When I did occasionally make the bus, I'd fall asleep in my seat before I even arrived at school. I would end up with my head on the desk; eyes closed in every class. Teachers would send me to the principal or to sick bay and accuse me of all sorts of things like; faking illness, staying up too late at night and being an attention seeking trouble maker. Thanks to my gaunt and frail appearance, I was even accused of being anorexic and was forced to eat my lunch in front of a supervising teacher. It was absolutely humiliating!

I felt like nobody believed what I was going through; not my teachers… and certainly not my parents.

Without doubt, one of the worst days of my entire life occurred on a particular school day when my father happened to be home instead of at work.

I was in bed when I heard Mum and Dad in the kitchen talking loudly about me not wanting to go to school. I'd told them a hundred times, it wasn't that I didn't *want* to go, it was that I physically didn't have the energy to. They didn't believe me.

It was about 10:00am and the school day was already underway. I'm lying there listening to the argument unfold, when all of a sudden they both burst in my room and rip the covers off me; ambushing me in my own bed!

"Get up Sophie! You're going to school!" demanded my father.

"I can't go Dad; I am absolutely exhausted. I haven't slept all night," I cried; tears already stinging my eyes from listening to their discussion in the kitchen.

"I don't care. You can't lie in bed all day. You never go to school and you're not learning anything by staying at home. You're going… now get up!" his voice loud and harsh.

"Dad… I'm sick. I can barely get up. How am I supposed to learn anything when all I do at school is sleep with my head on the desk in every class!" The realisation that neither of my parents believed how bad I was feeling was too much to bear. Tears began to stream down my face.

"Sophie, how many doctors have we seen? Seven… eight… nine? None of them know what's wrong with you. I think you just don't want to go to school!" said my mother unforgivingly; with no clue she'd just broken me in one heartless statement. It proved they had absolutely no idea of the turmoil my body was going through; not to mention my mind.

"I'm not going!" I said defiantly.

"Yes you are! Now get up!" My father's voice was brimming with anger.

"No!" I grabbed the covers and pulled them back over me.

It was at this point my nightmare began. Things turned to shit *real* fast!

My mother walked around to the other side of the bed and ripped the covers off me. They both grabbed one of my arms each and dragged me out of bed.

"Get dressed Sophie. We're driving you to school!" she snarled.

"No! I'm not getting dressed and I'm not going to school!" I yelled; trying to wriggle from their grasp. "I'm sick! Why won't you believe me?"

"Well if you're not going to get dressed, you can go in your pyjamas then," said my father without a shred of pity.

"You can't take me to school in my pyjamas! Don't make me go… please!"

We were standing in my bedroom and they were both holding onto me; one arm each. It was like a scene from a movie set in a mental hospital, with the nurse's man-handling the crazy patient.

"Oh you're going! If you don't want to get dressed, then that's your choice!" my mother snapped.

Every word they spoke highlighted the sheer lack of trust they had in me.

They honestly think I'm making this shit up! Bastards!

I couldn't believe what was happening, I wanted to drop to my knees and bawl my eyes out but I couldn't because the two 'psych ward nurses' wouldn't let go of me.

Even as I describe it to you now, more than sixteen years later, the recollection of this nightmare makes me anxious and upset. It was harrowing.

My parents then proceeded to drag me through the house towards the back door; full blown 'mental-patient-in-a-straight-jacket' style. Now keep in mind I wasn't a baby, I wasn't even a child anymore. I was a teenager, a woman, and my parents were treating me with malicious disrespect; like some kind of malingering liar. I was horrified at their lack of compassion and understanding.

With a great deal of effort on their part, they eventually succeeded in pulling me out of the house before physically forcing me into the back of the car. I was now faced with the harsh reality that they were seriously going to do this; take their sick, exhausted daughter to high school in her pyjamas!

This can't be happening! It's not real! It can't be happening! I tried to wake myself up from this nightmare. I was sitting in the back of the car, no bra, no shoes, hair a complete mess and I was howling in distress. I still didn't want to believe they were actually going to take me to school like this. I was in utter denial.

In hindsight, as soon as they got in the car I should've opened the door and made a run for it but I suppose I wasn't thinking clearly. I was frightened and in shock; probably couldn't have run if I tried anyway, and no doubt they would've just caught me then forced me back in the car again. I didn't bother trying.

The engine started and my father began to drive.

"Please don't take me to school Dad," I sobbed. "Please!"

No response.

"Mum? Make him turn around!"

"Sophie you've missed too much school… you're going!" she said without giving an inch.

I took a second and calmed myself. I thought maybe I had a chance at reasoning with them if I could just manage to relax and get control of my emotions.

"Ok I'll go," I said as calmly as I could. "Just let me go and get dressed first."

The car had now passed the front gate of the farm and was on the main road.

"Too late Sophie, we're already in the car!" she snapped again. "You had your chance!"

"Please don't take me to school like this! I haven't done my hair or anything! I don't even have a bra on!" I implored. "Just take me home and let me get ready. I promise I'll go, just let me get dressed."

I was begging for mercy but my attempts were futile.

"No! We're not turning around. You're going to school right now!" my father growled.

"I don't even have any shoes on! I don't have any lunch or my books! Why won't you listen to me?"

Neither responded.

The realisation of what was happening hit me like a bus. *Fuck! There really taking me! Assholes! Fucking Assholes!* I was filled with rage.

Being driven to school in my current state initiated a horrifying fear inside me unlike anything I'd ever experienced before. I'd tried to reason with them but neither my mother or father were going to save me. It's like they'd both committed to this crazy plan and neither one of them had the guts to back down in front of the other.

I sat in silence for a few minutes; tears still streaming down my face. As irate as I was, I thought I'd try one last-ditch attempt at reasoning with them before completely losing my shit. I wiped my tears and took a few deep breaths.

In the calmest voice I could muster, given the circumstances, I begged one final time. "Mum… Dad, please take me home. I'll get cleaned up, put my uniform on and you can take me to school. I promise I'll go. Please don't make me go like this."

I held my breath, waiting for them to realise they'd succeeded in breaking me and that they could finally put an end to the madness, but once again there was no response. Just silence, except for the sound of the car and my distressed sobs.

The fact neither of them responded to my final calm and rational attempt to reason with them, immediately indicated there was no escape from the nightmare I was trapped in; a nightmare which was about to get even more horrific once we pulled up at school. Visions of me getting dragged out of the car in front of a few hundred students flashed through my mind. The sheer embarrassment and fear would be more than I could handle. I lost it.

"Turn the fucking car around!" I screamed in total desperation. "If you take me to school like this I'll never speak to you again! Turn the fucking car around… now!" I was completely out of options; anger and threats were all I had left.

My father spun around in his seat. "Sit there and shut your mouth!" he snapped; eyes flaming with anger. He turned back to the road.

"Watch your mouth Sophie! Now sit there and be quiet!" my mother hissed; equally aggressive.

I buried my head in my hands and slouched forward in the seat. I was a devastated wreck; a shattered mess.

As we arrived at school I glanced at the clock in the car; 10:40am.

Oh my god... it's recess!

Every single student was out of the classrooms and busily playing and chatting in the school grounds. My heart pounded; I couldn't breathe. I think I was seriously having an anxiety attack. Literally my worst nightmare was about to unfold, but what hurt me the most, what cut to the bone and was the utterly devastating part about the whole situation was the two people who I loved more than anything, who were supposed to love me back, believe in me, protect and trust me were the ones who were putting me through it.

They say the love a parent has for their child is unconditional, well apparently not. There is one condition... don't get sick!

Now to top this whole fucked-up story off, we didn't pull up on the road outside the school; oh no, my father actually drove into the fucking school grounds, right up to the front office! This grabbed the attention of every single student within sight of the car. I wanted to disappear.

In an eerily calm voice, Dad spoke. "Get out."

I think he realised what he was about to make me do and finally understood how much it was going to hurt me. It didn't stop him though.

"No Dad, I can't. I'm begging you... *please* take me home," I wept. I could barely speak but tried one more time. I prayed that my mother and father would save me... save me from each other! "Mum... please! Please tell him to take me home!"

"Lynn, help me get her out of the car."

My heart felt like they'd pulled it out of my chest and stood on it; squashing it into the concrete driveway. My parents failed me in the worst way a teenage daughter could ever be failed.

They got out of the car and pulled me from the back seat. I didn't resist, I couldn't; I had nothing left. I closed my eyes so I didn't see the hundreds of faces staring at me, watching my public humiliation unfold. As they dragged my exhausted, lifeless body by the arms towards the principal's office, I could hear a few laughs and giggles in the distance.

"What's going on here?"

I opened my eyes to see the principal standing in front of us; a very concerned look on his face.

"We want to know why Sophie doesn't want to come to school? What's going on at this place?" my father demanded.

"Mr. Taylor, we don't have any idea what's going on. Sophie spends most of her time in sick bay when she is at school and I've had a number of her teachers complain that she constantly falls asleep in class."

Finally, I thought, hoping my parents would believe me now. I prayed they'd take me home.

"Well you're running this place, so find out what the hell's going on! We want to know why she doesn't want to come to school anymore. She's been to the doctors and they can't find anything wrong with her, so it must be some problem here at school."

I craved an end to this nightmare; any end. I couldn't take any more. I know it sounds drastic, but a lightning bolt through the top of my head would have saved me from such torture.

"Well you should have a talk with Sophie because we can't get anything out of her," added Mum; stepping on my ripped out heart a couple more times.

"Make sure you get the bus home," said Dad coldly as he let me go and got back in the car. Mum followed him.

As the car started and reversed out of the drive way, my parents leaving me in a state of absolute humiliation, I mustered all the strength I could not to collapse on the ground in a devastated heap. The principal walked over and put his arm around my shoulders then led me into the office. He knew the pain and embarrassment I'd just experienced and quickly provided me with the protection needed. He ushered me into the sick bay and I lay down on the bed. One of the female teachers brought me a blanket and draped it over me. I pulled it up over my head and closed my eyes.

I was no longer sobbing and I didn't bother wiping my runny nose, I couldn't; I was completely drained. Instead I just let the tears flow down my cheeks and onto the pillow.

There's no doubt about it, I was in a state of shock. I simply couldn't believe what had happened. The feelings of betrayal, humiliation and anger were raw and painful, and the only emotion I felt more was sadness; deep, cold sadness. I felt completely alone and at the mercy of my *monster*, who now it seemed had two willing subordinates to help inflict its wrath.

The doctors didn't know what was wrong with me, my parents didn't believe me and in that moment I felt like nobody even cared. I needed Jake. I knew he was the only one who could save me.

I stayed in the school office for the rest of the day; hidden in the safe confines of the sick bay. Some of my friends came to the office to visit after they'd seen what happened that morning, but I asked the office lady not to let anyone in. I was just too embarrassed to face anyone; not even Kylie or Sara.

I must've drifted off because the piercing ring of the school bell woke me up. It was 3:20pm. Instantly, I started to panic again. I knew I had to go outside to catch the bus home, and the fear of having to leave the safety of the office only to brave the exposure of the school yard was overwhelming.

I asked the lady at the office to tell me when my bus arrived at the front of the school, that way I could go straight from the sick bay and onto the bus as quickly as possible without having to wait amongst the other students. Remember I was in my pyjamas; no shoes, no bra and unshowered; a complete train wreck!

She came in and told me my bus was here. I took a few deep breaths, composed myself as best I could then walked out of the office; briskly down the footpath and straight onto the bus. I didn't make eye contact with anyone. As soon as I got on the bus I heard my name.

"Sophie come and sit here." It was Kylie.

I moved down the aisle and sat closely beside my best friend. She put her arm around me and I buried my head against her chest. Once again tears sprung from my eyes and rolled down my cheeks.

During the bus ride home Kylie softly spoke to me with reassuring and caring words. I listened to her voice and it felt nice to have my friend beside me. I didn't speak and I didn't look up for the entire trip.

"It's your stop Soph. Do you want me to come home with you?" she offered.

"No it's ok. I'm going straight to bed."

"Ok. Well call me later if you need anything."

"Thanks." I looked up at her and noticed she was upset too.

As I hastily exited the bus I heard a few quiet giggles from some of the other students on board; one final stab of humiliation and embarrassment. I stepped off the bus and walked up the dirt track towards my house. I didn't have to look back to know there were a bunch of kids staring at me through the bus windows. It hurt terribly.

I hadn't eaten all day and was completely devoid of energy, so walking up the hill was a struggle. As I slowly made my way home I thought of some different ways I could handle my parents. As much as I wanted to let them have it with both barrels, I just didn't have the strength; eventually deciding the best approach was to ignore them and go straight to bed. So that's what I did.

Dad was up in the shed and didn't see me arrive home so I walked straight into the house, past Mum who was in the kitchen and into my bedroom. I crawled into bed and curled up into a ball under the covers.

I spent the next four or five hours in my room clawing at my legs and arms. It was as though my weakened state had allowed the 'bugs' free reign to ravage my limbs. I craved the soothing hot water of a shower on my skin but I didn't want to face my mother and father. Eventually, I heard the TV turn off and my parents go to bed. I got up, had a shower and something to eat before going back to bed and finally drifting off to sleep. The worst day of my life was over.

So as you can see by the traumatic experience I just outlined, my *monster* caused me more than just physical pain; unfortunately, on more than one occasion. In the beginning it was impossible to detect and it had the ability to turn the people who loved me, against me. It was savage.

I never received an apology from my parents for how they treated me, and quite a few years passed until I told Jake about that awful day at Crystal Creek High. I suppose I didn't want him to dislike my parents and chose instead to protect *them*. How ironic.

I'll talk more about my illness as this story progresses, but at this point the main thing I want you to understand is once the symptoms of my illness began, every meeting with Jake thereafter was bitter-sweet. I say bitter-sweet because although he always listened to me and provided me with the care and affection I craved, at the same time I was constantly in pain from being attacked by the 'bugs'. He opened my heart and body to amazing pleasure and love, but each time we were together I knew it would inevitably end and I'd have to go back to the isolation of the farm; alone and at the mercy of my *monster*.

The first year with Jake was the best, and worst of my life; bitter-sweet for sure.

CHAPTER TEN

SLEEPOVER

Two weeks had passed since that memorable walk in the woods with my lover; his piercing eyes still vivid in my mind, looking up at me as he licked and teased my nipples. Over the phone we talked about the 'hideout' experience and often discussed what other exciting *firsts* we could share with one and other. I'd like to say I had the self-control not to let my hands wander as I listened to his voice, but to be honest I did have the odd moment of weakness.

We were not only surprised, but delighted that we'd managed to convince our parents to allow us to have a sleepover. Providing Jake was prepared to ride his bicycle all the way out to the farm, some fifty-odd kilometres from Sunbury, they all agreed he could spend the night and ride home the next day. It seemed fair, since a one hundred kilometre round trip for a fifteen-year-old would be a bit much in one day. We were both ecstatic that our parents shared the same view as us.

It was about 9:00am on Saturday. I was sitting at the kitchen table eating some breakfast; eager for Jake to arrive anytime within the next hour. He had decided to leave Sunbury at 7:00am and estimated it would take about two and a half hours to ride out; given the journey to our farm would see him tackle a number of large hills. I knew he was fit but I still couldn't believe he was riding all the way out to see me. It wouldn't be easy.

Jake often made the promise that he would do anything for me. I already believed him but I'm sure he saw this ride as his first chance to prove it; the first of many. Over the course of our lives together, I've lost count of the number of times Jake has upheld that promise to me.

'I would die for you' is a line you hear in songs and movies all the time. I can't even begin to describe what it feels like to know you have someone who would actually give their life for yours; without hesitation. It's a rare kind of devotion which gives you a feeling of safety and security that words simply can't explain. I'm telling you, with all my heart, that's exactly what I felt from Jake.

As this story unfolds I will talk about him being my saviour, but in addition you will also learn he was my protector… a guardian angel.

As I sipped on a cup of tea and ate some toast, Mum entered the kitchen. "Now, obviously you'll be sleeping in separate rooms," she said sternly.

"Of course Mum. I'll make up the bed in Dylan's old room."

It was right next to mine.

"Actually, I think it's probably best to make up Shaun's old bed," she suggested.

There was no reason to put Jake in Shaun's old room, other than the fact that it was further down the hall from mine. I didn't say anything though, I knew I was lucky to have him sleeping over in the first place and I wasn't about to push the boundaries.

"Ok. I'll make it up after breakfast."

"Now Sophie, your father and I don't want to hear either of you creeping around in the middle of the night. Is that understood?"

"Jeez, what do you think we're going to do!" I exclaimed; overly defensive. I had to at least make it *sound* like I didn't want him in my bed. I don't think it worked though.

Mum had obviously been a teenager once too, and given she was pregnant with her first child at the age of seventeen, she would've known exactly what was going on in my head; not to mention my body.

"I'm just letting you know we expect you both to behave yourselves. Your father and I, and Jake's parents for that matter, are putting a lot of trust in you two. Having a sleep over at your age is not ideal, and it's only because he's riding so far to see you that we've allowed it."

Her comment made me smile on the inside for a couple of reasons. Since I'd met Jake, I think it was the first time I was actually *glad* we lived a fair distance apart. I know if he had of lived closer then neither of our parents would have given permission for him to stay over. And secondly, at Mum saying it wasn't *ideal* for him to be sleeping over. I agreed completely. *It's not ideal... it's absolutely perfect!*

"I promise we'll behave. Jake will stay in his room… and I'll stay in mine," I replied convincingly. I hated lying to my parents.

"Good, that's all I wanted to hear;" her voice relieved.

Oh the guilt.

I finished breakfast and brushed my teeth. I was already showered and dressed since I'd woken up so early. I was actually getting used to the early starts on the days I was going to see Jake; the early starts and the sleepless nights beforehand. It's amazing how excited anticipation and teenage hormones can upset your sleep patterns.

I went outside and waited on the back veranda in the sunshine. From where I was sitting I'd be able to see him ride the last two hundred meters before reaching our gate. I couldn't wait to see him ride around the bend towards my house… towards *me*!

After a while I went inside and checked the clock. It was just after 9:30am; he'd be arriving any minute. *Welcome back butterflies.*

I returned to my seat on the veranda and resumed my fixed stare on the bend in the track from which he would soon appear.

When I first saw Jake ride into view, I remember being overwhelmed with both pride and gratitude. I could tell by the way he was pedalling, how tired and worn out he was; his legs must have been exhausted. It wouldn't have been an easy journey at all and he'd made it; I was so incredibly proud of him. I was also grateful that he'd subjected himself to such a physical test just to see me.

Nobody had ever done something so romantic for me before, and it felt wonderful. He was a man of his word.

I stood up and ran to the front gate to greet him, and as he rode closer I could see the effect the epic journey had taken on him. He was absolutely drenched with sweat. His t-shirt was saturated and he had sweat running from his forehead, down his cheeks and dripping off the bottom of his chin. He was breathing heavily, like he'd just finished a race, and when he spoke I understood why.

"I got here… as fast as… I could Soph," he puffed loudly; drawing deep breaths between words.

He *had* been in a race, only there were no other competitors. He was racing to see me.

"Hi Jake, I hope your ride wasn't too hard?"

"It was ok… I fuckin' hate hills though!" he panted. "Oh… and the wind… I hate that too!"

I couldn't help but laugh at his outburst.

As Jake recovered his breath, he unclipped his helmet and leaned his bike against the gate post then wiped the sweat from his face with his t-shirt.

"Come here gorgeous," he smiled; arms open wide.

I moved closer and he gripped me firmly by the waist, one hand on each hip, then kissed me passionately on the lips.

Oh that feels good! I relished in the warmth and affection.

As we kissed, his grasp on my waist became even firmer. To have his hands on me again felt amazing; to feel his strength and to taste his lips… just to have him with me again. Each time I greeted Jake I realised how much I missed him when we were apart. The emptiness when we weren't together would vanish as soon as we touched, as if a missing body part had been returned to me. Being reunited with Jake was like having my heart put back in my chest. It was like being brought back to life.

Jakes lips tasted salty from the sweat. It was different, but not unpleasant.

"You're soaked." I ran my finger down his arm, touching his wet skin which was surprisingly cool.

“I was pretty cold when I left this morning, but as soon as the sun came out so did the sweat. I’m looking forward to a shower and some dry clothes.”

“Well come inside and get cleaned up. You’re probably hungry are you?”

“Yeah I’ve well and truly burned up my toast and cereal from this morning. I’m starving!”

“I’ll make you something to eat while you take a shower then. Will bacon and eggs on toast do?”

His eyes widened at the suggestion of a hot meal. “Oh hell yeah! That sounds great Soph!”

We went inside and Jake talked with Mum and Dad for a while about the ride out. Dad asked him which way he rode from Sunbury to the farm. It turns out he went the long way; adding at least ten or so kilometres and a few more hills to the trip.

“Probably explains why I’m so stuffed! I don’t think I could ride over one more hill if I tried.”

We all had a good laugh at Jake’s expense; him included.

I led him into the bathroom and handed him a fresh towel from the linen cupboard.

“Need any help in there?” I whispered as I handed him the towel; shooting him a sleazy grin.

“If you wouldn’t mind. I could sure use a couple of extra hands,” he whispered back; his expression serious before cracking a smile.

“I’ll leave you to it then.” I bit my bottom lip as I closed the bathroom door behind me.

I headed into the kitchen and started on breakfast.

“Are you cooking Jake breaky Soph? You don’t even cook for us!” Dad joked.

“I do so… sometimes,” I replied; knowing full well I hadn’t cooked Mum and Dad breakfast for at least six months, probably since the last mother’s or father’s day. “Well Jake rode all the way out to see me, the least I can do is cook him a meal to show my appreciation.”

It really was the *least* I could do. I planned on showing him my appreciation in far more intimate ways. I squeezed my thighs together at the thought.

As I cooked the bacon and eggs I could hear the sound of the shower coming from the bathroom. I pictured the hot water spraying from the shower head and running all over Jakes naked body; steam filling the room. I hadn't seen his bare chest since I met him at the lake, but I could still see his hard and clearly defined muscles vividly in my mind. Knowing he was only meters away from me, completely naked in a hot shower, was driving me wild. I visualised what it would look like to watch him washing his body; lathering up every sculptured inch of himself.

Stop Sophie! I tried to focus on cooking to divert my mind, but the sound of the shower made it impossible.

I imagined how amazing it would be to spy on him right at that moment. To gaze at him while he washed his chest, shoulders and arms. To watch his hands gliding over his defined stomach before venturing even further south; the feeling of warm water and soap sliding over his manhood making him *grow*.

My mind raced, and with each second of delicious fantasy I could feel myself become increasingly slippery. My groin tormenting me with an intense and demanding ache; desperate for soothing attention.

"So what are you kids going to do today?"

My erotic visions exploded in a cloud of white smoke as my mother's voice snapped me back to reality.

"Umm… sorry… what did you say?" I fumbled.

"Earth to Sophie!" she teased. "What are you going to do today?"

"I thought Jake might like to take me for a ride on the motorbike around the farm."

"Can he ride?" questioned Dad.

"Yeah he said he can. He's actually saving up to buy a motorbike when he is old enough to get his licence; so he can ride out here and see me," I smiled.

"Ok just be careful. We don't want you two ending up in hospital with broken arms and legs."

"We'll only be cruising around the farm and up to the lookout. I'll make sure he takes it slow."

I already knew I wouldn't have to tell Jake to be careful with me on the bike. I felt completely safe whenever I was with him, and was certain he wouldn't put me in danger by riding too fast. I was right.

After showering, Jake emerged from the bathroom looking refreshed and immaculate. His hair was tied back perfectly neat; not a strand out of place. He had a pair of dark blue cargo shorts on and a white printed t-shirt. As soon as he entered the kitchen I could smell his cologne.

Mmm... he smells so good!

"I hope you're hungry, I've cooked you up a huge breakfast." I pointed to the pan with the spatula.

"That looks delicious. Thanks Baby."

I blushed instantly at being called *Baby* in front of my parents, and I glanced over at them to see their reaction. Mum was smiling but Dad was just sitting there, both eyebrows raised; surprised I guess.

"Take a seat and it'll be ready in a sec."

Jake sat down at the table and I presented him with a plate full of bacon, eggs, toast, sliced tomatoes, and a glass of juice.

"How many people are you going to feed with all that Soph!" exclaimed Mum, shaking her head at the pile of food on the plate.

Jake laughed. "Don't stress Mrs. Taylor. I'll get through it all... no problem."

So I've already told you a fair bit about Jake, but there's one thing I haven't mentioned until now. When it comes to food... he eats like a horse! Without a word of a lie, I've never met anyone who can eat so much. It's not that he's a pig; I guess it's just that he's so active it takes a mountain of food to replenish his energy. To this day, I'll often serve his meals on two plates; one with meat and the other salad or vegetables. I still find it hilarious when he sits down with two plates of food in front of him, and I'm still trying to comprehend how he managed to eat a one-kilogram steak in one sitting! I wouldn't have believed it if I hadn't of seen it with my own eyes.

The boy can eat!

As Jake worked his way through breakfast, he spoke with my parents and I about the previous couple of weeks at school and his job as a trolley pusher at one of the supermarkets in Sunbury. He also asked about the farm and my brothers. I loved how comfortable it felt spending time together with my parents and boyfriend. There were never awkward silences and the conversation was always relaxed and easy.

Once Jake finished eating, I took his dishes and washed up. We headed down to my brother's old room and I showed him were he'd be sleeping. As soon as we walked into the room, away from the eyes and ears of my parents, Jake grabbed me forcefully; taking me by surprise. He pulled me to him and kissed me feverishly. With our bodies pressed together, our lips and tongues reunited with profound sensuality. Slowly, I pressed my pelvis forward; grinding against him. Without hesitation, Jake pushed back; deliberately pressing *himself* against me.

Oh my... he's so hard! I didn't mention the lustful feelings rapidly building inside me, or the explicit thoughts which raced through my mind. My body screamed for him to throw me on the bed and take me...*all* of me, right then and there! I wanted him desperately. I wanted to give myself to him.

"I'll get the bike out of the shed and leave it at the back gate!" Dad yelled from the kitchen.

We stopped kissing and I clung to Jake; squeezing him like a baby monkey clings to its mother.

"Thanks Dad. We'll go for a ride soon," I yelled back.

"So where are we riding to Soph? I can think of one place I wouldn't mind visiting again," he grinned evocatively.

"And where might that be?" I chuckled; blushing as I recalled our last trip up into the hills.

"Our hideout." He lowered his voice. "Remember? Where you basically *demanded* me to touch your…" his eyes darted south to my groin.

"Jake!" I whispered. "How rude."

"Yes *you* are… very rude. And I love it!" he snapped excitedly; squeezing my hips as he spoke.

"I don't think I demanded it," I replied coyly. "And even if I did… *you* didn't take much convincing!"

"True. I'm only human after all," he smiled. "So where to then?"

"I'll tell you where we are going once we're on the bike."

"OK boss," he joked; saluting me.

I laughed and hit him playfully on the arm. "I'm not your boss."

His gaze deepened; eyes dark and suggestive. "Baby… you can boss me around whenever you like."

"I like the sound of that." I wasn't kidding either. Every muscle in my pelvis tightened at the prospect of taking the lead.

After putting on some boots, we went outside and headed over to the back gate where the bike was waiting. The farm motorbike was pretty old and beaten up but it was still quite powerful, so Dad came over and gave Jake a quick run-down on what worked and what didn't.

"I might go for a quick spin before you get on the back Soph, just so I can get a feel for it."

"Good idea," agreed Dad.

Jake kick-started the bike and rode out the gate into the field. He twisted the throttle a few times propelling him forward with force before pulling a couple of sharp turns; dirt spraying up from the back wheel as he changed direction.

He rode back to Dad and I. "All good. Jump on Baby!" he smiled, tapping the back seat with his hand.

"Take it slow won't you? Especially in the long grass. There's a few large rocks lying around the place which you won't be able to see!" explained Dad loudly so as to be heard over the engine.

"Will do Mr. Taylor!"

I climbed on the back behind Jake.

"Be careful," Dad urged a final time.

"Sure will." Jake gave Dad the thumbs up then looked over his shoulder at me. "You ready?"

I wrapped my arms around his waist and gripped his butt and thighs tightly with my legs.

"Sure am. Ride towards the far gate." I pointed out across the field, halfway up the hill to a cattle gate in the distance.

"Righto."

Jake put the bike in gear and accelerated smoothly. He slowly made his way up the hill towards the gate I'd pointed out. It was so romantic; riding through the grass on the back of the bike. Jake was in no rush and I felt completely safe with him at the controls. I absolutely loved having him between my legs, a feeling which prompted the most erotic visions to invade my mind... again! Honestly, from the moment Jake arrived, they hadn't stopped!

We rode all the way up to the lookout at the top of the property. Jake killed the engine and we climbed off the bike. There was a clearing at the summit of the hill which allowed a beautiful view of the valley, and the clear skies meant we were able to see all the way to Sunbury.

Jake and I sat on the trunk of a fallen tree admiring the view; and each other. As we held hands, he spoke about how he constantly thought of me and missed me like crazy when we were apart. I knew exactly how he felt.

Reluctantly, I told him about some of the symptom's I'd started to suffer. At this point I'd only just began to experience the crawling sensation under my skin, and was yet to see a doctor. I was still oblivious to how bad things would actually get and the horrendous months to follow.

I was a little hesitant about discussing my health because even though deep down I knew he'd be supportive and understanding, I still had concerns that it might scare him away. After all, he was a teenage boy, and Mum had warned me about how quick they were to lose interest. But as I expected, Jake was sympathetic and caring;

displaying a level of sensitivity and concern which instantly reassured me that telling him was the right thing to do. He put his arm around me and held me close as I spoke about the torment of the 'bugs' and the sleepless nights which were starting to take their toll.

I know this sounds selfish, but it actually felt good to include him in my struggle. His caring and compassionate nature made me feel like I had somebody in my corner, to watch over me… to fight for me.

"I'm glad you trust me enough to share this with me Soph. You know you can tell me anything right? Nothing you say will ever scare me away. I'm yours." He was reading my mind.

"Thank you." I replied sincerely. "That really means a lot Jake. Hopefully when I see the doctors next week, we'll figure out what's going on and get it all sorted out."

If only I'd have known just how *wrong* I was.

Understandably, the conversation was heavy and quite serious so I wanted to change the mood. "Why don't we go and check out our hideout?"

"Sounds like fun!" he replied immediately; his over enthusiastic tone making me laugh.

Jake kissed me softly on the lips, helped me to my feet and then led me to the motorbike. He kick-started the engine and it roared to life. As soon as I climbed on behind him I could feel my mood change. Thoughts of my unexplained illness vanished and I was suddenly brimming with excitement and anticipation at the prospect of his hands all over me… and more. I could feel the vibration of the engine through the seat which only contributed to the tingling sensation in my groin. I longed for him to touch me again… I *needed* him to.

As we rode down the side of the hill towards the willow tree that I had recently become so fond of, I noticed my father driving slowly up the hill on the tractor. He was a few hundred meters away, so I pointed him out to Jake who stopped the bike.

"Shit! There goes that idea!" I said loudly. The realisation I wasn't going to get what I needed aggravated me.

"Don't stress Baby, we have the whole weekend together," he said with a smile, which served to reassure me that my sexual needs would be met at some stage before his departure.

He really is a mind reader!

I took him on a guided tour of some of the surrounding country side. It really was a beautiful day and the scenery around the farm was breathtaking; more so than usual. I think everything just seemed so much more magical when I was with Jake. It was a lot of fun cruising around with him, but in all honesty, I still think the best part of the whole ride was that I got to sit behind my man; squeezing him tightly between my thighs for an hour or so. Yeah no appreciation of the scenery for me! It was all about having Jake between my legs… what a tart!

Eventually we arrived home. I jumped off the back and Jake rode the bike up to the shed. Once inside, we grabbed a drink and headed into my room. I put on some music and we talked about our friends and what was happening at school. After a while we went out into the lounge room to watch a movie.

I loved being with Jake regardless of what we were doing. Sitting on the couch, snuggled up together while we watched a movie felt so comfortable; so natural.

We were relaxed and cosy until a sex scene began to unfold. Jake had his arms around me and I felt his grasp tighten. As the sexual energy between us grew rapidly, so did our body heat. So much so that I could've sworn someone turned the temperature up in the house. As we watched the actor and actress play out an exceptionally hot love scene, I knew exactly what Jake was thinking; I was thinking the same thing. There's no doubt that if we were alone in the house, I would've taken him by the hand, led him into my bedroom and given myself to him; letting him forever claim my virginity as his. The fact remained though… we weren't alone! Us two horny teenagers would just have to ride the waves of hormones and sexual tension until they eventually subsided.

At this point I was beginning to understand something about my body, in particular my sexual organs. When I had the need for sexual release and didn't get it, I would be left to battle a dull ache in my groin which seemed to take forever to diminish. It would vary in intensity, sometimes verging on painful, and I didn't like it… not one bit!

After the movie we had lunch then went outside with Dad. He was laying a new water pipe from one of the top dams down to the house, so he asked Jake to give him a hand.

Having a part time job as a trolley pusher meant Jake was no stranger to manual labour, and I could tell my father was impressed that this 'city kid' didn't mind getting his hands dirty.

I enjoyed watching them work together all afternoon. I never had a boyfriend bond with my father before, and it made me happy to know that Dad liked Jake. *You might as well get to like each other now, because one day you'll be in-laws,* I smiled to myself.

Over the coming years when Jake came to visit the farm, he often helped Dad out with work that needed to be done around the property.

Eventually it was time to head inside for dinner. We cleaned ourselves up and sat down for a roast, which Mum had spent the afternoon preparing; her signature dish. Afterwards Jake and I washed the dishes together. *So domesticated.* I found it amusing how Jake's involvement with something as mundane as washing up, somehow made it so much more enjoyable; even fun. It once again proved that it didn't matter what I was doing with him… I was happy.

The four of us sat down and watched some television before Mum and Dad announced they were going to bed.

"I think I might turn in for the night," yawned Dad.

"Me too," agreed Mum. "Don't stay up too late."

"We won't. Just till the end of this show," I explained.

"And make sure you remember which bed you're supposed to be sleeping in Jake," teased my father, with a serious undertone that was impossible to miss.

"Will do Mr. Taylor."

"We don't want to hear any footsteps in the middle of the night… ok Sophie?" warned my mother. Clearly, she didn't have much faith in me.

"You won't Mum. We'll both stay in our rooms."

Of course you won't hear me creeping into Jake's room… I'm far too light on my feet! I thought to myself.

"Well good night kids. See you when I get home from work tomorrow." Dad was on night shift at the factory and would be leaving the house around 12:30am.

"Night Mum and Dad."

"Goodnight Mr. and Mrs. Taylor," Jake echoed.

Alone at last!

We sat together on the couch and I snuggled in close to Jake; resting my head on his chest. I lay their listening to the rhythmical thump of his heart.

I don't know if you've ever experienced it, but I had one of those moments when you just can't get close enough to the one you love. It still happens to me all the time. It's like being beside Jake and hugging him tightly just isn't close enough. I want to be so close that I melt into him; become a part of him. He says quite often he feels the same way about me too, and has also confessed to experiencing another desire which takes hold of him from time to time; a desire slightly more intense.

He's said that sometimes when he's kissing me, simply tasting my lips isn't enough. He craves *more* and literally wants to bite me… devour me. It usually results in him sinking his teeth into my neck, pretty hard too! He describes the feeling as though he somehow becomes possessed by me; so severely bewitched and enthralled that it reaches a point where he actually wants to bite a piece off me so I'm with him always. I know it sounds a little strange, but I can assure you the sensation of Jake's teeth clamping down hard on my neck leaves me weak at the knees. It's absolutely one of the hottest feelings ever. We both laugh at how crazy and savage it is, but at the same time I find it so powerful; so beautiful.

After an hour or so, I noticed that Jake looked a little tired.

I gently rubbed the side of his face with my hand. "Riding out to the farm has taken it out of you Baby?"

He closed his eyes at my touch. "Yeah I think it must have. I'm feeling a little sleepy."

"Why don't you go and jump in the shower and get ready for bed."

"Ok Baby. Sounds good."

He grabbed some fresh clothes and went to the bathroom. I stood right outside the door so I could hear everything! I would've killed for x-ray vision.

As soon as I heard the shower, I began imagining all the lovely places the warm water was lucky enough to flow. The *last* thing I felt like doing was going to sleep!

A few minutes later Jake emerged from the bathroom to find me standing at the door. He was so fresh and looked delicious in his singlet and boxer shorts; his hair still damp. I wiped a stray bit of tooth paste from his lip with my finger.

"What are you doing out here? You're quite the little stalker aren't you?" he joked.

"I just wanted to make sure you had everything you needed," I replied with a cheeky grin.

"Not quite everything." He grabbed the front of my t-shirt and pulled me towards him as he spoke.

Oh how I would've loved to take a shower with him. I fantasised about washing every inch of his body. Some places more thoroughly than others!

"Come with me, I'll put you into bed before I take a shower." I grabbed his hand; leading him down the hall to his bedroom.

I threw the covers back and Jake climbed into bed. It was fairly warm so I only pulled the sheet over his legs. I could still see the rest of his body. *Mmm.*

"Thanks Baby," he said sleepily.

"God I wish I could climb in there with you," I whispered.

"That could be dangerous."

I kissed his lips; savouring the fresh minty taste as my tongue explored his mouth. "I like danger."

"Really?"

"You'll find out soon enough," I grinned.

"I look forward to it."

I kissed him again. "Good night Jake."

"See you in the morning Baby."

I leant over and put my mouth close to his ear. "I have a feeling you'll see me before then."

He looked at me with blazing eyes; the sleepy expression from moments earlier nowhere to be seen. I smiled then winked seductively before walking out of the room; half closing the door behind me.

I showered and checked on my parents who were both fast asleep. It was just before midnight. I'd planned to wait for my father to leave for work, give it twenty-minutes or so to be sure Mum had drifted back to sleep, then go and pay Jake a visit.

I lay in bed, wide-eyed and waiting. It wasn't like I was ever going to fall asleep anyway; my *monster* always managed to keep me up well into the night. The 'bugs' under my skin were definitely getting worse by the day, but thankfully I hadn't yet reached the point where I was waking up covered in blood from scratching at my legs. That would come in the following weeks.

Eventually I heard Dad out in the kitchen, fixing something to eat and getting ready to leave for his night shift at the factory. I listened as the back door closed, then shortly after, the sound of Dad's car faded into the distance. I waited a little longer than planned just to be sure Mum would be fast asleep.

I climbed out of bed then quietly walked down the hall and stood outside my parents' bedroom. I listened carefully and could hear Mum breathing; slow and heavy.

She's sound asleep. Perfect.

The house was dead silent as I turned and walked towards Jakes room. I was holding my breath with each step, desperately trying not to make a noise. All I could hear was my heart, which was now thumping in my chest like never before. I swear I could literally hear it beating.

I reached his room and entered; closing the door behind me. It was a bright, moonlit night which made it easy to see in the dark.

I stood at the foot of his bed. "Jake," I whispered.

He was already awake.

"What are you doing in here?" he said, propping himself up on one elbow before quickly moving to one side of the bed and throwing the sheet back; welcoming me in beside him.

I wasted no time and climbed straight in; snuggling into him tightly.

"Do you know how much shit we'll be in if you're caught in here?"

"Of course I do, but Dad's gone to work and Mum's fast asleep. I figure if she comes to check on me and realises I'm in here with you, she isn't going to open the door anyway; she'd be too embarrassed. I couldn't sleep knowing you were so close to me."

"I felt the same. I was so tired on the couch while we were watching TV, but as soon as I got into bed I haven't been able to sleep at all. My mind hasn't stopped racing."

"What've you been thinking about?" I probed. "Tell me Jake… what's kept you up?"

He put his mouth next to my ear. "Why don't I show you instead?"

I looked deep into his eyes. "Ok."

I was feeling excited, but at the same time a little nervous because I wasn't sure how far he wanted to go with me. At that point, I was prepared to go *all* the way with him.

We started kissing softly, slowly twisting our tongues together; taking turns biting each other's lips. Jake gently pushed me onto my back and straddled me; one leg either side of my hips. He slowly moved his kisses from my mouth, across my cheek then down my neck. I tilted my head back while he licked and sucked the side of my neck; his teeth occasionally biting my skin like a vampire feeding on a helpless victim. Each time he bit down my whole body shivered deliciously. It felt like I had electricity flowing through my veins instead of blood. I was more alive than I'd ever been.

He reached down, grabbed the bottom of my singlet and slowly pulled it up over my stomach, then higher; exposing my bare breasts. I sat up so he could take it off entirely.

"You're so beautiful," he said, sitting up to admire my naked torso; delicately squeezing and massaging my breasts.

He leant forward, placed his mouth over one of my nipples and sucked firmly. A surge of pleasure ran through my body, intensifying as it reached my groin which was now positively saturated. Never had I been so sexually primed before; so *ready*.

While Jake paid equal attention to both my breasts, he slowly manoeuvred my legs apart and positioned his body in between my thighs. I felt vulnerable, but at the same time perfectly safe. He traced his hand down the inside of my thigh, caressing me softly for a moment before finding the edge of my underwear. Carefully, he pulled my panties to one side and I gasped as he exposed *me* to the cool night air.

Moving from my breasts back to my mouth, Jake kissed me tenderly as he slowly eased the tip of his finger inside me. It slid in effortlessly as I'd provided ample lubrication. I moaned with pleasure at his gentle touch; Jake alternating between teasing my now enlarged and incredibly sensitive clit, and shallow penetration with his finger. The combination was wonderful and it wasn't long before I felt the pressure building.

"That feels amazing!" I breathed into his ear. "You're going to make me come!"

"Let it go... come for me Baby," he whispered back as he increased his pressure and depth.

I was already on the brink, and hearing those words was enough to push me over. I erupted with pleasure; my hips thrusting back and forth against his finger; now buried deep inside me.

Jake withdrew, allowing me to catch my breath while he kissed me softly on the neck.

He held himself above me and look me directly in the eyes. “Can I taste you?”

Oh hell yes! I’d fantasised about this moment so many times I could hardly wait. As much as I wanted to grab his head and force him down *there*, I kept my cool.

“If you want to?” I replied calmly.

“I’ve wanted to for a long time Baby.”

He smiled mischievously then licked his lips as though he was about to dive into his favourite meal. I held my hand over my mouth to stop myself from laughing out loud.

Jake leant down and kissed me on the lips. “Let me take these off.”

As he grasped the waist band of my underwear I raised my butt off the bed and brought my legs together, allowing Jake to slide my panties down to my knees then completely off.

Surprised by my own confidence, I gradually opened my legs for him. He knelt between them; studying my body with wide eyes.

“Fuck I wish I could turn the light on!” he exclaimed, the moonlight obviously not giving him the visibility he so desperately wanted.

“I bet you do,” I giggled. “You’re like a kid with a new toy.”

“And I can’t wait to play with it!” he added quickly.

As I lay completely naked in front of him, it felt surreal; like I was dreaming. I felt so exposed but at the same time more comfortable and safe than ever before. I was bare and vulnerable, yet completely protected. As I said… surreal.

He grasped one of my legs and raised my foot up to his mouth. Placing light kisses on the top of my foot, he slowly worked his way down my calf, past my knee and across the inside of my thigh; stopping just before reaching my *warmth*. He was taking his time… and it was driving me wild!

Just when I thought he was going to give me what I needed, he reached over and grasped my ankle; repeating the tantalising process on the other leg. After trailing light kisses down the inside of my thigh, he paused achingly close to my wetness then inhaled deeply through his nose.

"Oh my god you smell incredible!" he exhaled.

"Jake!" I giggled; blushing at his blatant sampling of my intimate scent.

"Sorry, I couldn't help myself. You smell delicious!"

I smiled to myself. *Wait till you taste me!*

I couldn't wait any longer. I wanted, no… I *needed* to feel his mouth on me. I lay back on the pillow, closed my eyes and reached forward; my hands finding the back of his head. Gently I pulled him down between my legs.

The moment Jake placed his lips on my pussy for the first time was one of the hottest experiences of my life. The feeling of him greedily licking my clit before forcing his thick tongue between my lips, deep inside, sent me over the edge in a matter of seconds. I held my breath to silence the wild screams I so desperately wanted to set free as I orgasmed. I came hard, pulling his head against me, thrusting my hips against his face in sync with the waves of pleasure rushing through me. Jake moaned with satisfaction as I spilled into his mouth… and so did I.

The sensation of coming in my lover's mouth was addictive from that very first time. An addiction I still embrace today and suspect I will for the rest of my life. I love looking down and seeing his eyes staring up at me, burning with desire as his lips and tongue explore *every* part of me. Of all the sexual acts, having Jake go down on me is the pinnacle of eroticism.

Jake stayed down between my thighs pleasuring me again and again. It was bliss… paradise. There was no doubt that taking the next step in letting my man taste me, definitely bound us closer together. I was now giving him a piece of me… *literally*, and it was an act which served to deepen our love.

Jake took me to heaven multiple times with his lips and tongue, and I would've let him keep going too if it wasn't for the fact that I now had a burning desire to repay the favour.

I put my hand under his chin and lifted his head up to look at me; the moonlight glistened off his lips. Seeing *me* all over his mouth and chin looks so fucking hot!

“You’re covered!” I giggled quietly.

“I know. I thought you were going to drown me,” he grinned; wiping his mouth with his hand. “I loved it.”

“Me too, but now it’s your turn. Lie on your back,” my voice quiet yet authoritative.

“Are you sure?”

“Lie on your back Jake!” I demanded.

As we switched positions, I put my knickers and singlet on just in case we were interrupted. I know getting caught in Jake’s bed would have been bad enough, but having my boobs and ass out would’ve only made things worse.

Jake rolled onto his back and I lifted up his top; exposing his torso. I planted kisses all over his chest and lightly licked his nipples, just as he’d done to me. I was amazed when the small buds became erect like mine did; it was a huge turn on.

I ran my hand down his chest and over his smooth and perfectly toned stomach. I could feel each bump of his abdominals under my fingertips. I let my hand travel lower and grasped hold of his straining erection through his boxer shorts. He was so hard that it didn’t even feel like a body part, more like the handle of a wooden baseball bat! As I held onto *him* firmly, I heard a change in his breathing. It made me feel so powerful; as though I had total control of him.

I’d never touched one before and was eager to feel it in my hand; skin on skin. I let go then swiftly slid my hand inside his boxers before grabbing *him* again. It was surprisingly hot to the touch and I could feel it pulsing in my hand as blood pumped through its length. It was quite gratifying to know *I* was the reason he was so hard.

I began to massage Jake with a slow stroking motion; careful not to grip too tightly. His hips raised up and down in time with the rhythm I’d set, causing the feelings of power and control over him to intensify.

"Lie back Jake."

He let his head fall to the pillow. I repositioned myself so I was now hovering above his groin. Holding him firmly at the base, I leant forward and tentatively licked the end of his cock. I was surprised that I could already taste the unique flavour of his arousal; lightly seeping from the tip.

He's close and I haven't even started.

I'd certainly never done anything like this before, so I was paying particular attention to how his body and breathing responded to my touch. With my confidence growing, I began to lick up and down his shaft and around the pronounced head of his member. I sensed by his reaction that I was doing alright, so after a few minutes I went all the way; taking his length in my mouth then sucking gently.

"Oh fuck!" he gasped. "That feels incredible!"

I began to move my lips up and down his cock, occasionally pausing to lick around the head, which was easily distinguished from the rest of the shaft by a distinctive ridge. As I built up to a slow yet continuous rhythm, I could feel his dick swell and strain in my mouth. I was surprised by how the thick veins grew more prominent as I progressed.

After a few minutes I sensed he was *very* close.

"That's it Baby… that's it!" he encouraged with a strained whisper. "You're going to make me come."

I desperately wanted him to so I let him know by moaning agreeably.

I continued my steady rhythm, though slightly increased the sucking pressure. Jake's hips responded by thrusting harder. He grabbed the back of my head with both hands and I felt him thicken. He stopped breathing momentarily and his hips surged forward a final time. I felt him swell as a stream of come force its way through the length of his cock, before firing into the back of my throat; immediately followed by another jet of warm salty liquid… then another. The sensation of his erection pulsing again and again while he filled my mouth was absolutely mind blowing!

I quickly swallowed his creamy gift then took him in my mouth again. Jake quivered beneath me as I ran my tongue from the base to the tip, over every inch. As I licked him clean, I couldn't help but feel proud of my efforts.

Eventually he pushed me away. "Fuck that's sensitive!" he gasped holding my head back from his cock, which I was still grasping firmly like some kind of trophy.

I laughed quietly as I let go of him.

"How was that Baby?" I grinned; well aware that I'd done a brilliant *job*!

"Unbelievable! It felt amazing. Thank you so much Baby," he said gratefully, still slightly breathless.

"It was my pleasure."

"No… it was definitely *my* pleasure!" he smiled. "I can't believe you let me come in your mouth. Do you have any idea how fucking hot that is?"

"I thought you'd like that." I was so happy with myself for impressing him with my newly discovered skill.

"And even hotter is the fact you swallowed it! That didn't bother you?"

I shook my head. "Not at all. I actually don't mind the taste. Feel free to do that anytime," I urged.

"Give me twenty minutes?" he joked.

"I think we've pushed our luck far enough for one night," I replied, but not before giving serious consideration to his offer.

"We sure have Baby. You should probably get back to your bed," suggested Jake.

"Can we snuggle for a while?"

"Of course we can Soph."

I pulled up Jake's boxer shorts and cuddled him tightly. As we lay there in complete silence, relishing in the pleasure we'd just given each other, I'd never felt so connected with someone before. We had given each other something special, now we had a part of each other inside us. The experience all the more extraordinary because neither of us had shared it with anyone else before. Yet another sign that Jake and I were meant to be.

Exhausted from the waves of passion, emotion and pleasure over the last hour or so, I started to feel myself drifting off. I kissed Jake and told him I was going to go back to my room. I would hate to think what'd happen if I fell asleep in his bed. Mum was an early riser so I thought it better to be safe than sorry.

"Thanks for an amazing night."

"It sure was. Thank you. I love you with all my heart Jake."

"I love you too Baby," he replied as he kissed me on the forehead. "I'll dream about you."

"You'd better!" I joked, as I climbed out of bed and pulled the sheet over him.

"Good night Baby," I whispered as I kissed him on the lips. "I can still smell *me* on your mouth," I giggled.

He inhaled deeply through his nose. "Mmm," he smiled with satisfaction before closing his eyes. He was clearly exhausted.

I walked back to my room and climbed into bed. The night had been everything I'd hoped for and fantasised about. I felt like I had grown up in the space of a couple of hours. We were getting more serious and taking things further every time we met, and my mind raced at the thought of what our next meeting would hold. I knew *exactly* what I wanted, and after what I'd just done with Jake… I knew I was ready for it too.

CHAPTER ELEVEN

MAKING ME WAIT

'Just make sure he doesn't put any pressure on you. You know... pressure to do anything you don't want to do.' I vividly remember my mother's words of advice, given to me just before I went on my first date with Jake. I appreciated her protective guidance and I understood she was doing her job as a parent, but the irony of her concerns still makes me smile. The reason I found it ironic was because Mum was worried about Jake putting pressure on me to take our relationship further, but as it turned out, *I* ended up being the one pressuring *him* to take the next step.

You would've heard the old saying about people and money, and their inability to save it. The expression is something along the lines of *'It's burning a hole in their pocket'*, which can be used to describe somebody who has cash which they just can't wait to spend. Well after having Jake sleep over, which resulted in both of us eagerly reaching third base, I felt as though that particular expression could be applied to me; only it wasn't money that was burning a hole in my pocket, it was my virginity! I couldn't wait to give it to him.

The feeling of his mouth between my legs; his eyes staring up at me as I climaxed. Caressing his hard, throbbing cock with my hand before taking him in my mouth. Erotic images flashed through my mind constantly. His hands on the back of my head, holding me firmly as he let go; the sensation of his warm release sliding down the back of my throat. They didn't stop.

It wasn't just my heart that yearned for him when we were apart, it was my entire body. I absolutely ached for him to touch me, kiss me, and pleasure me all over. I wanted everything Jake had already given me and so much more. Making love to him was all I could think about.

This brings me back to the irony of Mum's words of protection. I really wasn't sure how I was going to bring the subject up with Jake. I didn't want to come across as 'easy', but the reality was that I desperately wanted to experience sex, and being madly in love only made the desire to go all the way even more powerful.

I wish I could say I didn't notice I was doing it, but that'd be a lie. In truth, I made a conscious decision to apply what I'd like to call a 'healthy' amount of pressure on him to sleep with me. *Sorry Mum.*

Now I've written it, I have to admit it does sound a little slutty. Oh well, what can I say in my defence, other than I was in love with Jake and wanted to prove to him how much.

I remember bringing it up a few days after our first sleepover. I thought approaching the subject via phone would be the safest option. *At least he won't be able to see me blush with embarrassment.*

"So… did you enjoy yourself the other night?" I asked coyly; wrapping the phone cord around my finger.

"Are you kidding! It was the best night of my life… hands down!" exclaimed Jake.

"I'm glad you had fun; I did too. I haven't been able to think of anything other than sneaking into bed with you… and what we did," I was serious too; it really was *all* I'd thought about since.

"Me too. The last couple of nights I've barely slept, and when I do finally get to sleep, all I dream about is you and all the things we did together," he confessed.

Jake's admission made me relax a little. It sounded like he was feeling exactly the same way as me, so I was fairly certain that what I was about to bring up wasn't going to be a surprise to him.

I took a deep breath. *Here goes nothing!*

'Jake?"

"Yeah."

"Um… I don't quite know how to bring this up, so bear with me ok?"

"Sure Soph. You know you can ask me anything."

"Well, I was… I… Um… I was wondering…" I couldn't get the words out. I was trying but was just too embarrassed, not to mention scared.

"Does it have something to do with what we did the other night?" he interjected cautiously.

"Uh huh."

"Is it about us taking the next step Baby?"

Jake 'the mind reader' strikes again!

"Yes!" I answered immediately; relieved I didn't have to say what I was thinking out loud.

"So you've been thinking about it too Soph?"

"Pretty much since you left the house on Sunday. I hope you're not freaked out. You're not are you?" I wanted to make sure we were definitely on the same page.

"Freaked out! More like the exact opposite! I really want to take things further with you too Baby."

I was so relieved. I honestly don't know how I would've handled it if Jake hadn't responded the way he did. In hindsight, I should've known he was going to be ok with it. After all, we had an incredible time together a few nights earlier. The thought making me smile to myself. I have to say though, I sure wasn't prepared for what he said next.

"I want to sleep with you more than anything Baby, but can I ask you a favour first?"

"Of course… anything."

"You promise you won't get upset?"

"I promise Jake."

"Would it be ok if we waited… just until I turn sixteen?" He spoke softly, as if he was delivering bad news. "I just want to make sure I'm ready, and more importantly… that you're ready too."

I couldn't believe it. I had heard so many girls at school talk about how their boyfriends were always putting the word on them to have sex; pressuring them constantly. Even to the point where some guys would actually break-up with girls who wouldn't open their legs for them. I had always thought of teenage boys, especially the ones at my school, as sex crazed who thought of nothing else but getting into a girl's pants. But here I was, practically confessing to Jake that sleeping with him was all I could think about, and *he* was the one asking me if we could wait. I wasn't disappointed or upset. I think I was just blindsided by the fact that in one softly spoken sentence, he'd just obliterated every teenage boy stereotype.

Now I think about it, when my son becomes a teenager I hope he is as gentle, patient and caring as his father was; and still is. I'd be so proud of my son if he has the same respect and thought for his girlfriend, and views their virginity as important and special as Jake saw ours.

"Oh Jake, of course I'll wait for you. I'd wait for you forever." I was doing the math in my head as I spoke. *Just over two months.* I was also rejoicing that he didn't ask me to wait until *I* turned sixteen, which would have meant I'd be waiting close to ten months! *Phew.*

"Thanks Soph, it means a lot to know you'll wait a little longer… until I'm ready. It's not that I don't want to sleep with you right now, because I do. I just feel like waiting till after I'm sixteen will give both of us a bit more time to make sure we're ready to take our relationship to that level."

"Of course. I completely understand. Thanks for being honest with me."

My respect for Jake, not just as my boyfriend but as a man, was growing by the second. It didn't matter how many times he'd shown me how different he was to any other boy I'd ever met before; he had amazed me once again. It was almost like Jake had already lived a lifetime. He had a kind of wisdom seen in people ten to fifteen years older; maybe more. I think it was why I trusted him completely.

From that moment on, I regarded Jake as so much more than just a teenage boyfriend. I looked up to him, and still do to this day, as someone who could be counted on for advice and guidance in many aspects of my life. Not only has he been a guardian angel, but a *guiding* angel as well.

"Besides, your sixteenth birthday is only a couple of months away Jake. I'm sure I can hold out until then. That is as long as you promise to look after me like you did the other night until your birthday arrives?"

"Now that's a promise I'll be more than happy to keep," he laughed.

Over the next couple of months, Jake stayed out at the farm a few more times. Needless to say we became quite good at creeping around the house in the dark. I'm reasonably certain my parents knew we would visit each other in the middle of the night, but they never brought the issue up with either of us. Maybe because I was the third child, my parents had relaxed a little. Either that or they were just too uncomfortable to bring the issue up. Regardless, I was happy not to have the discussion with them.

Honouring my declaration to being totally open and honest throughout this story, I feel obliged to make the following admission. Every time Jake and I were together in bed, perfecting our various *techniques*, I'd inevitably end up asking if he would take things to the next level with me; actually… it was more like *beg* him to. I tried not to pressure him but I just couldn't stop myself. He would get me so turned on and horny that even after giving me my final 'big' orgasm, which should have seen me satisfied, I would still crave him inside me. I wanted to know what intercourse felt like more than I wanted to breathe.

"Sophie, you really have no patience at all do you?" he would tease. "I'm not sixteen yet am I?"

"I know, but there's no harm in asking though is there?" I'd reply in an innocently sweet voice with accompanying pout.

It almost became common protocol for me to ask for sex every time we pleasured each other orally. It actually got to the point where he would look into my eyes after going down on me and say, "Anything you want to ask me?"

"Yes," I'd reply unashamedly. "Will you have sex with me *now*?"

We both found my persistence amusing, and it was good fun, but the humorous part of the whole situation was that Jake thought I was only joking around, when in actual fact I really *did* want him to fuck me! I would only laugh with him because I'm a good sport! Anyway, I was glad my pressure to have sex with Jake had turned into a game between the two of us, because it meant he didn't actually feel pressured at all.

Remember how I said that I hope my son turns out to be the type of teenager Jake was? Well, when my daughter becomes an adolescent… I hope she's nothing like me!

As the weeks passed, Jake and I became increasingly proficient at pleasuring each other during his visits to the farm. Unfortunately though, our skills in the bedroom weren't the only things that were progressing. The symptoms of my mystery illness were becoming even harder to ignore. My *monster* was on the offensive.

I'd started to show visible signs that something wasn't right. Jake had begun to notice the small dots and scratches on my legs, as well as my rapid weight loss. I had visited a number of doctors and undergone a variety of tests and skin treatments, but at this stage nothing was working. I was still a long way off a confirmed diagnosis.

I remember one particularly horrible night with Jake. I'd snuck into his room and we were in bed together. I was kneeling up in bed with my legs folded underneath me, hunched over in a ball with my head against my thighs; the only position I felt remotely comfortable in. Tears rolled down my cheeks as Jake cuddled me; attempting to sooth me by softly tickling my face and back. I'd already tried a hot shower to find some relief but my skin was still crawling, and I had scratched my legs so much they were bleeding. I was in pain and completely exhausted, but worst of all was the embarrassment of having Jake see me that way. He sat beside me all through the night, until the sun came up. We didn't sleep at all, nor did I go back to my bed in the morning like I usually did. The next morning Mum came down to my brother's old room where Jake and I had spent the night together. She knocked on the door. I wasn't even worried that we'd been caught out, because the fact was I felt like death. I'd spent the night crying and in pain, and Jake had been the one who got me through it.

"Come in," I said weakly.

Mum opened the door and looked at me; hunched over on my knees in Jakes bed. He was still beside me with his arm over my shoulders.

"Sorry Mrs. Taylor," Jake said immediately. "Sophie's had a rough night so I thought it would be ok if she stayed in here while I looked after her."

Mum looked at me. My eyes were puffy and red; face gaunt and grey, and my bare legs were littered with scratches and dried blood. I was a mess.

I know her first thoughts were about me spending the night in Jake's bed, but once she realised the condition I was in and that Jake had obviously sat up comforting me all night, she didn't even mention me being in his room. I was so grateful because I simply didn't have the energy to be reprimanded, let alone get into an argument.

Mum sat on the end of the bed, the sadness in her eyes clearly highlighting her concern. "Have you guys been up all night?"

"Pretty much. I had a hot shower but it did nothing. I couldn't lie down either. Kneeling up like this is the only way to stop the crawling and itching in my legs," I explained.

"I think it's because having your knees bent and sitting on your legs like that actually cuts off the blood supply, making your legs go numb," suggested Jake.

"That's kind of what it feels like; they hurt for a while but then I can't feel them anymore, which means I can't feel the crawling either."

"You both must be exhausted. Stay in bed a while and I'll go and put on some breakfast," she said sympathetically.

I was relieved Mum understood that having Jake beside me was so comforting, and along with making my legs go numb, was the only thing to ease the pain and stop me from going completely crazy.

"Thanks Mrs. Taylor. That'd be great," smiled Jake appreciatively.

"That's ok. Thanks for looking after her."

It must have felt strange for Mum; thanking a teenage boy for looking after her daughter. After all, I was her little girl and she'd been looking after me my whole life. Mum was the one who would put her arms around me when I was sick, in pain or upset, and now for the first time, she was watching somebody else fill the role. Her baby girl was growing up.

Don't get me wrong, I still needed my mother; it's just that I wanted Jake more. The connection I had with him, the love I felt from him, the way he wrapped me firmly in his arms and softly caressed my face… that was my medicine. Nothing came close to the power of Jake's affection.

"I haven't been able to do much besides tickle her face and rub her back. I wish there was more I could do," Jake sighed.

"Well sometimes that's all you can do Jake. Hopefully the next doctor we try can figure out what's going on with her. We'll be seeing another specialist in Sunbury this week; maybe he'll have some answers," explained Mum.

He didn't.

Once my mother left us alone, we lied down and Jake cuddled me against his chest. I closed my eyes and listened to the strong thump of his heart; beating its mesmerising rhythm. It's a song I've listened to hundreds of times since. The sound of Jakes heart has always had a soothing, almost pacifying effect on me. I feel safe when I hold my ear to his chest and listen to it thumping loudly. It sounds as though it will beat forever.

"It kills me to see you like this Baby. I just hate feeling so useless." He was clearly frustrated. "I can't begin to understand what you're going through, but I want you to know that if I could take away your pain, somehow absorb it into me, I would in a second."

I looked up at his face; tired and worried yet still so beautiful. "I know you would Jake… but I wouldn't want you to."

He looked drained and his eyes were red; not from a lack of sleep either. He was upset and fighting hard to stop the tears from escaping. I welled up instantly at the thought of seeing him cry. Knowing that my suffering was hurting him as well was more than I could handle. I put my head down and pressed my cheek against his chest again, but I couldn't hear his beating heart anymore; it was drowned out by the sound of my own sobbing. Jake cuddled me tightly as I wept. He didn't say anything; he couldn't speak. I knew he was crying too, because I felt one of his tears land on my cheek. It broke my heart… completely shattered it to pieces.

I'd always seen Jake as strong and powerful; unbreakable. He was my protector, my champion, and now he was reduced to tears. I felt like I'd broken him. It was a feeling a thousand times more painful than the physical attack from my *monster*.

Even though I knew it wasn't my fault, I still cried because I'd hurt my man. I also cried out of fear. Fear that one day Jake mightn't be able to handle the pain I caused him.

Still to this day, almost two decades later, with my relentless *monster* subjecting me to illness after torturous illness, the same fear lives with me… that one day enough will be enough for him.

How much can one person take?

Well the answer is a hell of a lot. I say this because throughout our time together, Jake has never once waivered in his compassion and devotion to me. When he said *'He'll be mine forever'*, it wasn't an empty promise. Even though I'm still scared that one day he will reach his limit, I have no proof or reason for thinking he even has one.

I wish I could put into words how much I love *my* Jake.

My young mind and body was in complete sensory overload. From one day to the next I was experiencing euphoric highs and breathtaking pleasures with Jake, then in stark contrast I was being subjected to devastating lows and horrible pain, thanks to my *'monster'*.

I was beginning to understand why I wanted my companion so much; why I wanted him to pleasure me constantly… to take me *all* the way. I realised that when Jake would do to me what he does best, my *'monster'* would fade into the shadows. I secretly hoped if he made love to me, then maybe… just maybe, by taking my virginity and giving me his, we would destroy my *'monster'* for good.

I prayed for the day.

CHAPTER TWELVE

NERVOUS

I was overflowing with excitement as Dad pulled into the drive way at Jake's house. In stark contrast, I was also worried; to the point of feeling nauseas.

The fact I'd never been to my boyfriend's house before was one of the reasons for my excitement. The other was that during the week my lover celebrated a milestone I'd been so patiently waiting for… his sixteenth birthday!

Finally! Now there's nothing stopping us from going all the way! I was more than ready to give myself to Jake, truth be told I'd been ready for months, and now that he was sixteen I knew he'd be ready too.

In contrast to my excitement, I was worried about him seeing me; considerably so. Over the past fortnight my physical condition had worsened significantly. I'd lost even more weight and was embarrassed by my emaciated appearance. My complexion was deathly pale and I looked frail and weak; exactly how I felt. I still had no idea what was wrong with me and by this stage I was up to my fourth or fifth failed diagnosis; probably that many doctors as well.

I'll never forget the look on his face when I arrived. He emerged from his house like a rodeo bull bursting out of its cage into the arena. The front door flew open with so much force it almost came off its hinges. With a huge smile on his face, Jake ran out into the front yard; his eagerness making me laugh.

The effect my deteriorated physical appearance had on him was immediately obvious. As I got out of the car, Jakes 'rodeo bull' eagerness vanished in the blink of an eye, along with his smile. He slowly approached me and carefully took me in his arms. The firm bear hug I'd grown accustomed to whenever Jake and I were reunited, was now replaced with a gentle, almost delicate embrace. It felt like he was cuddling me as though I'd break if he squeezed too hard. I wrapped my arms around him and closed my eyes.

"Hey Baby, it's good to see you again," he said quietly before placing a light kiss on my lips.

He's even talking to me gently! I must look worse than I thought. "Hi Jake, I missed you like crazy. Happy birthday!" I smiled shyly; feeling considerably self-conscious and awkward.

"Thanks Soph." He kissed me again.

Dad stepped out of the car.

"Hi Mr. Taylor."

"Hello Jake. Happy birthday mate."

"Thanks."

"Sixteen hey… all grown up!"

Dad's comment made me grin. *If only you knew!*

Jakes mother and father emerged from the house. As soon as Greg and Mary saw me, an obvious expression of concern appeared on both their faces. They too had noticed the rapid decline of my health.

"Hi Greg and Mary," said Dad; shaking their hands in turn.

"Would you like to come in for a cup of coffee before you head back to the farm David?" suggested Mary.

"That'd be great, thanks."

I grabbed my overnight bag and the five of us walked inside. Once we entered the house I was ambushed by Jake's three younger sisters. There was Alice, Kate and Samantha; who were fourteen, twelve and eight respectively.

Jake introduced me. "Girls, this is Sophie."

"Hi girls. You must be Alice, Kate and Samantha," I said, smiling at each of them in turn as I said their names.

"Are you Jakes girlfriend?"

We all laughed at the forwardness of Samantha's question; our parents included.

"Yes I am," I replied proudly; shooting Jake an affectionate smile.

"Would you like to come and see my room?" asked Alice. "You'll be sleeping in there with me tonight."

"Well that'll be lots of fun. We'll be able to have a pyjama party," I suggested excitedly; desperate to make a good impression with Jake's sisters.

I followed Alice down the hall to her bedroom; Kate and Samantha in tow. I sat down on her bed and she positioned herself beside me. Kate and Samantha sat on the floor. I giggled at how they all stared at me intently. The way the three girls looked at me, so interested and curious, it was like they'd never seen another human being before.

"Jake's never had a girlfriend sleep over before," stated Kate.

"You're the first," added Alice.

I couldn't help but smile to myself. *I certainly plan on being the first!*

The three of them were adorable as they began their questioning, taking turns quizzing me on all sorts of things. They wanted to know everything about me.

Kate started things off. "Do you live on a farm?"

"Yes."

Alice jumped in next. "You know our cousin Kylie don't you?"

"I sure do."

"Are you and Kylie best friends?" Samantha interjected quickly, joining the interrogation.

"Yes she is. We've been friends since I started high school."

Back to Kate, "How old are you?"

"Fifteen."

Alice, "Do you have any sisters?"

"No, but I have two older brothers."

Samantha, "We could be your sisters?"

She was so adorable.

"Well I'd love you all to be my sisters someday," I replied; caught slightly off guard by how fast this conversation spiralled into a 'deep and meaningful'.

"Did you know Jake told Mum and Dad that he wants to marry you?" Alice revealed. "He really did… I heard him say it."

"I heard him say it too," Kate said quickly, confirming her older sister's admission.

I can't begin to explain how good it felt to learn that he'd told his parents he wanted to marry me. Instantly I felt as though the temperature of my blood rose ten degrees. My entire body warmed at the thought of Jake proposing to me.

"Well that's a nice thing for him to say. I hope we get married one day too," I replied sincerely, trying my best to keep calm. Inside I was screaming with joy.

"If you and Jake get married then you really *will* be our sister," said Alice.

I was touched. I had only known these three beautiful girls for less than fifteen minutes, and they'd already shown enthusiasm towards the idea that maybe one day I would actually be their sister. I felt so welcomed by them and I fell in love with all the girls immediately.

Yet another sign that Jake and I are meant to be together.

I'm pleased to say over the course of my relationship with Jake, I really have become sisters with Alice, Kate and Samantha; sisters in every sense of the word. I have developed the most precious relationship with each of them, which I've treasured since that first day we all met, back when the girls interrogated me in Alice's bedroom. I love them all dearly and without a word of a lie, I've never had a run in with any of them. They truly have been fantastic sisters and friends to me, and I couldn't have dreamed of bonding with Alice, Kate and Samantha the way I did. It has been a blessing from the start.

"Come and have a look in our room," invited Kate.

"Yeah, I share my bedroom with Kate," explained Samantha as we walked back down the hall.

Their room was a little bigger than Alice's and contained two beds; side by side with matching pink and white covers. It was such a 'girly' room and was quite lovely. Both Kate and Samantha were quick to point out the large built in robes full of their clothes and accessories. Kate was a dancer so there were dresses and costumes busting out of the robe doors.

"You girls have a cool bedroom. It's so pretty. I really like it."

"Thanks," said Kate excitedly, as though she was relived it met my approval.

"Yeah, thanks," chimed Samantha; mimicking her older sister.

She's adorable.

"Jake's room is the one next to mine," Alice said; pointing back down the hallway.

"Do you want to have a look in there too?" asked Samantha.

"Yeah let's have a look in Jake's room," agreed Kate.

"We should probably let him show me," I urged, unsure as to how Jake would feel about his sisters going in his room without his permission.

"No he won't mind Sophie, we go in their all the time. Come on let's have a look," assured Kate as she walked towards his bedroom door.

It was refreshing to hear the girls were not afraid of going into Jake's room. It instantly gave me the impression he was close with his sisters, and cared for them a lot. The fact he'd dispensed with the usual 'stay out of my room' bullshit, showed his maturity. I could tell all his sisters really loved him and felt comfortable with him too, simply by how unafraid they were to go into their big brother's room without his permission.

"Are you sure about this?" I asked. "You're positive we don't have to ask Jake first?" I remembered how my brothers were whenever I went into their room. Going in there without asking was a definite 'no-no'.

"Jake! Can we show Sophie your room?" Kate yelled out towards the kitchen, where he was talking with our parents.

"Yep!" he called back.

"See we *told* you it'd be ok," said Samantha; shaking her head at me for not believing them.

The girls proceeded to show me around Jake's room. He had posters of martial arts movie stars; *Bruce Lee* and *Jean Claude Van Damme* stuck to his walls, along with various posters of superbikes and action movies.

"That one's Jake's favourite," Samantha said, pointing to a big poster of a bright red Ducati; smiling at it as she spoke. I noticed that she smiled every time she talked about Jake.

"I like that one too," I replied.

It was touching to see how much Samantha looked up to her brother, and as I got to know the girls more it was clear that she definitely shared a different kind of bond with Jake, compared with the other two sisters.

His room was tidy, in particular his desk was especially organised. Jake had mentioned that he did all his homework in his room, but even so I was still surprised by the order. I also noticed the stereo with a few cassette tapes stacked in a pile beside it; he was yet to upgrade to CD's.

I think the best thing about his room, apart from the fact that he didn't mind if his sisters were in there, was the smell. It was intoxicating, and I felt like I was surrounded by him. When I sat on Jake's bed I couldn't resist but smell one of his pillows. *Oh my god*, I thought as I drank in the scent. I wanted to climb under the covers, yell out his name and wait for him to come and crawl into bed with me.

Now, I was seriously debating whether to write this next part in my story, but at the time it was just so hilarious. After much deliberation I've decided to include it.

So there we were in Jake's room, me and his three sisters, all chatting about their brother. I think it was Kate who mentioned something about one of the *Van Damme* posters on the wall. He was in some kind of martial arts pose with his shirt off; displaying his muscled physique.

"Jake does karate too," said Alice, who was also looking at the poster.

"Yeah he's pretty muscly… sort of like that guy," revealed Kate; pointing at the actor. "Have you seen Jake's muscles before?"

Where are they going with this? I was slightly embarrassed by their line of questioning, and I could feel myself blushing. Obviously I needed an appropriate response as to when I had the opportunity to see Jake's muscles, other than when I'd sneak into his bed when he stayed at the farm. Luckily, I remembered the day at the lake.

"Yes… I have once. When I met Jake at the lake near Kylie's house. We went for a swim and I saw him without his shirt on then." I wasn't dare going to tell them about the *other* occasions I'd seen him shirtless. I desperately wanted to change the subject.

"Jake goes to karate and works out all the time, so he's got pretty big muscles now," Kate explained.

"Yeah well I've seen him in the shower and he's got a big willy too!" Samantha blurted out in a very 'matter-of-fact' tone; not even breaking a smile.

Alice, Kate and myself all burst into laughter. It was by far the funniest thing I've ever heard. It wasn't just what she said, but the way she said it which had the three of us in absolute fits.

"What's so funny?" asked Samantha naively, her age and innocence had her convinced there was nothing wrong with the information she'd just revealed.

The fact she wasn't laughing made the three of us laugh even more. I had tears rolling down my cheeks and my stomach muscles felt like they were going to cramp up. I will never forget it; it was absolutely priceless.

"What are you all laughing at?" asked Jake as he entered the room.

We all looked at him, desperately trying to get our laughter under control but failing miserably.

"Nothing," I fumbled between breaths.

"It can't be nothing… you're all hysterical!" he said; obviously suspicious.

"Really Jake, it was nothing," I explained, still trying to calm myself down.

"I was just telling Sophie that you had a big willy," blurted Samantha.

We all erupted into fits of laughter again; Jake included.

If I thought Samantha's statement was funny the first time, hearing her say it to Jake's face almost made me wet myself. It was side splitting.

"What the hell did you tell her that for Sam!" Jake exclaimed; red faced but smiling in a futile attempt to hide his embarrassment.

"I don't know. I just thought since we were talking about your big muscles I would tell her that was big too," confessed Samantha innocently.

"When have you ever seen it anyway?" he interrogated.

"She said she seen you in the shower," giggled Alice.

"Well shit! I'd better start locking the door from now on!"

"Probably not a bad idea," I added; still laughing uncontrollably.

"That's the last time I leave you alone with my sisters!" he laughed. "God only knows what they'll tell you next!"

I was relieved he saw the funny side to the situation.

"Anyway, I came in here to tell you that your Dad's heading off."

"Ok I'll come out and say goodbye," I replied; wiping my eyes and eventually getting control of myself.

The five of us made our way out to the kitchen. My father and Jakes parents were already at the front door.

I walked over and gave Dad a cuddle. "Bye Dad."

"Bye Soph. I'll be back tomorrow afternoon around five-thirty."

"Sure."

"See you later Mr. Taylor," said Jake.

"Bye Jake. Goodbye girls," Dad waved. He shook Greg's hand and said goodbye to Mary. We all waited out the front until Dad had driven out of sight.

"So what are you kids up to today?" asked Mary.

"I thought Sophie and I could walk down to the shopping centre and have some lunch, then maybe look around the shops for a while. We'll pick up a movie from the video store on the way home," Jake explained.

"Can we come too Jake?" asked Samantha.

It was so adorable that she wanted to come with us, to hang out with her big brother and his girlfriend.

"Jake and Sophie don't want us hanging around Sam," said Alice.

"What's say Sophie and I go down the street first, so we can spend a bit of time together, and when we get home we can go for another walk to the park with you," Jake suggested.

"That sounds like fun Sam," Mary said; convincing her it was a good idea. Jakes Mum knew we'd be busting to spend some time alone with each other.

"Alright, but you have to promise to take me to the park when you get back!"

"We promise," Jake said; smiling at her then at me.

"Promise," I echoed.

With the next few hours planned, Jake's family went back inside and left us alone out the front. He wrapped his arms around me again and gave me a proper kiss. It was so nice to feel his lips on mine, and I was instantly reminded just how much I missed the feeling. Being in his arms and kissing passionately made me feel renewed. I guess it was the intense feelings of safety, comfort and affection which had that effect on me. Cocooned in his arms was exactly where I wanted to be.

I used to think home had to be a place, but now I know it can be anywhere that you feel happy, content and protected. Home truly is where your heart is, and my heart belongs to Jake. He *is* home.

We went inside and grabbed a drink before setting off on our walk to the shopping centre.

"How far is it Jake?" I questioned less than five minutes into the walk. I prayed it wasn't too far since I was feeling quite weak and lethargic.

"We're going to cut through the park, so it will only take about twenty minutes at this pace. If you get tired and need to rest, we can stop at any time."

It was clear that Jake had already considered the need for me to take it slow, given my physical condition and subsequent decline in fitness.

How things have changed. I cast my mind back to when he and I ran down the hills and through the fields on our way back to the farm house only a few months earlier. It was really starting to dawn on me just how fast I was deteriorating and it scared the hell out of me.

As we strolled together, hand in hand in the sunshine, we reached the start of a walking track which paralleled a small creek. The track wound its way along the bank of the stream and eventually led to a beautiful big park. It was peaceful and there was no one else around.

Jake seemed unusually quiet and I could sense he wanted to talk to me about something. I decided not to break the silence; instead gave him a chance to say whatever was on his mind. A couple of minutes passed, eventually he brought up the topic of my health.

"So still no luck with the doctors Baby?"

I could tell by the concern in his voice that he was worried. It was obvious he wanted to know what was happening to me.

I sighed. "I'm getting so sick of doctors telling me that it's eczema, or dust mites… or food allergies. Not knowing what's wrong with me is driving me crazy. I think my parents are starting to think it's all in my head."

He looked at me; confused. "In your head... what the hell are they talking about? It's blatantly obvious it's not in your head!"

"I know, look how sick I am?" I agreed.

"Exactly! I mean you scratch your legs until they bleed for fuck's sake!" he snapped, no doubt furious because I still wasn't getting the help I needed. "It's clearly not just in your head!"

"I know that's what I keep telling them, but since the doctors are struggling to find a diagnosis it seems like Mum and Dad think I'm doing it for attention, or just to get out of school."

Little did I know the nightmare I described earlier, when my parents dragged me to school in my pyjamas, would happen the following month.

"The thing is… I love school. Why would I want to make up some bullshit illness just to get out of going?" I hissed; unable to hide my own frustration and anger.

"Surely they're going to figure out what's wrong. It's ridiculous that it's gone untreated for this long already."

"You're telling me!"

"What about your weight loss? Do you still feel hungry or are you too sick to eat?"

"I've lost my appetite but I really do try and eat. I can see that I'm losing weight but I'm so tired and fatigued; I just don't feel like I can stomach anything. I know I need food to feel better, and when I do eat I have a fair bit, but I'm just struggling to find any sort of appetite. I also have a weird feeling in my neck which is making it hard to breathe and eat. It feels like someone has their hands around my throat… strangling me."

I would later learn that I actually had a swollen lymph node in my throat which was compressing my wind pipe, making both breathing and swallowing food difficult.

Jake held my hand firmly. "Well all I can say is your parents and these doctors better start taking this shit seriously. Your Mum and Dad see you every day so they probably don't notice the changes in you as easily as I do, considering I'm only seeing you every two weeks or so."

After hearing him say he was noticing my physical changes from week to week, my anger and frustration was quickly replaced with sorrow. I always took a lot of pride in my appearance, and even more so when I knew I was meeting up with him. I always wanted to look my absolute best for Jake and it hurt me to know he wasn't seeing me that way; the dead opposite actually.

As any typical teenage girl would, I had thoughts about my boyfriend not finding me attractive anymore, and it frightened me. When I got ready in the bathroom that morning, I could clearly see what I looked like in the mirror. Not only did I feel like shit, I could see for myself that I looked like it as well.

I was already self-conscious about my sickly appearance, and I know hurting me was the last thing Jake wanted to do when he brought up the issue of my health, but I turned my head away from him anyway; embarrassed and ashamed. It's not that I didn't want to look at him because I did, Jake was all I ever wanted to look at, I just didn't want *him* to look at *me*! His sick, skinny… ugly girlfriend.

"Are you ok Baby?" he asked sincerely, already knowing I wasn't.

I didn't answer or look at him; keeping my head turned away so he couldn't see my face. We were still walking hand in hand.

"Sophie?"

Again I didn't answer. Tears had already built up and were just about to spill over my eyelids. I was trying with everything I had not to cry. I was sick of crying in front of Jake. He didn't deserve to have to deal with this bullshit every time we met. The limited amount of time we were able to spend with each other was supposed to be fun, happy and carefree; the way teenage lovers are meant to be when they're together. But because of my stupid *monster,* it seemed like we were forever discussing my ill health, and I'd always find myself getting upset and crying on Jake's shoulder. I felt like I was fast becoming a burden on him.

Don't cry Sophie! Don't cry... not now! I thought in an attempt to will myself from breaking down.

"Sophie… look at me," his voice was soft and calm. "Stop walking for a second… please."

Jake turned and faced me, he grabbed my other hand as well. I kept my head to the side and stared down at the ground. I knew if I looked into his eyes… I'd lose it.

"Sophie… look at me Baby. It's ok. Everything will be ok."

"I don't want to look at you because I don't want you to look at me. I'm sick and ugly. I don't want you to see me like this." My voice was shaky. It was as inevitable as the sun rising, I was going to burst into tears… again!

"Sophie, you're not well Baby. You feel terrible and I know you don't feel pretty at the moment… but you're not ugly."

I was still looking away from him as he spoke.

"I understand why you don't want me to see you like this, but that doesn't change the fact that *I* want to see *you*." Jake lightly placed his hand on my cheek. Slowly he turned my head to face him. "Sweetie you're the only thing I *ever* want to look at! To me… you're always beautiful… you're my angel."

I held my eyes closed tight but I could already feel the tears escaping, trailing one after the other down my cheeks. He softly cradled my face with his hands and I could feel him edging closer to me. I kept my eyes shut; arms hanging lifelessly by my sides. I could sense he was right in front of me, then I felt his lips. It wasn't a normal kiss though, Jake just held his lips against mine, lightly touching, not moving. The tighter I squeezed my eyes shut, the more the tears flowed. I could feel them running down my face onto our lips but Jake didn't move. I felt like my whole body was twisting into a knot. The thought of my tears trickling into our kiss was a painful image which still haunts me today. It was as if Jake was somehow sealing our future together; a future where these types of moments, painful and heart wrenching, would be a frequent occurrence. As my tears flowed into our kiss, I knew in that moment that no matter how bad things got, he would be by my side.

Eventually I opened my eyes; Jake was still kissing me. His eyes were open and staring straight into mine. I pulled away from him and wiped my face. He gave me a moment to compose myself and then wrapped me protectively in his arms. I buried my head under his chin against his chest and he squeezed me tightly; kissing the top of my head.

I've always felt so calm and safe whenever Jake would hold me the way he did on our walk to the shopping centre that day. Still now, whenever things aren't going so well, he will hold me tightly and almost instantly I feel myself relax. It's like a wave of calmness washes over me when I'm in his arms.

"Are you ok Baby? Did you want to keep going or did you want to head back?"

"No I don't want to go back. I'll be fine." I answered hastily. "Don't worry about me I'm just being stupid."

"Sophie, you're not being stupid at all. You're going through a real tough time at the moment; that doesn't make you stupid. You're upset and I don't blame you."

"But don't you think I'm silly for crying all the time?"

"I've *never* thought that, not even for a second!" he answered with conviction. "It hurts me to see you upset, but I've never thought you were stupid or anything like that; not ever! I only wish you were better. I wish I could *make* you better!"

"Thanks Baby," I smiled, as I kissed him on the cheek. "Thank you for everything."

"No need to thank me Soph. I love you… no matter what."

We continued walking to the shopping centre. For the rest of the journey we didn't talk much, instead just enjoyed each other's company. It was a comfortable silence and I loved that neither of us felt like we had to say anything. We could just be together, appreciate each other and enjoy the energy that flowed between us. If my body would have allowed it, I would've walked with Jake in the sun for the rest of the day.

Once we arrived at the shopping centre we had some lunch at a café, then browsed through some of the clothing stores and various retail outlets. Since I lived out on the farm, it was always a real treat for me to come into Sunbury to do some shopping. Jake must have sensed I was enjoying myself, because he never rushed me or tried to talk me out of looking through yet another shop full of women's clothing or jewellery. I think we browsed for a couple of hours at least, and the whole time he stayed by my side, patiently waiting until I had my fill of retail therapy; even if I was only window shopping.

Before long I was starting to feel quite fatigued, and was well aware that we still had to walk all the way home. "I'm getting a bit tired. We'd better start heading home, otherwise I mightn't make it back."

"Good idea. I'll gladly piggy back you all the way home though, if you're not up to walking," he said; completely serious.

I had no doubt Jake would carry me home if I needed him to.

"I still feel ok, so I should be right if we go now."

We left the shopping centre and walked back to Jake's house, stopping at the video store and picking up a movie on the way. Turns out I didn't need the piggy back after all, and I was relieved to be able to make it all the way without his help.

As soon as we walked in the door Samantha ambushed us.

"Are you still taking me to the park Jake?" she beamed excitedly.

Jake turned to me, knowing I was exhausted already. "The small park at the end of the block isn't far. Did you still want to go Soph?" he asked.

Samantha looked at me and unknowingly flashed me a look which perfectly resembled a sad puppy dog. I couldn't say no to her.

"Of course. I should be fine. I might have to take you up on the piggy back offer though Jake," I smiled.

"Yay!" yelled Samantha.

Jake called out to Alice and Kate to see if they wanted to come for a quick walk to the park as well. They both emerged from the lounge room and joined us.

The five of us walked to the park, which turned out to be less than five minutes away. *Thank goodness*! Jake and I played on the swings and slippery slides with his three sisters. It was so much fun getting to know the girls and joking around with them. I'd always wanted a sister and now I felt like I was very close to having three of them. It was a fantastic first day with Alice, Kate and Samantha and I bonded with them instantly.

"Had enough of the park for one day Samantha?" Jake asked, after playing for about half an hour or so.

"Are we going back now?" she replied.

"Yeah, we've had enough swinging and sliding for today Sam," said Alice.

"Push me on the swing one more time before we go Jake… please!" Samantha begged.

"Ok one quick go and then we'll walk home."

I smiled to myself. *I guess Jake's a sucker for a sad face too!*

As soon as we arrived home, Mary announced she'd made us some afternoon tea. We sat down at the kitchen bench for a drink, some sandwiches and fruit. It was a real novelty for me to spend time with Jake's family. At home on the farm I was so used to keeping my own company, and the house was always so quiet with only Mum, Dad and myself living there. It was a stark contrast to Jake's house; with his parents and three sisters around there was always something happening. Talking, laughing or the occasional argument between Alice, Kate and Samantha ensured the house was always alive. It was a refreshing change from the silence and isolation of the farm.

The rest of the afternoon Jake and I stayed in his room listening to some of his old tapes, talking, and of course kissing. It was nice to be able to close the door and have some privacy with him. I think Jake's parents understood that the girls would've been looking in on us every five minutes if his bedroom door had to remain open, so we were allowed to have it closed. I was grateful because this also gave us the privacy we needed to discuss a very important subject.

We were lying side by side on his bed, Jake was gently tickling my face. "So your sixteen now Baby?" I smiled coyly.

"It would appear so," his lips curling into an equally cheeky grin.

My feelings towards going all the way with Jake hadn't changed, but now we were about to discuss the subject, I started to feel even more self-conscious about my current appearance. To be honest I was actually frightened at the prospect of undressing in front of him; something I never had a problem with doing before. I was afraid these new insecurities which had developed over the past few weeks would prevent me from having the courage to actually take the next step with him.

"Jake?"

"Yeah Baby."

"I'm a bit nervous about sleeping with you. I really want to, I have wanted to for ages, but I'm worried about how I look at the moment. I look sick. I know I do."

"Awe Soph," Jake sighed sympathetically. "I understand you're not well, but that doesn't mean I'm not still attracted to you. I love every square inch of you and *nothing* will ever change that."

"I just don't want to disappoint you that's all."

"Nothing you could do would ever disappoint me, and don't for one minute think you have to sleep with me if you're not comfortable or ready. I'll wait for you forever."

"I just feel stupid, because all this time *I've* been the one pressuring you to sleep with me, and now I'm the one who is getting all nervous and scared. I'm not nervous about making love… I'm nervous about how you see me."

"What's happening to your body is not your fault. Believe me when I tell you that you're the most beautiful person I've ever met. You're gorgeous, and sexy, and I'm attracted to you as much as I ever was."

I forced a smile. "Thanks Jake." I really wanted to believe him, and even though I didn't understand how he could possibly still think I'm beautiful, his words were making me feel better; they always did.

"I only want you to be happy Baby. That's all I've ever wanted since we started seeing each other. If sleeping with me will make you happy then I'm ready, but if waiting a little longer is what you want then I'm fine with that too. Just remember I will love you regardless of your decision."

I kissed him softly on the lips. "You're amazing Jake. What did I ever do to deserve someone like you?"

He laughed. "I feel the same way about you Soph."

I snuggled into his chest and closed my eyes. I'd made my decision. I wanted him, more than ever, and I wasn't about to let my *monster* stand in the way.

"I've made up my mind!" I whispered; my head still tucked under his chin. "Do you think maybe I could visit you tonight?"

He put his hand under my chin and gently tilted my head up so he could look at me. His eyes burned with desire. "You sure Baby?"

"I'm sure. Do you have a lock on your door?"

"No I don't. Shit!" He paused for a moment; looking at the door. I could tell his mind was ticking. "I know… I'll wedge my baseball bat between the door and my desk so it can't be opened. That should work."

"Good. Well I'll wait for Alice to go to sleep then I will sneak in and see you tonight. At least your house doesn't have wooden floors like mine. It'll be a lot easier to creep around without making any noise."

Jake laughed. "Yeah your house is so noisy! Your parents must be able to hear us walking around in the dark."

"Do you have any… protection?" I whispered nervously; blushing slightly.

He nodded. "I picked up a couple of condoms from a service station on the way back from Melbourne last weekend."

Jake had been to the city for martial arts training. He was on the Victorian State Team and had to travel to the city on a number of occasions to train with the state coaches.

"I'm so excited… and nervous," I confessed.

"Me too Soph. We'll just take it slow so don't be scared. I'll take good care of you."

"I'm sure you will Baby." I smiled; kissing him again.

From the moment we planned our midnight rendezvous, I felt like a giant bundle of nervous energy; my belly bursting to life with the fluttering butterflies. I couldn't believe that tonight was *the* night. I'd waited so long to give myself to Jake and now it was only hours away. For weeks I'd dreamt day and night about what it would feel like. Knowing these dreams were about to become a reality triggered my heart to race, and a familiar ache to rapidly intensify deep inside me; right where I wanted him. I was excited and eager but at the same time, absolutely petrified.

Jake and I sat down with the rest of his family for dinner which was great fun. There was lots of discussion and laughing while we ate. I must have been asked about twenty questions by Greg, Mary and the girls, but I didn't mind though because I was learning a lot about them as well.

Mary was soft and warm, and I liked her a lot. We have developed a fantastic relationship over the years. I'm proud to say that we'd consider each other to be the best of friends, still to this day. In contrast Jake's father, Greg, was fairly stern and direct. It wasn't that he was unlikeable, I mean he was always kind and polite to me, I just got the feeling that he liked to be in control; the man of the house. A few times I heard him say things to his children and to Mary which gave me the impression he liked things *his* way. He was still pleasant though and didn't make me feel uncomfortable, but the vibe in the house was definitely different when Greg was home.

After dinner we crammed into the lounge room and watched the movie Jake and I hired. There weren't enough seats so Kate and Samantha sat on the floor on some pillows but they didn't seem to mind.

I wouldn't be able to tell you what the movie was because my thoughts were elsewhere; and by *elsewhere...* I mean in Jake's room! My eyes darted back and forth from the screen to the clock and as the minutes ticked by I knew bed time was fast approaching. The aching between my legs which began hours earlier, certainly hadn't subsided. In fact, it was getting stronger!

After the movie, the girls took turns using the bathroom and showering before bed; Greg and Mary retreated to their bedroom. Jake and I stayed snuggled up on the sofa in the lounge room; waiting for our turn in the shower.

"So… you still coming to visit me tonight?" he whispered in my ear before softly nibbling on my ear lobe, making me giggle loudly.

"Only if you want me to?" I teased.

"Yes… yes… yes!" he whispered again; taking a deep breath in and smelling my hair before proceeding to bite and suck the side of my neck. "Does that answer your question?" he smiled before ravishing me again.

It felt so good that I couldn't help but moan quietly. "Oh stop it Jake… you're killing me," I breathed; closing my eyes and relishing in the sensation of his mouth on my neck.

"Shower's ready!" yelled Kate from the bathroom.

"Looks like you're up Soph. Wish I could join you," he smirked.

"I wish you could too," I smiled back as I got up from the couch and headed to the bathroom; relieved that I was about to have a shower. My current state of arousal had left me absolutely saturated.

After showering I went into Alice's room where she had my bed made up on a mattress on the floor. I sat down on her bed and talked with Alice about her school along with some other girly topics while Jake had his shower. The whole time I could hear the running water, prompting images of my naked man to fill my thoughts. I've got to say, it was making it extremely hard to concentrate.

After about five minutes, Jake emerged from the bathroom and joined us in Alice's room. He stood in the door way, drying his hair with a towel. He looked so fresh and smelled absolutely delicious.

"What are you two talking about?"

"Never you mind… just girl talk Jake," I replied; smiling affectionately.

He looked so good, standing there in his black boxer shorts and white singlet; the hot water from the shower making the veins in his arms and shoulders stand out. He looked so strong; so capable, and as I studied him a different breed of nerves washed over me.

It wasn't fear in its purist form, but as I began to question my physical size compared to Jakes, I definitely felt as sense of trepidation. He was so masculine and developed, and I was only a girl; a small petite one at that! I know it sounds silly, but the question of '*Will he fit?*' kept replaying in my head. I'd never been so anxious in my life, and as hard as I tried I couldn't ignore the feelings of doubt that crept into my head. I began to worry. *Can I go through with this?*

Jake's Mum came down the hall to Alice's bedroom.

"You all set down here Sophie?"

"Sure am Mrs. Freeman."

"Goodnight kids. Don't stay up too late."

Mary kissed Jake and Alice before walking down to Kate and Samantha's room to say goodnight. I was surprised she didn't comment on us staying in our beds or say something about me not sneaking into Jake's room during the night. I guess she was too embarrassed to bring it up. Either that, or she'd already had the discussion with Jake earlier.

We had planned on 'going to sleep' quite early, in the hope that Alice would also drift off, giving me plenty of time with Jake during the night. He went and hung his towel up in the bathroom then came back into Alice's room. I watched as he tied his hair back into a pony tail.

"Want me to tuck you in?" he asked.

"Sure," I said as I climbed off Alice's bed and lay down on the mattress.

Alice giggled as she watched her older brother fussing over his girlfriend. It must have looked quite foreign to her.

"Well I'll see you tomorrow," Jake grinned covertly before kissing me briefly on the lips.

"Goodnight Jake. See you in the *morning!"* I emphasised.

Probably just after 12am! I smiled to myself.

"Night Alice."

"Goodnight." She was still giggling.

He switched off the light before leaving us and retreating to his room.

Alice and I talked for another half an hour or so before I suggested we get some sleep. She switched off her bedside lamp, and after talking for a few more minutes in the dark the conversation eventually stopped. I lay awake looking at the ceiling. I knew Jake was only meters away doing exactly the same thing… waiting.

At least forty-five minutes past. I listened carefully to Alice's deep, rhythmical breaths. She was asleep.

"Alice… Alice… Alice!" I whispered. "Are you asleep?" I had to be sure.

No response.

This is it Sophie. I slowly pulled back the sheets and crawled carefully out of bed. I could hear my heart thumping like a drum. It was so loud I was surprised Alice wasn't woken up by it. I could see clearly as the hall light was left on for Samantha. Like me, she wasn't a fan of the dark.

It was only a few steps to Jake's bedroom door; my footsteps were completely silent on the carpeted floor. *So much better than the creaking floorboards at my place.*

Jake's bedroom door was already ajar so I slowly pushed it open. As the hall light filled his room I could see him lying on his bed. He was staring straight at me.

"Hello," he said quietly.

I entered the room and closed the door. He turned on the bedside light and draped a t-shirt over it to dull the glow, then climbed out of bed; naked except for his boxer shorts. As planned, he wedged his baseball bat between the door and his desk; jamming it shut. Nobody was getting in, and I felt like I wasn't getting *out* either.

He turned to face me. I watched his chest expand then relax as he took a deep breath to calm himself. The t-shirt over the lamp caused the dull lighting to cast dark and unusual shadows on Jake's face and across the muscles of his naked torso. To be honest he looked intimidating, almost like some kind of beast. The burning stare of his eyes combined with his physical appearance made me feel small and helpless… as though I was about to be devoured.

Thump, thump, thump, thump. The sound of my heart was deafening. I was excited and petrified at the same time. I could feel my hands shaking so I closed my fingers into fists in an attempt to stop them trembling.

"Are you ok Soph?"

Thump, thump, thump. I could barely hear Jake's whisper.

I nodded slowly; reassuringly. But to be honest though, I wasn't sure if I was ok at all.

I had only ever felt safe and secure with Jake, but now, as I regarded the hunger in his eyes and listened to each powerful breath, he resembled a fearsome breed of ravenous animal. I was afraid of him; more so of what he was going to do to me. I knew he wasn't a predator, the opposite was true, but it didn't stop me from feeling like the *prey!*

He took a step towards me and I inhaled sharply. I held my breath as he reached forward and ran his hand up the back of my neck and into my hair, before pulling me towards him and kissing me passionately. My knees buckled immediately.

With his fingers twisted in my hair, he slowly pulled; tilting my head back. I opened my eyes just as he bit his teeth into the side of my neck causing me to gasp with surprise. *Holy Fuck!*

I could feel the tension in his arms, his grip, his bite… his whole body, and I wanted him to relax a little. He felt like a bomb about to explode. I didn't want to say anything but I had too.

"Gently Jake." I whispered. Even I could hear the shattered nerves in my voice.

"Oh shit… sorry Baby," he said in a soft apologetic voice.

He released his grasp then gave me a hug and gently kissed me on the forehead.

"I'm sorry. I didn't mean to scare you."

"It's ok."

"I'm just so turned on; I feel like I want to rip you to pieces. Sorry Baby, I just need to relax."

Throughout our relationship I've seen that 'beast' emerge on more than one occasion, and I can assure you that if I let it take over him completely, once he's finished with me I really do feel like I've been ravaged by some kind of savage animal! To be taken so forcefully is an amazing feeling, and I've come to appreciate it, though I definitely have to be in the right mood. Tonight was definitely not one of those nights.

"Come here." I put my hands on his arms and kissed him delicately until I felt the tension in his body dissipate. "That's it…

just relax. I'm not going anywhere so take your time with me," I smiled.

Almost immediately I could sense the change in his energy. My fear faded away and the familiar safety of being with Jake returned. *Much better.*

I climbed on his bed and lay down on my back. Jake straddled me and I put my arms above my head as he planted soft kisses all over my face, lips and neck. Now *I* was starting to relax and feel more comfortable; definitely more at ease.

"Sit up Baby."

I sat up and he pulled my singlet over my head; exposing my naked breasts. I lay back down and Jake slowly worked his kisses from my neck down to my boobs, which were increasing in sensitivity by the second.

"Oh Jake," I moaned softly; my nipples standing to attention.

As he continued to kiss and lick my breasts, he slid his hand into my pyjamas pants. I deliberately wasn't wearing any underwear, and I giggled at Jake's surprised expression after he made the discovery.

A wicked grin quickly emerged. "How rude," he whispered; gently sliding a finger in between my *lips*.

Delicious pleasure forced me to close my eyes as he began to delicately massage my clit; already swollen and hyper-sensitive. Jake teased me to the brink before sliding one, then two fingers deep inside me. Instinctively I pushed my hips up off the bed to meet his touch, and as he began to rub me in exactly the right *spot,* I climaxed within a matter of seconds. I held my breath to prevent an audible outburst as a deluge of liquid spilled from me; coating his fingers.

Turns out an orgasm was all I needed to calm my nerves. I was now completely relaxed, primed and eager. I was *ready*!

I reached down and put my hands on either side of his face. I lifted his head up to mine and kissed him feverishly; pushing my tongue into his mouth. "I want you now. Make love to me Jake," I breathed.

Every part of me was ready for him, and every fibre in my body wanted him. The moment had arrived.

"You're a hundred percent sure?"

I nodded. "Yes… I'm sure."

My insides contracted over and over. My orgasm hadn't done anything to quell the dull ache in my groin, which had now progressed to a relentless throb. I wanted him inside me; no question.

"Me too," he smiled. "I'm nervous… but I'm ready."

"Let's just take it slow and we'll be fine," I suggested; a subtle reminder to refrain from his earlier over-eager approach.

"I will… promise." Jake's sincerity was reassuring.

He reached over to his bedside table and pulled out a condom packet. As he knelt up and ripped the seal, I reached down and freed his rock hard member from his boxer shorts. It literally sprung with force from the waistband of his underwear.

Wow... I'm not the only one who's ready! My eyes widened at the sight of *him*.

As Jake removed the condom from the packet, he knelt above me for a moment, motionless; letting me survey his manhood. His cock was straining and I could see the thick veins; swollen and protruding along his shaft. My earlier concerns as to whether it would fit quickly flooded back into my mind. *Fuck!*

He arched his back and thrust his pelvis towards me while I stroked his erection with my hands. It was so hot… I mean *literally* hot! The smooth skin of his shaft was scorching to the touch. As I ran my fingers over the head of his dick, I could feel slippery pre-cum trickling from the tip. Again, my insides clenched firmly as my body pleaded with me to receive him.

I watched like a voyeur as he rolled the condom over his erection. It was the sexiest thing I'd ever seen. He stood up and let his boxers fall to the floor, then I lifted my feet so he could slide my pyjama pants off.

As I lay there completely naked, Jake looked me up and down lustfully. "Your beautiful Soph… absolutely beautiful." His words and the sincerity with which he said them went a long way towards banishing any self-conscious thoughts I had about being naked in front of him.

I gradually opened my legs… wide. Jakes eyes immediately darted down to my virgin entrance; vulnerable and untouched. Well, untouched except for the countless times I'd allowed him to slide into third base!

He climbed back onto the bed and positioned himself between my thighs; my wetness open and inviting; his hard cock only centimetres away from her. I could smell the mixed aromas of his fresh aftershave, my own arousal and the unfamiliar smell of latex. A combination of fragrances I'd soon develop a craving for.

Jake supported himself on one hand and reached down to his groin with the other. He grasped hold of *himself* and lined up to my opening. I grabbed a firm hold of his hips and slowly pulled him closer, until I felt his tip gently touch my *lips.* I inhaled sharply and held my breath as I pulled him even closer.

"Are you ready Baby?"

I nodded. "Yes," I surrendered.

Bit by bit, Jake entered me. I closed my eyes and exhaled slowly in an attempt to relax my *tightness*. He pulled back a little, giving me a moment to take another breath before sinking in deeper. I appreciated his level of caution, and even though my eyes were shut I could feel him staring directly at my face; watching for any indication that I wasn't ok.

I felt a small spike of pain which caused me to wince, followed by a warm, almost burning sensation as Jake edged in all the way. I could feel him stretching me… *filling* me! I pushed his hips with my hands and he slowly withdrew before sliding in again. This time, he let out a quiet moan as he buried his length inside me.

Everything was going ok. He was being perfectly gentle and controlled, when all of a sudden I started to feel anxious and uneasy. I tried to push the thoughts from my mind, letting him withdraw then sink into me again, but my anxiety grew stronger still.

Relax Sophie... just relax! I attempted to talk myself through it as he pulled back and plunged into me for the fourth time, then the fifth. I looked down to see his entire length disappearing.

Fuck! Fuck! I felt him swell inside me and the stretching sensation intensified, prompting me to wince again, then to panic. *No more! I can't do this!*

"Stop Jake! Please stop!" I said anxiously, and way louder than intended. Using both hands I pushed on his hips and forced him out of me, leaving me with an empty, hollow feeling. "I can't do it."

It wasn't that it was too painful, and Jake certainly wasn't rough. After all, *I* was controlling the movement with my hands on his hips. I really can't explain why I wanted him to stop. I just panicked and became scared all in an instant. I guess I was just overwhelmed by the whole sensation.

"Are you ok Baby? Did I hurt you?" he whispered with concern, displaying an expression I hadn't seen before. He was clearly mortified at the possibility that he'd caused me pain; the thing he loved most in the world. I'll never forget the hurt and regret in his eyes.

Jake immediately moved so I could bring my legs back together. He pulled the sheet over me, covering my naked body. I don't know if he did it deliberately, but he lay down on top of the sheet rather than under it with me, so the sheet served as a barrier between the skin of our bodies.

"Baby… I'm so sorry. Please tell me you're ok." He seemed to be growing increasingly distressed.

I grabbed hold of his hand. "I'm ok. I just freaked out. I don't know why," I replied.

"I feel so terrible. I hurt you didn't I?"

"No Jake, I'm ok." I tried to reassure him but I knew he didn't believe me.

He let go of my hand and climbed off the bed. "Let me get your clothes." He passed me my singlet top and pyjama pants.

What happened next broke my heart.

Jake turned away while I climbed out from under the sheets and got dressed. It was as if he was so ashamed of himself for hurting me, that he didn't deserve to see me naked. In the space of a few minutes he'd gone from a man, burning with passion and desire, to a scared, nervous teenage boy who couldn't even look at me.

I felt a lump building in my throat as I watched Jake pull his boxers back on after disposing of the condom. He still had his back to me.

"I'm so sorry," he repeated.

Standing behind him, I put my hands on his shoulders and rested my head on his back. "I'm ok Jake. Really… I'm ok."

His head hung down, shoulders hunched over; body limp. He was upset, and the sight sent a spear of pain straight through my heart. I didn't know what to do, and I still don't know if I did the right thing, but all I could think was to leave him alone and go back to Alice's room.

"I should go back to bed," I said calmly; already feeling like I wasn't handling it right.

He nodded then turned around and cuddled me. I put my head on his chest.

"Please forgive me Soph," he whispered in my ear before kissing my forehead and letting me go. There was nothing more I could say or do. Jake was convinced he'd hurt me, and it'd cut him deep.

He pulled the bat away from the door and slowly opened it for me. As I walked through I lifted my hand up to his face, but before I could touch him he grabbed it, lightly kissed my knuckles then let go. As I turned the corner to Alice's room, I heard his door close behind me. I climbed into bed, buried my head into my pillow and burst into tears.

I understood it was nobody's fault. We were only young and taking such a serious step in our relationship, but I couldn't help but feel like I had completely ruined what was supposed to be the most magical and beautiful moment we could ever hope to share. I'd ruined our first time. The most painful part though was that I knew

Jake was now alone, lying in the dark, with the firm belief that it was all *his* fault.

Not only was I completely devastated, but absolutely terrified at the thought of facing him the next day.

CHAPTER THIRTEEN

ALONE AT LAST

I know I cried a lot that night but eventually I must have fallen asleep, because I was roused by the touch of Jake's lips on my forehead. I smiled before opening my eyes to see him hovering above me.

"Morning sleepy head. Getting up anytime soon?" he asked, kissing me again; this time on the lips.

"Why? What time is it?" I replied sleepily.

"Almost ten."

"You're kidding me?"

"I would've let you sleep longer but I missed you," he said; gently running his fingers through my messy 'bed' hair.

I looked beside me and discovered Alice's bed was empty. She must've crept out without waking me. I couldn't believe how late I'd slept in. The emotional roller coaster I rode the previous day and night had obviously taken its toll on me.

"I came in earlier but you were still fast asleep so I thought I'd leave you alone to catch up on a few hours. I've already been up and had breakfast."

"Thanks Baby," I replied appreciatively. "I was exhausted from yesterday."

He lay down beside me and I snuggled into him. I closed my eyes and inhaled deeply. *I could get used to waking up to this!*

I could hear talking and the sound of clattering dishes coming from the kitchen and living area of the house. The noise of Jake's family travelled down the hallway to the bedroom where Jake and I lay in silence. There was definitely an 'elephant in the room'. We both knew we needed to discuss what happened last night, but neither of us wanted to be the first to bring it up.

I still had my arms around him with my head against his chest; the beat of his heart playing its soothing rhythm. *Here goes!*

I took a deep breath. "Jake… can I tell you something?"

"Sure Soph… anything."

"You have to promise you'll believe me, and trust that what I'm telling you is the absolute truth."

"Ok Baby… I will. What is it?"

I moved so I could see his face. "Promise me Jake, promise you'll believe me."

"I promise," his voice and eyes sincere. "Just tell me."

I lowered my voice just in case we were suddenly interrupted. "When I asked you to stop last night…"

Jake immediately broke eye contact before I could continue. I reached up and placed my hand on his cheek, gently turning his head back to face me.

"Look at me."

He slowly lifted his eyes to meet mine.

"Believe me. You didn't do anything wrong last night. You didn't hurt me Jake," I whispered. "Not at all!"

He went to drop his head again but I stopped him with my hand under his chin.

"When I left you alone in your room I know you were upset… upset because you think it was your fault that I wanted to stop."

"Because I *did* hurt you!" he emphasised.

"No Jake you didn't. I'm telling you it wasn't your fault… not at all."

"So what happened Baby?" he asked; clearly confused.

"To be honest, I don't know exactly. I really thought I was ready…" I lowered my voice further, "…ready to sleep with you. But when we started I just freaked out. There's really no other reason. I tried to keep going but I was just too nervous and scared, so I had to stop."

"Well in that case, I'm glad you *did* stop me. I would've felt terrible if you had of kept going for my sake." Jake's expression changed to one of relief. He knew if I didn't stop him, the situation could have turned out far worse. "How about we don't count last night as our first time? Then, when you're ready, we can try again some other time?"

"Sounds good to me Baby." I was so relieved he was feeling better about the whole situation.

"I love you so much Sophie. Thanks for being so open with me."

"I love you too. And I also want to say thank you."

"For what?"

"For being so understanding. You mean the world to me." I kissed his lips then hugged him firmly.

"If you need to talk anymore about it then let me know?"

"No, I think I'm ok now," I smiled.

He exhaled. "That's good. I'm so relieved. I barely slept last night because I was so worried you'd be upset with me."

"I know what you mean, I was worried too. But everything's ok Jake. I love you and you love me. That's all that matters."

"You're right. As long as we're in love and talk to each other about everything, we'll be together forever."

"Exactly!" I smiled. "Forever."

"Why don't you jump in the shower then come out for something to eat?"

"Sure. I'd kill for a cup of tea."

Jake helped me up from the mattress. I gathered my clothes and toiletries then headed into the bathroom. As I stood under the shower, the hot water on my body felt like it was washing away the last pieces of embarrassment and awkwardness from the night before. But the truth was, our discussion and willingness to be honest and open with each other was the catalyst for my vastly improved emotional state. I emerged from the steamy bathroom, clean and refreshed… ready to put last night behind me and start over.

For the rest of the day Jake and I stayed around the house. We spent some time outside with his sisters, playing in the yard with his dog Lucy, a black Labrador, and riding bikes up and down the street. Although I only rode a couple of laps before being out of breath and needing a rest. We also played music in the family room and watched Kate practice some of the dancing routines she'd been working on.

Jake took the opportunity to teach me some steps from a couple of Latin American dances, the *Jive* and the *Cha Cha*. It was so much fun. I already loved dancing but having him teach me how to do a proper ballroom style routine was the best, and without sounding too up myself, I actually picked up the steps pretty fast, which was surprising considering how distracted I was by my teacher! He and Alice also showed me some of their old routines from the days when they did ballroom dancing competitions. They were fantastic together, which would explain the array of trophies in Alice's room that she and Jake had won as a couple. It had been a few years since they'd competed, but they made dancing seem so easy. It looked like they hadn't forgotten a step. I hoped one day I would be able to dance with Jake like that.

I really didn't want to go home that afternoon. I was going to miss Jake for sure, but I was also having a great time with his sisters and I knew I would miss them as well.

At one point during the day while I was caught up in the dancing, fun and laughter, I had a strange moment. It was more of a thought, like a light bulb was suddenly switched on in my head; hitting me in an instant. *I actually feel good!*

I wasn't tired or nauseated, and the *crawling* under my skin had seemed to ease as well. I didn't feel like scratching my arms or legs at all. It really was as if my *monster* was on vacation. I think the distraction of Jake's family had allowed me to successfully put my ill health to the back of my mind, to such an extent where a few hours had passed and I'd forgotten how shit I actually felt.

Almost as quick as my light bulb moment appeared, it was extinguished. The realisation dawned on me that once I returned home to the isolation and silence of the farm, my *monster* would resurface with a vengeance. I didn't want to leave… I *never* wanted to leave.

About an hour before I was due to go home, Jake led me by the hand to his bedroom. He wanted me all to himself before saying goodbye. We lay on his bed with some music playing quietly on his old stereo. For a while we didn't say a word, we just looked at each other with our heads resting on his pillow.

I loved staring into his eyes, they were like a window into his heart. I could tell what he was thinking just by looking at those piercing baby blues.

"I'm getting really sick of having to let you go all the time," he said softly; his tone sombre.

"Tell me about it. I hate saying goodbye too. At least you get to live here with your sisters. It's so much fun at your place. I have to go back to the farm and sometimes it just gets so boring out there."

"You really like my sisters that much?"

"Yeah, of course I do. I've always wanted to have a sister. It's amazing you have *three*! I mean what are the chances you have younger sisters and I have older brothers?"

"I know. It's almost like a sign that we're perfect for each other because I've always wanted an older brother. When we eventually get married, I'll have two, and you'll end up with three sisters."

I giggled at his open admission with regards to marrying me one day. I couldn't help but smile, even laugh whenever I thought about walking down the aisle and seeing Jake waiting for me at the altar. Truth be told, if he had asked me to marry him right then and there I would've said yes without any hesitation; regardless of my age. There wasn't a doubt in my mind that I wanted to spend the rest of my life with him. I wanted to be with him forever.

I took the opportunity to search for confirmation. "Tell me the truth, do you *really* think we'll get married one day?" I know it was direct, but I wanted to hear him say it again.

"I'm certain of it," he replied with conviction. "Every time I have to say goodbye it hurts. If we're married, we'll never have to say goodbye to each other again. I don't think you realise how much I love you Sophie. I lay awake some nights looking at the ceiling, thinking about you. And some days at school, entire classes pass by and I haven't heard a word the teacher's said because I've been day dreaming about you."

I could feel my heart fluttering in my chest. It was so wonderful to know I was always on his mind; just as he was always on mine.

"Not only do I love you Baby… I *need* you."

"Oh Jake," I breathed; kissing him briefly on the lips, "That's exactly how I feel. I still can't believe I found you, and I just can't imagine not being with you for the rest of my life. I know we're young and that we've only been together for a few months, but I know you're the one. I feel it with all my heart."

I'd looked into a crystal ball at my future and in every scene of my life Jake was there. It was our destiny to be together, forever. I was certain of it.

Before long we heard the doorbell ring. I knew instantly it was my father, and Jake knew it too. He kissed me passionately; taking full advantage of our last moments of seclusion in his bedroom.

"I'll miss you Baby."

"I'll miss you too, and I promise the next time we're together I won't freak out."

"Hey don't worry about that. When you're ready you'll know. There's no rush remember?" he smiled affectionately.

"Thanks Jake. That really means a lot to me."

Ironically, the way Jake had handled the situation from last night, treating me with such understanding and compassion, now made me feel more ready than *ever* before. He had proven that sleeping with me meant more to him than simply having sex. He wanted it to be beautiful and perfect, as special as such an important experience should be. I knew he respected me, and that meant everything.

We kissed one last time before leaving his bedroom; a deep sensual kiss that made me wish we had more time… and the house to ourselves!

We walked out into the family room, Jake's parents and sisters were already outside talking to Dad. As we reached the front door, he grabbed me by the wrist, spun me around and kissed me hard on the lips; exploiting every last second of privacy. It was so hot to be taken that way, and I was definitely becoming more welcoming of Jake's ferocious side. When he wanted me, I knew it! I could feel the sexual desire bleeding out of his skin. I vowed to myself, the next time we were together I would be *ready*.

I was no doubt looking a little flustered as we emerged from the house. It was a thought which made me blush. I said goodbye to Greg, Mary and the girls. I really was sad to be leaving but I assured Alice, Kate and Samantha that I'd be back soon. Jake opened the car door and gave me a conservative peck on the lips before I climbed into the passenger seat. I heard Samantha and Kate giggle at their brothers display of affection for me. Jake and I grinned at each other.

"See you soon Baby."

"Bye Jake."

He said goodbye to my father, who was already in the driver's seat. He reached over and shook Dad's hand before stepping back and closing the car door.

As the car reversed out of the driveway, I remember seeing Jake and his family all standing at the front of the house; waving. I started to laugh because they looked like a TV family, all waving and smiling together. *They're the Huxtables, or maybe the Brady Bunch,* I smiled to myself.

I would miss them; most of all… my Jake.

I hadn't seen Jake for over a month because each weekend he had to travel to Melbourne for training with the state karate team. Thankfully though, the Nationals were almost here so he would have his weekends back soon. More importantly, *I* would have his weekends back.

Over that time my health had deteriorated even further, and at some point during those weeks we'd been apart, the horrendously embarrassing experience of being dragged to school by my parents had unfolded. I hadn't told Jake about it, even though I wanted to. I don't really know why I felt like I should cover for them. Maybe deep down I knew if Jake found out what my parents put me through he'd never look at them the same way again, and I didn't want him to resent them.

The feeling of my head resting on Jake's chest, listening to the soothing beat, couldn't come soon enough. I was feeling mentally and physically shattered and I needed the love and protection of my saviour more than ever.

The school holidays arrived and we'd arranged with our parents for me to stay at Jake's house for a few days; three whole nights in fact! I was bursting with excitement because such a long stay meant that I wouldn't have to say goodbye to Jake so soon after seeing him. It felt like forever since I'd last seen his beautiful face. I missed him so much, and it would've killed me to say goodbye after only spending one night with him.

Over the past few weeks I'd thought a lot about our failed 'first time'. I came to the conclusion that the reason I freaked out and called the whole thing off was I knew the rest of Jake's family was in the house. I think I was just too worried about the possibility we would be interrupted during our secret rendezvous; so scared in fact that I completely lost my nerve. Instead of being calm and relaxed, I became frightened and tense which subsequently destroyed my desire to progress any further. So once I realised this and explained it to Jake, he and I decided we wouldn't make the same mistake twice. We agreed the only way we'd try to have sex again would be if by some chance we found ourselves completely alone in the house. I simply couldn't bear the thought of sneaking into his room at night, getting him all worked up and excited, then freaking out again. I wasn't about to take the chance.

Now that we had our plan, Jake and I were both on high alert from the moment I arrived at his place. We were on the lookout for any opportunity where we may be left alone with the house to ourselves. It was mid-week, which meant his father would be at work each day, so it was just his mother and sisters who needed to be occupied.

Shouldn't be too hard.

On the first day, Mary announced she was going to do some shopping for a few hours. Jake and I started to get our hopes up until she informed us we'd be babysitting his sisters while she went on her own. We were so close.

On the second day I must have been feeling particularly aroused. I remember having a discussion with Jake about the possibility of going for a walk up in the hills near his place. Sure we would have privacy, but we both agreed we wanted our first time to be in the comfort and *guaranteed* privacy of his bedroom. Being busted by an unsuspecting bushwalker wasn't my idea of romantic! We wanted our 'first time' to be perfect, so we shelved the idea of faking a hiking expedition just to have sex. Needless to say, that's exactly what we did a number of times in the future.

So we were two days down and still hadn't been presented with an opportunity to be alone in the house. Our time was quickly running out and I couldn't sleep another night knowing Jake was in the next room… so close to me. So on the second night, after waiting for Alice to fall asleep, I paid him a midnight visit.

As agreed, we didn't attempt to have sex, but that didn't stop us from releasing the build-up of sexual tension in other ways; ways that we'd practiced and perfected over the past few months. By now we knew exactly what each other liked and were experts in the provision of such *therapies*.

Oh how I loved Jake's mouth between my thighs. I'm as addicted to it now as I was back then. I've trained him well. Even as teenagers, as soon as my underwear hit the floor, he could unravel me with a magnificent eruption of pleasure in less than sixty seconds. I'm not just saying that either… we timed it! I would also like to add that I had my oral sex routine down to a fine art too. It's all about eye contact. Well that, combined with just the right mix of lips, tongue and caress would have him 'boiling over' in no time.

So we didn't have sex that night, but at least we wouldn't have to endure the following day literally bursting out of our pants with sexual tension.

"So what are your plans for today Mum?" It was the third day and Jake was fishing for information while we all had breakfast. He wanted me alone.

"Well I was actually going to head over to your Aunty Jill's place for lunch." Jill was Mary's sister. "I'm taking the girls. You two should come. Jill would love to meet Sophie."

"What time were you going?" Jake was stalling. He didn't want to appear too eager to knock back her offer.

"I was planning on going around at twelve thirtyish."

"Umm, Soph and I were actually thinking about walking down to the video store and hiring a couple of movies. We were going to get some snacks from the supermarket too and spend the afternoon watching movies."

Nice one Baby. I was impressed with Jake's believable alternative to going for lunch at his Aunties house.

"Are you sure? You could still come over for lunch, then watch a movie when we get home," suggested Mary.

You're right we could, but that wouldn't give me the opportunity I need to sleep with your son, I thought slyly; grinning on the inside.

"Nah, we might give it a miss Mum… if that's alright? We'll stay home and watch a couple of flicks instead."

"Fair enough. Are you up for a walk though Sophie?" asked Mary directly.

I still looked like shit, and I think she had her doubts as to whether I would actually be able to walk to the video store and back in my current physical condition.

"Yeah I should be ok Mrs. Freeman."

"We'll take it slow," assured Jake, looking at me sympathetically. He knew I wouldn't be able to walk at speed anyway.

"Alright then. Well I guess we're all sorted for the day," smiled Mary.

"We'll be leaving shortly Mum, so I'll take a set of house keys in case you have already left by the time we get back."

"Good idea. Make sure you take it easy, and don't walk too fast." she urged.

"I'll look after her. We aren't in any rush."

We finished breakfast, had a shower and got dressed, then headed off on our walk.

"I can't believe we're finally going to have the house to ourselves Jake!" I beamed as we walked in the morning sunshine.

"I know. I was beginning to think we were never going to be alone. You do know this doesn't mean we have to take things further, just because we have the house to ourselves. I don't want you to feel pressured or anything like that."

I could tell by the tone of his voice, he wanted me to be one hundred percent certain I was ready this time. I had absolutely no doubts, but still appreciated him reinforcing that there was no pressure on me.

"Jake… I'm ready. This time will be different, I promise. I'm sure I'll be far more relaxed knowing we're alone in the house. I want to sleep with you but just as you've said to me, I don't want you to feel pressured either."

"I don't Baby, not at all. I want you… today!"

As Jake looked directly into my eyes I could feel his intense craving for me; his hunger. My insides clenched tightly at the thought of finally going all the way with him.

We reached the video store and hired a couple of movies. Jake made sure we hired two that we'd both seen before. That way we wouldn't need to watch them, but if by chance we were quizzed about the storylines, we would have the answers. *Clever boy.* We picked up some chips, lollies and soft drink from a nearby take away store. We had all we needed for a believable afternoon of movies on the couch.

As expected, the walk back was slow. We had to stop a couple of times so I could catch my breath. He tried to bring up the subject of my fading health, but I shut him down as soon as he mentioned it. I wanted this day to be romantic and special; perfect. Talking about how sick I was would not be the best foreplay that's for sure. Plus, I knew if we started discussing my illness, I would've probably ended up telling him about being dragged to school by my parents. I sure as hell didn't want to relive that horrible experience; especially today.

"Can we not talk about that today? I know you care, but I just don't want to think about being sick."

"Sure Soph. I'm sorry Baby."

"No, you don't have to be sorry. I just want today to be perfect," I replied in a gentle voice, after realising my previous response probably came out quite terse. "I want you to help me forget about all that."

"Me too Sophie… me too," he smiled warmly.

We arrived home just as Mary, Alice, Kate and Samantha were heading out the door. It was only 11:45am.

More time with Jake!

We said goodbye to his Mum and sisters, and were already back inside before the car left the driveway.

As I walked into the lounge room, I heard a loud metallic 'click' as Jake locked the front door. I turned around to face him. He was a few feet away and stood in front of me with his hands behind his back. We stared at each other, eye to eye, in silence. For the first time ever, Jake and I were speechless. It wasn't awkward though, not at all; more like the calm before the storm. We were savouring every second of the entire experience; both of us well aware of what was about to happen.

It was as though we were communicating telepathically, but even so, it didn't seem to be helping. We didn't know where to start, or who was going to make the first move.

"Come here Jake." I raised my hand and motioned with my index finger for him to move closer.

He took a step forward and was now standing directly in front of me; his arms remained by his sides.

"Kiss me." I closed my eyes, puckered my lips and stood still; waiting for my man to make his move.

I sensed his face edging closer to mine. My heart pounded like a drum, and I knew the second our lips locked… it would begin.

I kept my eyes shut as Jake placed his hands softly on my cheeks, the warmth of his palms on my skin felt incredible. It was like every single hair on my body was a sensory receptor on high alert. Even the lightest touch sent delicious shivers through me.

"I love you Sophie Taylor," he said; kissing me tenderly on the lips before I had a chance to respond.

His gentle kiss quickly escalated and our lips parted, allowing our tongues to feverishly explore each other's mouths. He gripped me firmly on the back of my neck and held me in place while we 'French' kissed with searing passion and lust. I couldn't help but moan into his mouth. His other hand dropped down to my waist and immediately I could feel the pressure and strength in his grasp on my hip; a clear warning that his inner beast was lurking just below the surface.

I turned my head slowly, breaking contact with his lips, then ran my hand up the back of his neck. I leant forward and put my mouth close to his ear.

"Make love to me," I whispered sincerely.

As we stared enticingly at each other, our breathing slow and heavy, I could feel the energy in the room; it was electric. There was absolutely no doubt the outcome of lying down in Jake's bed was going to be vastly different to our first attempt some weeks earlier. Although I was still nervous, the fact we were alone had ensured I was significantly more relaxed. I was as ready as I was ever going to be.

The stars had aligned for Jake and I. We were both about to lose our virginity, and the most beautiful part of all was that we were going to give it to each other. A unique bond was about to be forged between us, which could never be replicated with any other soul on earth.

His voice was tender and calm. "Come with me," he said as he grabbed my hand; leading me out of the lounge room, down the hallway towards his bedroom.

I was relieved to see his body language had changed, and although he still seemed eager, he was noticeably more placid. I think he realised he started off fairly strong last time, maybe even a little forceful, so he was remaining relaxed and composed. My nerves were thankful and had subsided considerably. I felt completely safe with Jake, and I was ready to give my body to him… to do as he pleased.

He opened his bedroom door and stood to the side. "After you my love," he said, ushering me into his room; a true gentleman.

"Why thank you," I replied with a smile.

He pulled the cord, closing his curtains to reduce the bright sunlight beaming into the room. I collapsed on his bed and laid back; resting my head on his pillow with the scent of my man all around me.

"Comfy Baby?"

"Yes… but it could be better though," I smirked.

Jake climbed onto the bed and straddled me; pinning me beneath him with his thighs either side of my hips. I was immobilised and at his mercy.

"How about now?" he asked with raised eyebrows; grinning.

"Much better." I ran my hand up the back of his neck and pulled him towards me. After kissing my lips, he lightly trailed kisses across my cheek to my hairline; just behind my ear. Carefully he licked and sucked the side of my neck, occasionally nibbling on my earlobe which sent glorious shivers right through me.

"Oh that feels so nice," I breathed.

"Good. I want *everything* to feel nice."

Slowly he moved to the other side of my neck where he continued his delicate teasing. I could feel my body priming itself for the pleasure that was about to commence. Jake pushed himself up; leaning back onto his knees so he could pull his t-shirt over his head. Without hesitation, I placed both hands on his chest and ran my fingers all over his naked torso. Gliding my hands over his muscles, I was instantly reminded by the strength he possessed, and was once again relieved that the beast I'd been introduced to in the past was nowhere to be seen.

"Can I undress you?"

He certainly wanted to make sure I was going to be ok every step of the way. I didn't mind though. At least it slowed him down, and I appreciated the chance to gather myself at each opportunity.

I nodded. "Of course."

He grabbed me by the hand, sitting me up slightly so he could slide my t-shirt over my head.

"Take my bra off too," I directed politely.

He unclipped my bra and hung it on the bed head. His eyes feasted on my bare breasts and erect nipples. "Mmm," he moaned; his lips curling into a cheeky grin.

I laid back and he dropped down on top of me; pressing his chest against mine. The feeling of our naked upper bodies against each other, skin on skin, was incredible. We took a moment to savour the feeling of body heat building between us; kissing passionately as the temperature rose. Jake slowly moved down the bed and began to lick and suck my breasts and nipples. I moaned as my body entered its next stage of preparation. With every deliberate tease and sensual bite, I felt my pelvic floor muscles contract and then relax, causing a familiar combination of pleasure and moisture to build between my legs.

As he run his tongue down the centre of my stomach to the waist band of my pants, I couldn't help but push my hips up off the bed towards him. It was obviously permission enough, because he didn't ask to take my pants off. He quickly popped the button and unzipped my jeans; exposing the front of my knickers. I knew Jake liked them, so I made sure I was wearing my white cotton panties.

He slid my jeans down a little lower. "Someone's excited," he teased, referring to the wet patch on the front of my underwear, which had rendered them almost transparent and subsequently provided Jake with a partial view of my aching pussy.

"Well what do you expect, you're driving me crazy with that tongue," I breathed, the pleasure in my voice clearly audible.

"I haven't even *started* with my tongue yet Baby."

"I like the sound of that," I giggled as he lifted my legs up and pulled my jeans and underwear off completely in one swift action.

Jake grasped me by the ankles and held my feet together in front of his face; pausing momentarily before slowly pulling them apart. As he gradually opened my legs wider, inch by inch, his eyes moved further south. I watched intently as his chest expanded then relaxed; breathing deeply as he surveyed my exposed entrance. It was such a turn on to see the effect I had on him, and by the time my legs were as far apart as they could go, I was absolutely gushing with slippery arousal.

"You look so good. I have to taste you," he said; right before diving head-first between my legs.

There were no gentle kisses on my inner thighs and around my groin; teasing me like he usually did. No, this time he buried his face into my pussy, wasting no time driving his tongue deep inside me. I grasped the back of his head and moaned loudly as I thrust my hips towards him. It was less than thirty seconds and already I could feel myself on the verge of climaxing.

My breathing quickened as the carnal pressure reached boiling point. I bit down on my bottom lip to silence my pleasurable outbursts, but then remembered we had the house to ourselves. There was no need to be quiet. I opened my mouth and let go; emanating a drawn-out squeal which lasted as long as my orgasm. As I released my nectar into Jake's mouth and over his lips, it felt exhilarating to allow such natural noises to escape so freely. I don't know why, but being noisy made every glorious sensation even more intense.

Until now I hadn't had the opportunity to show Jake just how noisy I was when I climaxed. I was always forced to hold my erotic melodies inside, since we had only ever fooled around at night when our parents were asleep in a nearby room; or at our secret hideout which was obviously outside, so I couldn't really let go there either. It sucked because I absolutely loved being noisy and I knew Jake would appreciate it too.

Whenever I masturbated at home, if there was nobody else in the house I would allow myself to completely let go as I came. This usually meant my orgasms were accompanied by a rather loud scream, which peaked in volume at the height of pleasure before gradually drowning out as the sensation faded. To tell the truth, I hated having to be 'quiet' and I still do. There's no doubt I always have the best orgasms when I can let myself be free, and right there in Jake's bed was one such opportunity.

"Whoa Soph. What was that!" Jake beamed with astonishment.

"Sorry." I giggled; slightly embarrassed.

"Don't apologise for that Baby. You sound amazing!"

"Really?"

"Hell yeah! I love it!"

"My orgasms are way stronger when I'm noisy," I confessed.

"Then don't ever be quiet again!"

"Yeah right. Imagine if I did that in the middle of the night with your family at home!"

Jake laughed. "I see your point. Well they're not home now!" he grinned before burying his face between my legs again; eager for another erogenous tune. I was happy to oblige.

He plunged his tongue deep inside me; penetrating me over and over again. Gently, he licked and sucked my clitoris which was always super sensitive to any attention; fingers or tongue! Before long I erupted like a volcano, emitting another pleasurable scream as I drowned my lover.

"Damn you sound so good! I love it!"

In contrast to being embarrassed I was actually rather proud of myself. "You like that Baby?" I grinned.

"Uh huh," he nodded; eyes blazing with primal lust.

I knew exactly what he wanted.

"I'm ready Jake," I whispered, granting the permission he was waiting for before daring to proceed further.

He stood up and hastily removed his jeans; his hard rod springing from his briefs as he slid his underwear down to the floor.

"You look amazing too," I said as I studied him from head to toe and back again; my gaze lingering for an extended time at his straining erection which was pointing to the ceiling. There was absolutely no doubt… he was ready too!

Jake grabbed a condom from his bedside table and quickly removed it from the packet. With both interest and utter visual pleasure, I watched as he rolled the rubber film over his shaft. I was thankful for the extra lighting compared to last time as it allowed me to clearly see, and fully appreciate, just how fucking hot it was to watch my lover prepare his manhood for me.

I extended my hand welcomingly. He grabbed it and I pulled gently, inviting him back onto the bed to take his position between my legs which were still positioned where he left them… wide open.

He laid down, supporting himself on his arms as he leant forward and kissed me. I could smell and taste *myself* on his mouth which is a huge turn on for me. As I licked every last drop of slippery residue from Jake's lips, I reached down between us and grasped hold of *him*. It was warm, throbbing, and hard as stone. It felt like a hot rod of steel between my fingers.

Brace yourself Sophie, I thought as I held my lover.

I looked directly into Jake's eyes as I lined *him* up with my opening. "You ready Baby?" I smiled, surprised by my confidence.

He nodded. "Do I feel ready?"

I gave his shaft a gentle squeeze. "Uh huh," I grinned.

I kept his gaze then slowly guided him inside me, just the tip, before pushing him back slightly then easing him in a touch further. I repeated the process once more then released my grasp; trusting that he had the pattern figured out. I grabbed hold of Jake's arms which were pressing into the bed beside my head as he continued the rhythm; pushing himself inside me before withdrawing slowly, then sliding back in… a little deeper each time. Every controlled thrust was gentle and deliberate.

I waited for a sharp sting or any form of pain, but it never came. Only pleasure; fascinating, delicate, perfect pleasure. My eyes rolled back in my head as Jake fed his entire length into me; stretching and filling my body in the most wonderful way. It was such an amazing sensation, the greatest I'd ever experienced; I couldn't believe how connected I felt to him. Having my lover inside me for the first time not only united us physically, but it was as though our souls were also merging together… uniting as one. It was so incredibly beautiful.

"You ok Baby?" Jake whispered in my ear before kissing the side of my neck.

"Perfect. Keep going."

As he increased his rhythm ever so slightly, I re-focused on his face; watching his eyes as each slow blink lasted longer than the one before it. He was enjoying it as much as I was. We settled into a slow, sensual rhythm and it wasn't long before I felt Jake throb inside me. My insides tightened firmly and I knew I was ready to let go whenever he was. I desperately wanted us to climax together.

"That feels amazing." I moaned breathlessly. "Don't stop."

"Oh my god Soph… I'm not going to be able to last much longer!" he confessed as his rhythm increased again; seemingly out of his control.

I let go of his arms and grabbed him by the hips; gripping them firmly as he thrust back and forth. Magnificent, mind blowing, even surreal don't come close to accurately describing what it felt like to hold my man's hips while he drove his length into me over and over again! In that moment I knew I was hooked… instantly addicted.

I felt his shaft throb for a second time. I was right on the brink and couldn't hold off any longer, and by the feel of *him*… neither could he.

"Sophie!" he gasped; his voice straining.

I squeezed my eyes closed as Jake's cock swelled to what felt like double its size; escalating the feeling of fullness to my physical limit. Holding my breath in an attempt to keep myself in one piece, I thrust my hips back and forth against him. Every part of me felt his shaft pulse again and again as he ejaculated; grunting like and animal as he came. The feeling of him letting go inside me sent a shock wave of pleasure through my entire body, eliminating my ability to control the fusion of squeals and groans that filled the air. Wave after wave of pleasure surged from my pussy throughout every cell in my body, giving me my first taste of pure euphoria. *This is what heaven must feel like!*

Breathing heavily, we both collapsed in a hot tangle on his bed; the weight of Jakes relaxed body crushing me.

"You're squashing me," I gasped.

"Shit! Sorry Baby," he said as he lifted his weight off me; both of us laughing out loud.

My laughter soon dissipated when I felt *him* move inside me. "Out Jake," I snapped. My 'sensitivity level' was off the charts; reducing my request to a cold, two-word demand.

Slowly he disengaged, subjecting me to a strange sensation which caused me to wince until we were apart. Immediately I was overcome with a feeling of emptiness, like I'd just lost a vital organ.

Jake rolled over and lay beside me, still breathing rapidly with a light bead of sweat on his forehead. We both looked at each other and I couldn't help but giggle coyly. It was the only reaction I could muster. I was just so happy; he was too.

"Thank you so much Jake. I can't begin to describe how good that felt."

"No… thank you. Do you have any idea how incredible you make me feel? I've never felt so close to someone, so in love as I do right now. I feel like nothing can ever separate us."

"Me too, I feel exactly the same way."

Giving each other our virginity had lifted our relationship to new heights. There was no doubt making love had united our spirits, forever locking them together as one; never to be alone again. The other change I experienced was a powerful, unmistakable feeling of maturity. I immediately felt like an adult; a woman in *every* sense of the word, and Jake most certainly felt like my man.

"It didn't hurt?" he asked tentatively, tenderly caressing my cheek with the back of his hand.

"No Baby. I thought it might hurt a little, but it didn't. Thank you for being so gentle; I think it really helped me to relax. It felt wonderful from start to finish," I replied honestly.

"Good. I wanted our first time to be perfect Soph."

"It was," I smiled; hugging him tightly. "It was perfect."

"We'd better get up." Jake kissed me on the lips before standing up, kindly giving me the opportunity to examine his naked body one last time.

He reached his hand out and helped me to my feet. My legs felt quite unstable and I took a second to steady myself.

"You ok Baby?" he grinned, noticing my lack of balance.

"Yeah, my legs are like jelly though!"

"That's no good," he smiled proudly. Obviously pleased that his efforts had left me 'jelly-legged'.

I grinned back at him. *Cheeky bugger*.

We both got dressed and tidied up the bed before heading into the bathroom to fix our hair. 'Sex hair' would have been a dead giveaway to how the two of us had spent our time with the house to ourselves.

For the rest of the afternoon I felt like I was floating. 'Cloud nine' I think the expression goes, and my lover had a stupid grin from ear to ear until the sun went down. I couldn't help but giggle every time we made eye contact, and I revelled in the fact I could still feel exactly where *he'd* been; even hours later!

The entire experience had been as perfect as I could ever have hoped for. Turns out having an unfavourable 'practice run' a few weeks earlier wasn't such a bad thing after all! Jake was a pure gentleman, from the nervous beginning until the glorious conclusion. He was tender and caring, treating me like a precious jewel from the moment he put his hands on my cheeks and kissed my lips.

So that was officially our 'first time'. I'd given him all I had to offer, and in doing so had never felt so safe and protected in all my life. If I thought I was madly in love with Jake before, now I was completely and utterly infatuated with him.

CHAPTER FOURTEEN

BARE

Over the next few months my health deteriorated even further. I'd never felt so sick in all my life, and I was scared.

"Alright Sophie, I'll need you to come with me into the surgery next door, so I can take a couple of biopsies from the sores on your legs. I'm also going to do what's known as a bone marrow aspiration from your sternum," explained my newest doctor, a blood disorder specialist by the name of Dr. John McDowell. It was the first time I'd met him and already I was getting a good vibe. He seemed like a man of action, and I had high hopes that he was going to find out what was wrong with me.

The thing I liked most about Dr. McDowell was that he always looked me in the eye when we spoke; he treated me like an adult. All the other doctors I'd seen would talk directly to my parents, and more often than not I'd be left sitting there like a child and not asked for my input at all. I was sick of being talked *about* and not *to*. Considering I was the one with the problem, none of the other doctors actually let me describe what I was going through. They'd always look to Mum and Dad for answers, which was hopeless because their belief in the seriousness of my condition was questionable at best. Dr. McDowell asked me questions directly, listened intently to my responses, and most importantly he believed what I was saying.

Finally, someone who actually listens! I remember thinking within minutes of our first consultation.

Without being too dramatic, Dr. McDowell really was my last hope. I'd now been at war with my *monster* for close to a year and I was losing badly. My weight had plummeted from sixty kilograms to a waif thin forty-six. Considering that twelve months ago I was an athletic teenager with a full figure, I now resembled a skeleton covered in skin. I was literally fading away to nothing. At this stage my bony legs and arms were littered with sores, scabs and scars, and my skin was pale and grey. My face was gaunt and my eyes were encircled by black rings from months of insomnia, thanks to the crawling sensation under my skin which made sleeping impossible. Imagine a fifteen-year-old girl in the worst possible physical condition, literally a walking corpse, and you would have a pretty good image of what I looked like.

Still to this day I don't know how Jake didn't run for the hills at the mere site of his frail and withered girlfriend, let alone sleep with me. But over the past few months his devotion had not faulted. He continued to make love to me in the most delicate and tender way, providing me with the only means to escape the seemingly endless pain and suffering. I will forever be indebted to him for all he did for me during the darkest and most frightening period of my life.

The surgery was located next to the consultation room, and as Dr. McDowell went to prepare for my procedure, I changed into a hospital gown and waited for him to call me in. He reappeared sometime later, dressed in light green surgical scrubs; face mask in place.

Shit! This is getting serious!

"Ok Sophie I'm ready for you," he said, the mask across his mouth moving slightly as he spoke.

As I followed the doctor into the surgery, I was absolutely shitting myself. I hadn't planned on an operation today and I didn't feel at all prepared. I thought it would be like *all* the other doctors' visits I had been to over the past year… all talk and no action. I have to say though, despite being scared, I was still relieved something was actually being done.

"I've moved the bed closer to the door, so you can hold your fathers hand while he waits outside."

Dad and Mum had come with me to the consultation, but Mum was a bit squeamish with medical procedures so she opted to go back out to the waiting area until we were done.

"David I'm going to have to ask you to stay outside the surgery with the door closed as much as possible, so we can keep the risk of contamination to a minimum," explained Dr. McDowell. "Reach in so you can hold her hand though."

"Sure," replied Dad. I could tell he was worried.

I found it strange he would go to so much trouble moving the bed near the door, just so I could hold Dad's hand. Within the next few minutes I'd completely understand why.

I climbed up on the bed and lay my head on the pillow. I looked up at the lights on the roof; they were bright and made me squint slightly.

"Ok Sophie. I'm going to do the biopsies on your legs first. This will involve me cutting away a couple of the scabs with a scalpel, so I can send them away for testing. Are you comfortable?" he asked, as he wiped antiseptic liquid all over the centre of my right thigh; it felt cold on my skin.

"I'm ok," I replied nervously; my trembling voice highlighting just how 'not ok' I actually was.

Dr. McDowell turned around to a trolley which had a number of instruments laid out on the top shelf. I closed my eyes as he turned back to me and placed his hand on my leg.

"Are you ready Sophie?"

"I'm ready."

"You might feel a little sting," he warned.

I closed my eyes and braced myself; one arm stretched above my head towards the door so I could hold onto my father's hand who was just outside.

Fuck! I winced with pain. Tears immediately formed and squeezed from my eyelids as the scalpel sliced off one of the scabs from the middle of my thigh. I can only assume he didn't use a local anaesthetic due to the scabs being so small and on the surface of the skin.

"Ok I just need one more. Are you alright?"

I nodded; still squeezing my eyes closed tightly.

Fuck! The second slice from the scalpel was equally as painful as the first. The doctor carefully cut another scab away from the centre of my right thigh, next to the other biopsy site. I let out a small squeal as the sting from the incision intensified.

"I'm sorry Sophie. I know that must've hurt," he said empathetically.

He immediately placed a sterile dressing over the two incisions and secured it with surgical tape, then handed me a tissue to dry my eyes.

"I'll give you a minute to compose yourself before the next procedure."

I sniffled as I wiped my eyes. I looked up and could see Dad through the opening of the surgery door; a look of concern still etched onto his face.

"Are you ok Soph?" Dad asked; squeezing my hand lightly.

"Yeah, I'm alright," I replied; lying to make him feel better.

He forced a smile. "Almost done Soph. One more to go."

I turned back toward the lights on the roof and prepared myself for the next procedure.

"I need you to take your arms out of the gown so I have access to the centre of your chest," directed Dr. McDowell.

I took my arms out of the gown and folded it down to my waist. Thankfully I'd left my bra on, but I still felt exposed and vulnerable as I lay on the bed under the bright glare of the surgery lights.

"I'm going to wipe some antiseptic on your chest. It will feel a little cold."

I nodded.

He was right. I flinched as soon as the cold liquid touched my skin. Once he finished, I looked down to see the dark brown colour painted onto the centre of my chest, directly down my sternum.

"Now Sophie you'll feel a little sting as I inject a small amount of local anaesthetic into the aspiration site on your chest. This will numb the area for the bone marrow removal. Are you ready?"

"I guess," I nodded reluctantly.

I closed my eyes. The small sting of the anaesthetic syringe made me gasp. I held my breath for a few seconds until the pain quickly subsided.

"Now we'll just wait a few minutes for the local to kick in, and then I'll begin."

While we waited, Dr. McDowell proceeded to give Dad and I a description of what he was going to do next. I know he just wanted me to be prepared but I think it would've been better if he just went ahead and did it, because I remember feeling quite anxious as he described the details of the procedure.

"The tool I'm going to use is a manually operated surgical drill."

He held up the instrument but I didn't look at it.

"I'll have to put a fair amount of pressure onto the drill, which I'll slowly turn by hand. The drill bit will burrow into your sternum, then I'll be able to collect a sample of your bone marrow from the tip of the drill bit. Are you ok with that?"

No, but what choice do I have? I nodded anyway.

The doctor's description had me feeling even more anxious.

"Can you feel this?"

He pricked my chest with something sharp; testing to see if the anaesthetic was working yet.

"I can feel pressure, but no pain."

"Ok we're ready then."

Dr. McDowell lowered the bed slightly then put one knee up on the mattress so he was positioned directly above me. I caught a glimpse of the surgical drill and immediately closed my eyes.

"You ready Sophie?"

I nodded again. I was so scared.

"Starting now," he said calmly as he placed the tip of the drill onto my chest.

As the drill made its way through the thin layer of skin covering my sternum, I only felt a small amount of pressure, but no real pain. *The anaesthetic must be working,* I remember thinking. A thought which quickly dissipated as the doctor applied more pressure, causing the drill to chew its way into the bone of my sternum.

Holy shit!

I squealed loudly and squeezed my eyelids together as hard as I could; tears rushed down both cheeks. I gripped Dad's hand firmly as searing pain radiated from the centre of my chest. Dr. McDowell pushed down with so much pressure, I thought he was going to drill straight through my rib cage and into the bed.

"Almost got it Sophie. Nearly there."

He increased the pressure on the drill and continued to turn it slowly. I was trying with all my might not to scream, but with each turn of the instrument the agonising pain intensified, taking me to breaking point. I was just about to cry out for him to stop when he announced he'd finished.

"All done. I'm very sorry to put you through that, but we really need a sample of your bone marrow."

I opened my eyes. The room was bright and my vision was blurry. I wiped my face and looked up at Dad to see his eyes red and puffy; cheeks wet with tears. I can only imagine what it must've felt like for him to see one of his children in such pain. It was a vision which had obviously taken its toll on him.

I was still sobbing quietly as the doctor removed the bit from the drill and tapped it lightly against two glass slides. I watched as tiny pieces of my bone marrow fell onto the thin rectangles of glass. He then placed cover slides on top of each; securing the extracted samples for the lab.

"You were very brave Sophie. I know that must've hurt," said Dr. McDowell sympathetically as he placed a surgical dressing over the small hole in my sternum, which was actually bleeding less than I thought it would be. He secured it in place with tape, as he had done with the biopsy incisions on my leg.

"The small hole from the drill should heal up nicely within a few days. It may leave a tiny scar… but hopefully not."

It did.

Dad was yet to speak. I think he was still trying to get himself together.

"Just lay there for a moment. Take your time getting up," suggested the doctor as he pulled my gown down; covering my chest.

I let go of Dad's hand, and as I slowly put my arms back into the gown, every movement caused a sharp sting of pain from the extraction site. I sat up on the edge of the bed and the doctor motioned for Dad to come into the room with us. The procedure was over and my wound covered, so there was no longer a risk of contamination.

Dad gently rubbed my back. "Are you alright?"

"I'll be ok, it just hurt like hell," I replied with a shaky voice. "Are *you* alright?"

"Yep. It was hard to watch you go through all that," he said, wiping away the last of the stray tears which had escaped.

I think in those moments my father realised how much pain and suffering I'd been in for so long. I don't doubt he was crying as a result of watching his little girl go through an extremely painful procedure, but I also had the feeling he was upset because seeing me like that prompted him to reflect on his lack of trust and belief in what I'd been telling him for so long. I'm sure the day he and Mum dragged me to school while I begged and pleaded for them to take me home, had made its way to the forefront of his mind. Now he could see how serious the situation was, and he would've felt terrible for not believing me sooner. I loved my father and it hurt me to see him upset.

Although I'd felt betrayed, even to the point where I'd almost lost faith in them completely, I forgave both my parents. I only hoped that I'd receive their absolute trust, understanding and support from here on in.

"I'll be fine Dad," I felt like I had to pull myself together for his sake; to be brave for him too.

"You can head back into my office and get dressed. I'll be in shortly to finish up the consultation," said the doctor.

"Can you give me a hand to get dressed Dad?"

"Sure," he said; helping me down from the bed.

I slowly made my way next door where Dad helped me out of the surgical gown and back into my clothes. It took longer than I thought, as I was reduced to slow deliberate movements to minimise the pain radiating from the fresh wound in my chest.

Dr McDowell returned; handing me a glass of water and two tablets. "Just some paracetamol to take the edge off the pain."

He concluded the consultation by explaining that the results of the biopsies and aspiration would be back within the week. "I'll be marking these as urgent so I'm hopeful they'll be back within a few days. Then we will have some answers."

"Have you got any ideas at this stage as to what might be causing the sickness?" queried Dad.

"Well there are a few possibilities, but I don't want to jump to any conclusions yet, not until I have the results to confirm my diagnosis. So for now I'd rather not say because it may mean a weeks' worth of worry for you all, then turn out to be something entirely different. It's best we wait for the results and then we'll know for sure. Are you happy with that Sophie?"

"Yeah that makes sense," I replied, once again appreciating him for addressing me directly.

The tone of Dr. McDowell's voice indicated that whatever he thought may be wrong with me, was serious. It wasn't a surprise to me though, considering how bad my physical condition was.

We finished the appointment and headed back out to the waiting area. Mum got up immediately and rushed over to me. She could see I'd been crying and could obviously tell that I'd been through a fairly painful ordeal. The way I was hunched over and moving gingerly verified her concerns.

"Oh Soph, are you alright Honey?" she said caringly; gently putting her hands on my shoulders.

"Yeah I'll be ok… just a bit sore."

"So what did the Doctor say?" she asked, directing her question to my father.

"He said the results will be back within the next few days, so we'll just have to wait until then."

"It doesn't sound good though," I added.

Mum looked at me with an expression of deep concern. "Are you in much pain?"

I nodded. "I just didn't expect to be having anything like that done today."

"No neither did we. It must have been a bit of a shock for you."

"It was, but hopefully it will be worth it. I need to know what's wrong with me."

We slowly made our way back to the car which was located a short walk from the building. It had been a tough day, but there was one bright side to the entire experience. Dr. McDowell's rooms were located in Sunbury, and since it was a Friday afternoon I'd arranged to be dropped off at Jake's house after my appointment. I would be spending the entire weekend with him.

"Are you sure you're feeling up to staying over at Jake's place?"

"I'm sure Mum, I'll be fine."

In truth, I was busting to see him as always, and I know my parents were doing their best to comfort me but the only person I wanted was Jake. I needed him to hold me, to look into my eyes and tell me everything was going to be ok. I needed him to kiss me and make me forget about the *monster* wreaking havoc inside me.

Mum looked at me in the rear view mirror. "Ok. Well just make sure you give us a call if you want us to come and get you early."

I nodded. "I will… promise."

No chance!

We reached Jake's house at about 4:00pm. He was already home from school and in typical Jake fashion, busted out of the front door like a raging bull at full charge. He raced over to the car, opened my door and held out his hand to help me out of my seat.

He wasn't aware I'd undergone a surgical procedure that afternoon, but as soon as he seen how slow and careful I was moving, he knew something must have happened at the doctor's appointment.

"Hey Baby. Hi Mr. and Mrs. Taylor. Shit Soph! What's happened? Are you ok?" He was talking flat out.

"Help me inside first, then I'll fill you in."

As he helped me out of the car, Jake asked my parents if they'd like to come in for a coffee.

"No thanks mate. We have to pick up a few things from the supermarket before heading back out to the farm, but thanks for the offer," replied Dad.

My parents got out of the car and gave me a kiss goodbye. Dad handed Jake my overnight bag.

"Make sure you give us a call if you need anything."

"I will Mum."

"We'll bring Sophie home on Sunday arvo… sometime around five if that's ok?" confirmed Jake.

"Sounds Good. Alright we'll be off then. Have a nice weekend." Dad kissed me on the cheek again. "I love you."

"I love you too Dad. Love you Mum."

Mum also kissed me again. "Love you Honey."

I couldn't help but feel as though that day was a definite turning point with regards to how my parents viewed my illness. It felt good to have their trust and support; to know they'd believed and understood just how terrible I was feeling.

My parents returned to the car and waited until Jake and I were inside before driving away. As soon as I walked through the front door, I was greeted warmly by Mary and the girls. Greg was still at work.

Over the past few months I had stayed at Jake's on a number of occasions. I'd developed a wonderful relationship with his family. We'd grown close and they could all tell I wasn't doing too well.

Mary, Alice, Kate and Samantha all took their turn at giving me a gentle hug and a kiss on the cheek. It was so lovely to be welcomed with such warmth and affection. I felt like I'd arrived *home* again.

"Sit down in the lounge room and I'll make you a cup of tea," Mary ordered politely.

"That'd be nice, thanks Mary." She had asked me to dispense with the Mrs. Freeman title months ago.

Jake led me to the lounge room and sat down on the couch beside me; his sisters followed us in. Whilst I drank my tea, I described the procedure I'd just endured to my attentive audience. They all listened in silence as I described how Dr. McDowell collected the samples for the lab. Jake held my hand as I spoke, and every time I looked at his face I could see deep sadness in his eyes; immediately causing a lump to form in my throat which made it hard to talk.

"I should've been there with you," said Jake regretfully; shaking his head with regret. "I should've been there and I feel like I've let you down."

I told him my parents looked after me but I don't think it eased the disappointment he had in himself; not in the slightest.

Earlier in the week we had planned on going to the movies after my doctor's visit. At the time, I wasn't aware the appointment was going to be anything more than talking.

"Are we still going to the movies tonight Jake?"

"No. I didn't think we would… considering what you've been through today." He had a confused look on his face, as if to say, '*Of course not. You're in no shape to go out to the movies!*'

"I'm feeling a lot better though. I was given a few pain killers and I think they've started to kick in. I'd still love to go. Besides, I will only be sitting there snuggling up with you, which is what I'll be doing if we stay home anyway."

"Well if you're sure you'll be ok; we can still go. I've checked the start time of the movie and it's not for a couple of hours, so if you change your mind we'll stay home."

"Ok, but I think I'll be fine. I really want to see Titanic."

"Me too, but we can go to the movies anytime. I don't want you to feel like you *have* to go just for my sake. I'll be just as happy staying at home on the couch with you."

"Thanks Baby."

Mary and the girls talked with me for a little while longer before leaving us alone in the lounge room.

We sat cuddling on the couch. Jake tickled my face and hands; occasionally kissing me on the forehead. It was so good to be in his arms again, and it never ceased to amaze me how much better I felt when I was with him. From the lightest touch, his energy and love would flow into my body; and like magic I could feel it reviving me.

Before long it was time to get ready. We showered, put on some fresh clothes and had some dinner. Greg had arrived home from work and sat down to eat with us, so we were able to catch up with him before leaving.

After dinner Mary dropped us off at the cinema and told us to give her a call when we were ready to be picked up.

"The movie's over two hours long so we'll give you a buzz as soon as we're out Mum."

"Ok, that'd be good Jake. You two have a nice time."

We said goodbye and went into the theatre.

Watching '*Titanic*' with Jake was such a bitter sweet experience, not that I told him. On one hand it was a fantastic movie to see on a date as a teenager, so full of love and passion, but on the other hand I was still in a fair amount of discomfort from the procedure. Nonetheless, I made it through the film.

I was deeply touched when I noticed tears rolling down Jake's cheeks at the end of the film; I was crying too. It's one of the things I find most endearing about him; the way he openly displays his emotions, especially in sad movies. Even as a teenager he'd give no thought to looking silly or weak by letting a 'tear-jerker' move him to tears. He has always worn his heart on his sleeve, and ironically, the fact he doesn't try to hold back the tears makes him seem even more masculine. It's like he has the courage to feel what is happening around him and let those feelings out, with no regard for what somebody else may think of him.

It makes me smile now, all these years later, that our son Nathan is exactly the same. I've lost count of the amount of times we've been watching a movie as a family, and I've looked over to see both Jake and Nathan with tears rolling down their cheeks. Seeing the sensitive side of my two brave boys brings me undone instantly.

Once the movie ended, we gave Mary a call to come and pick us up; we waited for her on a bench outside the theatre. The air was rather cool so I sat on Jake's lap while he wrapped his arms round me.

We were talking about the movie and soaking up the atmosphere of a busy Friday night in the city centre; always a good place for people watching. Initially it was a lot of fun because there are always some interesting sights, but it wasn't long before I realised that *I* was the one being watched.

I noticed that a lot of people would take a second glance at me as they walked past us; most with a look of concern on their face. I knew I looked bad but I was beginning to feel very uncomfortable as a result of the stares and expressions I was seeing on passers-by. I tried to ignore it, but eventually it just got to me. I put my head on Jake's chest; closing my eyes and tucking my head under his chin like a scared child seeking protection.

"I wish your mum would get here soon," I said quietly.

He put his hand on my head and held me close. "Are you alright Baby?"

"I just want to go home."

"You sound upset Soph. You're not ok are you?"

I was starting to well up. I kept my eyes closed tight. "I can feel people looking at me, like I'm some kind of freak. I need to get home."

"Awe Baby," he said softly. "Just stay close to me. Mum will be here any minute."

Jake didn't try to convince me that people weren't staring, which could only have meant he'd noticed them looking as well. I was so embarrassed, and it hurt like a dagger through the heart to think he might have felt embarrassed by me too. I didn't ask because I knew he'd never tell me even if he was. Jake always said he'd protect me, so there was no chance he was going to give me an answer that would have cut me to the bone. The thought of him ever being ashamed or embarrassed by me was too much to bear, so I tried desperately to push the idea from my mind.

"Don't worry about them Sophie… I'm here. I love you Baby. Everything's ok."

I love you too Jake, I replied in thought. I couldn't bring myself to answer out loud for I knew I would've burst into tears.

"Here's Mum now," he said, looking to the corner.

Thank fuck! Get me outta here! "Good… lets go," I said; curbing my emotions.

Jake held my hand as we walked to the curb. Mary saw us and double parked right in front of the cinema so we didn't have far to go. He opened the back door for me and I stepped in. Once we were inside the car I immediately felt better; protected from all those staring eyes. We clipped our seatbelts on and I snuggled in next to Jake as he draped his arm over my shoulder.

"How was the movie guys?" asked Mary.

"Was it good? I can't wait to see Titanic," added Alice who was sitting in the front passenger seat.

"It was absolutely brilliant. Probably one of the best movies I've seen," Jake replied enthusiastically. "I'll definitely be going to see it again."

He wasn't joking either. In total he ended up going to see '*Titanic*' at the cinema four times. Twice with me, once with his family and once with some of his friends from school. And yes… he cried *every* time.

Mary glanced at me in the revision mirror. "How are you feeling now Sophie?"

"Not too bad. It's been a big day though and I'm starting to feel worn out."

"We'll be home soon Baby," said Jake; rubbing my thigh as if to warm me up.

I looked at him and smiled.

It was close to 11:00pm by the time we arrived home, I was completely exhausted and ready for bed. I would've given anything to be able to crawl into bed with Jake and fall asleep in his arms, but I was still restricted to sleeping in Alice's room; understandably so. After all, we were only teenagers.

Once inside, I sat down at the kitchen bench and had a cup of tea with Mary and Greg while Jake and Alice made my bed up in her room. Kate and Samantha were already asleep.

"Your bed's ready when you are Soph."

"Thanks Alice."

I finished my tea, said goodnight to Greg and Mary then made my way into the bathroom where I brushed my teeth and changed into my pyjamas. Jake was waiting in Alice's room to tuck me in. He helped me by the hand as I carefully laid down on the mattress, then he pulled the covers over and tucked me in snug. Alice was already in bed, smiling with approval as she watched her brother fuss over me.

"You sure this mattress is comfy enough? You can have my bed and I'll sleep in here?" he offered.

"No this is ok."

"Well if you get too uncomfortable, come and wake me up and we'll switch."

"It's fine… really."

He turned the bedroom light off and lay down beside me on top of the covers.

"I'll tickle your face until you go to sleep Baby."

"That'd be nice."

"Why don't you just go and get into Jake's bed now! I know you'll be sneaking into his room once I fall asleep anyway!" joked

Alice, obviously well aware of my late night stealth missions, which usually commenced as soon as she drifted off.

The three of us started laughing and neither Jake nor I tried to deny it. It was pretty clear she knew what we'd get up to. After all, she was only a year younger than me and apparently not so easily fooled.

"Well I would Alice, but your Mum and Dad are still up," I whispered.

"Just so you know, you don't have to wait for me to fall asleep anymore. If you want to go into Jake's room I'm never going to say anything. I know you two are in love," she whispered; looking down from her bed at Jake and me.

It was such a sweet thing to say. Without even realising it, she'd given my late night meetings with Jake so much more meaning than simply sneaking in to his room to have sex. I really appreciated what she said because she was right… she *got* it! Jake and I loved having sex with each other, but even more than that, we just loved being together. I was glad Alice could see it too.

The feeling of Jake softly stroking my face was hypnotic, and it wasn't long before I drifted off to sleep. It'd been a hell of a day and I was completely drained. I didn't even have the strength to scratch my legs. For all I cared my *monster* could do whatever he liked. I was exhausted.

I don't know what time it was but I woke up feeling like my bladder was about to burst. The house was dead silent as I climbed out of bed and went to the toilet. Jake and I hadn't planned to meet up in the middle of the night like usual, as I was feeling too sore and tired from the day's events, but on my way back to bed I thought I'd take a quick look in his room to see if he was awake.

As I slowly opened his door, the dim hallway light seeped into his room. I could hear his deep rhythmical breathing, indicating that he was sound asleep. I stood in the doorway for a moment, staring at him; so peaceful and beautiful. I couldn't take my eyes off him and I certainly couldn't bring myself to go back to bed, so I stepped forward and closed the door behind me.

In all honesty, I never intended to have sex with Jake. I just wanted to lay beside him; to snuggle in close. Oh well… I guess plans change!

I walked over to his bed and slowly pulled back the covers, just enough so I could climb in. He stirred a little when I slid in beside him. With my back to Jake, I lied on my side and wiggled myself into a comfortable spooning position; my butt pressed up against his groin. Jake still hadn't woken up.

After maybe twenty minutes or so, I wiggled about in an attempt to *accidently* wake him up but he was still out cold. I wasn't getting back to sleep any time soon, so selfishly I set about seducing my man while he remained fast asleep.

I reached behind me and quickly found his flaccid member. I grasped it gently on the outside of his boxers which caused him to stir. Then I proceeded to lightly massage and stroke *Jake*, an act which aroused me even more, especially when *he* began to grow in my hand; thicker… harder!

"Are you awake," I whispered, thinking surely he'd couldn't still be asleep.

Still no response.

Holy shit! These things really do have a mind of their own! I thought, amazed that he could still be sound asleep while sporting a raging hard-on!

I remember Jake explaining to me how males would sometimes get random erections without having to deliberately think about anything sexual. I didn't know whether to believe him; convinced that he was *always* thinking about sex anyway. Well I certainly believed him now, because I was currently holding his rock hard, throbbing cock and he still appeared to be fast asleep!

It would've been a crime not to put it to good use, so I let go of *him* and slid my pyjama pants and knickers down; exposing my bare behind and wetness to Jake's groin. I reached behind me and located the waist band of his boxer shorts, then gently pulled his underwear down; just enough to set *him* free. Immediately, I grasped hold of his bare cock. I couldn't believe how hot it felt in the palm of my hand.

"Jake… Jake… are you still asleep?" I whispered again.

He *still* didn't answer.

The whole ordeal had now become a bit of a game for me. The fact I'd managed to enter his room, climb into his bed, arouse him to a nice hard erection, pull my pants down and free his cock all while he was asleep definitely excited me. I was now determined to see how far I could go before he did wake up.

I manoeuvred my hips so my saturated opening was directly lined up with my lover's throbbing shaft. Slowly I moved my hips back towards him until I felt his tip touch *me*. I rubbed it against my wet lips; lightly coating *him* in my natural lubricant. I pushed my hips back a little further and using my hand as a guide, slowly fed his cock inside me. I closed my eyes; pushing my hips back even further until I'd taken most of his length into my aching tunnel. I exhaled deeply as I was overcome with the most amazing feeling of fullness. I felt whole again; complete. The feeling of his hot shaft inside me, skin on skin for the first time, was phenomenal.

I felt Jake move and was sure he'd woken up.

"That feel good Baby?" I whispered as I slowly ground my butt against his groin; barely moving but still gently fucking him.

Once again, no response.

You've got to be shitting me! I was amazed he could still be asleep.

I could feel him getting harder and it was at this point that I started to freak out a little. My challenge to see how far I could get without him waking up had landed me in a precarious position. Here I was, slowly fucking his deliciously hard cock with absolutely no intention of stopping, and all the while knowing I hadn't put a condom on him!

Stop Sophie... right now! Stop! Just fucking stop! My subconscious may as well have been speaking Spanish, because I couldn't understand a word she said. The truth was I wouldn't have been able to stop if my life depended on it. It was without question the best I'd felt for days, so selfishly I kept grinding against him. In my defence though, I did move a little more vigorously in an attempt to wake him up, in the hope that *he'd* have the self-control to stop. It worked… well kind of.

"What are you doing?" Jake's drowsy voice sounded.

I answered with a soft moan, and he grabbed hold of my hips; pushing himself hard into me.

Oh my god! Heaven! I pushed back to meet his thrust.

As it turned out, Jake had about as much self-control as me… absolutely none! Either that or the feeling of being inside me, bare skinned, was just too much for him to resist.

This is your last chance Sophie. Stop before it's too late! Yet again I ignored the annoying voice!

I felt Jake throb inside me; a definitive signal that he was only seconds away.

Fuck it! I'm not stopping now! Finally, my subconscious was talking my language.

I felt Jake's fingers grip me hard by the waist as he buried the full length of his shaft into me, again and again. His mouth was right next to my ear, and I heard him hold his breath as his body strained with the escalating pressure of his imminent orgasm. His erection swelled, and I gasped as he thickened; stretching me to my limit. I winced with a combination of pleasure and fear… fear that I was going to be split in two!

I was only seconds from letting go. Then, like an atomic explosion… *boom!* With what felt like the force of a geyser spraying boiling water and steam high in to the air, Jake erupted; groaning in my ear as he let go. The absence of our usual rubber barrier meant I could feel every surge of hot come as he blasted deep inside me; over and over. It was an unparalleled feeling of euphoria which threw me into the most powerful orgasm I'd ever experienced; so strong it caused my entire body to spasm violently. The fact I couldn't scream resulted in an enormous build-up of pressure in my head; I'm actually amazed I didn't suffer a brain aneurism. The level of pleasure I experienced as my lover came inside me for the first time was like nothing I'd ever felt before. It was so intense, almost beyond comprehension, and the fact it was so forbidden only served to enhance the strength and duration of my own release even further. I thought it was never going to end… and I didn't want it to.

Trust me, I'm well aware of how irresponsible and dangerous it was to sleep with Jake without protection at such a young age. I know that if it had of resulted in me falling pregnant then the course of our lives would have changed dramatically, but I can't stress to you enough just how sick I was feeling. I looked like death warmed up, but I felt like death full stop! The sensation of Jake releasing inside me literally felt as though I'd been injected with a burst of energy… of pure life! My mind, body and spirit had all been awakened in an instant. I could actually feel him healing me, and it felt absolutely fucking incredible! Now I think about it, it makes perfect sense. People have sex to *create* new life… but I was having sex to *save* mine!

It's funny how a moment of utter exhilaration and joy can immediately turn into a situation of panic and regret. Jake slowly pulled back from me, severing our intimate connection, and I rolled over to face him. Neither of us spoke.

Am I in trouble? Is he angry? Is he upset? Holy shit, what have I done? Jake's expression was hard to read.

"Are you ok Jake?"

"Yeah I'm fine. I'm just disappointed with myself for not stopping. I know I should have. I hope you're not upset with me?"

"I'm far from upset with you," I reassured sincerely. "I can't describe how good that made me feel."

"I suppose I'm just worried about you falling pregnant. We're always so careful… I just couldn't stop."

"Hey I'm to blame as well. I didn't stop either!" I confessed, trying to make him feel better. "Look, don't worry about me falling pregnant. The truth is, I'm so sick I haven't had a period for months. My body has never been in worse shape than it is right now, so the chance of me falling pregnant would be next to nothing."

He didn't say anything; my explanation doing little to ease his concern.

"I wanted you Jake. I *needed* you. Having sex is the *only* thing that makes me feel human. I've told you how good I feel when you're inside me, but I truly don't think you understand. It's like… every time you sleep with me… you bring me back to life. You're my medicine Baby."

I didn't go into detail about the *monster* that lived inside me and tortured me constantly, but I knew Jake was the only thing strong enough to fend of his vicious attacks.

"Try not to be upset. I'm so grateful for what you just gave me and I don't want you to be disappointed… at all! I know we should've stopped, I know it would have been the right thing to do, but making me feel like I have a chance is also the right thing too. I love you with all my heart Jake… and I always will."

"I love you too Baby," he whispered.

I felt him relax but I could tell he was still worried. "Everything will be ok… trust me," I said reassuringly before kissing him on the lips. "Can you give me a minute?"

"Sure."

I climbed out of bed and went to the bathroom to clean up. When I returned Jake had the covers peeled back so I could climb in beside him.

"I'm glad I made you feel better," he smiled. "And I'm not worried anymore."

"Good. Just remember… you *save* me." I kissed him tenderly. "You save me every time you hold me, or kiss me… or *make love* to me," I grinned.

"It helps that much?"

"Oh Jake, you will *never* know how much you help." I snuggled into him and he wrapped me in his arms.

I closed my eyes and drifted off within minutes.

"Sophie! Get up!"

I opened my eyes to see Alice standing in front of me.

"Dads already up! You should come back to my room now!" she snapped anxiously.

Crap... I've slept in!

I threw back the covers and wearily climbed out of bed as quick as I could, which wasn't too fast considering how sore my chest was. We made our way back to her room and got in our beds.

I heard the hall door open; it was Greg.

Shit that was close! Seconds later and I would've been busted!

"Thanks Alice, you're a life saver."

"That's ok. I didn't want you and Jake to get into trouble," she said innocently, not fully realising the disturbingly awkward situation she'd just prevented.

"I owe you one Alice."

She giggled. "Really it's no big deal."

We both laughed quietly together. I adored her so much and was grateful to have another Freeman in my corner.

As I lay on the mattress in Alice's room looking up at the ceiling, all I could think about were the events of the previous night. For someone who felt like they were on the brink of death, I was sure living life on the edge!

I closed my eyes, took a deep breath then exhaled slowly; unable to erase the satisfied smile as the soothing feeling of *Jake* between my legs lingered on.

CHAPTER FIFTEEN

LONELY RIDE

It was the following Friday, exactly one week since my visit with Dr. McDowell. I dragged myself out of bed feeling worse than ever. Every muscle and bone in my entire body ached, the crawling under my skin was driving me to the brink of insanity, and when I looked in the bathroom mirror my reflection frightened the hell out of me. I was so pale and thin; the prominence of my cheekbones and jaw line emphasised just how gaunt and haggard I'd become. My eyes looked as though they'd sunken into my head and the dark grey circles that encompassed them were only a single shade from black.

What the fuck is happening to me!

When my brothers lived at the farm I would watch horror movies with them; I'd seen more than I could count. As I stood in the bathroom, studying my face in the mirror, I was convinced I could've been cast as a frightening ghost, ghoul or zombie in a horror movie of my own. It was like the *monster* inside me was working its way to the surface, and as a result my physical appearance now resembled the evil which had taken over my body.

It must have been a pupil free day or maybe a public holiday, because Jake had the day off from school and was riding out to spend the weekend with me. I cringed at the thought of him seeing me like this, and to be brutally honest, it was probably the first time I didn't want him to see me at all. I hated myself for even thinking such a thought, but the reality was I couldn't help feeling like it was only a matter of time before he found me unattractive; even turned off by me. I wouldn't have blamed him though, considering I was already turned off by my own reflection. I hated what my *monster* had done to me and I was terrified at the possibility that I may never escape the firm grasp it had, not only on my body, but every other aspect of my life as well. It had its claws buried in me, like an eagle holding a rabbit; its razor sharp talons biting deep into my flesh. Making an escape seemed all but impossible.

I climbed into the shower and blasted my frail body with steaming hot water, so hot it felt like my skin was cooking, which seemed to be the only way I could get myself going in the morning. Still to this day, I have my showers ridiculously hot, to the point where Jake struggles to stand with me under the water without complaining that it's going to melt his skin off.

I emerged from the shower and started to dry myself when I heard a knock on the bathroom door.

"Sophie?"

"Yeah."

"We just got a call from Dr. McDowell. Hurry up in there so we can tell you what's happening," said Mum with a definite air of urgency in her voice.

"Ok… I'll be out in a minute," I replied as I towelled my hair.

I quickly dried myself, got dressed and hurried out into the kitchen.

"So what's going on?"

Dad looked at me; clearly distraught. "Dr. McDowell has received your results…" He paused momentarily, as if choosing his next words carefully. "And it's not good Honey. He's booked you into the Royal Children's Hospital in Melbourne, and has told us to get you there as soon as possible."

"Melbourne!" I exclaimed, already feeling myself starting to panic. "Did he tell you what's wrong with me?"

"He said we'd get a full rundown on why you're so sick from one of the doctors who works at the hospital; a Professor Ericson. He didn't go into any great detail over the phone so we'll have to wait and see what the professor in Melbourne says."

The tone of Dad's voice and his body language did little to quell my suspicions that he'd already been told what was wrong with me. I had the distinct feeling that he was trying to hide something... something big! Turns out... he was.

"So when are we leaving?"

"As soon as we pack our bags, so go and get your things together," he directed.

"How long will I be staying?"

"Dr. McDowell said to plan for two weeks at least."

"Two weeks!" I snapped. "What the hell are they going to do to me!"

"Don't panic Sophie," said Mum, trying to calm me down. "Wait until we get there and find out more about what's going on."

"I've got to call Jake first to let him know not to ride out today."

"Ok but make it quick, we really need to get on the road," she said calmly. She must have been able to sense I was getting flustered and was trying to remain composed herself, in an attempt to prevent me from completely freaking out.

I called Jake's house, praying he wasn't already on his way out here. "Hi Mary, its Sophie. Has Jake left yet?" I asked hastily.

"Oh hi Sophie, yeah he left a little over an hour ago. Why?"

Fuck! He's already on his way!

"The doctors think they've found out what's wrong with me and I have to go to Melbourne today. It means Jake won't be able to come and stay for the weekend." The disappointment in my voice was obvious.

"Awe that's no good. I hope everything's ok?"

"We don't know much at this stage. My doctor said we'll find out more when we get to Melbourne."

"When are you leaving?"

"Right now actually. I just wanted to call and tell Jake not to worry about coming out, but since he's left we'll have to meet him on the road."

"Oh ok, well I won't keep you then. Take care and I hope everything turns out alright."

"Yeah me too. Thanks Mary. I'll see you in a couple of weeks."

"Ok. Bye Sophie and good luck."

"Thanks. Bye."

Jake didn't have a mobile phone, making it impossible to contact him and tell him to turn around. We would have to meet him somewhere on the road as we drove into Sunbury; prior to taking the turnoff to Melbourne.

"We have to leave straight away!" I snapped. "Jake will already be over half way out here. I don't want him to get all this way just to have to turn around and ride home again."

"Ok… then let's get moving," urged Dad.

The three of us left the kitchen and went to pack. I threw a heap of clothes and toiletries into a bag and was back out in the kitchen in no time. Moments later Mum and Dad emerged from their room, packed and ready to hit the road. We locked up the house and climbed in the car. As we drove out of the front gate, Mum and Dad discussed who they'd call to look after the farm and feed the animals while we were away. They planned on organising someone once we had reached the hospital.

We headed off towards Sunbury with our eyes peeled, scanning the road ahead; searching for Jake as he pedalled his way out to see me.

I felt sick in the stomach at the thought of telling him he had to turn around and ride home. I knew it wasn't my fault, but it didn't stop me from feeling guilty for making him ride all this way for nothing. I dreaded the look in his eyes when I told him that our weekend together wasn't happening, and that I had to go to Melbourne immediately.

We were about twenty kilometres or so from the farm on a straight stretch of road. I looked to the next hill in the distance and saw a person riding a bike on the opposite side of the road; just cresting the hill.

"There's Jake!" I yelled; pointing him out to Dad.

"I see him," he said as he pulled the car over to the side of the road.

Jake was powering down the hill towards us at break-neck speed. His head was down, arms tucked in by his sides and his legs were pumping hard on the pedals, like pistons in an engine. It was clear he wasn't out for a leisurely ride, and in that moment I understood why he'd be so exhausted every time he rode out to the farm. Jake was a man on a mission and it made my heart ache to see him riding with such determination to reach *me*.

"Flash the headlights David or he'll ride straight past us," suggested Mum.

Dad flashed the lights and immediately Jakes position on the bike changed. Realising it was our car which was parked on the side of the road, he sat up and stopped pedalling. As he rolled towards us, he checked for traffic then crossed to our side of the road before pulling up in front of the car; a confused look on his sweaty face. I climbed out of the back seat and walked to the rear of the car; it would be all the privacy we would get.

He rested his bike against the bull bar, hung his helmet on his handle bars and took his sunglasses off. He waved and said a quick hello to Mum and Dad as he walked over to me.

Immediately, he grabbed me by the waist and looked into my eyes; a worried expression etched into his face. "What's going on Soph?"

"Oh Jake." I kissed him briefly. "I'm so sorry I couldn't get hold of you. I rang your house but your Mum said you'd already left. I have to go to Melbourne."

"Melbourne? What? Why?"

"The Doctor called and said I need to get to the Royal Children's Hospital as soon as possible." I was already starting to well up.

Mum and Dad stayed in the car while we talked. As a car sped past Jake moved me further off the side. It was a one hundred zone and standing too close to the road wasn't a good idea.

"How long will you be gone Baby?"

"Maybe two weeks. We're not sure at this stage."

"Do you know what's wrong?"

I lowered my voice. "I think Dad knows but he's not saying anything yet. He said we'll find out when we get there"

"Shit Baby, it sounds serious," his voice now matching the concern in his eyes.

"I know."

My eyes stung as the first of many tears escaped and trickled down my cheeks.

"Hey… everything's going to be ok Baby," Jake wrapped his arms around me as he spoke. "I know you're scared but at least you're going to the best hospital, and I'm so glad something's finally being done to help you. I wish I could go with you Soph." His head and shoulders sank as he realised he wasn't going to be with me for the next few weeks.

"I know. I wish you could come with me too." I put my head against his chest and wept. "I need you."

Everything hit me at once. Going to hospital for weeks to get God knows what treatment, combined with the fact I would be so far away from Jake with absolutely no idea when I'd see him again; it was all too much for me.

He put his hand on the back of my head and held me firmly against him.

"Don't be scared Soph. Everything will be alright. I know it will."

"I can't help it. I know it's not good news. I mean why would they want me in Melbourne so urgently. I'm really freaking out, and seeing you… out here… like this…"

A feeling of dread washed over me like a giant black wave of pure fear. I'd been sick for so long and had literally felt like I was dying for months. The possibility that maybe I *was,* drained the blood from my face. The whole situation was a horrible nightmare, and for the first time thoughts of the worst possible kind flooded into my head.

What if I don't make it through this? What if the Doctors can't help me? Is this the last time I'm ever going to see Jake?

I tried to push the notions from my mind but they were planted firmly. The mere thought that I might never see him again caused my legs to weaken and buckle beneath me.

"Hey are you ok Soph?" Jake said as he tightened his grasp on me; preventing me from falling in a limp, lifeless heap on the ground.

My weeping turned to gasping sobs. I couldn't get control of myself; I was losing it. Standing on the side of the road out in the middle of nowhere, cars rushing past, my parents only meters away and not saying what was wrong with me, my lover having just ridden all the way out to see me only to find out it was all for nothing, my *monster* as determined as ever to break me to pieces, and now a head full of the darkest possible thoughts ever to have flowed through my mind. It was too much. I felt like I was going to black out.

As I cried uncontrollably, Jake held me close to him and did his best to calm me down. I knew Mum and Dad would be watching us in the revision mirrors; I was grateful they decided to wait in the car and let Jake console me. After all, he'd had a tonne of practice over the past eight or nine months getting me through breakdowns just like this.

"I know everything looks bad Sophie, but you have to believe it will all turn out ok in the end. I know you're afraid of going to Melbourne but I have a really good feeling about it. I honestly believe this will be a turning point for you, so try and stay positive Baby. Keep thinking about the future… *our* future."

"I just can't get these horrible thoughts out of my head. I keep thinking I'll never see you again." There was a sickening fear in my voice; I knew Jake could hear it too.

He put his hands on my cheeks and tilted my head so I was looking directly into his eyes.

"Sophie, I love you."

"I love you too," I breathed.

"And do you trust me?"

"Yes… of course I do."

"Then trust me when I say this is *definitely* not the last time you'll see me. You and I are destined to be together forever! I've never been more certain of anything in my whole life." His voice trembled slightly but he fought back the tears. "We have a lot of things we need to do, and I know with all my heart that we'll get the chance to fulfil *all* of our dreams together."

"Oh Jake," I sniffled; his vision for us giving me the hope and faith that I was so desperately lacking.

"Baby, if you only ever do one more thing for me for the rest of my life…"

"Anything Jake!"

"Please promise that you'll never have horrible thoughts like these again."

My bottom lip trembled.

"These dark thoughts aren't real, will never be real, and will only bring you worry and pain. It's so important for you to stay positive and believe the future we've dreamt of will come true. I know it will Soph… I just know it."

As he spoke, I could feel the blackness which had invaded my mind slowly fading. I pictured Jake standing at the altar, turning around to see me walking down the aisle towards him; a huge smile on his face. I imagined us holding a newborn baby together with tears of joy in our eyes, and I could see myself walking slowly through a park with Jake, both of us old and grey; still holding hands after decades of love and life. My heart melted as the bright visions over powered the darkness.

I've often heard that just before you die, your entire life flashes before your eyes. Well standing on the side of the road that morning in Jakes arms, my *future* flashed before mine. It was a future worth fighting for, and I was ready to fight!

Once again, Jake had pulled me back from the edge. He always seemed to know exactly what to say at exactly the right time. I've already referred to him as my guardian angel, and this was just another situation where he wrapped his giant white wings around me; providing the protection and love I so desperately needed if I was to have any chance of survival. Jake… my *angel*… forever.

"You guys had better get going."

"I wish we could drive you back to Sunbury but your bike won't fit in the car. I'm sorry you had to ride so far for nothing."

"I didn't ride all this way for nothing Baby. I rode all this way to see you, and I did," he smiled. "I think it was supposed to be like this so please don't feel bad for me. I'm grateful for every minute I get to spend with you. The truth is I would've ridden ten times as far to see you for less than I have today."

I believed him.

"Anyway… don't worry about me, it's time to focus on you now. I want you to put all your energy into getting better ok?"

I nodded, hugging him tightly and pressing my cheek against his chest before looking up and kissing him passionately. I knew we were going to be together forever and I believed everything he said, but just in case, I wanted our last kiss to be filled with all the love and adoration that overflowed from my heart. I didn't care if Mum and Dad were watching, I needed Jake to feel how much I loved him and a shy peck on the lips just wasn't going to cut it.

I must have kissed him for longer than I intended because Dad sounded the horn; interrupting our steaming hot, tear soaked kiss.

"I guess this is it Baby," he said softly as he stared deep into my eyes; his hands firmly around my waist.

I could tell he didn't want to let me go.

"I'll call you as soon as I can," I said, still sniffling as my persistent tears caused my nose to run.

As per usual when Jake and I would say our goodbyes, the familiar feelings of sadness began to creep into my body. My heart ached torturously.

"I don't know when I'll see you again. I'm going to miss you more than ever," I cried.

"I'll miss you too Baby. I promise I'll be thinking of you every second of the day, and I will dream about you every night. Be brave Sophie, and remember no matter what happens… I'll always love you. You mean *everything* to me Baby. You're my world." He spoke with the deepest sincerity. I could *feel* the emotion and sentiment in his words.

I put my hand on his cheek. "You mean everything to me too and I love you more than words can describe. I'll be home soon and hopefully I'll be better; fingers crossed."

We hugged again and kissed one last time. He walked over and opened the rear door for me, then said a quick goodbye to Mum and Dad as I climbed into the car.

"Look after her for me guys. I wish I could've come with you all."

"We will Jake. Sorry we couldn't give you a lift back into Sunbury."

"No worries Mr. Taylor. I'll just take my time, besides it's a nice morning for a ride," he smiled, trying to find a positive in such a horrible situation.

He leant in the car and grabbed my hands. He kissed me again on the lips then lightly on the knuckles.

Dad started the engine.

"Goodbye Sophie," he said softly as he let my hands go.

"Bye Jake. I love you."

"I love you too Baby."

He stepped back and closed the door then walked around the front of the car and grabbed his bike.

As Dad waited for a passing car, Jake put on his helmet and sunglasses then climbed on his bike. I didn't take my eyes off him, not for a second. We slowly accelerated away, leaving my *angel* alone on the side of the road. I kissed the top of my hand where his lips had been only moments earlier, then turned around in my seat to look out the back window; hoping to wave goodbye just one more time. He looked up and gave me a final wave then began to ride. Tears streamed down my face as I waved back, my heart felt like it stopped beating altogether.

I'll never forget the image of Jake starting his ride home that day. It was as though he was a totally different person compared to the one I'd seen only minutes earlier, flying down the hill towards us, legs spinning frantically like he was in the final sprint of the *'Tour De France'*; so determined and eager to reach me. Now, with his shoulders hunched over and head hanging down, he turned the pedals over achingly slow. I could tell he was crushed, beaten; robbed of all motivation to ride the long, lonely journey back to Sunbury.

I can't even imagine how horribly sad he must have felt. One minute he was riding with everything he had to get to me as fast as he could, then in the next, he was riding back home from the direction he just came after seeing me for only a few minutes; knowing he wouldn't hold me in his arms again for weeks.

I watched as his silhouette faded into the distance and eventually out of sight. I turned from the back window and loosened my seatbelt so I could lie down on the seat. I covered my face with my hands and sobbed softly. Without question it was the worst goodbye I'd ever experienced. My heart twisted with the emotional pain of being separated in such hurried and uncontrollable circumstances.

Mum reached around and put her hand on my shoulder. "Oh Sophie, you poor thing," she said sympathetically as she rubbed my shoulder comfortingly. "Hopefully we won't be in Melbourne too long. I promise, as soon as we're home Jake can come and spend some time up at the farm. Would you like that?"

I nodded.

My parents were beginning to understand how much Jake and I meant to each other. Witnessing the torment I was suffering after saying goodbye, clearly highlighted the seriousness of our relationship; proving this was no ordinary teenager romance. The love which flowed between us was as pure and true as that of any couple who had ever been in love before.

As we drove towards the hospital, and my fate, all I could do was pray that I would soon find myself in Jake's arms again.

Throughout time, the names *Romeo and Juliet* have become synonymous with true love. Their story of devotion and passion has lasted centuries, and is still regarded as the epitome of love between man and woman. I can assure you whole heartedly, the depth and power of the feelings we shared rivalled even the most famous of love stories. But in saying that, I could only hope the love we had for one and other was where the similarities with *Romeo and Juliet* would end.

CHAPTER SIXTEEN

THE 'BAT CAVE'

After saying goodbye to Jake, I don't remember talking much at all during the four-hour drive to Melbourne; I was just too upset. I lay on the back seat with my head resting on a pillow; eyes closed. My body twitched and jolted continuously as my legs and arms were tortured by the relentless itching. I tried desperately to resist scratching and clawing at them constantly but it was a futile effort.

I pictured Jake, imagining every detail of my *love*. His eyes, hands, body and mouth; all the beautiful parts of him which brought me pleasure and happiness. I would've given the world to be with him, just the two of us in his bedroom. Words can't begin to describe the safety, comfort and pain conquering pleasure I felt when I was with him. *Jake... Jake...* His name floated hypnotically around in my head.

As we reached the outskirts of the city, I sat up and took in the sights of Melbourne in an attempt to divert my attention from the physical and mental anguish. I was always blown away by how busy the city was compared to the quiet and tranquillity of the country. The amount of cars, trucks and buildings was staggering.

Mum was in charge of the map while Dad drove, and as usual, they had a few colourful disagreements about which direction they needed to go. I guess it was inevitable considering they were so used to driving around in the country, where you could drive for kilometres without passing a single car.

We eventually reached the Royal Children's Hospital in the suburb of Parkville. As we parked the car I looked up and surveyed the sheer size of the building. It was at least ten stories high and was easily twenty times bigger than the hospital in Sunbury. As we walked inside, the enormity of the place didn't disappear.

The foyer was huge with a number of staircases heading up to different floors, ramps for wheelchairs, elevators, and people everywhere. One thing which really took me by surprise though was that it had its own *'McDonalds'*. I never expected to see a fast food restaurant in a hospital, but I would soon be grateful that some tasty junk food was close by.

As far as first impressions go, the most frightening aspect of the Royal Children's was the amount of sick kids I could see, of varying ages, walking or being pushed around in wheelchairs. I knew they were all sick because I lost count of how many children I saw with bald heads, face masks and even missing limbs. Some had oxygen tubes under their noses to help them breathe, and others had IV drips coming from their arms that were connected to carts they wheeled around with them. It was a sight I'll never forget, and it made my situation seem all the more real. If I was scared before, now I was totally fucking petrified!

We walked over to the main counter and Dad introduced us to one of the three ladies at the desk. She typed my name into the computer, then directed us to take a seat while she paged the people we needed to speak with. Mum, Dad and I sat down in the waiting area for a short while, then two women approached us. I can't remember their names, but I know that one was a nurse and the other was a social worker. They introduced themselves before asking us to follow them to a private office where we began the hospital admission process. I was actually quite surprised by the amount of forms my father had to fill out. There seemed to me a mountain of paperwork, which made me even more anxious to know what the hell was wrong with me. At this point, after seeing all the sick kids in the hospital lobby, I'd pretty much surrendered to the fact I was in some seriously deep trouble.

After we filled out the paperwork, the nurse measured my height and weight then fitted me with patient identity bands; one on my wrist, the other on my ankle. The whole process took half an hour or so. I remember the nurse and social worker being very friendly and helpful. It was clear they were used to working with children because as scared as I was, their compassionate and calm nature made me feel slightly more at ease.

Once the admission was complete, they led the three of us to an elevator; the nurse hit number '6'. As the elevator ascended they asked me questions about where I went to school and what it was like to live on a farm. I didn't feel like they were just making small talk either, they seemed genuinely interested in what I was saying. I guess living in the city sparked their curiosity about what life in the country was like.

The elevator stopped and the door opened. As I exited, I looked up at the large sign displaying bright red lettering; '*6 EAST ONCOLOGY WARD'*.

"Welcome to the oncology ward Sophie," said the nurse.

What's oncology? I remember thinking. *Sounds bad.*

"Now we're going to take you to a part of the ward known as the Bat Cave," she explained. "It's a small isolation room where patients come before they start treatment."

As I'm writing this part of my story, I recall it was around this point, talking about 'Bat Caves' and 'isolation rooms', where I really wish somebody would've told me what the fuck was wrong with me!

We reached the glass doors of the 'Bat Cave'. They were adorned with more red lettering; '*ISOLATION ROOM*'. It was an unusual setup whereby there was an outer set of glass sliding doors, then a small space big enough for two or three people; an initial containment area, then there was a second set of sliding doors which allowed access to the isolation room. I could see why it had the nickname the 'Bat Cave' because all the glass sliding doors gave the place a kind of secret hideout feel.

"This is where we say goodbye and hand you over to the nurses on the ward." As the admission nurse spoke, another nurse emerged from the 'Bat Cave' and waited in the containment area. She was in full scrubs, complete with hair cover and face mask. She was holding a hospital gown, a robe and some other items. "I will take your Mum and Dad to get gowned up and they will be in with you shortly."

"Bye Sophie, it was nice meeting you, and good luck with everything," said the social worker. "I'm going to have a chat with your Mum and Dad before they come in and see you. I will come and check in on you from time to time during your stay at the hospital."

I gave Mum and Dad a kiss and said thank you and goodbye to the two ladies who had been so kind and helpful. The nurse in the containment area pushed a button on the wall and the outer doors opened. I walked inside and they immediately shut behind me.

"Hello Sophie, my name's Jill and I'm one of the oncology nurses." As she spoke she pulled across an internal curtain; blocking the view from the outside hallway. "I will need you to take your clothes off and hop into this gown. Is that ok with you?"

"Sure," I answered nervously.

Jill helped me undress. I was moving slow and was surprised by how hard I was finding it to get changed into the gown. I think the long car trip and emotional turmoil of the day had finally caught up with me.

"You can leave your bra and knickers on Sophie." Jill, like the other two ladies I'd already met, was also really friendly which went a long way towards alleviating my anxiety.

In one change of attire I had transformed. I was officially a hospital patient… a frightened one.

"Don't be afraid. We'll take good care of you Sophie. You're in one of the best hospitals in the world, and lucky for you, I'm one of the best nurses in the world."

I could tell she was grinning under her mask. She could obviously sense I was nervous and her little joke made me smile.

I will always remember how great the staff were at the Royal Children's Hospital. It takes a special kind of person to be able to look after sick children, keep them positive and free from fear; to keep their mind from focusing on the pain and suffering. They're true angels, every single one of them.

Jill put all my clothes in a plastic bag and sealed it shut. We both washed our hands then she pushed another button on the wall. The second set of doors opened and I followed her into the isolation room. It was quite small and only had four beds. Three of the beds were empty but in the fourth was a young girl, about seven years old. She was awake and lying on her side; curled up in the foetal position. I could hear her moaning quietly; in terrible pain. Her body was frail and her face was gaunt and grey in colour; eyes dark and sunken. This poor little girl looked like she was dying. *She looks exactly like me!* A lump formed in my throat at the sight of her, and it broke my heart to see a young child in such terrible condition.

Throughout my time in the 'Bat Cave', her parents came in and out, as did mine. Occasionally they'd talk with Mum and Dad. Unfortunately, all the parents in the hospital had something in common… *very* sick kids!

As the nurse directed me towards one of the empty beds, opposite the young girl, she gave me a brief explanation of the room in which I was now staying. "Ok Sophie. At this stage you'll remain here in the isolation room for at least a week while you start your treatment. Have you been told what treatments and procedures you're due to have?"

"No. I haven't even been told what's wrong with me yet. Nobody's telling me anything!" I replied desperately.

"Well I don't have any information I can give you at this stage, but I'm sure you will be told everything by your doctor soon."

I was disappointed she couldn't tell me anything, though I don't think she would've been allowed to even if she knew.

"Okay, the purpose of the isolation room is to keep you in an environment that's as sterile as possible. This will give us the best chance of keeping you free from things like viruses or infections. Everyone who comes to visit you over the next few days will have to be brought through the containment area, wash their hands and be dressed in a gown, hair cover and face mask; just like you and me.

That way if they have something like a cold, we will be able to reduce the chance of that virus being passed onto you. It's very important, especially in the early stages of your treatment, that you don't get struck down with another illness. Even something as simple as a cold can make things very difficult here."

As I listened to Jill's explanation, I climbed into bed and laid my head down on the pillow. She tucked me under the covers.

"Thanks," I said weakly.

"Have you got any questions?"

I shook my head.

"I'll be back to check on you in a minute Sophie. Your parents won't be far away either."

"Ok."

I was the newest resident of the 'Bat Cave' and as I lay in bed waiting for Mum and Dad to come in, I think I'd reached rock bottom in terms of my physical condition. I felt like I'd been deteriorating from the moment I woke up that morning. I was completely exhausted and weaker than ever. I was struggling with even the smallest movements, even keeping my eyes open felt like it took every ounce of determination and energy. You would think being so weak and tired, I would have just fallen asleep, but sleep was literally impossible. The crawling, itching assault on my legs and arms was at its all-time worst. To give you some idea of what it felt like, picture having your arms and legs covered in hundreds of tiny cuts, before being tied down onto a bull ant's nest to be ravaged by thousands of the tiny insects. Imagine them biting your flesh and crawling into the open cuts on your limbs; literally under your skin. Trust me it felt even worse than it sounds! It was torture… agonising torture. I couldn't stop scratching and clawing at my legs and arms. It was as if my *monster* was somehow aware that I'd been brought to the one place where he could be defeated. So in response to this threat towards him, he now attacked me with all the ferocity and savageness he could muster. It was crystal clear that my *monster* was trying his absolute best to kill me, and as each minute ticked by, he edged closer to succeeding.

Mum and Dad arrived at my bedside a short while later; dressed in a gown, mask and hair cover.

"What the hell's going on? I want to know what's wrong with me now!" I demanded. My voice was weak but my frustration was clearly audible. I was fed up with feeling like I was the only one who didn't know what was making me sick, and I couldn't take it any longer. I wanted answers and I deserved them! "Just tell me what's wrong with me… please!" I begged.

They both looked a mess. Mum had red eyes like she'd been crying and Dad looked like he was only just holding himself together. I knew full well they had a pretty good idea of what was going on.

"Sophie, I know your scared. Calm down and we'll tell you everything we know. We just spoke with a doctor, his name was Professor Adam Ericson and he's the man Dr. McDowell referred you too," explained my father.

Mum sat on the bed beside me and stroked my hair.

"What did he say?" I pressured.

"Tomorrow they're going to do a small procedure to remove a lymph node from the side of your neck. It will be sent off to the lab for tests and then they'll know exactly what we're dealing with."

"So you're telling me you still have no idea of what it could be?" I was looking straight into he's eyes but he was unable to look directly into mine.

"We just don't know anything for sure yet, so it's best to wait for the results of tomorrow's procedure."

I knew he was bullshitting me. He and Mum had been told what was wrong, they just didn't want to get me worried and upset. The problem was though… I was already absolutely terrified! They were forgetting that I was currently in an isolation room in the Royal Children's Hospital; a place which was full of the sickest kids I'd ever seen in my life, and that every person who was going to come into contact with me for the foreseeable future, including them, would be dressed in full hospital attire. Whether they were trying to protect me or not, there was no hiding the fact my condition was serious, and keeping me in the dark about the whole situation was only making it worse for me. At least if I had some idea of what was going on I could start to prepare myself, or at the very least begin to accept the fight which I had in front of me.

I knew I wasn't going to get anything out of them so I gave up asking. At the time I was utterly pissed off at my parents for holding out on me, but in hindsight I understand they'd never been in a situation where one of their children was dying right in front of them. So I guess Mum and Dad were only doing what they thought was best for me. Now, as a parent myself, I will always remember how I felt when I wasn't given the facts. God forbid, if ever I'm put in a similar situation with one of my children, I think I would handle it differently, especially if my sick child was in their teens as I was.

"Is there anything we can get you Soph?" asked Mum as she tickled my hair and face; trying to sooth me while I scratched and itched in bed.

I shook my head. There was nothing they could do to help me.

My parents stayed with me until dinner. The nurse brought out some hot food on a tray. I sat up in bed and tried to eat whatever I could. I can't remember what was served and I don't actually recall eating anything substantial; I was just too uncomfortable.

Soon after, Mum and Dad announced they would be leaving me for the night and would be back first thing in the morning. "We're going to head off now Sophie. We'll be staying across the road at a place called 'Mac House'," explained Mum.

Ronald McDonald House is a charity which provides emergency accommodation for families of children who were undergoing treatment at the Royal Children's. It was a short walk from the hospital.

"Ok," I nodded.

I wasn't worried they were leaving me because they both looked completely exhausted and in desperate need of some rest. There simply wasn't a lot they could do anyway.

"Try and get some sleep Soph and we'll see you in the morning," said Dad as he kissed me on the forehead.

Mum kissed me as well. "We love you Soph."

"I love you too."

Dad told a nearby nurse they were going for the night.

"No problems. We'll take good care of her," she replied.

They gave me a final wave and left the 'Bat Cave'.

Alone in the isolation room, except for the attending nurses and the sick little girl in the other bed, I will remember that night as one of the worst of my life. Agonising, horrendous, excruciating, harrowing; none of these words accurately describe the severity of discomfort and pain I dealt with on that first night in the Royal Children's. It was torture of the worst possible kind.

The room had to be kept cool, something about it being more sterile, so I was cold all night. The nurses did their best to comfort me but the care they were able to provide really only scratched the surface. There was only one person who had the specific skills and abilities to stop my *monster's* onslaught in its tracks, and I left him on the side of the road that morning! I needed my Jake more than ever. More specifically though, I needed the unique form of *therapy* he provided! It really was the *only* thing that helped distract me from the pain and I would've given anything to have him with me, but I knew it was impossible. I wondered if I was going to make it through the night with my sanity intact.

I remember lying in bed and watching the window slowly illuminate with the glow of the morning sun. I'd been awake all night and was completely exhausted.

Mum and Dad arrived fairly early. They had a cup of tea with me; I wasn't allowed to have breakfast due to the operation I was having later on. Even though I probably wouldn't have eaten much, breakfast would have been welcome because I knew today was going to be a struggle and I'd need every ounce of energy.

I guess it was about 8:30am when the nurse came to prepare me for surgery; the removal of the swollen lymph node from my neck. There wasn't much to do really, besides a quick shower and change into a fresh hospital gown. I was weak, so the help of Mum and the nurse was appreciated.

Once washed and changed, I emerged from the bathroom to see an orderly waiting out in the hall with another bed. I left the Isolation Room and climbed up on the bed as directed by the nurse. The orderly pulled a blanket over me before wheeling me to the elevator; Dad and Mum in tow.

I can't remember what floor we went to, but once the elevator stopped and the doors opened, the first thing I saw was a sign on the wall which read '*SURGICAL THEATRES*'.

The orderly pushed the bed towards a glass sliding door. "This is as far as your parents can go Sophie."

Mum and Dad moved to either side of the bed. "We'll see you as soon as the operation is over," said Mum as she kissed me on the forehead.

"You'll be ok Soph, these people are the best," Dad said reassuringly; trying not to look worried as he spoke.

"I love you Mum. Love you Dad."

Mum ran her fingers through my hair. "We love you too Sophie."

"Good luck, and we'll see you soon," said Dad as he leant over and kissed me on the top of the head.

"Yep," I nodded, trying my best to remain calm and keep my nerves under control.

The orderly pushed a button on the wall and the sliding door opened. As he wheeled me through, I looked back at my parents and gave them a final wave. They both looked scared and upset; surprisingly though, I wasn't too bad. I think I would've been far more anxious if I wasn't so sleep deprived and lethargic.

We reached one of the theatres and I was wheeled in, there were at least three people dressed in scrubs waiting for me. Things moved very fast from then on. I was slid from the bed to the operating table where I was bathed in brightness from the surgery lights.

"Hi Sophie, my name is Dr. Steven Tan and I'll be doing the biopsy on your neck today. Have you got any questions about the procedure?"

"Will I be going to sleep?"

"Ordinarily for a procedure such as this we would use a general, but due to your condition the anaesthetist and I have decided it would be a lot safer to do the procedure using a local anaesthetic."

Because of my condition! What condition! Again with the lack of information. I was starting to get used to not being told what I wanted to know. *Maybe it's the way things are in children's hospitals,* I thought to myself. *They only tell kids what they need to know so they don't worry.*

"So I'll be awake the whole time then?"

"Yes," he answered briefly.

"Am I going to feel it?" An obvious question.

"You will feel a bit of a sting as we inject the local into your neck, but after that you won't feel any pain, only some movement as we extract the lymph gland." His voice was calm and assuring, putting me at ease. "Are you ready for us to begin?"

I nodded and closed my eyes. I decided if they weren't going to put me to sleep, I could at least pretend I was. I gasped at the cold feeling of the antiseptic being applied all over my neck. It took me by surprise. They smeared the strong smelling liquid from the bottom of my ear to my collar bone.

The longest part of the procedure was waiting for the local to kick in. After the first injection, every few minutes the doctor would prick my neck and ask if I could feel it. If I replied 'Yes', he would inject some more anaesthetic; repeating the process until eventually my neck was completely numb. The first couple of injections stung like crazy but once the anaesthetic started to work I couldn't feel each individual needle; thankfully, because in all I had twenty-seven injections in the side of my neck!

"How about now Sophie? Can you feel that?"

"No."

"Ok we're ready to start," said Dr. Tan; prompting the theatre nurses to take their positions.

I remained as calm as I could up until the moment when I heard the metallic 'ting', as the doctor picked up the scalpel off the operating tray. My eyes were closed, but it didn't stop a horrifying vision from appearing in the forefront of my mind; the doctor's rubber gloved hand holding the shiny blade as it cut into my skin, causing a trail of blood to follow the incision; deep red liquid spilling from my throat. My state of calmness instantly evaporated, and was replaced with a heart pounding fear which gripped my entire body. Thankfully though, the doctor was right about the anaesthetic. Although I could definitely feel that *something* was happening to my neck, it wasn't painful. I kept my eyes closed tight and didn't listen too carefully to what the doctor and nurses were saying. Even if they were trying to comfort me and keep me relaxed, I wouldn't have heard them. It's rather ironic, because up until that point, all I wanted was to know what was going on with me, but now I didn't want to know anything! I just wanted the procedure to be over.

I tried desperately to keep my mind focused on anything other than the fact that my neck was being sliced open with a razor sharp scalpel… while I was awake! It really was the stuff of horror movies. The only thing which seemed to allow my mind to escape the reality I was now trapped in, was to think of Jake.

I pictured our night together at Kylie's Debutante Ball, which was close to a year ago. I thought about how completely magical it was; a night as perfect as any teenage girl could ever have imagined. That first moment when our eyes met from across the crowded room, and the way my heart pounded in my chest as he walked across the dance floor towards me. The feeling of his hands on my hips as we danced, and how I felt like we were the only two people on the planet, even though the room was full of people laughing and talking. I thought about the way he looked at me, and how his piercing eyes caused my insides to contract and my knees to weaken. It was as though he could see directly into my heart… into my soul. I pictured every minute detail, as we sat outside in the cool night air and embraced before stealing our first kiss; the electricity that raced through my veins as our tongues met. It was like a dream; simply life changing. A night so special, so powerful, that it was getting me through this operation. My *guardian angel* was still protecting me, even though he was hundreds of kilometres away! Just the thought of his love and the effect it had on me, was enough to give me the strength I needed on the operating table that morning.

Before long I was snapped back to reality with Dr. Tan's hand on my shoulder.

"You can open your eyes Sophie, we're all done."

I opened my eyes and immediately squinted; forgetting how bright the surgery lights were.

"Everything went well, you did an amazing job Sophie," Dr. Tan said reassuringly.

"You're a brave girl," added one of the nurses.

I looked at her and smiled weakly.

"We'll get these off to the lab as a matter of priority. Prof Ericson will have the results on his desk within a couple of hours. I envisage that he'll come and see you as soon as he gets the pathology results of the biopsy," explained the doctor.

Finally, I may actually find out what's wrong with me!

Dr. Tan and the nurses said goodbye after switching me to the orderly's bed. I was then wheeled back to the 'Bat Cave'. My parents arrived after being debriefed by the surgeon. "So Dr. Tan said the procedure went well. Did it hurt Soph?" asked Dad, looking at the fresh bandage on my neck.

"Not really, the first few injections hurt a little though."

Mum kissed me on the cheek then sat on the side of the bed. "Did he mention that Professor Ericson should be coming to see you sometime this arvo with the results?"

"Yeah he mentioned something like that. I really want to know what's going on," I added.

"I know you do Soph. Not long now," Mum replied; knowing she couldn't keep avoiding the truth much longer.

The rest of the day was a battle for the precious sleep I'd missed out on the night before. I would try to close my eyes and forget about the itching, but all up, I doubt I would've got any more than an hour of broken sleep in total.

I also remember leaving the isolation ward a second time and going to radiology for a gallium scan. I distinctly remember this because staying still while the machine took the images of my torso was almost impossible with the relentless itching. Nonetheless, I was able to remain still long enough for the radiographer to get the images the professor required.

It was late afternoon when one of the ward nurses came over and informed my parents that they needed to go down to Professor Ericson's office for a meeting. I figured he had the results and wanted to talk to them before breaking the news to me, which I had already decided was going to be pretty horrible at best!

"Hopefully we won't be too long." Dad forced a smile to mask his concern. It didn't work.

"We'll be back soon Sophie." Mum didn't even try to hide the fact she was petrified.

They left the 'Bat Cave'; waving from behind the glass before disappearing out of sight.

As I waited for my parents to return, thoughts of the worst kind raced through my head. I cast my mind back to the previous morning. Standing on the side of the road with Jake and the promise I made to him after confessing my fears; the worst of which was that I might never see him again.

'Please promise me you'll never think dark thoughts like these again.' I could hear Jake's voice as the words played over and over in my mind. I tried desperately to honour my promise to him, but some things are easier said than done. I was convinced my parents were going to return with bad news, and there was no possible way I was going to like what the Professor had to say. The tormenting thoughts continued to plague me and I fought to push them out of my head. *What if I don't make it? Could I really be dying?* It frightened the hell out of me, but just as terrifying was the thought of never seeing Jake again; I couldn't bare it.

I could feel my level of anxiety escalating, but suddenly *something* revealed the light through the clouds. I'm not exactly sure what allowed me to clear my mind of such despair, nor what gave me the ability to think rationally in such a terrible situation, but I was truly thankful.

Jakes words from yesterday sounded in my ears. '*It's so important for you to stay positive, to believe with all your heart that the future we've dreamt of will come true.*' I realised I couldn't change what was happening to me, I could only change how I reacted to it. This moment of clarity also prompted me to make a promise to myself. It was then that I vowed, regardless of what the professor had discovered was trying to kill me, that I wasn't going down without a fight! As scared as I was of all my dark and horrible thoughts, I made the conscious decision to never give up. I wanted my life back. There was no way I was about to let my *monster* steal my future.

Mum and Dad returned with who I assumed was Professor Ericson. The redness in both my parent's eyes was definitive evidence that they'd been given the bad news. I sat up and prepared for the worst.

"Hello Sophie. My name is Professor Ericson."

"Hi," I replied weakly.

His face mask covered his mouth and nose so I could only see his eyes, but I guessed he was in his mid-sixties.

"So I imagine you're probably feeling pretty terrible at the moment."

I nodded.

"Alright, I'm not going to beat around here. I understand you want to know what's causing all your symptoms. I have already discussed your condition with your parents and we thought it best that you hear the results of all the tests from me."

I looked at Mum and Dad; their expressions were unmistakable.

Brace yourself Sophie!

"Now all the tests you've gone through, including the biopsy on the lymph node we took from your neck this morning, the bone marrow aspiration Dr. McDowell performed last week, along with all the other scans, have confirmed that you have a disease called Hodgkin's Lymphoma."

I had so many tests over the last week that it was hard to keep track. I'd had lymph node biopsies, chest x-rays, CT scans of my chest and abdomen, a gallium scan, full blood examinations, liver and renal function studies and an echocardiogram. Clearly, the diagnosis was irrefutable.

The professor continued. "Hodgkin's attacks your lymphatic system. It causes your lymph nodes to become enlarged; eventually forming painless tumours."

"Was that what was taken out of my neck this morning?"

"Exactly. This type of cancer damages your lymphocytes which make up part of your immune system, so your body becomes less able to fight infection. That's why we have you up here in the 'Bat Cave'. We can't risk you getting even something as simple as a cold."

I was listening to everything the professor was explaining, however there was one word which really stood out from the rest… cancer!

I have cancer! Fucking cancer! I couldn't believe it. I thought maybe I misheard him.

"So I have cancer then? That's why I'm so sick?"

"Yes Sophie, unfortunately you do. But the good news is we now know what we're up against, which means we will be able to start treatment immediately."

The tone of Professor Ericson's voice suggested he was very optimistic, which was confusing considering how visibly distraught my parents were. *If the professor's so optimistic, then why are my Mum and Dad so torn apart?* I guessed there was still more to the story, more I wasn't being told. I was right.

I took a deep breath and rather than push for answers, decided there must be a reason I wasn't being given the full story. Maybe they were all trying to protect me from worrying too much. Once again I had to remind myself that I was in the *Children's* Hospital. I bit my tongue and didn't press the point. It didn't matter to me anyway, because I'd already decided I *was* going to beat this.

Years later, I eventually found out how far my disease had spread. It was classified as Stage IV Hodgkin's Disease, and to cut a long story short, there is no stage five. Stage IV is deemed 'widespread disease', meaning the cancer had spread outside the lymph nodes to one or more organs. I had it in my lungs, specifically a *'mediastinal enlargement'*, which is a tumour in the membrane that partitions the lungs. In no uncertain terms, my disease was in such an advanced stage that I was literally days from death!

My parents told me they had been advised that due to the advanced stage of the disease, there was an extremely high chance treatment would prove unsuccessful. So it wasn't until some years later, I understood why Mum and Dad were so distressed on the day of my diagnosis. The harsh reality was… their baby girl was dying.

"So what kind of treatment do I need?"

"Well as I said Sophie, we're going to start treatment immediately. You'll be having your first round of chemotherapy within the hour. There are a number of types of chemo drugs which we use to treat all kinds of cancers, and it will be our best chance of getting rid of this disease. As well as chemo, you will be having a blood transfusion. This will boost your blood volume and help with your energy levels, so you will cope better with the first round of chemotherapy. I will also be putting you on a drug which will boost your appetite considerably so you can start to put on some of the weight you have lost in the last few months."

Professor Ericson went through a few more details about my treatment plan for the coming months. My brain had reached the maximum amount of information it could assimilate, so the rest of my involvement in the conversation was somewhat of a blur. All I could think about was calling Jake. I knew he would be busting to hear any news, good or bad, about what was happening here at the hospital.

"So I'll see you at some stage tomorrow Sophie. Your first couple of rounds of chemo will be administered to you here in the isolation room. One of the nurses will be in to give you the injections shortly. Do you have any questions before I go?"

"No… I don't think so."

"Alright. Well I'll see you tomorrow. David… Lynn, call me if you have any questions."

"Thanks Professor," replied Dad.

As soon as he left, I turned to Mum and Dad who cuddled and kissed me. I had kept my emotions at bay while the professor was there, but now I couldn't hold them back any longer. I burst into tears as my parents embraced me; they were crying as well. It was absolutely horrible.

I had so many reasons to cry. I was weak, tired and in terrible pain. I had cancer, and I was dying! There was nothing anyone could do or say to make me feel better. All I could do was let the sadness and frustration poor out of me, in the hope that once I pulled myself together I would at least be able to think a little clearer about what was happening.

Mum and Dad let go of me. We all wiped our faces and took a moment to compose ourselves.

"I need to call Jake. I need to tell him what's going on."

"I don't think you'll be allowed to leave the room Soph," Mum said as she looked around, presumably for a phone.

"Well I need to talk to him. Can you ask the nurse how I can make a call?" I said desperately.

"Maybe you'll be able to use the phone at the nurse's station," suggested Dad. "I'll go and talk with the nurse and see what I can do."

Mum looked at me. "Are you sure you want to call Jake?" she asked. I could tell she was concerned as to whether I could handle such a serious conversation at the moment.

"I *have* to call him Mum. I know he'll be worried."

Dad returned with the nurse.

"Hey Sophie, your father tells me you want to use the phone to give your boyfriend a buzz. What's his name?"

I could see under her mask that she was smiling.

"His name's Jake… Jake Freeman." I couldn't help but smile as I said his name.

"Nice name. Well if you're able to get out of bed, you can come and use one of the phones at my desk. You'll have to make it quick though."

"Thank you so much, I really need to talk to him," I said gratefully as I pulled the sheets back and climbed out of bed; pausing to ask what day it was.

"Saturday Soph," Dad confirmed.

Good, Jake should be home.

I walked over to the nurse's station and stood behind the desk. She handed me the phone.

"Dial nine for the outside line, then Jake's number," she explained before leaving the station so I could talk in private.

I punched in the numbers and listened to the phone as it rung Jake's house.

"Hello, Alice speaking."

"Hey Alice, its Sophie."

"Hey!" she beamed excitedly. "How are you?"

"Not so good actually."

"Awe that's no good. I hope everything is ok?"

I dodged the question. "Sorry Alice I can't talk for long. Is Jake around?"

"Oh sure, I'll go and get him for you."

"Thanks Alice."

"Ok, see you later Soph. I hope you feel better soon."

I heard Alice place the phone down on the bench as she yelled out to Jake.

"Hey Baby, how are you?"

As soon as I heard his voice a huge lump formed in my throat. I tried to answer him but I couldn't speak.

"Sophie?... Baby?... Are you alright?" he asked sincerely.

"Jake." It's all I could say; my voice soft and broken.

I closed my eyes and swallowed in an attempt to find my voice again. I did my best not to burst into tears.

"Baby I'm right here. Take a few deep breaths. It's alright… I'm right here." He could tell I was on the verge of breaking down and did his best to calm me.

I did as he said and took a few deep breaths.

"Take your time Baby. When you're ready, tell me what's happened."

"Professor Ericson just left. He told me… what's making me sick."

Jake didn't say anything; instead waited patiently for me to break the news.

I took another deep breath. "I have cancer Jake," I whispered regretfully.

I could tell by his silence that he was trying to process what I'd just told him.

"It's a type called Hodgkin's Lymphoma."

"Shit! I don't know what to say Soph. I'm so sorry Baby."

I bit my lip as a teardrop rolled down my cheek.

"Are you alright? How are you handling it?" The concern in his voice was clear. I knew he'd be suffering as a result of not being able to be with me when I needed him.

"I'm ok. The professor said I will start chemo today. He seems very optimistic."

"Well I'm glad they're not waiting to get started. Are you still in pain?"

"I am; the itching is killing me. God I hope this chemo stops the itching fast."

"Me too. I hate knowing you're in pain; I can't stand it. I hate feeling so god damn helpless!"

"It's alright, there's nothing you could do here anyway," I lied. I needed him more than anything.

"I don't care. I still wish I was there for you."

"I know you do Jake. I miss you."

"I miss you too… more than ever! So you start chemo today?"

"Uh huh. They're also going to give me a drug that'll make me hungry, so I'll probably be the size of a house the next time you see me," I joked, trying to make light of such a dismal situation.

"That's alright with me Babe. I'll still love you… fat ass and all," he said playfully.

It made me smile.

"I wish I was there with you. I just feel so helpless here," he repeated.

"I wish you were here too. I don't know when I'll be able to call you again."

"Don't worry about me, not for one second. Think only about yourself and getting better. We'll have plenty of time together once you're through this."

"I hope so Jake… I hope so."

"We will, I promise. We're going to be together forever… remember?" he reminded me reassuringly.

I closed my eyes again and prayed he was right.

"I'm on the nurse's phone, so I'll have to go now."

"Ok. Just remember how much I love you Soph. I always have, and nothing will ever change that; not even cancer."

"Good because I need you."

"And I need you too." The sincerity in his voice warmed my heart. "Good luck over the next few days and hopefully I'll talk to you soon."

"I'll call when I can. I miss you." I replied softly; again fighting back the tears.

"Be strong Baby. I'll be praying for you."

"Bye Jake," I stammered in a broken whisper.

"Take care Soph."

I hung up the phone and thanked the nurse before walking back to bed.

Mum helped pull the covers over me. I put my head on the pillow, closed my eyes and pictured Jake lying in bed beside me; wrapping me tightly in his arms. My heart ached for him, and knowing he was so far away trying to digest everything I'd just told him, only made my heart hurt even more. I prayed he would be ok after our call.

It was a day of victories for my *monster*. He had extended his reach to my parents and successfully turned their world upside down. And now that I'd told Jake about my cancer, my *monster* had well and truly sunk its claws into him as well.

For the first time I understood the hopelessness and despair that Jake had described, because now he was also suffering horribly, I could feel it, and there was absolutely nothing I could do.

CHAPTER SEVENTEEN

DAYS FROM DEATH

Through words alone, it's difficult to accurately embody just how important making love to Jake was throughout the course of my illness. Pleasure, pain relief and relaxation; it goes without saying that all these physical benefits were crucial, but I must emphasise what sex did for me on an *emotional* level too. It was magical, like medicine for my mind, and provided me the perfect escape from the prison I was trapped in; even if it was only temporary. Every time I slept with Jake I was able to clear my mind of the depressing, anxious thoughts that constantly whirled around in my head. I could devote every ounce of focus and attention on my lover, and being loved. Without the affection and the connection I was able to enjoy with Jake, I shudder to think what long term psychological damage I may have suffered.

Still to this day I'm absolutely convinced that sex saved me… *all* of me. It was pivotal in keeping my mind, body and spirit intact, and without it I would have surely suffered irreparable damage. But in saying that, there was one time where modern medicine rivalled the therapy which sex provided.

Every time I gave myself to Jake, my eyes would roll back in my head with pleasure as he gradually disappeared inside me. It was a sensation which successfully reignited my internal fire time and time again. A fire which was usually a dull flicker; constantly at risk of being extinguished indefinitely. It was as though I was being infused with pure love… pure life, and it was a sensation which couldn't be replicated. But I have to say as incredibly uplifting as my carnal therapy was, receiving my first blood transfusion came a very close second; exposing me to a very similar feeling of life and energy running through my veins.

The nurse inserted a cannula into my arm, then hooked my intravenous line up to two bags of O Negative, as prescribed by Professor Ericson. As each drop of blood flowed from the bag through the line and into my vein, I could feel my energy levels start to rise. I immediately felt warmer and the colour of my skin even changed, from a pale white to a faint but noticeable pink; especially my cheeks.

I was still in my bed in the isolation room with my parents beside me. I had my eyes closed, and as grisly as it sounds, was savouring the feeling of *somebody else's* blood running through my body! Now don't get me wrong, it was no steamy hot session with my man but it was still a pretty exquisite sensation nonetheless. It also distracted me from my itching for a while, for which I was very grateful.

The room was quiet and peaceful. The young girl in the other bed was asleep; her parents sitting either side of her in silence. I'm not sure how long the transfusion went for, but when the last drop flowed into me the I.V. machine made a beeping sound. I open my eyes and the nurse came over to unclipped the line.

"How are you feeling now Sophie?" She was smiling, assuming I'd be feeling better already thanks to the transfusion.

"I feel a lot better, like I have a bit more energy."

"Good. Yeah it's pretty amazing how quickly it can make you feel alive again. If you're ready, I can give you your first dose of chemotherapy now?"

"Do I need to go anywhere for it?"

"No, I'll give it to you here. I will be pushing it into the same IV line as the transfusion."

"Ok," I said nodding to myself; mentally preparing for my first round of chemo.

"I'll go and get it ready. Hold tight and I'll be back shortly."

I looked at Mum. “I hope this isn’t going to hurt,” I said; secretly looking for reassurance that everything was going to be ok.

“I think because it’s going straight into your vein it shouldn’t hurt too much, not like tetanus shots which go into the muscle,” she explained.

It was the answer I was looking for, even if Mum was only guessing.

The nurse returned with a cart. On top there were a few large syringes filled with liquid; one clear and one bright red. The other had a protective cardboard cover; I later learned it was light sensitive.

“Alright, first I’m going to push through some saline,” said the nurse as she pulled on a fresh pair of surgical gloves.

She undid the cap on the IV line and screwed on the first large syringe of clear saline.

“I’ll push it through slowly, but you will still feel a cold sensation run up your arm as the liquid goes in. Ok?”

I nodded.

The nurse started to push on the end of the syringe. I watched as the clear liquid ran through the I.V. line and disappeared into my arm. Just as she’d said, I felt the cold sensation slowly make its way up my arm. It wasn’t painful though. It was kind of like icy cold water running over my skin, except that it was under it!

Once the nurse finished the saline flush, she connected the first of the chemo drugs to the I.V. line. “This one’s called ‘MOPP’ for short,” she said as she injected the drug into the line.

The nurse then repeated the process with the other chemotherapy drug; ‘AVB’. Neither of the drugs hurt as they entered my body, all I felt was the cool feeling running up my arm as the liquids flowed into my veins.

“All done,” she said with a smile; unclipping the last syringe from the line.

And that was it, my first round of chemotherapy was complete. *Not so bad*, I thought.

The thing is with chemotherapy, everybody reacts differently and you never really know how your body is going to handle it until the drug is in your system. I didn't feel any different for at least an hour; no nausea or vomiting. Then I noticed my itching legs and arms began to gradually get worse… a lot worse.

I honestly think the chemo was the first real attack on my *monster*, and it didn't like it one bit; retaliating with a level of savagery I hadn't experienced until now. Up until this point all my defensive efforts were on a psychological level. Yes, my therapy with Jake was physical, but the love and affection he provided was only emotionally curative; it didn't do anything to actually *heal* my illness. In terms of truly fighting my *monster* through medicine, I mean really trying to kill it, my initial round of chemo was the first solid counter-attack in an attempt to save my life. The real war inside my body had now begun, and my *monster* was making it very clear to me it wasn't going to surrender and die without one hell of a fight.

The itching got so bad I couldn't lie down or even sit. Instead I remained standing; twitching and scratching, hour after hour. I was so weak and tired that Mum and Dad took turns holding onto me as I stood up; it was excruciating. My arms were bad and they hurt like hell, but it was my legs that really pushed me to the limit; to the brink of insanity. Without exaggerating, if a doctor had of came into the isolation room and told me he could get rid of the itching by amputating my legs, I honestly think I would have jumped at the offer. I know it sounds ridiculous, amputating your legs to stop an itch, but I can assure you this was no *ordinary* itch!

The analogy I gave earlier about being tied to an ant's nest would have seemed like a massage at a day spa compared to the agony I was in now. It was like I had starving bull ants burrowing under my skin, and they were now eating my flesh from the inside out. Amputation would have been merciful considering what I was going through. It was straight up torture!

I was up the entire night; not one second of sleep. It was just too painful to lie down, so for the most part I was standing up, or at the very least being held up by my parents or one of the nurses. I thought it would never end; the agonising assault on my body and sanity.

Shoot me! Just fuckin shoot me! I lost count of how many times I contemplated my options if this was going to be how I had to live from now on. I eventually reached the point where I wanted the pain to stop, more than I wanted to be alive. That's when I knew I was losing.

I remember seeing sunlight seeping through the window before everything faded to black. I guess all the pain relief the nurses had administered throughout the night and the utter exhaustion of unrelenting agony, combined with hours upon hours of standing, twitching, scratching and countless nights of insomnia had finally taken their toll on my frail body. I was done; tortured to within an inch of my life.

I don't know what time it was, but when I finally opened my eyes I'll never forget what I felt… absolutely nothing! My crawling, itching, agonising ordeal which had started over a year ago, and pushed me to the brink was over. I was lying in bed, perfectly still. I couldn't believe it, and I'm sure for a moment I thought I was dreaming.

It's gone! It's actually gone! I was in mild shock. The smile on my face was so big that my cheeks hurt. As I lay in the isolation ward in utter silence, what I felt was the absolute epitome of peace and tranquillity; my body heavy from the cocktail of medications that flowed through my system. The room was cool, yet I was warm under the covers. Best of all though, I was completely motionless; free from my usual twitching and clawing. I was all alone except for the sick little girl sleeping in the other bed and the nurse at her desk, so I was able to take in and savour everything I was feeling; every sensation. I felt as though I'd been reborn.

I'd finally won a round against my *monster*. It was like my first dose of chemo had given me a victory in the battle to win my freedom. I knew I wasn't cured by a long shot, and I was still not even close to being out of the woods yet, but I didn't care because I knew with all my heart I was going to win. All the proof I needed was to compare how incredible I felt now, to the last twelve months.

I could hardly wait for my parents to arrive at my bedside; I was elated and wanted to share the good news with them. They must have been exhausted as well, because they came in later; I drifted off to sleep before they arrived. I guess they were catching up on a bit of sleep too.

I heard Mum's voice and opened my eyes briefly to see her talking quietly to Dad; my vision was blurry.

"Hey Sophie, how are you feeling?" Mum said, as soon as she noticed I was waking up.

I blinked slowly; allowing my eyes to adjust. Her face was the first thing I saw clearly. Her eyes anyway as she was still wearing a mask.

"You've had a decent sleep. It's after nine-thirty," she added before I could answer her first question.

"Really? I feel like I only just drifted off," I replied, surprised at how long I'd actually been asleep.

"We got here over an hour ago but we didn't want to wake you."

"So how are you this morning… feeling any different?" asked Dad.

I slowly sat up and looked at them both, unable to hide my smile. "I'm not itchy anymore," I responded with bewilderment; my voice sounding as though *I* couldn't even believe what I was saying. "I've been lying here perfectly still and I haven't felt like I needed to scratch my arms or legs at all."

"Oh Sophie that's wonderful," said Mum. "I'm so glad you're not in pain."

"That's fantastic! We were really worried about how you would react to the chemo, considering how bad you were last night," Dad revealed; frowning as he cast his mind back to the horrendous condition I was in hours earlier. "So it just stopped… just like that?"

"Yeah, well I must have finally passed out last night from everything I'd taken. I was absolutely exhausted. Anyway, when I woke up this morning the itching was gone. I was lying here still, like I am now and I didn't feel like scratching at all."

"Well the professor said chemo was a very powerful drug, but I still can't believe how fast it worked," said Dad.

"I'm still really tired though. I feel like I've missed out on a year's worth of sleep," I yawned.

"Are you hungry?" asked Mum.

"Yeah I am actually, and I feel a bit grotty too," I added; sniffing under my armpits.

"I'll get the nurse and we will see what we can do." Dad made his way over to the nurse's station to get her attention.

The nurse came over to my bedside. "So I hear your hungry Sophie?"

I nodded. "I'd love some toast and a cup of tea. I'm also busting for a shower if that's ok?"

"Oh of course. What's say we get you washed, changed and I'll order you some breakfast from the kitchen. Do you have any pyjamas?"

"Actually I don't. I packed in such a rush I didn't put any in."

"Well we can dress you in a fresh gown for now. Just a thought, but the gift shop downstairs sells pyjamas," she smiled suggestively at Mum and Dad. "You'll be here a while, and pyjamas will be far more comfortable than a hospital gown."

"You hop in the shower Soph, and your mother and I will head downstairs and pick out a pair of new pyjamas for you. How's that sound?" smiled Dad under his face mask; immediately picking up on the nurse's hint.

"Sounds good to me," I agreed. The thought of a warm shower, fresh pyjamas, toast, tea… and no itching! *Heaven!*

Dad and Mum left the isolation room to visit the gift shop.

They must be getting sick of changing in and out of their gowns, mask and hairnet, I thought as I watched them leave.

"I'll help you in the shower if you like?" asked the nurse.

"No I should be fine; I'll just take it slow."

"Ok, well there's a button on the wall. Just press it if you need me and I'll come straight in."

"Sure."

I slowly got out of bed and walked to the shower.

"Stay in there as long as you like Sophie, and I'll bring your pyjamas in when your parents get back. You'll find towels in there already."

I walked into the bathroom, closed the door and turned on the shower to warm the water up while I got undressed. I took off my gown and put it in the dirty linen basket. I was standing in front of the sink, above which was a fairly large mirror; big enough that I could see most of my body.

As I looked at myself in the mirror, the joy and happiness I felt earlier disappeared. It was replaced with a sad, almost ashamed feeling. I looked absolutely awful, horrible… disgusting! There wasn't one part of me that wasn't a complete mess. My eyes were dark, my skin pale, face gaunt and hair dull. I could see all the bones in my ribcage, which were barely covered by the thinnest layer of white skin. My collar bones stuck out like they were on the outside of my body, and my shoulders were equally sharp and bony. I looked down at my skinny arms and legs to survey the damage of the night before. The futility of my attempts to resist scratching my skin raw was now blatantly apparent. Fresh sores and dried blood littered the entire length of both arms and legs. The tops of my thighs were so thin; resembling those of a nine-year-old girl, not a fifteen-year-old woman. I was emaciated; not a single curve or attractive feature in sight.

Emotionally, I must have been feeling a little stronger because I had one last look in the mirror, took a deep breath and turned around. The tears which should have flowed at the sheer sight of my reflection were wrestled back. *I win again!*

As I removed my bra and knickers, a brief flashback of undressing in front of Jake raced through my mind. His eyes watching my every move as he lay on my bed; waiting anxiously to ravish me. I smiled at the thought.

I stepped into the shower and let the hot cascade of water envelope my body; the warmth on my back felt wonderful. I closed my eyes and tilted my head back, letting the stream run over my face and down my chest. I must have stood with the shower blasting directly on my face for ages. I couldn't move, and even better was the fact that I didn't have to. I dropped my head forward and put my hands against the wall. The water flowed down my back, over my behind and down between my legs. I inhaled deeply, breathing an intoxicating combination of air and hot steam. It was like the heat of the shower was melting away a year's worth of pain and suffering. I will never forget how good it felt. Without question, it was the most amazing shower I'd ever taken.

I snapped myself back to reality and pumped some soap from the dispenser into the palm of my hand. I washed my face and body. My legs and arms looked so much better once I washed away the scattered drops of dried blood. Hundreds of red marks and scratches still remained though.

I was in the shower for at least twenty minutes when I heard a knock on the bathroom door. "Sophie… it's Mum. I've got your new pyjamas here," she said through the close door.

"Ok. Come in and leave them on the bench."

Mum opened the door and quickly put my clothes down. I didn't have a shower curtain or screen to hide behind, as the bathroom was designed so people in wheel chairs could be washed as well. She didn't look at me anyway.

"Thanks Mum they look really nice."

"I hope you like them. We got you an eight, so they should fit," she said; closing the door behind her.

I switched the shower off and towelled myself dry. My new flannel pyjamas fit perfectly, and they felt wonderfully soft and gentle against my skin. I platted my hair and emerged from the bathroom a new woman, well at the very least… a hell of a lot fresher!

The following day I was given my second dose of chemotherapy. To my absolute relief I didn't have to go through the same harrowing experience as the previous night. I actually felt my health improve even further within only an hour or so after the injections.

In all, I spent just over a week in the isolation room. It was a week of TV, magazines, and pills; around thirty a day! The other activity which took up a fair amount of time was eating. Oh my god… the eating!

The drug which Professor Ericson prescribed to increase my appetite was ridiculous. Ridiculous in the sense that it didn't matter how much or how often I ate, I was still utterly famished. I wasn't allowed to have anything other than hospital food while I was in the isolation room, but thankfully I was provided with breakfast, morning tea, lunch, afternoon tea and dinner; all of which I polished off with speed. In between each of those scheduled meals and snacks, I would be having countless sweet biscuits, cups of tea and sandwiches; made for me by the nurses from their kitchen. I was basically eating constantly, and when I wasn't eating, I felt like I was starving. The appetite pills were doing their job; I was gaining weight by the hour!

Once I was released from the isolation room and moved to the Oncology Ward, my appetite didn't slow down. As soon as I was allowed to eat something other than hospital food, I was so grateful for the '*McDonalds*' located in the foyer. The taste of my first burger, chips and '*Coke*' was incredible. There's a saying which goes, *'It's like there's a party in my mouth and everyone's invited!'* Such a perfect way to describe how good it tasted… absolutely delicious!

I can remember one occasion when I was allowed to go and spend the night at Mac House with my parents. I was feeling quite good so Professor Ericson thought it would be beneficial for me to get out of the hospital for a night. I woke up at about 1:00am with the worst hunger pains I've ever experienced. I needed something substantial and *'Maccas'* wasn't even going to cut it. I begged my father to go down to a 24-hour supermarket and by me some steak! My body must have been craving the protein and iron, because I couldn't rest until I sank my teeth into a nice juicy piece. I'm sure Dad would've rather stayed asleep in bed, but he dragged himself out, got dressed and headed off to the supermarket. It was well after 2:00am by the time I finished my steak, which Dad cooked for me in the Mac House kitchen. I crawled into bed and slept like a baby with a belly full of milk; dead to the world.

During my stay at the Royal Children's I would have eaten enough to feed a small village. With each meal I could feel myself getting stronger, and heavier too that's for sure. When I arrived at the hospital I weighed in at forty-five kilograms, but by the time I was ready to leave I tipped the scales at fifty-seven! The weight piled on so fast that I could literally feel myself growing day by day.

Every few days I was having gallium scans and x-rays to check the effect the chemotherapy was having on my Hodgkin's Lymphoma. To my absolute relief I'd showed continued improvement, which meant the treatment was working well, and just as exciting was that the positive results meant my two week stay at the Royal Children's Hospital was coming to an end.

It was the morning of the last day and I'd just finished my third round of chemo. The plan was to wait a few hours after the injections, then if I was feeling ok I would be released and allowed to go home. I couldn't contain my excitement. I had only been able to make a couple of brief calls to Jake and was busting to see him, and as vain as it sounds, I couldn't wait for him to see me either… to see the transformation I'd undergone over the last few weeks.

I said a sincere thank you and goodbye to the nurses who'd cared for me so well over the last fortnight. We also had a final visit from the professor. He gave me a review of my progress since commencing treatment and also booked me in for my next round of chemo, which would be in roughly four weeks' time. I hoped my parents were listening to everything Prof Ericson was saying, because I was so excited to be feeling better and going home that I was having trouble concentrating. I just wanted to get on the road.

"Thanks for everything professor," said Dad; shaking his hand appreciatively.

"Thank you so much," Mum added as she gave him a hug.

"I'm just glad you responded well to the first few doses of chemo Sophie. You must be feeling so much better?" Professor Ericson said; smiling warmly at me.

"I sure am. Thank you for everything you've done for me." I stepped forward and gave him a hug as well.

"Look after yourself Sophie. I will be seeing you again next month."

"Sure will," I smiled.

"You all have a safe trip home," he said before leaving my bedside.

There was absolutely no question he had saved my life, and I will be eternally grateful for Professor Ericson, as well as the rest of the team who worked on me at the Royal Children's.

Eventually, after Dad signed one last piece of paper finalising my discharge, we were ready to go. Walking out of the hospital feeling a thousand times better than when I arrived a fortnight ago was a fantastic victory for me. I was under no illusions regarding my health, knowing full well I was by no means in the clear, but I felt as though I'd taken back control of my life. My stay at the hospital had definitely weakened my *monster's* grasp on me. Sure he was still holding on, but his claws were no longer sinking quite so deep into my flesh. Now more than ever, I was convinced that I was going to beat him.

The drive home seemed to pass fairly quickly. I couldn't hide my excitement at the thought of seeing Jake again and I was far more talkative compared to the last time I was in the car; over a fortnight ago. Apart from that brief meeting on the side of the road I hadn't seen him for over a month. I missed him so much and it hurt me to be away from him for so long. I needed my Jake.

We arrived home late. I was tired… and of course hungry. I showered, had some dinner and gave Jake a quick call before bed.

We made arrangements for him to come out to the farm the following day; thankfully Jake's Mum agreed to drive him. I couldn't bear the thought of him having to ride all the way out for me again!

The call was brief, my belly full of food had resulted in the rapid onset of a serious food coma. I was like a huge bear that had fattened up for the winter and was ready for hibernation. I needed sleep, and as soon as Jake sensed I was tired he basically ordered me to go to bed. Apparently it had something to do with me needing all my energy for the next day! My mind raced at the prospect of being with Jake after more than a month apart.

We said our goodbyes, I brushed my teeth and crawled under the covers. As soon as I lied down in the familiar comfort of my own bed, I closed my eyes and was out within minutes.

I was standing at the kitchen sink, washing out a mug after my morning cup of tea, when I heard the dogs barking; signalling the approach of a visitor. Instantly, my lips curled into a cheek splitting smile. I knew my lover was here.

It was always an incredible rush in those few moments before being reunited with Jake, even though the excitement was usually short lived as it was quickly replaced with a horrible feeling of self-consciousness about my sickly appearance. Well not this time. I couldn't wait for him to see me. I looked so different from the last time we met. The skin on my arms and legs had all but cleared up; they were smooth and soft except for a couple of small marks that still remained. I was actually surprised my limbs hadn't scarred, considering they had been littered with hundreds of sores for months. I think the fact the wounds weren't very deep allowed them to heal without leaving a trace which was a huge relief. Thanks to my insatiable appetite over the last two weeks, my figure had completely transformed as well. Gone were the sharp bony protrusions of my ribs, shoulders, collarbones and hips. My body was now a beautiful array of healthy, feminine curves; especially my breasts which had at least doubled in size! *Jake will appreciate these*, I thought as I looked down at my chest; the shape of my full round breasts easily visible under my t-shirt. Probably the most noticeable difference though was my face. My pale grey skin and gaunt bony features were gone, and since I was now finally getting enough sleep, the dark circles around my tired eyes had faded considerably. My overall zombie like appearance had been replaced with a vibrant glow. My eyes were bright, skin pink and my face was full and plump. I felt amazing, and I have to say compared to a few weeks earlier, I think I looked amazing as well. *Jake won't believe his eyes.*

I don't know why but for some reason I didn't race outside to see him like I usually did, which turned out to be a great play. I could hear my parents talking with Jake and Mary, so I think my decision to wait for him to come inside probably had something to do with skipping the small talk and simply throwing myself at him as soon as he walked into the house. I stood by the kitchen table and waited for him to burst through the door. *Any second now!*

My parents and Jake's Mum were still talking outside when I heard the door handle turn. My heart thumped so hard in my chest that I could feel its rapid beat. The door opened and my *angel* burst into the house. I hadn't even taken a step towards him and already tears rolled down my cheeks. The pain of being away from him for so long was instantly replaced with tears of utter joy.

Jakes face said a thousand words. My transformation had clearly left him in shock. He raced over and wrapped his arms around me. I squeezed him so tight; I just wanted to melt into him. He let go of me and placed his hands on my cheeks, I still had my arms around him firmly, and I was never going to let him go again. We took a moment, looking into each other's eyes before reacquainting our lips; a gentle kiss quickly turning into a passionate exploration of each other's mouths. The entire world could have exploded around us and we wouldn't have noticed. I was thankful our parents were still outside, because there was absolutely no doubt if they had been present and bear witness to our embrace, and the passion with which we were kissing, they honestly wouldn't have known where to look.

I was happy to save them the embarrassment, and even more appreciative that Jake and I were able to reunite without having to hold back for their sake.

The back and forth caressing of our tongues against each other had me aroused in seconds. I hadn't spoken a single word to my lover and already I wanted him. A vision flashed into my mind, of Jake clearing the kitchen table with a single swipe of his arm before laying me down on my back and climbing on top, eagerly positioning himself between my legs then sliding deep inside; having his way with me. My pelvic floor muscles contracted with lustful anticipation.

"Sophie you look amazing! I can't believe my eyes."

"I know… I feel so much better too. God I missed you."

"I missed you too Baby." He kissed me again. "Look at your body!"

Jake took a step back and studied me from head to toe before grabbing hold of me again.

"It's amazing how fast my legs and arms cleared up."

"You look so healthy… and your face… you've completely changed. I always thought you were beautiful, but seriously… I'm blown away! I don't know what to say."

"Awe thanks," I blushed; batting my eyes playfully. "Do you want to know the best part though?"

"What… besides your boobs getting bigger!" he joked; obviously noticing the increased size of my *assets*.

I laughed out loud. "Yeah they've grown a fair bit haven't they?" I agreed; glancing down to admire them myself. "Well besides those, the best part is I'm not itchy anymore. I can actually lie in bed and fall asleep without having to scratch myself until I bleed. It's so amazing to be able to lie still and not feel like my skin's crawling."

"Soph… I'm so happy for you. I hated seeing you so sick, and I know you didn't want me to feel sorry for you but I did… I always did. It just wasn't fair you had to put up with all that pain for so long."

"I'm not out of the woods just yet, but the professor said so far I've responded really well to the chemo; he's definitely happy with the results."

"So am I Baby… so am I," he replied sincerely; wrapping me in his arms and squeezing me tightly. "I can't believe the difference two weeks in hospital has made. You look so bright and happy, which makes me feel the same way," he said as he held my head against his chest.

"I am happy, and even more so now that you're here with me." I looked up at him. "God I missed you Jake. You're all I thought about while I was lying in hospital these last few weeks."

We kissed again, stopping when we heard our parents nearing the back door, along with some other familiar voices.

I looked at Jake with a confused expression that quickly morphed into an excited giggle. *I know who that is!*

Mum walked in first followed by Mary, and to my surprise, Jake's three sisters. Alice, Kate and Samantha had come along for the ride and were now standing in my kitchen as well. They must have kept so quiet outside, because I really had no idea they were here until they all walked through the door; a fantastic surprise. I was caught completely off guard and couldn't help but let out a girlish shriek at the sight of them. They all raced over and wrapped their arms around me for a group hug.

"What are you girls doing here!" I beamed excitedly.

They all started talking at once. I couldn't tell who was more excited… me or them. Eventually they slowed down and took turns.

"You look so good Sophie. I can't believe how much you've changed," said Alice; scanning me from head to toe then back again.

"Your face has changed so much! You look totally different!" added Kate.

"Yeah look how much bigger you are! You've put on heaps of weight!" commented Samantha.

Everybody started laughing. I knew she meant well, but the way it came out was hilarious.

"Why thank you Samantha," I chuckled. It's not often a teenage girl could take being told that she's put on heaps of weight as a compliment.

Mary came over and gave me a hug. "Oh Sophie, I'm so happy for you Honey. You look so healthy; it's amazing!"

"Thanks Mary. I feel so much better."

"We have a present for you," said Kate.

Dad was standing in the doorway holding a box wrapped in pink paper. Kate walked over and he handed it to her.

"Oh wow… a present! You guys didn't have to do that," I said as Kate handed me the gift.

"Open it Sophie! Open it!" Samantha said loudly. She was so excited.

"She will Sam… calm down!" said Alice.

I gave them all a kiss on the cheek. "Thank you so much."

I was so touched they had brought me a present.

With Samantha right beside me watching eagerly, I sat down at the kitchen table and unwrapped it. *This kid loves her presents!*

Their gift was a bedside touch lamp made of brass and floral printed glass panels. It was so beautiful.

"Thank you all so much. I'm touched… I really am;" my voice breaking slightly as a lump formed in my throat.

Sensing that I was getting emotional, Jake came over and put his arm around me. I managed to hold myself together though.

"Well Jake said it was your birthday while you were in hospital, so we thought it would be nice to buy you a present," said Kate.

I had my sixteenth birthday a few days before being discharged from hospital. I have to say it wasn't the most memorable, though the nurses did organise a cake for me which I appreciated. It was nice to blow out some candles and make a wish on my sweet sixteenth.

"Touch lamps are really cool because you don't have to find the switch when you're ready to go to sleep. You just touch any part of the metal frame and it switches off," explained Alice.

"What a great idea for a present," said Mum.

"Thank you all again. I absolutely love it." I really wanted them to know how much I appreciated the thought they had put into my present. Just the fact they even brought me one in the first place was wonderful.

"Have you given Sophie your present Jake?" asked Samantha with excitement.

He looked at her with a 'thanks for ruining the surprise' expression. We all laughed.

"Well I haven't yet, but I suppose now is as good a time as any," he said; smiling at his little sister.

Jake went over to his bag and retrieved a fairly large box which was also wrapped in pink paper.

"Happy sixteenth birthday Baby." He gave me a sweet little kiss on the cheek as he handed me the gift. "I hope you like it."

As I accepted the present I couldn't help but look at Samantha's face; her expression of pure excitement made me giggle. I unwrapped Jake's gift. It was the most beautiful box set of *'Oscar de la Renta'* products; two bottles of perfume, a body wash and scented talcum powder. I could smell the delicious fragrance through the packaging.

"Thank you Jake. It smells gorgeous," I said as I gave him a hug and a kiss.

"I'm glad you like it."

I opened up one of the perfumes and each of the girls had a whiff of the fragrance; it was lovely and soft.

I was so happy. Not only was I feeling better but Jake was here, his sisters had come for a surprise visit, and I was given two lovely birthday presents. It really was a great morning and I felt full of light and happiness. I don't think I stopped smiling for hours.

After the presents, I gave Mary and the girls a brief tour of the farm before heading back inside for some morning tea. I knew they were interested to know what was going on so I gave them a run-down of the past two weeks in hospital. Although I didn't go into great detail, everyone went a little quiet when I mentioned that the treatment was far from over, and that I had quite a few more visits to Melbourne for chemo.

Mary and the girls stayed for about an hour before heading home. It was so nice to see them and it felt wonderful to know they cared for me so much. There was no question they felt like family, and I made sure I gave them each a big hug before they left.

Once Jake's mother and sisters had gone, I led him straight to my bedroom. I wanted to be alone with him; to have him all to myself! I knew I'd have to wait until late that night before I got what I *really* needed from him, but just lying on my bed cuddling and talking was fantastic. I literally had the man of my dreams lying beside me. What more could a girl want.

I rested my head on his chest and draped my arms and legs over his body; pinning him down. He wasn't going anywhere. Jake tickled my face as I lay there with my eyes closed; listening to the strong beat of his heart. My head would rise and fall in time with each of his slow, rhythmical breaths. The combination of his heart beat and the sound of air filling his lungs then escaping through his nose was hypnotising. It was the most beautiful song I'd ever heard, because not only could I hear it, I could feel it. The sheer comfort and absolute safety I felt in those moments was indescribable. It was like I had the protection of something more than just a man, something more powerful… more magical. The effect he had on me, it was like he was the polar opposite to the darkness of my *monster*; he was pure light. With absolute truth and sincerity, lying there with my lover's arms around me, I felt like I was wrapped in the wings of an angel.

I lifted my head and looked into his eyes. There was no hiding the desire fiercely burning inside me.

"What can I do for you?" he asked cheekily, obviously reading my mind. A salacious grin adorned his face making him look even more desirable.

"I've never wanted anything as bad as I want you right now," I whispered; my hand making its way under his t-shirt. I slowly walked my fingers up his stomach before running my open palm over the bare skin of his chest. I slowly thrust my pelvis forward; grinding my pubic bone against his thigh.

"I believe you. But unfortunately..." he lowered his voice, "you're going to have to get control of yourself Baby. Because as much as I would love to tear your clothes off and fuck you right now, you and I both know we have to wait until tonight." He knew talking to me this way would only add fuel to the fire.

I inhaled sharply through my teeth; feeling the effect of his comments directly between my legs. Hearing Jake's voice and watching his lips speak those words as he described how he wanted to fuck me, instantly caused my pussy to ache. It was like my *kitten* had morphed into a ferocious lion, and now had severe hunger pains of her own. There was only one thing which would satisfy her appetite.

I could feel myself getting wetter by the second, and I continued to grind my groin against his leg. My hand, still on his bare chest, transitioned from a gentle caress to deliberately clawing at his flesh; my fingernails slowly scratching across the surface of his skin. Now I understood how Jake felt when he would bite into my neck; with a look in his eyes like he wanted to devour me. In that instant, I felt exactly the same. As I clawed at him, my hand like a lion's paw, I literally wanted to tear a piece of flesh from his body.

"It hurts," I moaned; squirming beside him uncomfortably in desperate need of sexual release.

He laughed. "You've got it bad don't you?"

He's really enjoying this, I thought as I looked down at my watch. "Fuck! It's only eleven! I can't wait until tonight! I'm not going to make it!" I beamed louder than intended.

"Shh, keep your voice down Soph," Jake snapped, and rightfully so. I don't think my parents would've appreciated hearing how much their sixteen-year-old daughter craved her boyfriend's cock!

I'd worked myself up and there was no way these feelings were going to subside on their own. I couldn't wait. I needed him... I needed him now!

"Fancy a walk Soph? I think you could do with some exercise," Jake smiled suggestively; reading my mind… again!

My eyes lit up. "Where to? Did you have a particular place in mind?"

I already knew exactly where we were going.

"Well there's a little place not far from here which I think you might like. The last time I was there I seen the most *beautiful* view!" he emphasised; looking me up and down. I could tell by his expression that he was picturing me naked, just as I had been the last time we snuck away to our 'secret hideout'.

"Really? Sounds like a place I'd like to visit." My heart raced at the thought of Jake taking me back to our secluded hideaway in the woods.

"Oh you'll like it alright," he smirked before subtly biting his bottom lip. "We'd have to walk up a bit of a hill though, are you sure you're up for it?"

"Don't worry about me Baby, I'll be fine." I already knew it would be a struggle, but I would've climbed to the top of Mt Everest if it meant I was going to feel Jake inside me when I got there.

We emerged from my bedroom. My parents were still in the kitchen.

"Jake and I are going for a walk."

"Are you sure that's a good idea Sophie. You haven't done much physical activity in the last few weeks," said Mum with concern.

You're telling me! I don't think Mum was referring to the kind of 'physical activity' that I was preparing for.

"We won't go far. I just want some air and sunshine." *And Jake's hard…* I quickly pushed the image from my mind.

"Well if you feel a bit weak, have a rest then head straight back," suggested Dad. "Make sure you look after her Jake."

"Will do. I'll take a bottle of water with us."

We headed out the back door; destination… 'Secret Hideout'.

"Hey, besides that bottle of water, did you bring any other essential supplies?" I whispered.

"Sure did," replied Jake; tapping his pocket.

As we walked hand in hand through the open field in the sunshine, I was both excited and happy. Excited because the anticipation of having sex was so strong, it felt like it was my first time all over again. I felt better than I had in the past year, and although feeling healthy again definitely made me happy, I was equally joyous about having my soul mate back by my side. I wasn't just walking in a field that morning… I was walking in a dream.

We reached our secret hideout and did one final scan of the area; confirming we were alone before disappearing under the cover of the leafy branches. I'd forgotten how secluded it felt under there; a cave made of leaves. Immediately I turned around to face Jake and our lips locked together in a feverish kiss; tongues lashing each other.

Our mouths separated. "Oh Jake… I've missed you," I breathed before kissing him again.

He grabbed my pony tail and pulled gently, causing my head to tilt back slightly. "I've missed you too Baby." His eyes were burning wildly, glaring at me; over flowing with lust.

Immediately he latched onto my throat, thankfully the opposite side to the incision where the lymph node was removed, which was all but healed anyway. I could feel his teeth gently biting into my neck. The sensation caused my knees to weaken, and I moaned softly as he bit down harder. A shot of adrenaline raced through me as he bit down so hard that I thought his teeth were going to sink right into my flesh; he backed off just in time though. It was so incredibly hot and had rendered *me* completely saturated.

Jake trailed kisses up the side of my neck to my ear. "Do you want me?" he whispered. I could feel his breath on my skin.

"Yes," I moaned; closing my eyes as he nibbled on my ear.

"How do you want me?"

"I don't care… just do whatever you want."

He grabbed hold of my ponytail again and pulled. "Really? What if I want to *fuck* you?" he emphasised.

I knew Jake didn't want to simply have sex, he wanted to possess me. The biting and the way he held me in place with a fist full of my hair; all signs the sexual beast within was awake and ready to be unleashed.

"Then *fuck* me! Fuck me as hard as you want… as hard as you can!" I provoked.

Being apart for so long, combined with the ups and downs of the emotional rollercoaster we'd ridden over the last month, had resulted in a build-up of sexual tension stronger than anything we'd ever experienced. You could feel it in the air.

In the past I was so weak and frail, Jake always had to be gentle and careful not to hurt me. But now that I felt better and no longer looked so delicate, he wouldn't have to make love to me as though I was made of glass. He wanted to fuck me, and finally I had the energy to let him.

"Are you sure Baby?"

I could tell he was apprehensive.

"Yes… I'm sure. I want you to."

I was clenching my thighs together firmly. The aching between my legs had intensified to the point where it had become unbearable. "Fuck me now!" I commanded impatiently.

He reached down, undid the button on my jeans then unzipped me. Using his thumbs, he slid my knickers and jeans down at the same time.

He's not messing around!

I flicked my shoes off and as soon as I stepped out of my jeans and underwear, he dropped to his knees and buried his face between my legs; plunging his tongue between my lips. The feeling of his warm tongue licking inside me was incredible, causing me to moan loudly with pleasure. I grabbed hold of the back of his head with both hands and thrust my pelvis back and forth; grinding my pussy against his mouth.

"Oh Jake… that's it! I'm coming!"

On about the fifth thrust I erupted in orgasm, sending a flood of my slippery nectar into his mouth and over his lips. He held his tongue firmly in place until my release subsided, ensuring my wave of pleasure lasted as long as possible. I put my hand under his chin;

prompting him to stand. As soon as we were face to face, I kissed him. I loved the distinctive taste and smell of *me* on his lips; I always have.

"Turn around and grab that branch."

I did as he ordered; gripping the waist high branch which caused me to bend over slightly. Usually Jake and I loved foreplay, we both enjoyed pleasuring each other generously before intercourse, but not today. He didn't have to read my mind to know that all I craved was him deep inside me… he could see it. I was so wet that my state of arousal was running down the inside of my thigh. I'm not exaggerating either, it was literally trickling down my leg!

I heard Jake unzip and slide his jeans down, followed by the tear of a condom wrapper. I looked over my shoulder to watch him roll the latex film over his rigid length; a sight I'll never get tired of.

"Spread your legs."

Once again I complied immediately with his stern direction and took a step to the side. Grasping the branch firmly, I was now bent over and *open*; my welcoming entrance pointing directly at him. Jake grabbed my hip with one hand and his dick with the other. I closed my eyes and held my breath with anticipation. He took a small step forward, positioning himself directly behind me. I'd waited for so long for this moment, and now it was here… finally!

Jake held his cock, gently tickling and teasing *me* with the tip. "Are you ready Baby?"

I nodded and closed my eyes. Ever so slowly, he entered. In one gentle push he slid his length inside me. The full feeling I'd craved was a million times better than I'd remembered. We were together again; two souls reunited.

Jake held still for a moment, savouring the connection between us. Then it began. With one hand still on my hip, he grasped my ponytail with the other and pulled my head back slightly; pinning me in position. I gripped the branch with both hands and braced myself as he started to thrust back and forth; as deep as I could handle.

I couldn't believe how hard he was. "Fuck!" I gasped loudly. "Fuck!" It's all I could say.

Jake's pace quickened, and within a couple of minutes I felt him swell inside me. I knew he wasn't going to last long, but it didn't matter because I was ready to let go as soon as he was. The build-up to this moment had reduced our sexual stamina to almost zero. We were already on the brink of climaxing together.

He let go of my hair and grabbed my other hip. With both hands now, he pulled me back towards him as he thrust forward; driving into me with force. This wasn't making love; it wasn't sex either; hell it wasn't even fucking! It literally felt like he was *punishing* my pussy, and I loved every second of it! Apparently he was enjoying the domination aspect to our session as well, because it wasn't long before I felt his rock hard shaft throb again.

I bit my lip and winced as the feelings of intense pleasure fought a battled against the inability to scream my lungs out. *Yes! Yes! Yes!* I couldn't say the words, for fear that if I even tried to speak the entire valley would surely hear me screaming wildly.

I surrendered; coming hard as Jake erupted inside me. As he ejaculated, each pulsating throb of his cock intensified my own orgasm; which ripped through my entire body like an earthquake, with my pussy as the epicentre!

With a final thrust Jakes orgasm was over, and so was mine. My pelvic floor muscles twitched and spasmed a few more times before relaxing completely. He let go of my hips and collapsed against my back. We both puffed heavily; out of breath yet still connected.

"Oh my god Soph… that was incredible."

I didn't answer as I was still trying to catch my breath. He stood up and slowly withdrew; sending a not so pleasant shiver through me. My hypersensitive 'V-jay-jay' letting me know that it was a no go zone for a while.

For a moment I struggled to stand up straight, my arms and legs felt heavy and weak. I clumsily put my underwear and jeans back on. As Jake removed the condom, I stole a quick look at his cock before he pulled up his jeans. Who could blame me, I hadn't seen it for a while. He dug a hole in the soil with his heal; burying the evidence.

We straightened up our clothes and embraced for what felt like an eternity. I revelled in not feeling like hell as soon as we finished having sex, this time there was no pain to replace the pleasure as it usually did. I was invigorated and bathed in a post-coital glow.

"Until tonight Baby," he grinned.

I knew immediately he was referring to me visiting him in the middle of the night… for *round two*!

"Until tonight *Lover*," I echoed; mimicking his suggestive tone.

I kissed him again before leading us from our hiding place.

We walked home slowly, but for once not because I was tired. I needed time to allow my flushed complexion to stop glowing before getting back to the house, though there was absolutely no chance my wicked grin was going anywhere soon.

CHAPTER EIGHTEEN

TAMMY

A couple of months had passed, along with my second trip to the Royal Children's Hospital for treatment. I was feeling better and thankfully my scans were showing continued improvement as well. The chemotherapy was working its magic; my *monster* was slowly but surely being defeated.

I was feeling more alive than ever and I could feel myself growing stronger by the day. My improved health and new found level of energy was paying huge dividends whenever Jake and I would be together. Our relationship was soaring and now that I was feeling better, we were able to avoid the sad and depressing conversations we'd become so used to. I no longer felt like the sick girlfriend who absorbed so much sympathy. I absolutely revelled in the fact that every second I spent with Jake was positive, happy and passionate.

Life was good, and set to get even better. My treatment was on track and I, along with the professor, was optimistic that I'd make a full recovery. I desperately wanted to return to my best; for me and for Jake. Even though I knew he already loved me just the way I was, I still longed for the day when he could see me running on all cylinders.

I wasn't exactly sure when it started, but I woke up one morning and noticed my pillow was covered in a fair amount of hair. I was aware that hair loss was a side effect to chemo and I knew it was bound to happen at some point, but seeing so much of it on my pillow was still a shock.

I went to the bathroom to survey the damage. I flicked on the light and looked in the mirror. My thick brown hair, which was well passed my shoulders, looked normal enough.

Not so bad, I thought; turning my head from side to side. *I've got plenty left!*

Things changed though when I ran a brush through it. I literally filled the brush with one stroke, and the sight of the hairbrush caked with thick clumps of hair prompted me to put it back in the drawer immediately. At that rate I would've been bald by the time I'd finished doing my hair for the day!

Holy shit, I'm going bald! I took a few deep breaths to calm down, then reassured myself that I was already prepared for this to happen so there was no need to get upset.

My oldest brother, Shaun, and his girlfriend, Leah, were coming out to the farm for a visit later in the day; they were bringing Jake out with them. Leah was a hair dresser, so I decided that since I was inevitably going bald, I'd try a different hair style before losing the lot. I gave her a call and asked if she could bring out her scissors and some different hair colours to give me somewhat of a makeover before having to rock the standard chemotherapy hairdo; or lack thereof.

Shaun, Leah and Jake arrived just before lunch.

I rushed out to greet Jake with a firm embrace and passionate kiss.

Butterflies every time!

We all went inside and sat down for lunch. As we ate, we talked about what each of us had been up to in the last few weeks.

"So you want a new hair style Soph?" asked Leah, changing the subject from the mundane to the relevant; for me anyway.

"Yeah my hair's falling out by the brush full, so I thought I'd change things up before it's all gone."

"Did you have a style in mind?"

"Well I've had long brown hair for ages, so I thought I would go short for a change. Maybe even dye it blonde for a really different look."

"Short and blonde hey Soph? I won't recognise you," smiled Jake.

"Well look at the bright side, if it looks shit I won't have to put up with it for long," I laughed.

Nobody else thought it was funny but if I didn't joke about going bald at sixteen I would have cried instead.

Jake sensed my emotional struggle. In full view of everyone he grabbed my hand consolingly. "Don't be scared about losing your hair Baby. You'll always look beautiful to me."

I tilted my head to the side shyly and smiled. He leant over and kissed me on the cheek.

"What a lovely thing to say," said Mum.

"Well it's the truth," he replied; not taking his eyes off me. "You're *always* beautiful."

Jake's heartfelt declaration momentarily silenced the conversation. That was until my brother blurted out "Suck up!" which caused everyone to laugh.

"Stop it Shaun!" snapped Mum in Jake's defence.

"Now, I can cut your hair short and I've got enough peroxide to turn you into a blonde, but if you're up for it I have an even better idea?" Leah said with a grin.

"And what might that be?" I replied. Knowing Leah, it was going to be something on the wild side.

"Well what do you think about going pink… *fluorescent* pink?"

I burst out laughing.

"Only if you want to Sophie. I just thought it might be the only time you ever have a chance to do it; and as you said, if it doesn't look any good then you don't have to put up with it for too long."

I thought about it for a second.

"What do you think Jake?"

"Go for it; it'll be fun," he smiled, reaching up and running his fingertips through my hair, just above my ear and down the back of my neck. He always told me how beautiful my hair was and I could tell he was going to miss it… not half as much as I was though!

"Ok Leah, short and pink it is." I started to laugh at the thought of my beautiful brown locks being replaced with a funky, pink style.

"Are you sure?" asked Mum with a raised eyebrow; always so conservative.

"Yeah Mum, I might as well have some fun with it."

We finished lunch. Jake and Shaun did the dishes and tidied up the kitchen while Leah started on my hair cut. Within seconds my long ponytail was gone. I'd had long hair ever since I could remember; years of growing gone in one snip of the scissors. I looked down at the hair covered floor, and the realisation I was going to look completely different hit me instantly.

Once Jake finished with the dishes, he sat down at the table and talked with me while Leah cut my hair. Before long she was done.

"I don't want you to see it until I've put the colour through," she said.

"Ok Leah. I can wait. How does it look Jake?"

"It's very short. I think you're going to get a surprise when you see it."

Leah mixed two chemicals together into a paste then brushed the peroxide through my hair.

"We'll leave the peroxide in for a fairly long time so it goes completely white, then the pink dye will take to it better," she suggested.

After about thirty minutes we went into the bathroom and washed it out. I dried my hair and went back into the kitchen.

"Holy shit you look different," said Jake "It's amazing how much a hair style can change your appearance."

"Well it's not over yet," I giggled. I couldn't wait to see my new style.

I sat back in the chair and Leah began to spread the rich pink dye through my hair.

"It looks dark in the bottle, but once we wash it out of your hair it should be really bright," she explained.

Once all the dye was combed through we set the clock for another half hour. After the timer sounded we ventured into the bathroom to wash it out; and this is where things got interesting.

I knelt down beside the bathtub, put my head under the tap and Leah started washing out the dye. I squinted and could see the rich pink colour washing down the drain. Unfortunately, the dye wasn't the only thing that was being washed out. Within a minute the drain was completely clogged full… of my hair!

"Holy shit! Have I got any hair left?" I shrieked.

Neither Leah nor Jake responded straight away so I knew it was bad.

"Soph I think the peroxide and dye was a bit too much for your hair to handle. A lot has fallen out… but you still have some left," reassured Leah; her voice not instilling much confidence in me.

Some left! That doesn't sound good at all.

Jake hadn't said anything.

Leah finished washing the dye out, wrapped my head in a towel and gently dried it for me. She threw the towel on the floor, which was full of short pink strands, then squirted some hair gel into her palm and ran it through my hair; styling it with her fingers.

"So how does it look?" I asked.

"I'll say one thing… it's the *brightest* hair I've ever seen," said Jake.

"Maybe you should just check it out in the mirror for yourself," suggested Leah.

I took a deep breath and hesitantly turned to the mirror, almost too scared to look.

"Oh Fuck! What the hell happened to my hair?" I snapped.

Jake was right, my hair was bright and definitely pink, but there was basically none left! There were large patches missing and the hair that was left was so thin that you could see straight through to my white scalp. It looked absolutely shithouse!

"So do you like it?" asked Leah.

I didn't know whether to laugh or cry. I knew she would have felt terrible, considering just over an hour ago I had beautiful brown hair and was now left with a style which resembled that of a fluorescent pink, mangy dog!

I looked at her with a raised eyebrow. “Look. I know it’s not your fault, but this is the worst hair style I’ve ever seen in my life!” I made sure my tone was friendly so she knew I wasn’t having a go at her. “So yeah… I absolutely love it!” I joked.

The three of us started laughing, which was fine for me; quite frankly I was sick of crying anyway.

Jake put his arms around me. “Oh Soph… you poor bugger.”

“Well it’s not staying like this, that’s for damn sure!” I clarified sternly.

“What do you want us to do?” asked Leah.

“Jake, get the razor,” I demanded. “It’s all coming off. It’s going to happen eventually anyway so we might as well do it today.”

“Are you sure about this Soph?” he said.

“Positive. It needs to go… all of it.”

He opened up the vanity and grabbed the clippers Dad used to trim his beard. “I’ll cut it really short with these first and then run the razor over the top.”

I think Leah sensed this was something Jake and I needed to do together. “I’ll leave you guys to it.”

“Thanks for all your help Leah, sorry it didn’t really work out,” I said.

“You don’t have to apologise… not at all. I think the peroxide and dye was just too strong for your hair. At least you got to try something a little different,” she smiled sincerely before leaving us alone in the bathroom.

It didn’t take long at all. Jake trimmed my hair short all over, like a soldier ready for boot camp. Then he grabbed some shaving cream and lathered my head up. With the basin full of hot water, he proceeded to shave my head; rinsing the blade with each pass.

“I hope you don’t think I’m ugly when all my hair’s gone?” I whispered.

Let me tell you, being a teenage girl and having my head shaved by my boyfriend was a very tough experience; a real knock to my self-confidence. I always wanted to look nice for Jake but now I just felt so bare; so exposed and ugly.

"I'll always think you're beautiful… no matter what," he replied putting his hand on my shoulder and squeezing gently to comfort me. I reached up and put my hand on top of his.

"Are you sure? I just feel so ugly."

"Well then it's my job to make sure you never feel ugly again," he replied, leaning down and kissing me on the cheek; his words and affection making my heart flutter.

Before long my head was completely bald. Jake wiped it down with a warm face washer and then rubbed some moisturiser into my scalp.

"You know… you do have a pretty nice shaped noggin!" he announced as he kissed the smooth skin on top of my head.

I stood up and looked in the mirror, ready to be shocked by my reflection… for the *second* time in one day!

Jake stood behind me and looked over my shoulder at my reflection. As I studied my new appearance I rubbed my head with my hand. I was yet to speak.

"You look beautiful as always. I love you." He kissed me on the cheek again and hugged me tightly.

"My head feels really cold. I look like one of those kids on the 'Camp Quality' ads on TV."

"Look at the bright side… hair grows back."

"Are you sure you don't think I'm ugly?"

"Not one bit. Honestly, it's actually a bit of a turn on," he smiled; rubbing his cheek against my bald head.

"You're a real sicko, you know that?" I laughed.

"Yeah I know," he smiled coyly.

I pulled my hoodie over my cold head and emerged from the bathroom. Mum, Dad, Shaun and Leah were all sitting at the dining table, waiting anxiously to see my new style. I flipped my hoodie back to reveal my 'cue ball' head. I think Mum's expression was the best; utter shock.

They were all very supportive and managed to not make me feel like a freak. It was quite funny when my brother pointed out that Jake, who still had a pony tail, was the one in the relationship with the long hair. It prompted us all to erupt with laughter; especially Jake.

For any teenage girl, looks are an important part of self-esteem and confidence, and it did take me a while to come to terms with being bald. Even when I did get used to it, I would still wear a bandana when I was out in public. There was no question, Jake's constant reassurance that I was still beautiful and his continued reassurance that he was still crazy about me, helped my confidence to no end. The way he would look at me with complete adoration, the love he had in his eyes, it never faulted; not once.

I'd returned to 6 East Oncology Ward for another round of chemotherapy. It was supposed to be a routine trip, whereby Dad and I would drive to Melbourne and be back home later that night, but when Professor Ericson came to visit me and asked how I was feeling, my response prompted him to order a set of blood tests which threw a spanner in the works. I'd been feeling a little off for a few days, and considering how good I *had* been, he thought it better to be safe than sorry. The professor decided a set of blood tests would guarantee an explanation as to why I was feeling so out of sorts.

The results came back and unfortunately it turned out I had a blood infection. Normally, in a healthy person, something like that could be treated with some oral antibiotics and wouldn't be too much of a concern, but for somebody with cancer and an extremely low immune system, it could be disastrous.

Professor Ericson ordered me to stay in hospital on I.V. antibiotics, until the infection cleared, which was going to be a few days at best. Dad had to return home that afternoon as planned. He'd already had a heap of days off work due to my visits to the city for treatment, and simply couldn't afford to take any more time off from the factory. I wasn't too worried about staying in hospital on my own. I'd become familiar with a lot of the nurses on the ward already, and I felt comfortable with Dad leaving me there for a few days.

I was lying in bed with I.V. fluids running into my arm. The room I was in had two separate areas with six beds in each, and a nurse's station. From where I was, I had a clear view of all the beds in my area as well as a few in the other section. Almost all of the beds were occupied with small children, and most had one or two parents sitting beside them. Some of the kids were colouring in, others were watching TV and some were fast asleep; *all* of them though looked sick. After all, this was the 'Oncology Ward', so it was a safe assumption every one of them had some form of cancer or other serious illness.

I noticed a young girl walk in with her parents and a nurse. She was about nine and looked as frail and weak as I did before I started treatment. She was sick, very sick, and looked absolutely petrified. I recognised the looks on her mother and father's faces; I'd seen my parents with the same expressions of worry and fear when I was admitted to the Royal Children's for the first time.

It's just not fair! Sometimes life can be so cruel and unforgiving.

Watching the little girl and her parents was surreal. I felt like I was looking into the past and watching my own hospital admission from the third person. I knew how she was feeling; so scared and daunted by the size of the hospital. Seeing all the doctors, nurses, machines and countless sick children would be terrifying her. It was heartbreaking to watch such a young child, so small and innocent, having to endure such a horrible experience.

I couldn't hear what they were saying, but I gathered the nurse was explaining a few things about the oncology ward and the hospital in general. The adults talked for about ten minutes or so while the little girl sat on the bed; still and silent.

The nurse pulled the curtain around the young girl's bed so they could change her into a hospital gown. Once the curtain was drawn back, I noticed that the poor little thing looked even more frightened.

I wondered if maybe she was going to have some sort of biopsy done, like I did when I was first admitted. It would explain why she and her parents were looking so anxious.

The nurse left them alone for thirty-minutes or so before returning with an orderly who wheeled another bed over to the young girls bedside; confirming my earlier suspicions regarding surgery. The father helped the girl onto the orderly's bed and they all left the ward together. I went back to reading and watching some TV while my antibiotics continued to drip into my arm; fighting my infection.

Around two hours later, the nurse and the orderly returned to the ward with the little girl. She remained fast asleep as they carefully transferred her back to her bed. Her parents weren't back yet and the nurse returned every ten to fifteen minutes or so to check on her. I gathered she was still sleepy as a result of the anaesthetic because she would stir every so often then drift off again.

Her parents still hadn't returned and it had been a while since the nurse checked on her. I could see she was stirring so I got up and walked over to the little girl's bedside; moving slowly as I wheeled my drip with me. It was on a trolley which looked kind of like a stainless steel hat stand.

I sat down beside her bed and gently grasped her hand. She was stirring quite a bit now and I could tell she was going to wake up any minute. The thought of her waking up alone in a strange place was awful, so I held her hand and was ready to comfort her as soon as she opened her eyes. I looked down at her medical wrist tag which read '*Tammy Jacobs.*'

She stirred again and her eyes began to open; blinking a few times before closing again. This happened for a couple of minutes, until she finally woke up properly. I still had hold of her hand as her eyes opened fully; she was finding it hard to focus. After blinking a few more times to clear her vision, she looked straight at me.

"Hey Tammy, your Mum and Dad won't be far away," I said calmly; knowing her first question would be as to the whereabouts of her parents.

Tears formed in the corners of her eyes and her lips began to quiver. She was frightened.

"Don't be scared. My name's Sophie. I'll sit with you until they get back." I put my other hand on her shoulder to comfort her. "Are you in any pain?"

She shook her head.

"Where's my Mum and Dad?" she whispered; her voice was shaky. She was trying to hold back the tears but a couple of strays escaped and rolled down her cheeks. I grabbed a tissue from the bedside table and handed it to her.

"They're probably with the Doctor. I'm sure they won't be far away. Do you feel like you need to be sick?" I thought I'd ask since it's quite common for people to throw up after anaesthetic.

She shook her head again. "No."

"Can I get you anything?"

"My mouth is really dry and yucky. I need a drink."

I looked above her bed head and hit the assistance button. The nurse was with us promptly.

"Oh look who's awake," said the nurse as she arrived at Tammy's bedside. "How are you feeling?"

"I'm ok," she replied timidly.

"Thanks for sitting with her Sophie, how thoughtful of you," smiled the nurse.

"I just thought she wouldn't want to wake up alone. Tammy was wondering if she could have some water?"

"Of course, I'll be back with some iced water in a minute." The nurse left us to get Tammy a drink.

We sat in silence for a short while, Tammy was still grasping my hand. I looked at her small innocent face; her features petite and soft. She was the most adorable little girl.

"How old are you Tammy?"

"Twelve."

Oh my god she's so small! The seriousness of her condition hit me like a tonne of bricks. I had guessed she was about eight or nine when I first saw her. She looked so small and fragile for a twelve-year-old.

"Wow! Soon you'll be a teenager. How exciting!" I replied; hiding my shock.

Tammy returned the question. "How old are you?"

"I turned sixteen a couple of months ago. I actually had my birthday in this ward."

"Are you sick too?" she asked, glancing at my bald head.

"Yeah I am, but I'm getting better," I responded confidently, even though on that particular day my blood infection had me feeling like shit.

"Why has all your hair fallen out?"

"The medicine I'm taking to make me feel better can sometimes make your hair fall out. It grows back though," I added optimistically. "Did you just have an operation?"

"Yeah. I have a lump on my back and the doctors don't know what it is, so they cut a piece of it off."

"Ouch!" I sympathised.

"I think they're testing it to find out what's wrong with me."

"Well I hope it's nothing too serious. I'll keep my fingers crossed for you."

I sat with her for a while, talking and keeping her occupied until her parents returned. Among other things, I learnt she was from Melbourne and had a younger brother and sister; Ben and Elise.

Eventually her parents returned. They looked extremely worried, and I could tell by the look in their eyes that they didn't have good news.

I stood up immediately, said goodbye to Tammy and walked back to my bed. Tammy's mother forced a smile when we made eye contact.

I climbed into bed and watched as her parents hugged and kissed her. Her mother started to cry and Tammy's father walked to the other side of the bed and comforted his wife with a hug. I felt so bad for them. I assumed they'd just come from talking with a Doctor who had given them Tammy's diagnosis. Judging from their body language… it was serious.

Tammy must have told them I sat with her while she woke up, because both her Mother and Father looked in my direction at the same time. I gave them a brief wave and her Mum got up and walked over to my bedside.

"Sophie is it?" Her eyes were red and puffy. She looked a wreck.

"Yes."

"My name's Kerry and that's my husband Thomas. I just wanted to thank you for sitting with Tammy while we were with the doctor."

"That's ok. I just thought she might have been scared if she woke up and nobody was there with her."

"Well it was a lovely thing to do, so thank you."

"I hope she is going to be ok,' I said sincerely.

"We do too." Her eyes started to well up.

"I looked as sick as Tammy a few months ago, but after a few treatments of chemo I'm feeling much better," I said in an attempt to give her something positive.

"I hope Tammy responds to the treatment like that." Kerry was obviously sad but I could hear the hope in her voice.

"I guess we will be seeing you around Sophie."

"You sure will. Good luck."

"Thank you," said Kerry before returning to her daughter's bedside.

So that was how Tammy and I became friends. It seemed like fate, because in all bar a couple of my remaining trips to the Royal Children's, Tammy was there as well. We developed a close bond and so did our parents. Mum and Dad would stay at Mac House and they met up with Kerry and Tom on quite a few occasions, so they spent a fair amount of time together as well. They were all lovely people, but it was horrible that we had to meet them under the worst possible circumstances.

A couple of times Tammy and I were put in beds beside each other and since neither of us were going to school anymore, we missed our usual friends. I think that's why the bond between us developed so quickly.

I was surprised by how mature Tammy was for a twelve-year-old, and I found it really easy to talk with her about all sorts of things. She was always asking me questions about what high school was like, as she was due to go the following year. We would talk about our friends and siblings, and I told her stories about life on the farm. Oh, and of course I talked to her about Jake. I know she was interested in hearing about him, but it actually helped *me* even more. When I wasn't with Jake, talking about him was the next best thing. It made me feel close to him. Tammy and I would also talk about our illnesses and how our treatment was going. Unfortunately, her *monster* seemed to be a lot stronger than mine, which meant she not only had to undergo chemo, but radiation therapy as well. From what I understood, radiation was far more aggressive, and fairly dangerous for such a small child, but what other choice did they have?

Tammy had a large tumour in her back, which had grown in and around her spinal cord making it impossible to remove via surgery. The only treatments I was aware of her having was chemotherapy and radiation, but I wouldn't have been surprised if the doctors tried other treatments like bone marrow transplants as well. She was a sick little girl and the harsh treatments prescribed to treat the tumour were taking their toll on her.

My treatment was on track and I was getting stronger as the weeks rolled by. I did however suffer a huge set back, thanks to one nurse who was a little *too* eager injecting the chemo into my arm. In short, when she was administering my chemotherapy she pushed the drug through too fast. Instead of the usual cool feeling, a painful burning sensation raced up my arm. It's almost like the chemo burnt the inside of my vein and caused it to collapse; rendering it unusable.

Once he found out what had happened, I remember seeing Professor Ericson give the nurse an absolute face ripping. I actually felt a little sorry for her. After the incident, he made the decision that I was not to have chemo 'pushed' through any more.

The result of the veins collapsing in my arm was that I needed to have a 'Hickman Line' inserted. This would negate the need for chemo to be injected into my arm via an I.V. line. Unfortunately, in order to have the Hickman put in I would have to undergo another operation. I would be put under a general anaesthetic and the silicon line would be inserted straight into my jugular vein in the bottom of my neck. Two tubes would be left sticking out of my chest with protective caps on the ends. The nurses would be able to attach the syringes to these tubes and inject the chemo straight into my blood stream via the central line; no more needles in my arms. The Hickman would stay in place until the end of my treatment.

I couldn't help but feel like this whole situation was just my *monster* trying everything he could to bring me down. It was as if he could feel the medicine slowly destroying him over the last few months, and he was getting desperate. So preventing me from being able to be administered my life saving chemotherapy was a direct counter attack against me.

I was fairly nervous about this procedure, the whole idea of messing around with my jugular vein had me a little freaked out. I had talked to Jake about my concerns and he said he wouldn't be letting me go through another operation alone, especially one I was so anxious about. I asked my parents whether it was ok if he travelled with us to Melbourne to be with me for my operation. They didn't mind as long as it was ok with his parents. I remember Jake telling me he got in a fairly decent argument with Mary and Greg about whether he should come to hospital with me. They brought up the issue of him missing school, and that maybe my Mum and Dad didn't actually want him to come; hinting that maybe he'd just be in the way. Jake wasn't going down without a fight, and fight he did. Eventually he convinced his parents that it was totally irrelevant if he missed a few days of school, because knowing I was having a serious operation meant he wouldn't be concentrating in class anyway. He also told them that it wasn't about what my parents wanted, it was about what was best for me and my recovery.

Thankfully Jake was able to persuade Greg and Mary that it was the right choice to let him go.

When I asked him what convinced them he replied, "I told them straight up, the most important thing for your recovery is to keep you calm, positive and happy, and if that means me going to Melbourne to be there for you then that's what's going to happen. They both realised I was never going to back down so they eventually said yes."

I would've loved to have been there to see Jake fighting for me; fighting to be with me when I needed him the most. I'm pretty sure that particular conversation was most likely the point where Jake's parents realised just how serious our relationship was.

Since then Jake has been by my side for every one of my operations, and I can assure you that over the coming years… there were plenty.

The day of my operation had arrived. Jake was standing by my bedside as I waited on the gurney outside the surgery doors. I was still scared, but without question having him holding my hand and telling me that 'everything's going to be alright' made all the difference. I believed everything he said.

Mum and Dad gave me a cuddle and a kiss on the cheek then wished me luck, before stepping back so Jake could do the same. He grabbed hold of both my hands, kissed them one at a time, then looked directly into my eyes and smiled.

He leant forward and kissed me softly on the forehead then on the lips. "I'll be the first thing you see when you wake up Baby. Just stay calm and remember… everything will be ok."

He let go of my hands and I wrapped my arms around the back of his neck; holding onto him tightly. "I love you Jake," I said quietly.

"I love you too Baby. I'll see you soon."

I let him go and he stepped back from the bed so the orderly could take me.

"We love you Soph," said Mum as I was wheeled through the doors and into the hallway adjoining the surgical theatres.

Unlike the operation to remove the lump from my neck, this time I was having a general anaesthetic which would put me to sleep for the entire surgery.

The last thing I remember was feeling a little sting in the top of my hand where the anaesthetic was injected, then being told to count backwards from ten.

"Ten, nine, eight… seven… six…" I was out.

I slowly opened my eyes; squinting as though I hadn't seen daylight for weeks. Everything was blurry so I blinked a few times to adjust my vision.

"Sophie… it's Mum."

Her face slowly came into focus.

"You're in the recovery ward. Everything went well Honey"

"Jake?" I whispered; my voice croaky thanks to a dry mouth and throat.

"Sorry Soph. They'd only let one of us into the recovery ward. Jake was happy for me to come in. He's waiting for you with Dad back at your bed in oncology. We will be heading over there soon."

"I think I'm going to be sick," I sat up, pressed my lips together tightly and put my hand over my mouth. Mum, who had a container ready, handed it to me quickly and I vomited as soon as I got my mouth over it.

Coming out of the anaesthetic had caused the nausea and vomiting. I handed the dish to Mum and lay back down; relieved that Jake wasn't there to see me emptying my stomach. I closed my eyes and drifted off again.

I don't know how long I slept for, but as I started to wake up I could feel somebody tickling my face; the gentlest fingers running across my forehead and down my cheek. I knew who it was instantly, there was only one person who touched me like that! I decided not to open my eyes straight away, instead I just laid there for a moment; savouring the sensation of my lover's touch. When I finally opened my eyes, Jake was looking back at me; eyes soft, lips smiling warmly.

"Hey Baby," he whispered before leaning over and kissing me on the cheek. "The doctor told your parents that everything went really well. I'm so relieved." He grabbed my hand and lightly kissed my knuckles.

"That's good," I mumbled; my mouth still dry. "I need some water." I looked around and realised I was now back in my bed in the oncology ward.

"Sure. I'll be back in a minute."

Jake got up and went to get me a drink. I rolled over to see both my parents sitting there. They'd been there the whole time.

"Hey Sophie are you still feeling sick in the tummy?" asked Mum.

"A little bit queasy… better though."

"How does your chest feel? Are you in any pain?" Dad leant over and kissed the top of my head after asking how I was.

"I'm a bit sore. It hurts to move."

Jake returned with a jug of iced water and a glass. I drank two full glasses, one after the other.

I carefully lifted the neck of my gown up and looked down at my chest. I took one glance then quickly looked away; slightly shocked with what I'd just seen.

Jake sat down beside me. "Are you ok?"

I took a deep breath then looked again. There was a thin white tube about as thick as a piece of spaghetti sticking out of my chest at the top of my cleavage. It branched off into two ends; one with a red cap, the other blue. There was a clear adhesive covering stuck to my skin to protect the incision site where the tube entered my chest. I could see some blood around the cut and the protruding tube. It didn't hurt, but I think the sheer sight of it just caught me by surprise.

I looked up at Jake and my parents, all three of them wanted to know what I'd just seen.

"Okay then! I have a tube sticking out of me!" I said in a cheerful voice, as if to make light of the situation even though I was obviously shocked. “I would show you all but I don’t have a bra on and it’s sticking out from between my boobs.”

“That’s ok, you don’t need to show us,” said Mum.

“It looks really freaky.”

“Hey at least you don’t have to have any more needles now,” added Jake.

“True… I definitely won’t miss those.”

“Professor Ericson said you’ll be having your next dose of chemo tomorrow. The nurse will be using the central line you had fitted today,” explained Dad.

“Well I hope it works. It’s going to feel weird having the chemo pushed straight into my neck.”

I was right.

I was in two minds whether to include this next part in my story or not. First of all, because it’s fairly outrageous and I feel a little embarrassed sharing the details. Secondly, because most people wouldn’t believe it was true anyway. But when I started writing I made a promise to tell my story as it happened, so to stay true to that promise, and myself… here it is.

For the rest of the day, Jake never left my bedside. My parents were there as well, only leaving to get some lunch. They brought something back for Jake so he could stay with me the whole time. It was so nice having him there; to talk to, help me go to the bathroom, hold my hand, and tickle my face while I dozed in and out of sleep. I was thankful that strict visiting hours weren’t enforced, so Jake was able to stay with me the entire day and into the night. I guess scheduled visiting hours in a children’s hospital weren’t preferred, as it would be too traumatic for younger kids to have to stay on their own if their parents were made to leave at various times of the day.

It was some time around 6:30pm, when my parents decided to go back to Mac House for the night.

“Did you want to come with us Jake,” asked Mum.

"No thanks. I'll walk over later on and have something to eat after. I really want to stay here with Soph if that's ok?"

"Ok. Well come over at seven-thirty. Sophie will need an early night."

"Sure thing Lynn."

"Thanks Mum," I added.

"We'll be back in the morning Soph. Try and get a good night's sleep," said Dad. "See you after Jake. We'll save you some dinner."

"Thanks David, I'll be over right on seven-thirty."

Mum and Dad gave me a kiss and headed back to Mac House.

The nurse brought my dinner over just as my parents left the ward. I ate as much as I could; Jake polished off the rest.

"Do you want to see the central line?"

"Only if you want to show me Baby, you know you don't have too."

"I want to show you. I haven't even had a really good look at it yet."

Jake stood up and moved closer. I pulled the neck of my gown forward and we both looked at the silicone tube which was protruding from the centre of my chest. It was going to take me some time to get used to it.

"It doesn't bother you?" I asked; already self-conscious.

"Of course not. Nothing that's going to help you get better bothers me… how could it? I just hope it isn't hurting you?"

"No it doesn't hurt, it just looks gross; I mean it's right between my boobs!"

"It's not gross Baby. Honestly, it doesn't bother me. Can you shower with it?"

"The clear plastic covering is completely waterproof so showering is ok. I wouldn't risk a bath though."

"Yeah it looks like it could get infected fairly easy."

I covered myself back up and lay down.

"Thank you so much for being here Jake and looking after me. It makes such a huge difference having you beside me."

"I wouldn't want to be anywhere else Baby."

"Mum and Dad are fantastic and they help me out a lot, but it's just different when you look after me."

"What do you mean?"

"I think it's because, to them I'm still their little girl, so I kind of feel like a child. I don't feel that way when you're here though."

"I think you stopped being a child a long time ago!" Jake grinned cheekily.

"Well I suppose… all thanks to you." I returned a suggestive smile. "I wish I could come and sleep in your bed at Mac House. It's going to kill me, knowing you're so close but I can't be with you."

"It's ok Baby, you're in no condition to share a bed with me anyway," he joked.

"That's what you think. Whatever drugs I'm on are doing the trick because I'm not in the slightest bit of pain. I'm pretty sure I'd be able to handle *snuggling* up with you."

"Do you really think you could control yourself? Remember… I know what you're like Sophie Taylor."

"I don't know what you mean," I replied in the most innocent voice I could muster causing Jake to laugh.

I could see where this conversation was going, and all this sexual innuendo was making me feel a little flustered.

"I think we should change the subject."

"Why?" Jake smiled. "Getting a little warm?"

I nodded.

"Maybe even a little bit… *wet*!" he whispered with emphasis.

"Stop it Jake." I closed my eyes, took a deep breath and exhaled slowly.

As soon as I saw his lips say the word 'wet', I couldn't help but squeeze my thighs together; a futile attempt to extinguish the tingling sensation that was gradually developing between my legs.

Jake noticed me moving under the sheets. "Feeling uncomfortable are we?" he teased.

I nodded again; frowning at him.

"Awe Soph… what's the matter?" he said in response to my sulky expression.

"I have an itch," I pouted.

"Really? I thought the chemo got rid of that," he smiled.

"Not that kind of itch!" I snapped.

"Oh… *that* kind of itch! Whoops… I hope it's not my fault."

Jake was clearly enjoying himself at my expense. He'd worked me up and he knew it. I was now grinding my thighs together, as subtly as I could, which wasn't helping the situation at all.

"Gee, you're a bit of a wriggle worm!" he smiled; chuckling under his breath.

I bit down on my bottom lip. "Stop teasing me… it hurts," I whispered; referring to the dull ache in my groin.

"You poor thing. I thought you said the drugs were working, you shouldn't be in any pain?" he grinned.

"Yeah… well they're not helping the *pain* you're causing!" I frowned; maintaining my sad face whilst trying desperately not to laugh as well.

"Baby what pain could I possibly cause you?" he asked ever so innocently.

"You know *exactly* what you're doing to me."

"Maybe we should ask the nurse if there's some medicine you can take?"

"There's no medicine for this," I replied, replacing my sad expression with a suggestive stare. I glared at him; eyes burning.

"Well that's a real shame." He looked directly into my eyes; mimicking my lustful glare. "I wish there was something I could do for you."

"Maybe there is," I hinted.

He raised an eyebrow.

"Come here Jake… come closer to me."

He edged his chair closer.

"Put your hand on the bed," I ordered.

He obeyed. I slid my hand slowly out from under the covers, grabbed his wrist and discretely pulled his hand back under the sheets.

"What do you think you're doing?" he whispered; scanning the room.

There were other parents sitting by bedsides and a couple of nurses at the nurse station. Everyone was preoccupied and paying us no attention. Luckily my bed was next to a wall, and the bed on the other side was vacant, so we had a little bit of space and privacy… all I needed anyway.

"You do know you're out of control Sophie?" His voice was quiet, yet his eyes blazed with desire.

"I'm not crazy…" I slowly moved my legs apart, just enough to place Jake's hand under my gown on the bare skin of my inner thigh. "Just horny," I smirked.

He closed his eyes momentarily as he squeezed the soft skin of my thigh.

"Now who's got an itch?" I teased.

"You're evil."

I knew he would be getting harder by the second. The thought of his erection straining in his pants was more than I could handle. I couldn't help myself. I still had hold of his wrist and slowly slid his hand up the inside of my thigh. I watched Jake's face intently. The higher I moved his hand, the deeper his breaths became, and the longer his eyes remained closed with every blink.

"You want to touch *me*… don't you?" I whispered ever so quietly.

He nodded subtly.

Moving slowly, careful not to attract the attention from anyone else in the room, I repositioned myself so I could discretely spread my legs wider under the covers; just enough for Jake to gain the access he needed.

I let go of his wrist and slid my panties to the side. "Then touch me," I challenged.

Jake slowly trailed one finger to the top of my thigh, then gently ran it directly up the centre of my aching pussy.

I was facing towards Jake, away from the rest of the room, so I closed my eyes and inhaled deeply; savouring the feeling.

"Fuck you're wet Baby!" Jake whispered; so quiet that I only just heard him.

I nodded; barely moving my head.

He slowly moved the tip of his finger in small circles over my clit. I couldn't help but gently push my pelvis towards his hand.

Jake leant forward and put his mouth closer to my ear. "Hey… no moving! We're not exactly alone. Stay still or I'll stop!" he said quietly, yet firm enough to let me know he was serious.

"Ok… sorry," I whispered, the corners of my mouth curling up into a mischievous grin.

I closed my eyes and Jake continued; softly massaging my clit while he caressed my face with his free hand. To a bystander, the scene would have appeared innocent. Me, asleep, with my man soothing me by tickling my face. If only they knew how he was *really* caring for me.

Jake moved his attention from my clit; gently spreading my *lips*. I gasped lightly as he slowly slid one finger inside me and I held my breath as he eased in another. The sensation causing me to exhale blissfully.

"Oh Jake." It was taking all of my self-control not to thrust my hips against his pleasuring touch.

"Stay still Baby," he cautioned. "Don't move… just let it build."

I nodded again.

He curved his fingers up, applying just the right amount of pressure to my g-spot; massaging it with a slow and methodical rhythm. Since being with Jake I'd given him detailed instruction as to how he needed to touch me, now I could *feel* how well I'd taught him. He knew every part of *me* so well, almost better than I knew myself. Longer fingers I guess!

As Jake administered my 'therapy' he continued to lovingly caress my face, putting me into such a relaxed state that I couldn't have opened my eyes even if I wanted to. The way he touched me, it was so beautiful, tender and delicate; perfect in every way. In fact, so perfect that the soothing pleasure radiating throughout my body soon morphed into something far stronger. I may have looked like I was asleep, but looks can be deceiving. I was like a dormant volcano with hot lava bubbling deep down inside; ready to erupt any second.

I groaned quietly as my climax loomed. My lover's fingers, so familiar, had rapidly delivered me to the edge.

"Don't move, and don't make a sound," he warned; knowing that my intense orgasms were always accompanied by violent thrusts from my pelvis, and distinctly pleasurable moans; screams when we had the house to ourselves.

He increased his pressure; massaging the inside of my pussy a little firmer whilst maintaining a slow, deliberate pace. My breathing was now shallow and rapid. I was mere seconds away from release. The fact I couldn't make a sound resulted in such intense pressure that it pushed my pain meds to the limit, and I began to feel the tender incision site from my surgery. I probably should have taken it as a signal to stop, but I ignored the sting.

I was ready to give in, to surrender to the pleasure. "I'm going to…"

"Keep still… and no sound," he warned again with a stern whisper, worried that I was going to explode uncontrollably; alerting everyone else in the ward as to what mischief we were up to. Not that moaning in a hospital is out of place, but I'm pretty much certain the kind of moaning I wanted to let out wouldn't be mistaken for discomfort.

I bit my lip as hard as I dared and held my breath. Every single muscle in my body contracted as I let myself go, and a glorious orgasm raced through my entire body. The fact I couldn't move or scream with pleasure, trapped it inside me, which meant it lasted forever! I had to fight with everything I had not to convulse and squeal. The intensity of my release, combined with my attempts to not let it escape, made my head feel like it was going to pop. Eventually it subsided and I was able to exhale. My body was so relaxed and heavy, I felt like I was sinking into the mattress. I could feel come trickling out of me and gradually sliding down between the cheeks of my butt. I was dripping… literally! Jake carefully removed his fingers and straightened up my underwear.

I opened my eyes. Everything was blurry but as soon as Jake's face came into focus I smiled at him graciously. I couldn't help blushing.

He looked at me; both eyebrows raised in utter disbelief at what just transpired. "Well then… I guess I should say you're welcome," he grinned.

"Oh you're welcome anytime," I responded gratefully.

He leant forward and kissed me on the lips.

"Oh my god Jake… that was so intense."

"It didn't hurt you did it?"

I shook my head. "Hurt? Not one bit. I felt amazing… perfect." I chose to omit the details about my incision sites stinging a little. Besides, the pleasure I felt from my orgasm far outweighed any pain from the surgery.

Jake tickled my face gently. "I love you so much Sophie."

I could tell by the way he spoke and how he looked into my eyes, that he was glad he could do something to help me. And it really *did* help. Jake would tell me how useless he felt sometimes because there was nothing he could do to help with my disease. He really had no idea the power he possessed, and what an integral part of my treatment he was.

"I love you too." My heavy eyelids causing me to blink slowly as I spoke.

I felt as though I'd been drugged. The operation, the medication, the stress, the pleasure; everything caught up to me at once. My body was exhausted and relaxed. Sleep beckoned and I struggled to open my eyes again.

"Is there anything you need before I go?"

I didn't answer, nor did I open my eyes, I just shook my head a little.

"I'll stay here until you fall asleep. See you tomorrow Sweetie."

He kissed me on the lips, sat back down and kept tickling my face until I drifted off.

The feeling of my *angel's* loving caress worked faster than the anaesthetic I had before my operation. There was no counting backwards from ten… I was out before I knew it.

The following day I was due to have my next round of chemotherapy and as Dad had mentioned, the nurse would be pushing it through the Hickman line.

Jake and my parents arrived just after I finished breakfast. The nurse had already helped me shower and mentioned that she'd be back shortly to give me the chemo.

"Come and give me a kiss," I said to Jake as soon as he reached my bedside.

He leant over and kissed me briefly on the lips. I stared at him; my eyes thanking him for last night. He smiled back; shooting me a discrete wink which made me blush. I could feel the warmth in my cheeks and hoped my parents didn't notice.

The nurse returned with her trolley of large syringes. She pulled the curtain around my bed; blocking the view of all the other people in the room.

"Now I'm going to need access to your line. Are you happy for your parents and Jake to be in here?" asked the nurse, referring to the need to expose my breasts.

"I'll wait outside," said Dad.

"I think I might be a little squeamish so I'll wait outside as well. We'll let you concentrate," added Mum.

I got the feeling Mum sort of implied that Jake should wait outside with them.

"You're not going anywhere Jake. I want you beside me," I said directly.

He grabbed hold of my hand. "I'm staying right here."

Mum and Dad looked at each other; eyebrows raised.

It was almost as funny… actually, *funny* probably isn't the right word. It was almost as *awkward* as the time Professor Ericson asked me if I was sexually active. Really it wouldn't have been a big deal, except that my parents were sitting either side of me! He brought the topic up when discussing the possibility of the treatment affecting my chances of having children later in life. The expression on their faces when their teenage daughter replied 'yes' was absolutely priceless. I'm fairly certain they already knew, but to hear me actually admit it out loud definitely took them by surprise.

"We'll be out here if you need us Soph," said Dad.

"Thanks," I smiled appreciatively.

Mum and Dad pulled the curtain back a little and stepped out of view.

The entire process only took about ten minutes. It didn't hurt, but feeling the cold liquid running up and down a major vein in my neck was unusual to say the least. As the medicine flowed straight into my jugular vein I tried not to think about it too much, choosing instead to focus my attention on Jake's eyes… a perfect distraction.

After the nurse finished administering the chemo, we waited for a few hours at the hospital to see how I reacted. I wasn't feeling sick and my central line felt fine, so after a quick visit from Professor Ericson to discuss my progress and the plan for the next few months, I was discharged and allowed to go home.

The trip was going well up until the thirty or forty-minute mark. I don't know what the hell happened but I went from feeling fine to awful in a matter of seconds; as if somebody flicked a switch inside me. My stomach churned and I started to vomit profusely. The professor warned us this might happen so we were somewhat prepared for it, and thankfully had a stash of sick bags in the car.

The entire trip home Jake sat with me in the back seat, holding the bag for me while I vomited countless times. Dad would pull into every rest stop to dispose of the used sick bags and tissues Jake was using to clean me up. It also gave me a chance to get out of the car for some fresh air.

It was by far the worst car trip of my life. The nausea and vomiting was relentless for the good part of three and a half hours. When I wasn't vomiting I was lying with my head on Jakes lap, eyes closed as he softly stroked my face or rubbed my back, trying his best to keep me calm and soothed. I felt terrible that he had to endure this with me; seeing, hearing and smelling me emptying my stomach over and over, but at the same time I'd never been so grateful that he was there with me… *for* me. I honestly believe it was experiences like those, even though they were horrendous, that forged a bond of unconditional love between Jake and I which has held strong since the beginning, and will continue well beyond the end.

When a couple say their vows on their wedding day they often include the line '*In sickness and in health*', but to be honest… they're just words. What really matters are actions. Over the course of my life with Jake, I've lost count of how many times he has been there for me, 'holding the bucket'. Actions always speak louder than words, and at just sixteen, Jake had already proved to me that he *was* definitely going to be there in sickness. I hoped and prayed he would get a chance to be there for me in health someday too.

As soon as we got home, Jake and Mum tucked me into bed. I was shattered, utterly exhausted and in pain. The violent contractions from vomiting all the way home had left every muscle in my body aching and sore. Mum brought me a glass of water and some pain killers then said goodnight.

Just as he'd done the night before, Jake sat beside me and caressed my face until I drifted off. Once again I fell asleep with my *angel* watching over me; protecting me. I adored him beyond words.

The rest of my chemotherapy treatment went fairly smooth, except for when my Hickman line got infected somehow. I was always so careful but it was a constant danger, and as I've learnt to accept, if there's ever a side effect to a treatment or something which could potentially go wrong… it will.

I had to stay in hospital for a few days on I.V. antibiotics, as I'd done when I contracted a blood infection earlier on, so being left at the hospital while my parents went home without me was a bit of a setback. There was an upside though because I did get to spend some more time with Tammy.

Our friendship grew stronger every time we met at the hospital, and I think the battle we were fighting against a common enemy had bonded us together; close and fast. It was as if we'd been friends for years, when in reality we had only met on five or six separate occasions; though some for days at a time. When I was with her I couldn't help but feel like her older sister. I cared about her deeply.

Tammy always asked me how Jake was and would listen intently when I talked about him. Sometimes I would catch her staring into the distance; smiling, like maybe she was imagining her future and secretly hoping that one day she would find herself in love with someone the way I loved Jake. I often prayed that she would.

Tammy always seemed so much older and mature than a regular twelve-year-old, well beyond her years, which is a feeling I could relate to. I think it's part of being struck down with an illness at such a young age. It forces you to grow up and get serious about life because you learn, first-hand, how precious it really is.

The hard part about my relationship with Tammy was not seeing her health improve the way mine was, even though she was having far more aggressive medicines and treatments than me. Each time I saw her, it was clear her health had declined even further. The doctors were having real trouble treating her because she was just so small and frail. The aggressive treatment to combat the growth on her spine was taking its toll. I could gradually see her body getting weaker, her voice quieter and her movements slower. I could see the pain in her eyes constantly. The worst part though was her beautiful smile, which I loved seeing so much, had all but disappeared. It was as if Tammy's *monster* had control of her, turning her like a 'dimmer switch'; gradually fading her light from a bright illuminating glow… to darkness. It was heartbreaking to watch, and I made sure that every time I said goodbye to Tammy I would always give her a firm hug and wish her the best of luck.

A few more weeks passed and I'd reached the end of my scheduled chemotherapy treatment. Jake had come with my parents and I to the Royal Children's. I was due to have another round of scans to determine if the treatment over the last six months had worked; ridding me of Stage IV Hodgkin's disease. Clear scans this time around would mean I was officially in remission.

Once the scans were completed, the results were sent to Professor Ericson. We all met at his office, including Jake, to hear whether the treatment had been a complete success or if I needed to have another course of chemo.

The professor stood up from his desk and shook each of our hands as we all entered his office. Mum, Dad and I sat down and Jake stood behind me with his hand on my shoulder.

Professor Ericson started the conversation. "So how are you feeling Sophie? I mean… compared to say… six months ago?" he said with a smile.

"Well six months ago I felt like I was dying. Now I feel full of energy… I feel alive!" I replied excitedly.

"That's great. I guess you want to know if your Hodgkin's disease has cleared and whether you need to have any more chemo."

"Yes. I have my fingers crossed."

He looked over at his computer screen.

"I have all the results here, and it's very good news indeed."

I think all four of us exhaled at the same time; utterly relieved.

"We already knew the mediastinal enlargement in your lungs was responding rapidly to the treatment and shrinking each month. The latest scans show it has completely disappeared… which is excellent!"

The smile on my face grew even larger. I felt Jake squeeze my shoulder with excitement. I reached up and put my hand on top of his.

"The other good news is that all the enlarged lymph nodes, which had subsequently turned into tumours like the one we removed from your neck, have returned to normal. All bloods have come back normal as well."

"So does that mean I don't need to have any more chemo?" I asked anxiously.

I think I heard Mum, Dad and Jake all take a deep breath in anticipation of the answer.

"In my opinion Sophie, you're in remission which means no more chemo."

I was so happy that I felt like bursting into tears. Jake leant forward and kissed me on top of the head, and Mum and Dad both leaned in and gave me a hug. We were all smiling and laughing, including Professor Ericson. Dad stood up and shook his hand again.

"Congratulations Sophie," said the professor.

"Thank you so much, you saved my life."

"It is my pleasure, but I can't take all the credit. The support your parents gave you through all of this is always so important, and I am sure the man standing behind you had more to do with your recovery than we could ever hope to understand. It's amazing how strong humans can be when they have someone worth fighting for… and someone fighting for them."

He gets it! I was touched by the professor's words, and it meant a lot to know that he understood how important Jake had been in my recovery.

I'll never take anything away from the love and support I got from my parents, and the amazing treatment I received at the hands of Professor Ericson. But knowing how close to death I actually was, I've always felt like Jake was the one ingredient that made all the difference. His love for me never faltered. Not when I looked like death; skin and bones, covered in scabs and sores, nor when all my hair fell out, or the countless times he held the bucket while I vomited violently through the night. Jake loved me through it all, and I always felt that love. It gave me the strength I needed to keep fighting my *monster*, no matter how hopeless victory seemed sometimes.

So that's how I survived cancer. My *monster* had given me a pretty good battering, but for now I was smiling. I had beaten him. He had retreated into the darkness and I wouldn't feel his presence again for many years to come.

My life was mine again.

I will never forget it. The phone rang and Dad answered. I was in the lounge room with the TV on so I couldn't hear who he was talking to or what it was about. As soon as he hung up he called out for Mum to come and talk to him.

"Lynn! Can you come inside for a minute?"

I didn't think anything of it; assuming it was one of my brothers or a relative, so I went back to watching my show.

Probably ten minutes or so later, Dad and Mum came into the lounge room. "Can you turn that off Soph?" he asked; clearly worried.

I looked at Mum and she was wiping her eyes with a tissue.

Initially, I thought it must have been the professor and that something was wrong with me again, but it had been a couple of months since I'd last seen him and I felt great. I was actually ready to start looking for a job.

As I picked up the remote and switched the TV off, it hit me like a tonne of bricks.

Oh my god... Tammy!

With the noise of the television gone, the room was silent except for Mum's sniffle as she tried in vain to muffle her sobbing cries.

I turned to Dad. "What's happened?"

"Sophie…" he paused; searching for words.

"Just tell me!"

I could already feel the sadness growing inside me, and my eyes were starting to sting with the impending tears.

"It's Tammy."

"No… no!" I shook my head as if to convince myself that whatever Dad was going to say next wasn't true.

"Sophie… she's gone love."

I tightly squeezed my eyes closed as tears instantly streamed down my face. I was crying but there wasn't a sound; I couldn't breathe. All the pain and suffering I'd endured over the last eighteen months was nothing compared to the anguish I felt right at that moment, and I would have gone through it all again to bring her back. Finding out Tammy had lost her battle was devastating.

Mum sat down beside me and put her arm around my shoulders. As soon as she cuddled me I broke down; sobbing uncontrollably. She was a mess too.

Dad sat on the other side. He held my hand and rubbed my back comfortingly.

"When?" I sniffled; my blubbering voice barely comprehendible.

"She passed away yesterday. It was her birthday Soph."

Mum tightened her grip on me as I cried; howling with raw and painful grief.

Dad waited for me to get myself together before continuing. It took a while.

I wanted to know what had happened so I tried desperately to stop crying and get some kind of control over myself. I wiped my eyes on my sleeve and looked at Dad; he told me the rest.

"That was Thomas on the phone. He said she wasn't doing too well, so the doctors had her staying in hospital as a full time patient." He spoke slowly; pausing to let me absorb what he was saying. "Tammy wanted to go home for her thirteenth birthday and spend it with her younger brother and sister. The doctors decided she could spend one night at home and then return to the Royal Children's the next day, so Tom and Kerry organised a small party for her with some close family and friends."

While I listened to Dad talk me through his conversation with Tammy's father, I was on the verge of breaking down with every word, the lump in my throat was literally choking me.

"Late in the afternoon Tammy started to feel tired, so she said goodbye to everyone then Thomas carried her to bed to get some rest." Dad paused for a moment; swallowing the lump in his throat. "Everyone at the party decided to leave, so the house would be quiet. Kerry went back in to check on her… she was already gone."

It was the most heartbreaking thing I'd ever heard. To be told my friend had passed away, and on her birthday, was too much for me to handle. I needed to be alone to process the whole situation.

"I'm going to bed for a while… I need to be alone."

"Ok Soph," Mum sobbed; wiping away the tears.

I stood up, gave Dad a hug and went to my room. There was no doubt Tammy's death had hit Mum and Dad hard as well. It was very close to home for them, considering they almost lost me to a very similar illness less than a year ago.

I climbed into bed and buried my head in a pillow.

Visions of Tammy smiling and laughing in the hospital bed beside me raced through my mind. I knew she would have fought her *monster* with everything she had. The fact she held on until seeing all her family and friends on her birthday, was proof she fought for her life for as long as possible.

My heart was in pieces. The thought of Tammy lying alone in bed, sound asleep as her last shallow breath quietly drifted from her tiny body; leaving my friend peaceful yet lifeless… it broke me. I was so upset that I was finding it hard to breathe, and the realisation I would never see her again definitely left me in shock.

It just wasn't fair. I thought of all the things we talked about, and I couldn't help but feel angry at myself for talking so much about Jake; how happy he made me and how amazing it felt to be in love. I felt selfish for having so many wonderful experiences with Jake, yet Tammy had been taken so young, before she even felt the excitement and magic of her first kiss. I was guilty, angry and full of grief all at once.

Jake had shown me countless times how beautiful and amazing life is, but losing Tammy to such a slow and horrible illness showed me first-hand how cruel and unforgiving it can be as well.

I cherish every moment I spent with Tammy, and I make sure I think about her regularly. Whenever anything good ever happens in my life, I pray she is looking down from above, smiling and laughing… sharing it with me.

Tammy Jacobs… forever beautiful, innocent and brave.

You were an angel long before finding your way to heaven.

I will never forget you.

CHAPTER NINETEEN

BOOT CAMP

The strength of our relationship was proven. Together we'd fought and won what looked like an impossible battle, against a horrible disease which almost claimed my life. Jake's devotion and loyalty to me was without question, and there wasn't a doubt in my mind that he and I would spend the rest of our lives together. My fight against cancer had forced both of us to grow up faster than usual, which resulted in us openly discussing different aspects of our future that most teenagers wouldn't even be thinking about yet. Of all these topics, there was no doubt that the one closest to my heart was marriage.

"I've thought about it a lot Baby… about our future together. I love you more than anything and I already know I want to spend the rest of my life with you. I promise that when we're old enough… I'm going to marry you."

Jake was only seventeen when he made this promise, but it wasn't something he said simply because he knew I wanted to hear it. Don't get me wrong… I did, but his promise was so much more than words alone. He'd actually put a great deal of thought into how our future was going to become a reality. Jake had a plan.

"I finish year twelve at the end of next year, so I'm going to need a job. I've thought about university but it's going to be at least three years of study before I actually make any money. So I've decided the fastest way for me to make decent money and be able to provide you with the life you deserve, is to join the army."

I was thrilled that he had the same amount of enthusiasm and excitement about our future as I did. I have to say though; I was a little worried about his plan to join the military.

"If I work my ass off from now until the end of next year, I think I'll be able to get a good enough score in my Higher School Certificate to get into military college. But I've done some research, and even if I get the score I need there's a fairly intense selection process to get through as well. So I have decided to join the Army Reserves as soon as possible to get some experience and improve my chances of being accepted into college."

"Military college? Where is it?" I asked.

"All the training is done in Canberra at a place called Duntroon. The whole course goes for eighteen months."

"And it's hard to get into?"

"Apparently. That's why I think joining the reserves now is a good idea. It might give me an advantage during selection if I already have some military experience."

"So when do you think you will join the reserves?"

"Well since I'm already seventeen, I can apply whenever I want. I was thinking about doing the six weeks basic training over the school holidays at the end of this year. That way I will be able to do some time in the reserves and get some experience while I complete my last year of school."

"You'd be away for the entire six week holidays?" I was already dreading the fact that I wouldn't see him for so long.

He nodded. "I know it's a long time but it'd work in perfect with school. It will be hard to be away from you for so long and I know it will be tough on you too, but believe me… I'm thinking of the bigger picture. It'll be worth it."

"Tell me about the bigger picture," I prompted; unable to hide my eagerness to hear more.

I loved listening to Jake talk about our future. I trusted and believed in him with all my heart. He made me feel like my hopes of us being together forever were more than just dreams. They were going to come true, and he was going to make sure of it!

"If I get accepted into military college after year twelve, I'll spend eighteen months in training then graduate as a Lieutenant. I'll be an Officer in the Australian Army, which is a secure job and the money will be pretty good, considering I'll only be nineteen when I graduate…" he paused, his lips curling into a grin, "…and you need money if you want to start a family."

He'd only just finished his sentence and my cheeks were already killing me from the ridiculously large smile plastered across my face. Jake had *really* thought this through, and his comment about starting a family filled my heart with happiness. I was so overwhelmed I wanted to cry.

I'd always wanted to have children young, and it wasn't like Jake and I hadn't talked about it already, it's just that now we were actually making plans which made the dream seem more realistic than ever. I'm sure our parents would've been mortified if they knew Jake and I were discussing children, given that I was still only sixteen; but as I said, we'd grown up fast. I didn't even *feel* like a teenager anymore.

Jake always said he'd protect me and promised he would do everything he could to make sure I was happy. Even though he was only a teenager in year eleven at high school, he was so organised and determined. I already felt so secure with him, and deep down I knew he would keep me safe well into the future too. I believed every word he said; I definitely had no reason to ever doubt him, and in that moment I was certain I would be loved, looked after and provided for… for as long as I lived.

"That sounds amazing Jake. You really want to start a family young?"

"Of course I do Baby, but not until I know I can provide the best life for all of us."

I kissed him on the lips. "I wish you knew just how much I loved you."

"I already know Soph…" He grabbed hold of my wrist and held my hand against his chest, directly over his heart. "I can feel it."

Where did he come from? I felt so moved, almost overwhelmed by his gesture. It was beautiful.

"So what do you think? It's the best plan I've got at the moment. I know I won't be in the army forever but it will allow us to get married and start a family as soon as possible."

He could obviously see I was getting excited. Maybe it was the clapping hands which gave it away!

"It still might take two or three years by the time I finish year twelve, get accepted into military college and pass the course, but it will come around fast."

"I'm with you Jake. Whatever you decide is best for us… I'm in."

He wrapped his arms around me tightly in a warm embrace.

There was no question my battle with cancer and subsequent near death experience had affected both of us profoundly. Normal sixteen and seventeen year olds are talking about going to parties, sneaking into night clubs and getting drunk, but we were already passed all that. The ordeal Jake and I had been through had matured us in a matter of months. We weren't going to take anything for granted… especially time. He and I both understood how precious life was and how fast it could be taken away. We were determined to make every single day count. We knew what we wanted in life and now were planning how we were going to get it. To be honest, I already felt like Jake and I were married. We were already working together as a team and putting the best interests of each other first. From the moment I met Jake, all I ever wanted was for him to be happy and I trusted that he wanted the same for me too. He would not disappoint.

"I've done a lot of research on the army and what it takes to be a soldier. I don't want you to think this will be the easiest road. What I'm saying is, it will be the fastest and most secure to get us where we want to be. If we're going to do this, you have to understand it will mean some time apart."

"Jake." I said firmly. "Considering the test we have already gone through, the army will be a walk in the park. I know you'll have to go away sometimes, but if it means we can start our lives together sooner, then I'm willing to accept that. I can't say I will enjoy being apart but as you said, it won't be forever."

"Well apparently absence makes the heart grow fonder Baby. Besides, we've already been living in a long distance relationship since we got together."

"Jake… I couldn't get any *fonder* of you if I tried," I smiled.

He smiled back. "Well I guess that's that! I'll go into the recruiting office this week and find out exactly what I need to do to apply."

"Have you talked to your parents about it?"

"I've mentioned it to them and they think it's a good idea, which is great but to be honest, it was *your* approval I needed Soph. After all, it's *our* life we're talking about."

I don't know how he managed to do it, but every time he spoke I felt myself being drawn closer to him. It's a strange feeling, when you think you love someone with all your heart and soul, only to hear them say something which sweeps you off your feet and takes that love to a completely new high. Then just when you think you couldn't possibly love them anymore, they do it to you again.

It was a fairly brief conversation, and although we were taking the decisions we were making seriously, I don't think we fully appreciated the speed at which our lives were about to change.

The discussion we had about Jake joining the military happened after the most horrendous eighteen months of my life. The next three years however, would include some of the most amazing experiences I could've ever imagined, with a couple of struggles thrown in for good measure. The fairy tale I'd always dreamt of was fast becoming my reality.

You'd be forgiven for doubting the extent to which Jake mapped out our future at just seventeen, so it's important you understand what kind of person he was, particularly in terms of making plans and setting goals. I think it stemmed from the discipline, structure and focus of his martial arts training.

I remember him telling me about his instructor; a quietly spoken man who was very strict and traditional in his teachings. Jake would call him 'Shihan' and had enormous respect for him. Shihan must have seen something in Jake because he pushed him to his physical and mental limit, and at just fourteen, removed Jake from the junior classes and had him training a minimum of four nights a week with the men. It forced Jake's discipline and physical ability to extend far beyond that of a regular fourteen-year-old, so by the time he was seventeen, his level of maturity was extremely well developed. It explains why I never really saw Jake as a boy, because he had already been expected to behave and think as an adult for years.

I don't know if it was his martial arts training, or if he had it in him already, but the one trait he possessed which would ensure the success of every plan he set, was his determination. Jake was absolutely relentless in his pursuit of whatever goal he wanted to achieve; I could see it in him when we first met, and it has never left. This unrelenting determination and focus made it impossible not to believe in him, which is why I so willingly followed.

'Talk's cheap… actions count!' It's a saying Jake still uses to this day. He said he was going to protect and provide for me; give me everything I ever needed or wanted, and that's exactly what he set out to do.

True to his word, Jake applied and was accepted into the Army Reserves. He was due to go away to boot camp at the beginning of the school holidays. I remember saying goodbye to him before he left; it was horrible. His training would see us separated for the longest period of time since we started seeing each other.

A couple of days before he was due to leave, Jake stayed with me for a night at Shaun and Leah's place. I was doing some part time work at Leah's hair salon until I found a full time job, so I was staying at their house for a few weeks.

The entire night we were inseparable; talking about the past, the future and constantly maintaining physical contact. I felt like I was never going to see him again, and I wanted to get as much of him as I could before we had to say goodbye. Jake made love to me that night and I savoured every touch, taste, sound and feeling; letting every sensation and emotion burn into my memory so it would last me until I saw him again. It was as sad as it was beautiful, and burn into my memory it did. I've never forgotten our final night together before he left for the army.

It turned out that he would be gone for a total of forty-two days, which was actually *seven* weeks, not six as we first thought. Seven weeks away with very limited contact, even by phone. When Jake did have time to call, his entire platoon of more than thirty soldiers would have only half an hour or so to use the two available phones. As a result, calls were restricted to a couple of minutes so that everyone had a chance to ring their loved ones. For example, a call from Jake basically consisted of him telling me he was still alive, that he missed me and how much he loved me. He'd make sure I was ok and then he'd have to go. Jake told me there were people in his platoon who were struggling with being separated from family, especially the older recruits who had children. He didn't want to use up too much time on the phone, which meant they could talk longer with their wives and young children. I could tell he wanted to talk to me for hours like we always did, but knowing Jake, he would rather have seen his peers feeling better after talking with their wives and children; even at the expense of time talking to me.

I knew he missed me and his family, and even though he assured me everything was fine over the phone, I could sense that he wasn't finding boot camp easy. I knew Jake, and I could tell he was putting on one hell of a brave face to keep those feelings from me so that I wouldn't worry.

The most effective way for us to communicate was through letters. Jake described how his platoon would line up in the hallway of their barracks each night, ten minutes before lights out, and the platoon sergeant would read out the names of recruits who had received mail. He said it was the best feeling in the world when your name was read out, and he loved seeing the smiles on the faces of all those who had received a letter from their families.

"Some days were really tough and you wonder how you are going to get up the next day and do it all again. But whenever you got a letter from home, it gave you the strength to keep going and see it through to the end."

Jake told me this after arriving home. I only wish I knew how important my letters were because I would have sent one every single day.

I was spending a lot of time with Jake's family while he was away, often staying over for days at a time. Since it was school holidays, I hung out with his sisters almost every day that I wasn't working at the salon. It was so nice to be able to stay at Jake's place, even though he wasn't there, because just being in his house and around his family made me feel closer to him.

In my letters I'd always give him a rundown on what was happening at home, and quite often his sisters and I would all sit down and write letters to him at the same time. Alice, Kate and Samantha missed their big brother as well, and it was good to be able to talk about him with the girls. I think it made us feel like he wasn't so far away.

Here is one of the letters I sent Jake while he was at boot camp. It was only short but it let him know how much I was thinking about him.

29-12-98

Dear Jake,

Hello sexy, how are you. I'm doing ok, although I went to the pool today with Alice and Kate and got a little sunburnt.

I'm having a really good time with your sisters, but I wish you were home with me. I wake up in Kate's room and look down the hall to your room, but you're not in your bed. I miss you so much. When I see you, I'm going to give you the biggest hug and I'm not letting you go... ever!

I'm always thinking about you Jake. I love you, and don't forget it.

Oh yeah, your mum's having the carpets cleaned on Monday so we had to lift all the furniture up. But don't worry I got our condoms out of your room. Good thing I remembered... that would have been embarrassing!

(Jake used to hide his condoms under the bottom draw of his desk. His mum would have surely discovered them whilst moving all the furniture, if I hadn't remembered they were there and got to them first.)

By the way, whenever you ring me at home, make sure you reverse charge the call ok?

I also wanted to tell you that I'm going to the doctors on Wednesday because I'm going on the pill. I hope it doesn't make me FAT!

Well, not a lot has happened since Christmas and I've run out of things to say. So goodbye Baby, and remember how much I love you, and how proud of you I am.

Only 28 more days. That's not long.

Bye bye.

Love Sophie. XXOO

P.S. I'll send you a kiss goodnight.

(I put bright pink lipstick on and kissed the bottom of the page)

P.P.S. I Love U, I Love U, I Love U, I Love U, I Love U, I Love U, I Love U, I Love U, I Love U, I Love U, I Love U.

Jake only wrote a few letters to me because he was under such strict time constraints. Whenever we talked he would apologise for not writing to me, but explained it was because he was being run off his feet almost every minute of the day.

I did receive one particular letter, which was memorable to say the least. Memorable not only for its content but the way in which it was scribbled down, with heaps of crossed out words and sentences. It looked like a rough draught. He later told me that he only had a few spare minutes to write it and didn't have time for a good copy. I didn't mind at all though. I really appreciated how little spare time he must have had to write it for me. I don't know why, but this particular letter is so special to me. It's like he had this vision in his head, and had to get it down on paper and into the mail as fast as possible; mistakes and all. I could *feel* how desperately he wanted to get it to me and I loved it.

For ease of reading, I've neatened it up for you.

Sophie.

As droplets of warm water hit our naked bodies, our mouths and tongues embrace each other in a moist but tender wrestle. Our hands caress each other's bodies and gently touch the parts which are most sensitive to us.

The scent of love is in the air and our hearts beat simultaneously to a rhythm of passion. My mind is on fire as every square inch of my body feels the wetness of your mouth. I cannot put the amount of pleasure which fills my heart into words and as I stand back to view the beautiful female I have in front of me, I thank my lucky stars.

From the top of your head to the tips of your toes; my mouth tastes everything. The flavour and scent of the sweetest and most luscious part of your body excites me beyond belief.

As I become aroused due to the atmosphere we have created, we hold each other so close that we become one. With a slow and ever so gentle pulse, we move to an unstoppable rhythm. Our breaths become deeper and louder with every motion.

Although the shower has dampened our bodies, we have created a wetness that only lovers can understand. As our pace increases, you let out a quiet moan, almost a scream, as we reached the point of no return.

The ultimate climax draws near, until the split second where humans become animals arrives. Noises of passion fill the air until we have nothing left.

We hold each other on the shower floor and gaze into each other's eyes, never to part.

Love Jake.

I remember reading this letter countless times over; alone in my bedroom. The first time, I read it so fast I don't think any of it really sunk in. But reading it for the second time, slow and deliberate, I savoured every word. If Jake's intention was to make me miss him, want him, and *need* him, then he succeeded.

After reading the letter for the third time, I couldn't help but trail my hand down between my thighs. As I slid it into my underwear, I closed my eyes and pictured every detail of Jake's vision of us in the shower together. His words had served their purpose; I was wet and burning with the need for sexual release.

I lay back on my bed and held Jakes letter against my chest while I gently caressed *myself.* With my orgasm building, it was moments like these that I longed for my man the most. Of course I missed talking and laughing with Jake, and looking into his eyes, but as a sixteen-year-old girl with hormones racing through my body, there was no question what I craved most of all! It was making love to him… feeling him deep inside me… flooding my entire body with pleasure; pure and intense.

The feeling of my fingers sliding between my wet lips, combined with visions of Jake and I fucking, caused me to *arrive* within a couple of minutes. I raised my hips up off the bed and let myself go; a euphoric feeling raced through me as I climaxed.

I collapsed in a heap; relaxed and slightly breathless. I reached over to my beside table, grabbed a picture of Jake and gazed at it. It had been at least five weeks since I'd seen him and the emptiness I felt when we weren't together seemed to be growing by the day. I missed him so much that I couldn't help but cry.

With regards to him joining the military, I know I told Jake I was with him all the way, but I have to admit I was beginning to doubt whether I could handle being away from him for weeks, or maybe months at a time. I decided not to tell him how bad I was coping with him away at basic training. I knew if he thought I wouldn't handle the time apart then there was absolutely no way he'd sign up for full time military service like we planned, which would have caused our lives to take a very different course. I knew we had always promised to tell each other the truth, but on this occasion I was so glad I didn't raise the issue with him.

Eventually the end of Jake's time at boot camp had arrived. His family and I were going to the military base for his 'March out Parade'; a formal ceremony to mark the end of basic training. The parade would involve all the soldiers who'd passed the seven-week course. They would be dressed in their ceremonial uniforms and would march in formation to showcase the skills and training they'd mastered throughout the course; a display for family and friends.

I was so excited to see him again, and to be honest I had no idea how I would react at the sight of my man in uniform. My insides tingled at the thought.

I stayed over at Jake's house the night before the parade. I didn't sleep a wink… how could I?

When morning finally arrived, Jake's family and I all got up early. We raced around the house; eating breakfast, showering, getting dressed in our best clothes and doing our hair. I have to say I probably hogged the bathroom a little that particular morning because I wanted to look my best for Jake.

My hair had grown back and I was rocking a short blond look that I would style with bobby pins and hair gel. While I did my hair in the mirror, I wondered what Jake would look like with all his hair shaved off. The first time he called me from the base he mentioned how the barber had a huge smile on his face as he ran the clippers over his head, making short work of his shoulder length hair.

"I was the only male with long hair and the instructors couldn't wait to get me up to the barbers to shave it all off. I reckon it's pretty shit that all the girls got to keep their long hair, but I had to shave *my* head. Anyway, I was due for a change. Now I know how you felt when we had to cut all yours off."

I could picture Jake smiling while they cut his hair. I knew he would've been thinking about the day he had to shave mine. He would have seen the funny side of it, now the 'shoe was on the other foot'.

Once we were all ready, we piled into the minivan and headed off to the Army Recruit Training Centre. It was a little over an hour and a half drive to the base, and by the time we drove through the gates of the army barracks I was bursting with excitement. I think I was actually bouncing in my seat! I couldn't bear to wait another minute to throw my arms around my *lover*.

The army base was massive, and as we drove passed huge brick accommodation blocks, old army tanks and artillery guns on display around the grounds, you could feel the energy in the place. Seeing a group of soldiers running in step with an instructor barking commands at them made the hairs on my arms stand up. But it wasn't until I saw a bunch of soldiers doing push-ups out in a large grass field, that it felt like I had stepped into a movie. I was overwhelmed and actually a touch scared about being on the base. *This place is serious!*

I thought about Jake arriving on the bus on his first day. How scared he must have been driving up the road we were now on; not knowing what to expect, the realisation that he couldn't leave fast becoming a reality. I hoped he had been as strong and confident as he had sounded during our phone calls. I prayed it wasn't just for my piece of mind.

Greg followed the temporary signs marked 'March-out Parade' until we arrived at an enormous bitumen square which looked like a shopping mall car park without the parking space lines. It was perfectly smooth and clean, and must have been the size of at least two football fields. There was a knee high fence, made from a single strand of thick chain which ran the entire way around the outside perimeter, and on each corner was a show piece of military equipment. I remember one of them was a huge tank with the gun pointing out at a forty-five-degree angle, like it was protecting the parade ground. At one end was a grandstand for the audience, and in front of that grandstand was a stage with stairs leading up each side to a lectern and a number of chairs for the dignitaries. It was such an impressive location; the atmosphere of the place was like nothing I'd ever felt before.

All of us were talking and pointing out things we'd noticed. We were so excited and I could tell Jake's sisters were busting to see their big brother as much as I was. I could hear it in their voices.

There were men in uniform directing the traffic to the designated car park at the back of the grandstand. We piled out of the car and hastily made our way to the grandstand, which was already filling up fast. As we sat down, I looked around and noticed there were heaps of women who all had the same huge smile on their faces that I did. Most were older than me, but I knew exactly how they were all feeling. They too had spent the last seven weeks away from their lovers, and the anticipation and excitement of finally being reunited with them again was clearly visible. There were also heaps of older people, parents and grandparents, dressed in their best suits and dresses; looking so proud and excited. It was an amazing energy which filled the air.

There were quite a few young children in the stands, and I wondered how hard it must have been for them to be without their fathers for the past couple of months. I smiled knowing how anxious they must have been to see their daddy's marching in the parade.

Like all the other guests, we had arrived well ahead of time. We were seated for about twenty minutes when a voice came over the PA system, informing us the parade was about to begin. The crowd quietened down and looked out over the parade ground. Despite the fact that everybody was bursting with anticipation, you could have heard a pin drop.

Then we heard a loud voice coming from the trees behind the parade ground, about one hundred meters away. "Alpha Companyyyyy! Atteeeeennnnntion!" The Parade Commanders orders were loud and drawn out. "By the right! Quuuuuiiiiick!"

Then six loud beats of a drum; *BOOM BOOM BOOM... BOOM BOOM BOOM!*

The hairs on the back of my neck stood on end and a shiver ran through me like a pure shot of adrenaline. I looked at Jake's sisters, with their huge smiles and wide eyes; I knew they could feel it too.

The sounds of a brass band roared to life with a traditional marching band instrumental piece. Within seconds, I could see the first few soldiers emerge from behind the trees and onto the parade ground. One was holding the Australian Flag and he had two soldiers, both armed with rifles, marching beside him as though they were his body guards. The flag rippled in the breeze and I couldn't help but feel a deep sense of pride and patriotism wash over me.

Following the flag bearers was the band. There were at least twenty brass instruments and a variety of drums; snares and bass. I loved how the sun shone brightly off the polished metal as every band member marched in step. I was amazed at how they could play their instrument and walk in perfect unison so effortlessly.

Next in the formation, and the soldiers everybody had been waiting for, were the recruits. They were the newest members of the Australian Army, and *my* Jake was among them. The soldiers marched in perfect formation; a sight which resembled a huge green caterpillar worming its way out from behind the trees and onto the parade ground. A lump formed in my throat at the sheer sight of them, and knowing Jake was part of such a perfect moment in time was incredible. The parade commander shouted directions so loud he could be heard over the music of the band; the 'caterpillar' responding to his every command.

Jake said there were three platoons of thirty soldiers marching out, and that he would be in the last group. My eyes strained; searching for him among the sea of khaki green uniforms. The three groups of thirty were evenly spaced, one behind the other, with a leading officer out in front; sword unsheathed and held firmly. It was almost impossible to single Jake out from such a distance, when every soldier was marching in time and with perfect posture. They looked so well-ordered and coordinated; almost robotic.

The soldiers made their way along the far side of the parade ground then turned towards the grandstand. As they walked towards us in files of three, I could slowly begin to make out individual faces. People in the crowd were all pointing out loved ones. 'There he is!' and 'I can see her!', was repeated over and over.

The formation made a right turn and began to march parallel with the grandstand, about thirty or so meters in front of us. I looked at the corner; scanning for Jake's face as each trio made the ninety degree turn. As I briefly glanced at each individual face I could feel my level of excitement building, to the point where I was actually holding my breath. Then finally… I saw him.

I gasped at the sight of my *angel*, and in that second every other soldier on the parade ground vanished. It was as if I had tunnel vision. All I could see, in crystal clear focus, was him; everybody else was a blur. I couldn't take my eyes off him… not for a second. I heard Jake's sisters announcing in turn when they saw him, but my focus didn't waiver; my gaze transfixed, like a moth to a light.

"Alpha Companyyyyy… halt!" The caterpillar stopped instantly.

"Leeeeeft… turn!" Every soldier in the formation executed a perfect turn on the spot; stamping their foot down in unison.

Jake was now facing towards me, although he didn't make eye contact. Instead he stared straight forward, as though hypnotised. I studied his face under his hat, which had one side turned up displaying a polished gold 'Rising Sun' badge; a shiny silver badge adorned the front. His long hair was gone; replaced with short back and sides. He looked so serious and committed, like he was ready for something… anything. I wanted so badly to run out onto the parade ground and throw my arms around him. Having him so close yet being unable to touch him felt painfully cruel.

He was in the front row so I could clearly see his entire body; immaculately dressed in his ceremonial uniform. His black boots were highly polished; khaki polyester pants fitted and pressed like they were made for him. Pulled tight around his waist was a black belt with shiny brass buckles, his shirt was pressed and worn to perfection and strapped to Jake's right shoulder was a black and grey rifle. He was a vision, absolutely flawless, and I couldn't believe my eyes. I'd always looked at Jake as a man, but seeing him like this, I now had a totally new appreciation of how much of a man he'd become. Many times I had wondered what Jake would look like in a uniform, and how I would feel when I saw him. Now I knew. He looked hot, and as for how I felt… turned on… ridiculously!

I watched for any indication that Jake noticed me, but his intensive stare did not falter.

"Preseeeeennnnnt… arms!" The Parade Commander barked orders, requiring the soldiers to present their rifles in a salute to high ranking officers, who made their way onto the parade ground in cars escorted by military police on motorbikes.

Jakes focused and somewhat cold expression didn't change. I wanted him to look around, to try and find me in the crowd and make eye contact; signalling that he knew I was there, but he didn't. His eyes remained fixed to the front, like he was looking into nothing. He was so disciplined and I wondered if everybody was the same, so I scanned the other soldiers on the parade ground. Many of them looked straight forward as Jake did, but some were looking around with their eyes, even though their heads remained still. I started to feel unnerved by his focus. It was like I could *see* him, but the Jake *I* knew wasn't there. I started to worry that maybe he'd changed.

He was always so warm and sensitive. He was passionate and able to express his emotions freely, which is why I loved him so much. But what I was seeing now, the blank emotionless stare, suddenly made me consider the possibility that maybe his training had toughened him up to a point where he'd try to suppress those kinds of feelings. The more I looked at him the more I was afraid that the thing I loved most of all, his soft and gentle nature, may have changed.

The first part of the parade went for maybe fifteen minutes; all the official guests had arrived and were seated. The MC announced that the parade would now do a 'March Past', which would involve each platoon saluting the Commandant as they marched past the centre stage. He was the highest ranked officer on the base.

As the caterpillar started to move again, Jake still hadn't made eye contact with me. *Will he ever look at me!* I was anxious and starting to feel a little upset that he hadn't seen me yet.

The formation slowly made their way past the Commandant. Each platoon was given the command 'Eyes Right' and every soldier would snap their heads to the side; looking in the direction of the stage and the grandstand of family members. The Commandant would salute them in return.

The flag bearers, the band and the first two platoons had passed. Noticing how they all had to look in the direction of the crowd, I was sure Jake would see me now. As his platoon started their 'march past', I had my eyes fixed firmly on him. The Platoon Commander called 'Eyes Right!' and the soldiers turned their heads sharply. Instantly, Jake's eyes found mine; he knew exactly where I was all along. My heart pounded in my chest and I gave him the biggest smile I could muster; so wide it hurt my cheeks. I felt my eyes well up as he stared back at me. Making eye contact after so long caused tears to build and I tried desperately to fight them back. For a split second his lips curled into a cheeky smile, before his stare turned to the Commandant. It was only a few seconds, but the way he looked into my eyes was all the proof I needed to know that my *Baby* hadn't changed at all.

The parade went for another half an hour or so. The Commandant gave a short speech and some of the soldiers were called out to receive different awards. After the Commandant marched down the ranks and inspected all the recruits, the official guests exited via escorted cars, just as they'd arrived. I thought the soldiers were going to be dismissed straight away and allowed to reunite with their families, but much to my disappointment, they were all marched off the parade ground and back to their barracks. The MC announced that all the family and friends were to make their way to the 'Other Ranks Mess', the formal name for the dining hall, where we would be joined by the soldiers.

Jake's family and I made our way back to the car. We were all buzzing with excitement as Greg followed the long line of cars up to the OR's mess. It sounded like everybody was talking at once.

"I'm so proud of him," said Mary. I could hear the pride in her voice.

"Me too," Samantha added.

"Jake looked so grown up didn't he?" stated Kate.

"I couldn't believe how he didn't look around at all. I only seen him look at us when they marched past," said Alice.

"Yeah I was waiting for him to look over and see us too," I added. "Did you all see him smile at us?" I knew he was smiling at me, but hey… I'm not selfish.

"Yep! I saw him smile!" beamed Samantha. She was so proud of her brother; his whole family were proud of him.

Greg commented on the discipline and practice to be able to march perfectly in such a large formation. "They must have spent hours and hours out there marching around in the sun."

It was January and the past few weeks had been scorchers; over 40°C on some days. I can only imagine how unpleasant it must have been; practicing in the sun on the hot, black bitumen.

We parked the car and headed into the mess. The building was huge and immediately felt very *Army*. Everything was clean and polished, and the walls featured a number of military paintings along with other interesting pieces of memorabilia. There were already a couple of hundred people inside waiting for the arrival of their loved ones.

In the centre of the room was a long table full of cakes and sandwiches for morning tea, and on each end were a couple of huge urns of hot water for tea and coffee. While we waited for Jake, his parents and the girls had something to eat and drink. I was so excited that I couldn't stomach a thing. Alice did bring me back a glass of iced water though, which was appreciated considering how dry my mouth was.

Soon we heard someone yelling commands out the front of the building. I knew instantly that the soldiers had arrived. *Jake will be walking through the doors any moment.*

I couldn't make out any of the commands, except for one… a loud and clear 'Dismissed!', followed by cheers and whistles from all the soldiers.

Moments later soldiers started pouring in through the front doors of the mess. Family and friends rushed over to embrace the men and women they'd missed for so long. I scanned the crowd intently, searching for my *love*.

"There he is!" yelled Samantha as she bolted out into the crowd.

Jake opened his arms and she jumped up and hugged her brother. Sam was cuddling him so tight that she looked like she was going to squeeze the air out of him. Jake was unable to hold the tears back and unashamedly let them fall down his cheeks. A lump formed in my throat at the sight of his open display of emotion. *My soft hearted angel.*

Samantha missed Jake so much, she'd talked about him constantly while he was away. I was glad she was the first to wrap her arms around him because it really was such a beautiful moment; unforgettable.

Jake kept walking towards us, still holding his little sister in his arms. Sam was holding her feet up off the ground so he couldn't put her down. As we stared at each other, I could already feel tears trickling from my eyes.

As soon as he put Sam down I didn't wait a second longer. I rushed over to him; throwing my arms around his neck and squeezing him as hard as I could. Jake held me firmly against his chest. I tilted my head back and paused for a second to look into the beautiful blue eyes I'd been longing to see, then I kissed him passionately. The feeling of his lips against mine was incredible, and even though we had an audience I couldn't help but open my mouth; our tongues briefly reuniting.

Slowly, our lips unlocked. "Hey stranger," he smiled as he wiped a tear from my cheek with his thumb.

"God I missed you Jake. I missed you like crazy!" I gasped, still slightly out of breath from the 'knee weakening' kiss.

"Believe me, I missed you too Baby," he confessed before kissing me again.

The rest of Jake's family had been waiting patiently, so I thought I'd better let him go so he could give them all a kiss and a cuddle. Every member of the family had red eyes from tears of joy. Greg and

Mary had their boy back and the girls had their big brother again. We were all emotional, in the best possible way.

Once Jake was reunited with his parents and sisters, I moved back in and held him again. We were all crowded around him.

"Like my hair cut?"

"You look so different," said Kate.

"I love it Jake," I said, running my hand up the back of his head; my fingers coursing through the freshly shaven hair.

"You look like you could run all day," said Greg. "Have you lost a bit of weight?"

"Yeah I've definitely lost some muscle. All we ever seemed to do was run so I feel pretty lean."

I studied Jake's face and noticed he did look somewhat drawn in the cheeks.

"We just finished a field exercise too, so I'm pretty tired and worn out. Once I get home and back into some weights… and Mums cooking, I should be back to normal pretty soon," he smiled affectionately at Mary.

"The parade was so good Jake. You all must have practiced that a thousand times?" quizzed Mary

"It *felt* like a thousand times! They called it 'Drill Practice'. Standing on that parade ground in the midday sun was a killer. Even though we had drink breaks every fifteen minutes or so, people were still suffering with heat stroke."

"Did you get sick at all?" asked Samantha.

"No Sam, I made sure I drank heaps and heaps of water so I was pretty good. A few times I thought I was a bit dehydrated but I made sure to drink plenty as soon as I had a chance."

"You look like one of the youngest to march out. How did you go with the training compared to the older guys?" Greg asked as he surveyed the room; noticing that most of the other recruits were in their early twenties or older.

"To be honest Dad, all the physical stuff wasn't too bad; compared to some of the sessions I've done at karate. The weapons training and shooting was ok too. The main areas I struggled with were navigation and signals, but I got the hang of them both in the end."

"What were the other people like? Did you make any friends?" asked Kate.

"Yeah, some of the guys were really good fun and I like them a lot. It was a bit hard on the weekends though, when the bar would be open. Since I'm under age, I wasn't allowed to go up with them. A few of the other cadets who were under eighteen risked it and went up any way, but this place was bad enough without getting into trouble so I didn't go. I preferred to stay at the barracks with some of the other guys who weren't into a lot of drinking."

We stayed at the function for another half an hour or so; enough time to have a little more to eat and drink, and talk with Jake about his training. We also filled him in on what had been going on at home, since he'd missed Christmas, new years and the entire school holidays.

Jake introduced us to a couple of friends he'd made, and in turn they introduced their families. Surprisingly, all the soldiers who Jake talked with were a lot older than him; some already with wives and children. I guessed they were passed the whole 'getting drunk' stage, so I figured that's who he would spend his time with instead of going to the bar on Saturday nights. It filled me with relief to know he had made close friends, which would have made the seven weeks training far more enjoyable.

"I'll just say a quick goodbye to some of the other guys and we'll be able to go," said Jake.

I could tell he was well and truly ready to head home.

"What about your gear?" queried Greg.

"I've got it all packed and ready to go. After I say goodbye to a few people, I'll head back to my room and get it. Did you park just up the hill?" Jake pointed in the direction of the car park as he spoke.

"Yeah. We'll start heading to the car and meet you there."

"Sounds good Dad. Give me about fifteen minutes."

I squeezed his hand. I didn't want to let him go again.

Jake looked at me with reassuring eyes. "I won't be long Baby. I promise I'll go as fast as I can. See you in a minute ok?"

"Ok." I hugged him again and kissed him on the cheek.

"Geez… he'll only be fifteen minutes!" sighed Samantha.

We all laughed. She was still so young and didn't quite understand just how much I'd missed her brother. The rest of his family did though.

I let go of him and watched as he disappeared into the crowd of people; instantly feeling anxious the moment he was out of sight.

We left the mess hall and started to walk up the footpath to the car park. I listened as they all talked about the events of the day, and how different Jake looked, but I barely spoke a word. I know it was silly, but I had this unwarranted feeling of anxiety. I knew he wasn't going to be long, but I couldn't relax until he was back with me.

We waited for Jake in the shade of one of the large trees which surrounded the car park. I had a clear view down the road and the direction he would be returning from. I waited in silence, staring down the road scanning for him. I was so impatient.

Before long I spotted him walking up the footpath towards us. I knew he could see us but I waved to him anyway, though he didn't wave back as he was carrying two large bags of gear; one in each hand. Watching him walk towards me on his own, in uniform, was a sight to behold. I had to remind myself that he was actually *mine*, and I must confess, I couldn't wait to *show* him how much I missed him.

We all piled into the minivan and headed off on our journey home.

"I can't believe I'm finally going home," said Jake as the car drove out of the front gates of the base.

He held my hand firmly. I was so happy to be taking him back with us.

As Greg drove down the highway towards Sunbury, Jake told us a few stories about life at boot camp; many of them had us all in fits of laughter. There was absolutely no doubt he'd experienced a lot over the last few months, and I was filled with gratitude that he'd completed the first part of 'our' plan; just as he said he would.

Once we arrived home, Jake and I went into his room to unpack all his gear. It gave the two of us our first opportunity to be alone. As soon as we reached his bedroom, out of sight from the rest of his family, we embraced and kissed each other feverishly. I could feel the sexual tension in the air; the result of seven long weeks apart. I was overflowing with an insatiable lust for my man, and wanted nothing more than to rip his clothes off and throw him on the bed; to ravish him right then and there.

"Oh Jake… I missed you like crazy," I whispered between kisses. "I want you *so* bad." The suffering could be heard in my voice. I squeezed my thighs together in an attempt to smother the intense ache resonating from my groin.

"I want you too Baby. It's all I've thought about every single night since I left. Your naked body… making love to you. I can't wait."

I slowly and deliberately pushed my pelvis against him; grinding against his thigh.

"Stop it Soph," he whispered softly.

"Why? What's wrong?" I grinned mischievously; knowing full well that my advances were working him up.

Jake inhaled deeply and closed his eyes. "You're killing me."

"Killing you? I don't know what you mean," I giggled.

"Do you have any idea how horny I am?"

"Actually I do. I know *exactly* how you feel." I continued to grind against him.

"I don't think you do. I bet you looked after yourself a few times when you were alone in your bed at night." He raised his eyebrows as if to say, 'Go on… tell me the details'.

"I'm a good girl. I'd never do such a thing," I replied coyly.

"Yeah right Sophie. I know you, and there's no way you went all this time without…" he lowered his voice even further, "…playing with that beautiful pussy of yours."

I blushed as I watched his lips whisper the 'P' word; *mine* instantly moistening at the sound.

"How rude!" I scolded playfully; unable to hide my tell-tale smile.

Jake *did* know me, and truth be told I'd lost count of the amount of times I'd masturbated while he was away.

"And what about you?" I enquired; poking him in the stomach with my index finger.

"What about me?"

"Did you… you know?" I performed a 'wanking' gesture with my hand which made him laugh out loud.

"Not even once!" he replied proudly. "Honestly I didn't have the privacy, time or desire. Remember I've been living with a bunch of blokes for the past couple of months which far from put me in the mood."

"So you're a bit randy then?" I teased.

"Like you have no idea Baby! I hope you're not expecting an amazing performance tonight because I'm pretty sure I'll be over and done as soon as I get a whiff of you."

I burst into laughter. "Awe you poor thing. Don't stress, I'll completely understand if you *go* a bit early. As long as I have you I'll be more than satisfied."

"Well I promise I'll do my best," he smiled.

We stopped cuddling and started to unpack his gear; all the while laughing and joking about how sexually frustrated we were. It wasn't long before we had to change the topic though, as Kate and Sam ventured into the room to talk with us.

Now I know so far my story has included some hot and sexy chapters, and I'd love to tell you when I snuck into Jake's room that night we reunited by making passionate love for hours, but unfortunately that would be stretching the truth. After all, my story is real, and the reality was that Jake was a hormone fuelled seventeen-year-old who hadn't had an orgasm for over seven weeks. The joke he made about finishing as soon as he got a 'whiff' of me wasn't far off.

After dinner we spent a few hours in the lounge room talking with his parents and sisters. It was late in the evening and I could tell Jake was getting weary. He wasn't the only one either. Mary yawned loudly, took a final sip of her tea then announced that it was time we all went to bed.

Once I was in bed on Alice's floor, I waited as per usual so I could be pretty sure Jake's family would all be asleep. I knew I wouldn't have to wait long as it had been a big day with plenty of emotion and excitement; everyone was exhausted.

I quietly crept into his room and closed the door behind me. Jake had drawn his blind halfway so the room was dimly lit by the moonlight shining through the window. I could see him lying in bed.

"You still awake Baby?" I whispered.

"Of course," he replied; throwing the sheet back so I could climb in beside him.

I snuggled into him, rested my head against his chest and closed my eyes. It felt so good to be able to listen to the beat of his heart again. I felt so safe and protected.

"You smell good," Jake said as he nuzzled my hair and inhaled deeply. "I've missed your smell so much."

"What else have you missed?" I whispered suggestively.

"Do I even need to say it?"

"Yes Jake, I want you to tell me *exactly* what you've missed."

"Well… I've missed your eyes."

I looked up at him and batted my eyelids. He kissed them in turn.

"And…" I prompted.

"Your mouth… I've definitely missed your mouth."

He lightly kissed me on the lips.

"Yes… and…"

"I've missed your lips… and your tongue."

He kissed me again, this time licking my lips gently before slowly pushing his tongue inside my mouth. I sucked it firmly before lightly biting down; holding him in place momentarily before releasing him.

"What else?"

"Your legs… your beautiful legs."

Jake's hands slowly made their way down the side of my body to my legs. I was only wearing underwear and a singlet which allowed him to gently stroke my bare legs with his fingertips. I closed my eyes as my pelvic floor muscles contracted. It felt so good, and as each second passed I was getting more turned on; my breathing deep and clearly audible.

"Want to know what else I've missed?" he whispered; his tender caress venturing towards my inner thigh.

"Yes… tell me Jake," I breathed. I was already on the brink.

"Are you *sure* you want to know?" he teased.

"Yes!" I demanded; uncontrollably grinding my pelvis against him.

"Your soft, perky breasts… and those pretty pink nipples."

He slid his hand under my singlet and gently squeezed one of my breasts before delicately pinching my nipple between his fingers.

I groaned with pleasure.

"You like that Baby?"

"Love it," I gasped, as a jolt of sensual pleasure shot straight down to my groin.

He moved from one breast to the other; repeating the torturous nipple teasing which instantly caused the wonderful tingle between my legs to intensify.

"There was one thing I *really* missed though. Do you know what it was?"

"I've got a fair idea," I said as I grasped his hand and put it between my legs. I knew he'd be able to feel how wet I was because my knickers were completely soaked through.

"Fuck!" he gasped. "You're so wet."

"You miss that Baby?"

"Oh god yeah." He nestled into my neck and bit down softly.

"Then touch me."

He didn't need to be told twice; hastily pulling my knickers to the side then sliding a finger deep inside me.

"Oh fuck!" I exhaled; my hips involuntarily thrusting forward to meet his touch.

Jake slid a second finger inside; curling them up and rubbing my g-spot with perfect pressure, which instantly delivered me to the brink of orgasm.

"I'm going to come Jake!" I whispered loudly. My admission prompting him to slightly increase both pressure and tempo; forcing my body to let go. I bit down on my bottom lip to stop myself from crying out as I released my erogenous syrup around his fingers.

Jake gently massaged and tickled my pussy; carefully pinching my lips between his fingers and playing in my juices while he gave me a few moments to recover.

"I want you Soph… now!"

I reached down and grabbed hold of his straining cock through his boxer shorts.

"What are you waiting for then?" I challenged.

Jake ripped the covers off and threw them on the floor. We usually made love on the floor since it was quieter than his bed. He knelt down and I stood directly in front of him, before sliding my underwear down to my ankles; his eyes immediately fixating on my exposed pussy. I stepped out of my knickers and stood with my feet apart; giving him all the access he needed. Without hesitation, he buried his face between my legs and began licking feverishly at my wetness. He darted his tongue in and out of my tunnel before licking the entire length of my slit; long and slow. The roughness of his taste buds as they ran over my clit almost brought me undone again.

As good as it felt to have his mouth on me again, I needed him inside me… fast! I turned around then climbed down on all fours; tilting my hips up so my ass and pussy was angled directly towards him.

I looked over my shoulder at Jake. I could clearly see how turned on he was by the fiery glare in his eyes. "Fuck me Jake!" I ordered sternly. This wasn't the time for making love.

He reached under his pillow and grabbed a condom. I'd told him earlier that although I was on the pill, I needed to wait a few weeks for it to be effective. He ripped the packet and rolled the condom on. I was still looking behind me and couldn't help but smile when I noticed how Jake hadn't taken his eyes of my pussy as she waited patiently; open and inviting.

"I'll hold off for as long as I can Baby."

"I don't care… just fuck me!" I snapped harshly.

I was so turned on, and I knew I'd be ready to 'go' as soon as Jake was.

He positioned himself behind me and grabbed my hips firmly with both hands. I felt his tip lightly touch my opening, then in one smooth push… he filled me. My eyes rolled back in my head as my insides wrapped around his hardness. *Heaven!*

"Damn that feels good!" I moaned.

As soon as my lover started thrusting, I felt his cock throb inside me. I let my orgasm build almost instantaneously and did my best to hold onto it while I waited for his release.

Within a minute or so, I felt his grip tighten on my hips, and I winced as his erection strained inside me. He was so hard I thought it was going to tear me apart. Even though I'd masturbated while Jake was away, it had been a long time since I'd had anything *inside* me. I'd forgotten how much his cock would 'thicken' right before he blew, and was now receiving a very detailed reminder.

The intensity of his thrusts increased; it was time. I took a deep breath and held it to prevent a high pitch squeal from waking up, not just the house, but the entire neighbourhood. Jake exploded in orgasm; my hips jolted back and forth as I climaxed with him. I could feel his dick contracting over and over again as he came; pumping with such force that I was surprised his load didn't bust a hole in the condom! It was an absolutely glorious sensation, so intense that all I could think was '*Don't scream... don't scream*!' as my body pulsed and quivered with pleasure.

It was such a hard and fast orgasm that I was left panting; completely out of breath. I collapsed on my stomach with Jake still deep inside me; his cock as hard as steel, like he hadn't even climaxed.

"Don't move," I gasped breathlessly. It had been so long since Jake and I had united as one. I wanted to savour our post coital bliss just a little longer.

He laid down on top of me, resting his chest against my back as he too caught his breath. "Well I'm pretty sure that was a world record!" he joked, referring to the fact our entire fuck had lasted no more than two minutes.

I started laughing, and the contraction of my stomach muscles automatically started to force *him* out of me; a less than pleasant feeling which made us laugh even more. We quickly reduced our outburst to a quiet chuckle.

I reached behind me and pushed his hips back; completely disengaging from him. Jake rolled over and collapsed beside me. I turned onto my side to face him.

"Sorry Baby, I..."

I put my finger against his lips; extinguishing his sentence.

"Don't even say it Jake... it was perfect," I smiled appreciatively. "I'm actually surprised you lasted *that* long!" I giggled.

"To tell you the truth... so am I," he beamed.

He gave me an affectionate smile then snuggled his head against my chest. I ran my fingers up the back of his head and through his hair; a gesture which caused him to moan softly. It was his favourite.

"You spoil me," he breathed.

"Shhh... just enjoy it Baby," I whispered. "Relax and enjoy it."

My *angel* was home again, cradled in my arms; back where he belonged. I never wanted to let him go again.

CHAPTER TWENTY

YES

A couple of weeks after Jake returned from boot camp, I decided to have a party out at the farm to celebrate my seventeenth birthday. There were about thirty guests in all, including Kylie and Sara, both of whom I hadn't seen since quitting school. I'd missed so much time from school due to my battle with Hodgkin's disease that I never went back, even after my cancer treatment had finished.

Jake had borrowed his parent's minivan and brought out his sister Alice and three of his friends from school. As soon as they arrived and everybody had been introduced, I took Jake aside and quickly whispered a little secret in his ear which I knew would drive him wild the entire night.

I wrapped my arms around him and put my mouth next to his ear, "Guess what Baby?" I whispered; my voice soft and seductive.

"What?"

"I don't know if I should tell you," I teased.

"What is it?" he pleaded.

"Well… let's just say it's no big deal if you forgot to bring condoms out with you."

"Are you serious?" he replied excitedly.

"My pill should be working now, so next time we're together it will be skin on skin!"

His expression was worth a thousand words. I could instantly tell by the look in his eyes that he couldn't wait to get me alone… neither could I.

My seventeenth birthday party was a lot of fun. Dad made a huge bon fire and we all spent most of the night outside under the stars, laughing and joking around the warmth of the fire.

Over the course of the night, Jake and I snuck away from the party three times; retreating to the privacy of my bedroom to make love, which was actually more like fast, hot, frantic sex. We were never gone for more than five minutes at a time, so I was pretty sure nobody noticed. I guess the feeling of being inside me without the usual latex barrier between us was a huge turn on for Jake. That, combined with the fact we'd only slept together once since his return from boot camp meant he simply couldn't get enough of me. And when he did, the 'skin on skin' sensation was obviously incredible for him, because each time he would climax within minutes. Admittedly, he wasn't the only one who was insatiable. The feeling of Jake firing deep inside me, one hot climax after another, drove me absolutely wild and I was instantly addicted to the sensation of keeping a part of him with me after making love. I couldn't believe how something which already felt so good could possibly feel any better, and I vowed then and there to never go back to using condoms.

We slept together twice more that night, after everyone had fallen asleep in the early hours of the morning. I was amazed at how fast he was recovering after each passionate session, and it was a fascinating and powerful feeling to know I had such an effect on him. I was so glad I'd managed to convince my parents to let me go on the pill some weeks earlier.

The next day I was completely exhausted, and a little bit tender to say the least. I suppose five sessions in the space of twelve hours or so will do that!

It was without question the best birthday I could have ever imagined, and as it turns out, Jake and I weren't as covert as we'd thought. Most of my friends *had* noticed our sneaky disappearances after all!

Even though I'd spent a few weeks living with Shaun and Leah, the day after my birthday marked the official day I left home. I moved out to live with a couple of school mates in Sunbury; Tim and Charlie. I had talked to Jake at length regarding his thoughts about me sharing a unit with a couple of guys from school. Obviously I wouldn't have moved in with them if it bothered Jake, but he was supportive of the whole idea.

"I trust you Soph, and I think it's a great idea to move into town. That means you'll be able to start looking for a job since you don't want to go back to school. Plus I'll be able to see you all the time."

I was so grateful for the trust and freedom he gave to me so willingly. I don't know too many guys who would be happy with their girlfriend living with two eighteen-year-old boys!

I never felt like Jake was overprotective, but he did mention that even though *I* had known Tim and Charlie since the beginning of high school and trusted them, it didn't mean *he* did.

"I know what guys are like Sophie. Living with two of them means you should still be on the lookout for any flirting or unwanted advances… which could result in a problem," as he put it. "Just make sure the boys understand how much you mean to me, and what I'd do for you."

Although Jake didn't elaborate, I read between the lines. I sensed by the tone of his voice and the protective look in his eye that he wouldn't hesitate to sort out any 'problems' if my house mates over stepped the line. I'm pleased to say though, the entire time I lived with the boys neither of them made a move on me. Unfortunately, there were a few other aspects to their domestic habits which drove me out of my mind, but I suppose that's what you get when you live with a couple of teenage guys.

Moving into town was a good idea because within a week or so I managed to get a full time job at a clothing store. Jake and I were both so excited to be able to see each other whenever we wanted. It felt amazing to be feeling healthy, earning some money and having the freedom to do what I wanted, whenever I wanted. Life was good.

Jake's final year of high school was a balancing act between his HSC studies, part time job at a local supermarket, Army Reserves training… and me.

He was so disciplined throughout the course of that year; especially with his studies. Sure we went to a few parties and had some fun, but Jake knew it was important for us that he achieved a high enough score to get him into military college. Even turning eighteen and being able to go to nightclubs and pubs didn't distract him. I can only ever remember him going out maybe two or three times with some of his friends who were also eighteen. I can't say I liked the idea of him out on the town without me, but there was no way I wasn't going to give him my approval when he was letting me share a house with two guys!

I remember what it was like when I visited Jake while he was studying. If he had some school work to do he would set his watch for one hour intervals; spending an hour with me then an hour alone in his room at his desk. I would hang out with his sisters while I waited for his one-hour study blocks to finish. Jake hated locking himself away to study when he knew I was so close, usually right next door in Alice's room, but he would always tell me he had to keep focused on the bigger picture.

His regimented approach to study, his part time job and Army Reserve training was working. Jake was doing well at school and was on track to achieving the marks he needed for military college.

I remember being at Jake's house one afternoon when Mary called out to let me know I had a phone call. It was very unusual; nobody but my parents had ever called me at my boyfriend's house before.

"Hello, Sophie Taylor speaking."

"Hi Sophie," a friendly woman's voice replied. "I was just talking with your parents and they gave me this number to reach you. I'm a representative of 'Challenge', which is a charity organisation that was set up to help children fighting cancer."

"Oh I know about Challenge. They gave me some concert tickets when I was having chemo."

"That's fantastic. Well as you know, we help sick kids out with entertainment while they're in hospital; like celebrity visits from singers, actors and sports personalities. And for kids who are well enough to spend some time out of hospital, we also organise concert tickets and passes to sporting events; like we did for you."

I was listening intently. "So what can I do for you?" I asked.

"Well, every child who was a patient at the Royal Children's Hospital over the past twelve months went into a secret raffle, and your name was one of the tickets to be drawn out."

Now I was really intrigued. I'd never won anything major before and I thought maybe I'd won some concert tickets or something cool like that.

"But I'm not in hospital anymore. I stopped treatment about five or six months ago."

"That's ok Sophie, you're still eligible to claim your prize. Many of the children in the raffle have recovered from their illnesses, but all patients go into the draw regardless. By the way, congratulations on being in remission," she added sincerely.

"Thank you, it's a good feeling."

"I can only imagine. So would you like to know what you've won?"

"Sure!" I replied eagerly. I could barely contain my excitement.

Jake had come out to see who I was talking to. He was standing there smiling at me; obviously amused by my overly excited expression.

"Well I'm pleased to say, you've actually been one of ten people to win a ticket on our major annual holiday called 'The Trip of a Lifetime'. It's an all-expenses paid trip to America for two weeks!"

"Is this for real?" I asked cautiously; assuming I must be part of some kind of prank.

"Yes Sophie… it's real. You'll be flying over to the U.S. and staying in five-star accommodation the entire time. You all get limo driven wherever you go and you'll be attending all kinds of concerts, tours and sports events. You'll also be meeting heaps of different celebrities along the way. Everything on the holiday is donated to Challenge, and it really is *the* trip of a lifetime. Congratulations Sophie."

I started laughing loudly with sheer excitement. I really couldn't believe what I was hearing.

"What is it Soph?" Jake asked; waiting patiently to hear what all the fuss was about.

The lady on the other end of the phone continued to talk, so I held up my hand and mouthed the words 'hang on'; letting him know I was still listening to her.

She confirmed my address and told me I would receive an information pack in the mail with all the details I needed; including dates and an itinerary.

"I can't believe it. Thank you so much," I said excitedly.

"It's our pleasure Sophie. You deserve it after all you've been through, and I am so glad you're feeling better."

I thanked her again, we said goodbye and I hung up the phone.

"What's happened?" asked Jake. He too had a surprised expression on his face; mimicking my own.

"That was a lady from Challenge. She told me I just won a raffle for the trip of a lifetime… an all-expenses paid trip to America for two weeks!" I was bouncing up and down with happiness.

Jake wrapped his arms around me. "Awesome Soph! That's the best news ever! I'm so happy for you!"

"Thanks Baby. I told her I wasn't sick anymore but she said that was ok. All the patients at the hospital over the last year go into the draw and I was one of the winners."

"Do you know when you're going?"

"She's sending me an information pack with all the details. I can't believe it. I can't believe I won."

"Well you deserve it Babe. You've had a couple of shit years so it's about time you had some good luck for a change."

I gave my parents a call and told them the good news. As expected, they were over the moon for me.

It was about two months or so after I found out I'd won the trip and it was finally time for me to go. I was scheduled to fly out of Melbourne, and by chance Jake had a martial arts tournament in the city the day before I was due to board the plane to America. I travelled with Jake and his parents to watch him compete, then we spent the night at his auntie and uncles house.

Logistically it wasn't easy, but there was absolutely no chance I was going to fly to the other side of the world without one last steamy session with Jake before I left. I can assure you, he completed one hell of a covert operation that night; sneaking around the house and into my bed undetected.

It was well after two in the morning before Jake was confident enough that everyone in the house was fast asleep; giving him the opportunity to pay me a cheeky visit. I'd even fallen asleep waiting for him, but was more than happy when he eventually climbed into bed beside me. We made love that night. It was gentle, passionate and beautiful; not to mention perfectly silent!

As Jake lay on top of me, pinning me to the bed, I wrapped my arms and legs around him as tightly as I could and nuzzled my head into the side of his neck. I wanted us to melt together, for him to become part of me so I could take my lover with me the following day. Even though we had to be quiet, given his parents were in the room beside us, I treasured every pleasurable second he was inside me. As my release beckoned, I clamped my mouth onto the side of his neck in an attempt to muffle my pleasurable groans. A glorious flood of sensations and emotions washed over us in one beautiful wave as we climaxed together; leaving my body tingling all over.

As I recovered my breath, I couldn't help but feel a sense of sadness as Jake held me in his arms. Even though I was about to go on an amazing journey to see and experience things I'd only ever imagined, I already knew I was going to miss him like crazy. Being so far away from my *angel* was going to hurt.

As planned, Jake and his parents came with me to the airport the following day. I was met by the trip organisers, who were also going along as chaperones.

The four of us, along with the other nine winners and their families, sat through a short presentation about where we were going and what was planned for us. I was blown away by how many amazing things we were going to see and do.

After the presentation it was time to go through to the international check-in, which meant saying goodbye to Jake.

"Have the best time won't you Baby."

"I will Jake. Try not to miss me too much."

"Are you kidding? I already miss you," he replied hugging me tightly.

"I'll call you whenever I can."

"That'd be great, but don't stress if you're too busy. It sounds like you have a lot to get through over the next two weeks."

I said goodbye to Greg and Mary, who both gave me a cuddle, then I grabbed hold of Jake again. "I love you."

"I love you too Soph… always have."

"Always will," I smiled; kissing him again and squeezing him tightly for one last hug.

"See you soon, and be careful Baby." He leaned in closer. "And think of me every night," he whispered seductively in my ear, causing me to giggle. Images of the previous night's activities raced through my mind. I could feel myself blushing.

"I promise." I grinned suggestively. "Bye Jake."

I gave him one last kiss before letting go of his hands, then I followed the rest of the group through the 'International Departures' doors. Before they closed I looked back to see Jake waving goodbye. The lump in my throat was choking me, but I managed to blow him a kiss just as the doors closed between us.

The two-week holiday was jammed packed with things to see, places to go and people to meet. I could literally write an entire book just about the trip. The organisers must have spent months arranging the itinerary, and I'm sure if I had to pay for the same experience it would have cost tens of thousands of dollars. It was a trip I would never forget and I was absolutely privileged to be a part of it.

The other kids who were on the holiday with me ranged in age from ten-years-old right up to seventeen; I was the eldest. We were accompanied by four adults, one of whom was a nurse, and the others were representatives of the Challenge organisation. They were all amazing people and I got along with them well.

To be honest I would be hard pressed to pick a favourite moment; the entire trip was like a dream. We visited Disneyland and Movie World, watched an NBA Game at Maddison Square Garden, seen 'Footloose on Broadway' and watched Bruce Springsteen and the E Street Band in concert. We visited the stars on Hollywood Boulevard and watched the Chicago White Socks play the Royals from seats directly behind home plate. We visited the set of the TV show 'Party of Five' and met some of the actors, flew to Phoenix to watch the WNBA, saw the sights at Venice Beach in California and took a tour of the NASA space centre. We ate at Michael Jordan's restaurant, had high tea at the famous Waldorf Astoria, and spent a day with the members of the rock band 'The Living End'. We got a bird's eye view of New York City from the top of the Empire State Building and were driven around the Statue of Liberty in a speed boat. Our group went in more stretch limousines than I could count and we took at least 15 flights all over the country to see various places and shows.

I know all of this sounds hard to believe but they don't call it 'The Trip of a Lifetime' for nothing. It was the real deal and I've got the ticket stubs and photos to prove it!

I managed to call Jake a couple of times; he couldn't believe all the things I was getting to do. The only real problem with the whole trip was that I got to stay in some of the most beautiful hotels I'd ever seen but Jake wasn't there with me to make the most of them. Though I did end up sharing the bed in most of the hotels we stayed in with another teenage girl named Kathy; innocently of course. It was nice because I never felt lonely, plus she was quite attractive so

I didn't complain. Kathy had a boyfriend as well so we both kept each other company at night, which always felt like the hardest time to be separated from our lovers.

In all it was an unforgettable experience, and I'll always be grateful for the Challenge organisation for giving me the chance to experience such amazing and wonderful things. It certainly went a long way towards helping me forget about the previous years of pain and suffering that I endured whilst battling with my *monster*.

Once my trip to America came to an end, Jake travelled with my parents to pick me up from the airport in Melbourne. It felt so good seeing him standing there in the terminal, arms open wide… waiting for me. I couldn't help but do the whole 'run and embrace' movie scene re-enactment as soon as I walked through the 'International Arrivals' door. I threw myself into his arms and kissed him passionately. Even though I'd just finished an eighteen-hour flight, I felt alive and full of energy a soon as his lips met mine.

I gave Mum and Dad a kiss and cuddle; it was so good to see my family again. We collected my bags and I said goodbye to everyone who went on the trip with me. I gave Kathy a cuddle and thanked the four chaperones who'd been so fantastic the entire time. After that day, I didn't see any of the people from the trip again; that's not to say I'd ever forget them.

Mum and Dad had decided to stay in Melbourne for the night. Since I'd just finished such a long flight, they figured getting into a car for a four-hour trip home would have been the last thing I felt like doing; they were right.

To my absolute amazement they'd actually booked Jake and I into a separate hotel room to them. I couldn't believe it. *We have our own room*! My mind went into overdrive. Staying in beautiful hotels for the last two weeks, all I could think about was how amazing it would be to stay in one with Jake, and now it was actually going to happen.

It was about half an hour's drive to the hotel. I spoke about some of the amazing things I had seen and the people I'd met over the past fortnight. I sat in the back with Jake, holding his hand firmly the entire trip.

I was so happy Mum and Dad had arranged a separate room for us. I appreciated that they were taking our relationship seriously and allowing us time alone, which was exactly what Jake and I needed. We had a lot of 'catching up' to do.

By the time we arrived at the hotel and checked in, it was late afternoon. I was feeling pretty grubby from the flight and couldn't wait to get into a hot shower and freshen up. Knowing Jake would be able to join me made it even more enticing.

"I feel gross after the flight. I need to have a shower ASAP," I announced.

"Well you guys go and freshen up, and what's say we meet up in an hour and all head out for dinner together?" Mum suggested.

"Sounds good." I replied. *An hour should be plenty of time for Jake to give me a proper welcome home.*

Dad gave Jake the key and we made our way to the room, thankfully it was a few doors down from them. It was the first time we'd stayed in a hotel on our own before and I couldn't help but feel like I was on my honeymoon. My heart raced as I contemplated the possibilities.

As soon as Jake opened the door and dropped his bag and my suitcase, I pushed him onto the bed and dived on top of him.

"How cool is this?" I said; propping myself up on his chest.

"I know… a whole room to ourselves!"

"Whose idea was it to get a separate room?" I wondered if Jake had asked, or if my parents had offered. Jake had turned eighteen while I was gone, so I thought maybe that might have something to do with my parents agreeing to us sharing a room. That, and the fact I'd already moved out of home.

"Actually your Dad said on the drive down here that he'd booked a separate room for us. Maybe he and Lynn want some privacy so they can get up to no good!" he joked.

"Please… that's not an image I need in my head right now."

"They're probably going hard at it already," he laughed.

"Holy shit Jake! Are you trying to turn me off!"

"Sorry Baby." He was still chuckling to himself.

"So you should be."

"Hey did you hear that?" he said, quickly tilting his head to the side like he was listening for something.

"What? What is it?" I listened intently.

"I think I just heard Lynn scream out your Dads name!" He burst out laughing again.

I slapped him playfully on the chest. "You're a shocker!" I said; shaking my head in disbelief.

He was quite amused by the whole conversation.

"If you say one more thing about my parents having sex, I won't let you in the shower with me," I warned.

"Cross my heart Baby, no more talk about your Mum and Dad between the sheets." He was still smiling and I paused for a moment, half expecting him to make one last wise crack, but he didn't.

"So… how about a shower?"

"Hell yeah!" he beamed with excitement; his eyes blazing lustfully.

We walked into the bathroom and I turned around to face him. "I'm so exhausted. Do you think you could undress me?" I said playfully.

He didn't have to be asked twice. Before I knew it he'd whipped my t-shirt over my head, dropped to the floor and pulled my shoes and socks off, and slid my jeans down to my ankles. I stepped out of my pants and he took a step back; surveying me from head to toe as I stood there in my bra and panties.

"Look how brown you are!" he exclaimed.

"Yeah we spent a fair bit of time in the sun by the pool; usually in the afternoons when we got back from sightseeing," I explained as I looked down at my arms, legs and tummy. "I do have a pretty decent tan don't I?"

"You sure do!"

"Well I can't shower in my underwear."

Jake stepped forward, kissing me on the lips as his hands reached behind me and unclipped my bra. I let it slide down my arms and onto the floor.

"Now that's a hot look," he said, referring to the white triangles on my breasts; the pale skin which had been covered by my bikini top considerably lighter than the rest of my tanned body.

I turned to the mirror. It did look pretty hot.

Jake grabbed my hips and turned me back to face him. He hooked his fingers in the top of my knickers and slowly slid them down my legs. As his head passed by my groin, I heard him inhale deeply through his nose.

"Did you just try and smell *me*?" I snapped, somewhat shocked but at the same time turned on.

He looked up at me; smiling. "No… of course not!" he grinned, doing a terrible job of lying.

"You did so Jake. I heard you."

"Ok I'm sorry. What can I say, everything about you drives me wild; especially your scent."

"Well me and my scent need to have a shower before you're coming anywhere near me," I giggled as I stepped into the shower. As horny as I was, an eighteen-hour flight called for a freshen up first!

Jake undressed quickly and joined me under the hot cascading water.

"Careful with that thing… you'll take someone's eye out!" I laughed, referring to his erection which was pointing to the ceiling.

"It's a good thing I'm careful with it then," he grinned.

"He looks very dirty. Maybe I should give him a wash?"

"That's probably a good idea," replied Jake as he grabbed my hand and pulled it down towards his groin.

I immediately wrapped my fingers around his shaft and started to rub him up and down in slow deliberate strokes; prompting him to emit a subtle moan.

"He's missed you."

"I've missed him too," I confessed; Jakes hardness sliding between my fingers causing my own instrument of pleasure to prime herself.

He grabbed the back of my neck and planted a firm kiss on my lips, our tongues feverishly licking inside each other's mouths and twisting together.

"Oh Jake… I need you inside me… now!"

He reached down between my thighs so I moved my feet apart to give him easy access. Gently, he slid a finger between my lips; his eyes widened as soon as he felt my slippery entrance.

"You're ready for me," he breathed.

I replied with a subtle nod. I'd been *ready* for him since I wrapped my arms around him at the airport.

There was a narrow tiled ledge in the shower which was about waist high. The small hotel-sized shampoo and conditioner bottles were sitting on it. I raised one leg and positioned my foot on the ledge which caused my *lips* to part; ready for my lover to invade me under the warmth of the shower. Since I was practically standing on one leg, Jake wrapped an arm under my thigh to hold me steady.

With one arm draped over his shoulders, I grabbed my man's rigid shaft with my free hand and pulled him towards me. I caressed my clit and lips with the head of his erection; deliberately coating him in my slippery nectar before lining him up with my aching snatch.

"Push it in," I urged.

I closed my eyes as he plunged into me, inch by throbbing inch; filling my tunnel. The pleasure which flowed through my entire body like a wave caused me to moan loudly. The hot water running over my skin combined with Jake's cock slowly sliding in and out of me was heavenly.

"Fuck that feels amazing," I gasped in between thrusts; prompting my lover's pace to hasten which immediately delivered me to the verge of climax. He held my hips firmly with one hand, elevated my thigh with the other, then drove his entire length into me… hard. I let go; falling to pieces around him and screaming loudly as I came.

"Oh I missed you," I declared with sincerity as I regained my breath.

"I can see that," he smiled. "Ready for more?"

"Uh huh."

His pace, which had subsided after my orgasm, quickened once again; rapidly building me up towards another fantastic eruption of pleasure.

"Yes! Yes! That's it! Yes!" I came again; hard and loud. It was even more intense than the first, and my eyes rolled back in my head as pure ecstasy invaded my body.

I absolutely love being fucked in the shower. Perhaps it has something to do with being Aquarius.

Jake let go of my leg, allowing me to stand on two feet again. "Turn around and grab hold of the ledge," he ordered.

I did as he commanded; swiping the small bottles of shampoo and conditioner onto the floor before bracing myself on the tiled ledge.

"Feet apart."

Again I complied, spreading my feet wide and bending over from the waist.

Jake grabbed hold of my hips, then without warning rammed his cock into me; deep and with unexpected force. I let out a squeal as he impaled me; a sound which only served to provoke him further. He grabbed a handful of my wet hair and pulled my head back, causing my lower back to arch and my ass to point up towards him. He held me firmly in place so there was absolutely no escape from the vicious pounding I was about to receive.

I swear he could read my mind. Whenever we had sex, Jake could sense if I wanted to make love; passionate and gentle, or whether I wanted to fuck; hard and dirty. And right now I was definitely in the mood for the latter.

"I'm going too fuck you now Baby… I'm going to fuck you hard!" His voice was serious and I could sense his inner beast was present and ready to tear me to pieces.

"Yes," I replied submissively.

I trusted Jake completely and although I knew he was going to fuck me with the ferocity of a lion, he also knew my limits, which is why I had totally surrendered to him more times than I could count. Although I had to be in the right mood, I loved it when he pushed me to the edge; where the line between pleasure and pain blurred and I wasn't sure if I was screaming because I was erupting in orgasm or about to be split in two! I was definitely in *that* kind of mood.

With each powerful thrust, Jake pulled me back towards him by my hips and the handful of hair which he grasped firmly; an action which caused his cock to penetrate so deep that I could feel him hitting the end of my *tunnel.* I squinted every time the head of his slippery rod nudged my cervix, but there was no way I was going to stop. Nothing comes close to the feeling of being fucked so deep and hard that you're unsure as to whether you'll be in one piece by the end. For me it's not just a turn on… it's an adrenaline rush!

As Jake continued to pound me, the sound of his pelvis thumping against my ass cheeks became almost as intoxicating as the feeling of his balls slapping against my dripping pussy. To be honest the entire time I felt like I was in the middle of one giant orgasm; a timid squeal escaping from me with each violent entry.

My squeals quickly transformed into screams as his shaft throbbed inside me. It felt like it doubled in thickness as his release built quickly. I closed my eyes tightly and ceased all forms of audible noise. It was now Jake who was groaning loudly, he's beastly grunts more animal than man; music to my ears. He fucked me with everything he had until he exploded in orgasm; my body's ability to distinguish between pleasure and pain totally failing. Jake shot so deep inside me that I felt each individual hot jet of come, a sensation which instantly threw me over the edge and into my own Earth-shattering orgasm. He continued to thrust in and out of me until my hips finished their familiar pulsating rhythm. He wanted to make sure I wasn't left wanting.

Letting go of my hips and hair, he wrapped his arms around my tummy and rested his head on my back. My legs and arms felt so weak that for a moment I thought I was going to fall in a heap on the shower floor.

"Jake… hold me. I think I'm going to collapse."

He slowly withdrew and helped me stand up. I wrapped my arms around his neck and put my head on his chest while enveloped his strong arms firmly around my limp body.

"I hope that I wasn't…"

"No Jake!" I cut him off quickly. I knew he was going to say something about being too rough, he usually did after a session like that. I looked into his eyes. "That was so good. It felt like you were going to break me in half… but it was exactly what I needed."

"Ok Baby… I'm glad you liked it," he said with a relieved smile before kissing me on the lips.

"Like it… I loved every second of it! I can still feel you inside me," I grinned; running a hand over my stomach.

"After dinner I will be," he grinned.

Jake poured some shampoo into his palm then gently washed every square inch of my body. It felt so relaxing having his hands caress me tenderly; a stark contrast to the way he grasped me only minutes earlier. We finished our shower and he towel dried me.

"You're spoiling me," I whispered graciously.

"I'm allowed to," he smiled. "Now let me help you get dressed."

"All I want to do is climb in that bed with you and snuggle," I sighed; looking at the soft white linen on the double bed which seemed so welcoming.

I was feeling jet lagged from the flight, not to mention exhausted from the pounding I'd just received. I would've gladly traded dinner for sleep.

"I'll tell your parents that you're buggered so we'll go somewhere close for dinner. I think you'll sleep heaps better after a decent meal."

"You're probably right. The airline food wasn't great."

We went to my parent's hotel room to meet them for dinner. Jake and Dad talked about going to a restaurant close by so we wouldn't have a late night. We still ended up walking a couple of blocks but it was actually good to be able to stretch my legs out after sitting on the plane for so long. I must say though; I was a little wobbly on my feet after our escapades in the shower.

While we had dinner, I gave Jake and my parents a run-down of some of the things I did in the States. As I talked through the trip with them I was still surprised by how much we actually got to see and do, and meeting a heap of celebrities along the way was the icing on the cake. I couldn't wait to get my photos developed to show them just how amazing the experience was.

By the time we finished dinner, having a belly full of food combined with a huge dose of jet lag had left me feeling like my batteries had been completely drained. I needed sleep. As we started to make our way back to the hotel, I felt so tired I could barely walk. Jake told me to jump up onto his back and he piggy backed me all the way to our room.

We said goodnight to my parents, then as soon as I got into our room I collapsed on the bed. Jake undressed me and tucked me under the covers. While he brushed his teeth he gave me a piece of chewing gum so I didn't have to get up and brush my own. I loved how he thought of things like that. I watched as he undressed in front of me and climbed into bed. It was so nice to be able to snuggle up with him after sleeping in hotels for the last two weeks.

Just before I drifted off, Jake said the most amazing thing to me. I'll never forget it. He was lying on his side staring at me and tickling my cheek with the back of his hand. "Since you've been gone Baby, I've done some thinking."

"What about?" I said sleepily.

"Well I think it's time I talked to your parents."

"My parent's… why?" I asked; tired and confused.

"To ask their permission to marry you."

My ears pricked up. All of a sudden I was wide awake; he had my undivided attention.

"I don't really care if they approve or not because I'm going to marry you anyway, but I think it's the right thing to do. What do you think?"

I couldn't speak. All I could do was cuddle him with all the strength I had left. I closed my eyes and instantly felt tears building beneath my eyelids.

Eventually I answered. "I love you Jake. I can't believe it's coming true."

"What Baby?"

"My dream… my dream about marrying you. About us being together forever," I wept; burying my head under his chin. I wasn't usually so emotional.

He kissed me on the forehead. "Of course it's coming true. I promised you it would… remember?"

"I know you did. How could I forget?"

We didn't talk anymore about it; there was nothing left to say. Instead, we simply laid there in a warm and deliciously cosy embrace; the two of us savouring such a beautiful and utterly perfect moment until I drifted off to sleep.

After that night in the hotel room when Jake revealed his plan to speak with Mum and Dad, I lived in a state of permanent anticipation. Even as fast as things moved with him, I still found myself feeling impatient. I tried my best not to bring up the topic too often, even though I wanted to question Jake on a daily basis as to when he planned on discussing marriage with my parents. I fought hard to keep my questions to a minimum for fear I might be putting too much pressure on him, and god forbid, cause him to reconsider if it was the right thing to do.

I constantly reminded myself that Jake was only eighteen and completely focused on his HSC studies until the end of the year. Plus, he was busy working two jobs; the army and the supermarket. I trusted he had everything planned out, undoubtedly with my best interests at heart, and I was certain he'd already chosen the exact day he wanted to propose to me. I knew I had no chance of ever extracting the date from him. If there was one thing I was certain of it was when he did finally decide to pop the question, I wouldn't see it coming. He loved surprising me and wouldn't miss an opportunity as big as a marriage proposal to knock me off my feet.

In hindsight, I think he took great pleasure in knowing I couldn't wait for him to ask, even to the point where one afternoon we walked past a jewellery store and I joked that it would be fun to try on some engagement rings; never expecting him to agree!

"What a great idea," he said excitedly; knowing full well it would just drive me even crazier to see gold rings and shiny diamonds on my wedding ring finger.

Jake wasn't silly though and I'm sure he used the opportunity to see exactly what styles and designs I fancied.

Close to six months had passed. I was still working full time at the clothing store and Jake had finished his final exams and graduated from high school. It would be a few weeks until he'd get his results and find out whether he'd earned a high enough HSC score to apply for Military College. He'd put in so much time and effort that it would be absolutely devastating if he missed the mark. I had my fingers crossed for him.

It was a week before Christmas when I got a call at work from Jake.

My boss handed me the phone. "Hey Jake what's up?"

"Eighty-three point seven Baby!"

"Is it enough?" I couldn't remember exactly what he needed.

"Hell yeah it is! Only Just though," he replied excitedly.

I let out a girly squeal. I was so happy for him. All those times he'd been so disciplined; setting his watch for one-hour study sessions alone in his bedroom all the while resisting his biggest distraction, *yours truly*, had paid off. Proud doesn't even begin to describe how I felt. I was delighted, overjoyed… ecstatic!

"Oh Baby, I'm so proud of you. I can't wait to finish work so I can come home and kiss you."

"Thanks Soph. I was going to wait for you to get home, but I thought it might brighten up your day if you found out at work."

"Well it has, it most certainly has. I can't stop smiling."

I could hear Jake laughing.

"Well get back to work or your boss will give you the sack," he joked.

"I'll come over straight after work."

"Sweet, that'd be good. I'll see you soon. Love you."

"I love you too." I hung up the phone.

I was elated for him. The smile on my face lasted the rest of the day. I knew his HSC score was only one part of the selection process, and Jake had already told me that even if he got the score he needed he'd still have a fair few hoops to jump through before being accepted. So far though, everything was going according to plan... *our* plan, and the future we'd dreamt of was looking very bright.

That year we marked Christmas with the usual family dinners and celebrations. After having Christmas lunch with his family, Jake came out to the farm to celebrate with me. It was great because it gave me a chance to introduce him to some of my aunties, uncles and cousins whom he hadn't met yet.

The following week we spent New Year's Eve together at a pretty wild party at one of his friend's places. We celebrated as the year 2000 rolled in, and as expected, found out the dreaded 'Millennium Bug' didn't eventuate to anything remotely serious after all.

It was a great time for us. Jake had finished his studies and I was healthy, working full time and had recently changed address; moving in with my brother Shaun, which was far more comfortable as opposed to living with a couple of friends. Overall, life was good but there was still one thing I yearned for, *one* thing which dominated my thoughts day and night.

"Do you think we could go out to the farm this weekend Soph? It'd be nice to head out to the peace and quiet for the day."

It had been a few weeks since I'd seen my parents so I thought it would be good to catch up with them.

"Sure thing Baby, sounds like a nice idea. I know Mum and Dad would like to see us."

"Great, it's all set then."

I had my suspicions and desperately wanted to ask if he was going to have *the* talk with my parents, but decided to bite my tongue. *Be patient. He'll talk to them when he's ready!*

We drove out to the farm on Saturday morning. I'd brought a car shortly after my seventeenth birthday and was enjoying the freedom that having my licence and a vehicle offered.

We arrived around morning tea time, so as soon as we walked in the door Mum offered us a cup of coffee. We sat down with my parents, caught up on the last few weeks and discussed Jake's plans to apply for Military College; he was going to submit his application within the next week or so. Both Dad and Mum were very interested in what would happen if he was accepted, such as how long he would be away and where he would have to live. They were also curious about my thoughts on the whole idea, and how I would feel if he had to move away.

"I'll be going wherever Jake goes," I said directly. "There's absolutely no way I'll be staying in Sunbury if he has to live away for the next eighteen months!" I explained adamantly. "No way!"

My parents looked at each other, I don't think they knew what to say.

"Actually since you brought up the issue of Sophie and where she fits into all this, there is something I wanted to talk to you both about," announced Jake.

My heart stopped and the hairs on my arms stood on end. *Holy shit... this is it! He's going to ask them!*

Dad and Mum both looked at Jake; eager to hear what he was about to say next.

He looked down at the table, taking a moment to gather his thoughts. The silence was deafening; you could've heard a pin drop. Then he took a deep breath, lifted his head and looked directly at Mum and Dad.

"I want to marry Sophie." As he spoke he reached his hand towards me and I grabbed it immediately.

Inside I was screaming to the heavens. He was so brave. I wanted to get up and throw my arms around Jake and hold him as tight as I could. I stayed in my chair and tried desperately to control myself.

Before my parents had a chance to respond, he continued. "I know we're young, but we don't feel it. The last few years Sophie and I have been through a lot together, more than some couples ten years older have ever had to deal with, and it's definitely matured us. I love her and she loves me… and this is what we want."

There was a brief moment of silence. My parents looked at each other; their expressions hard to read.

"Well if that's what you both want to do. It really is your decision to make," said Dad. Mum still hadn't responded.

"It *is* what we want! It's *all* we want Dad!" I blurted out excitedly, before I had a chance to stop myself.

Jake glanced at me and smiled. He knew I was trying my best to stay calm.

"So when were you planning to get engaged?" asked Mum.

My head snapped sideways so fast I almost broke my own neck. I glared at Jake; waiting anxiously for my lover's response.

He grinned at me; knowing how desperately I wanted to know the exact day it would happen. I was now holding his hand with both of mine; bracing for a hint as to when he was going to ask me.

"Well… that's a surprise."

Argh, so close!

As I exhaled, Mum and Dad both chuckled at my disappointment.

"In a bit of a rush are we Soph?" teased Dad.

"No!" I scoffed, doing a horrible job of lying.

"Look, marriage isn't something either of you want to rush into. You need to be one hundred percent sure it's what you both want," explained my father.

"Have you talked with your parents about it Jake?" asked Mum.

"Actually no, I haven't… and I don't think I need to either," he replied confidently.

Jake went on to explain that his parents were going through a bit of a rough patch, and he already knew they wouldn't have thought us getting married at such a young age was a good idea.

"To be honest, I promised Sophie a long time ago that we'd be together forever. Getting married is only the beginning."

I think it was a polite way of saying '*This is going to happen with or without the consent of our parents.*'

"I'm going to look after her for the rest of her life."

My parents looked at each other again; Mum nodding to Dad with approval. "Ok then. Well as I said, if it's what you both want then Lynn and I will support you."

I jumped up and wrapped my arms around Dad then gave Mum a hug too. Jake stood up and shook Dad's hand; Mum gave him a cuddle and a kiss on the cheek.

I was so happy and grateful that my parents had given us their blessing. I hugged Jake and kissed him with all the love and emotion I could muster. I was so glad he'd finally asked my parents and the outcome couldn't have been better.

One step closer to being Mrs. Freeman. To say I was excited would be a complete understatement. I literally felt like I was floating on a cloud of happiness.

We stayed at the farm for a few more hours, before leaving at the same time as Dad who was heading into the factory for the afternoon shift.

I was driving and we had some music playing.

"Pull over Baby," said Jake as we approached the lake; pointing at a clearing near the gate.

"Why? What are we doing?" I asked. Immediately thinking we were going to find a secluded place for a quick 'session'. It definitely wouldn't have been the first time we'd spontaneously pulled off the road and made love in the car; especially out in the country.

"Just pull over and I'll show you," he grinned; his eyes seducing me already.

I was now totally convinced we were going to have a 'quickie'.

We parked the car under the shade of some trees. I could already feel myself getting *wet* at the thought of a spontaneous fuck. They were so much fun; a real adrenaline rush for me.

He turned to me and we kissed passionately. Now I was *really* primed and ready for him.

"Let's go for a walk Baby."

"Ok," I replied eagerly, although I was a little confused as to why we weren't just going to climb in the back seat.

I guess we're going to find a private place in the woods.

We got out of the car and walked hand in hand through the gate and onto the dirt track which ran alongside the water's edge. It was a beautiful day, the sun was warm and the sky was clear and blue. The sound of the water lapping against the bank was tranquil and soothing.

It was a short walk to the edge of the woods and the privacy offered by the thick flora.

"Stop here for a minute Soph." Jake pulled on my hand gently, causing me to stop beside him.

"Do you remember this place?"

We were standing beside a massive gum tree which grew out from the bank and hung precariously over the water.

"Of course I do. It's where we first met… right beside this tree."

"That's right," he smiled. "And do you remember what day it is today?"

"Um… the twentieth of January?"

"That's right. And do you know what happened on this particular day?"

I thought for a moment, not immediately realising the significance of the date.

"Think about it," he prompted.

"Oh, it's the date I was diagnosed with Hodgkin's disease."

"Exactly two years ago today," he added.

I cast my mind back to that awful day which seemed like a lifetime ago. "I remember it Jake. It was one of the worst days of my life. I remember the day before; leaving you on the side of the road on your bike, then driving away to Melbourne."

"Yeah that sucked," he sighed.

"I think I lied in the back of the car and cried nearly the whole way there. Then the next day I had the operation on my neck and they told me I had cancer. Both those days were horrible. I'll never forget them but I wish I could."

I was looking out over the water as frightening images flashed through my mind. Images of the hospital, operations, needles and the look on my parent's faces when confronted with the reality that their daughter was dying.

My mood had rapidly shifted from feeling aroused and sexual, ready for some fun, to dark and sombre. I was confused as to why he'd bring up such painful memories for me.

"Look at me Sophie."

I turned to face Jake. He grabbed both of my hands and stared into my eyes.

"I'm sorry if I upset you."

I forced a smile, but my expression was obviously displaying the sorrow I felt from having to relive such a horrible time of my life.

He continued. "I know that was a terrible day for you. The twentieth of January was probably the worst day of your life; full of pain and sadness. It tears me apart knowing I wasn't there for you. I'm so sorry I wasn't there Baby."

I could see the sincerity in his eyes and hear it in his voice. I felt my lip quiver.

"I've always felt like I failed you that day. I should have just left my bike on the side of the road, got in the car and went with you to Melbourne… but I didn't." He paused; his expression full of regret. "And I can't change the past."

My eyes began to water; I couldn't help it. It was so upsetting to learn that he honestly thought he could've done more for me. The truth was Jake's love and devotion had saved my life! He *had* done everything for me, he just didn't realise it.

"What I can do though… is change how you feel on this day from now on."

Jake dropped to one knee in front of me.

It took me a second to realize what was happening, but when I did I burst into tears. I was frozen; staring at Jake as he looked up at me from one knee. It was the most beautiful thing I'd ever seen. We had spent the morning talking with my parents about getting married, but never in my wildest dreams did I think he was going to propose to me on the same day. It was a complete surprise.

As Jake let go of my hand and reached into his pocket, I could hear myself breathing heavily; tears spilled from my eyelids. He held up a small white box and it was just too much for me; my legs completely turned to jelly. Rather than drop to the ground in front of him, I sat down on his knee and draped my arm over his shoulder to hold myself up.

"Sophie Taylor, you are the most amazing person I have ever met. I've loved you since the day I first saw you standing right here." He took a breath; his eyes were welling up. "I will love you forever, and I want to spend the rest of my life with you."

Seeing my *angel's* heartfelt sincerity only served to make me even more emotional. I completely gave up wiping my tears, instead letting them trickle freely down my face.

As Jake opened the box, the sun reflected off the diamond ring causing it to sparkle brightly. "Will you marry me?"

I looked at the ring then back to Jake's eyes before throwing my arms around him. It was such a surreal experience; sheer elation and happiness causing me to weep uncontrollably.

"Yes Jake… yes… of course I will marry you!"

I kissed my fiancé for the first time; passionately… perfectly.

Jake took the ring out of the box and I extended my left hand which was shaking uncontrollably. He gently grasped my hand and held it still before sliding the ring on my finger. It fit like it was made for me. I looked up at him and smiled before kissing him again.

"Look familiar?" he grinned.

"Yes." I replied, holding my hand out in front of me; admiring the sparkling jewels.

It was the ring I'd tried on in the jewellery store more than seven months ago; gold with a row of five diamonds across the top. I'd fallen in love with it the moment I tried it on.

"Just before we left the store that day, I waited till you weren't watching and told the lady who served us to put it aside. I went back later that week and put it on lay-by."

"You've had this planned since the middle of last year?" I beamed.

"Sure have!" he said proudly; knowing he'd successfully kept it a secret from me the whole time.

"So you knew you were going to propose to me on this exact day all along?"

"Yeah, and I wanted to come out and ask your parents because I knew it would throw you off track. Asking you on the same day would definitely be a surprise."

I laughed. "Surprise! I almost passed out Jake! I literally couldn't stand up!"

He started to laugh as well. I was still sitting on his knee so I stood up and helped him to his feet.

We embraced again. "Oh my god Jake, I love you so much."

"I love you too Baby."

We started to walk back to the car. "So we're not going to have sex out here then?" I asked.

He laughed out loud. "What are you talking about?"

"I thought when you told me to pull over that we were going to have a quickie."

"Are you serious?"

"Yes. I had no idea you were going to propose to me!"

"Well we can if you like, but I thought you'd want to go back to the farm and break the news to your Mum."

I thought about it for a second. I really did want to have sex but I also couldn't wait to show Mum my engagement ring.

Jake could see I was struggling to make up my mind. "How about we go and tell your Mum the news, then swing by the factory to tell your Dad on the way home…" He paused; grinning cheekily. "…and then I'll take care of you tonight?"

It was exactly what I wanted to hear. "Great idea Babe. Sounds good to me."

As we walked hand in hand to the car, my cheeks throbbed from the smile permanently etched on my face. I looked at the beautiful ring on my finger and thought about the hours and hours of work he'd put in at both his part time jobs to buy it for me. Jake worked hard, for minimum wage, and I was overflowing with gratitude that he would spend so much to give me the engagement ring I'd fallen in love with.

It was then that an unusual feeling washed over me, one which is rather hard to define. It was very similar to when Jake and I first made love; a combination of elevated maturity and appreciation. I think the feeling of maturity stemmed from the fact I was now engaged at seventeen. Yet another milestone of adulthood, reached before officially becoming one! When I woke up that morning I was a teenager with a boyfriend; now I was engaged to be married. I'd never felt so grown up and committed to something as I did in that moment. I was going to become Jake's wife and I vowed to devote every part of myself to him; my heart, my soul, my life… forever.

The feelings of appreciation are harder to describe. I mean how do you explain what it feels like when a dream comes true? I felt obliged to thank some form of higher power, maybe the universe or even God for bringing Jake to me. I just couldn't believe the magic which radiated between us when we first met, had continued to grow stronger with each passing day. You hear people talk about finding their *soul mate*, well words can't describe how grateful I was for the divine power which had landed me in the arms of mine.

It was the year 2000 and the 20th of January had officially been transformed from the worst, to the greatest day of my life.

Thank you Jake.

CHAPTER TWENTY-ONE

'I WILL FOLLOW YOU ANYWHERE'

As surprised as I was by Jake's proposal, it's safe to say Mum and Dad were totally blindsided by it! Even though they'd both given him their blessing only a few hours earlier, they were still shocked their teenage daughter was now engaged to be married.

Jake explained his reason for proposing on that particular day so they were clear on the motive behind his actions. Making a horrible day a special one was such a sweet and romantic idea, and it's definitely gone a long way towards erasing the painful memories I experienced on the 20th of February all those years ago.

Mum was clearly happy for us; congratulating Jake and I with a kiss and a cuddle when we broke the news to her. I think I even saw a few stray tears of joy, which was very touching. It felt good to have her support.

"Just promise us it will be a long engagement," she said, subtly hinting we shouldn't be in a rush to 'tie the knot'.

I think Dad said almost exactly the same thing when we arrived at the factory to tell him the news. Jake explained his plan was to wait until he graduated from military college before we had our wedding, which would be at least December the following year. This would mean our engagement would be close to two years. Mum and Dad both agreed it was a good idea to wait until Jake graduated, though not for the purpose of making sure it was definitely what we wanted, *we already knew that*, but more so because we would be financially stable once he was an Army Officer.

I must confess though, Jake's revelation about not wanting to get married until he graduated was a little unnerving for me, considering he hadn't even been accepted yet! I secretly wondered what would happen to his plan, more specifically when we'd get married, if he didn't actually make selection for military college. I never brought my concerns up with Jake because I didn't want him to ever think I doubted him, or his plan for our future. I wanted him to know he had my support one hundred percent, and be under no illusion of my trust and belief in him.

So the day was going well, Jake and I were engaged and my parents were both very happy for us. As we drove back to Sunbury, we discussed the reaction we thought we were going to get from his parents.

"Honestly Soph, I don't know how they're going to take it. Mum and Dad don't have the best relationship at the moment, which is why I didn't ask for their advice in the first place. I already knew they would've been against the idea of me proposing to you at this age."

Jake's words worried me, and I remember feeling a little uncomfortable at the prospect of having to announce our engagement to his parents; face to face. There was one consolation though, my relationship with both Greg and Mary was good; never a disagreement or ill word had been spoken between us. So although I was a little uneasy about it, I did my best to convince myself that everything was going to work out ok.

"I think they'll be fine Jake, after all your eighteen now… an adult. You're old enough to make your own decisions so hopefully they will respect that."

Jake turned to me and smiled. "That's exactly right Baby, which is why I was going to propose to you regardless of what anyone else said; your parents or mine. Look, however Mum and Dad take it, just remember we're doing what feels right for *us*. I love you and you love me, which is *all* that matters. It's our lives and we'll live them the way we want."

He put his hand on my thigh and squeezed gently. I took one hand off the wheel and put it on top of his. "I do love you Jake." I said sincerely. "If only you knew how much."

"I know you do. After all… you did say yes! Or was that just to get a shiny ring on your finger?" he joked.

"I would've said yes even without the ring!" I replied, taking another look at my new diamonds as they sparkled brightly on my finger.

Jake leaned over and kissed my cheek. "I know you would've Baby, that's one of the reasons I love you so much."

We spent the rest of the drive discussing how we thought his family would take the news, but it turns out nothing could have prepared us for the reaction we got.

When we arrived at Jake's place, only his father and sisters were home; Mary was still at work. She also had a part time job at a local supermarket.

After we said hello to everybody, Jake and I retreated to his room to discuss whether we should wait for Mary to get home before announcing our engagement. We concluded that maybe it was a blessing Mary was at work, because if we told Greg now and his reaction was bad, at least we'd only have *one* angry parent to deal with.

As we made our way to the lounge room where Greg was watching television, I was so nervous my hands were shaking. Jake could sense I was frightened.

"Calm down Soph, everything'll be ok," he said reassuringly as he squeezed my hand.

Greg was in the lounge room on his own.

"Hey Dad. Have you got a minute?"

"Sure. What's up?" he replied; turning down the television.

"Sophie and I have an announcement."

Greg's eyebrows raised, it was obvious he could sense it was something big. I imagined he had the words *'please don't be pregnant, please don't be pregnant'* repeating over and over in his head.

"Well exactly two years ago today Soph was diagnosed with cancer, and as you can imagine… it's a day she'd rather forget. So… I thought I'd make it a day she would rather remember instead," he said; smiling at me affectionately.

"Ok. Make's sense." Greg already looked slightly more relieved. No doubt at the realisation his son *hadn't* knocked up his seventeen-year-old girlfriend!

"Dad, today I asked Sophie to marry me… and she said yes!" beamed Jake proudly.

I swallowed and waited for Greg's reaction. It took him a second to process everything.

"Well congratulations," he smiled.

I exhaled and every muscle in my body relaxed as relief washed over me.

Greg gave Jake a hug and shook his hand, then he turned to me and gave me a kiss and a cuddle. Jake laughed then hugged me tightly. He knew I was relieved and I could see he definitely was too.

I raised my hand to show Greg my engagement ring.

"Very nice. Looks like you've been saving a while Jake."

"Yeah I put it on lay-by sometime around the middle of last year and have slowly paid it off. I'd hate to think how many trolleys I had to push to buy that."

Greg seemed to have taken the news pretty well, and unless I was mistaken he actually seemed to be proud of Jake and I for taking such an important step.

By this stage, Jake's sisters had come out to the lounge room to see what all the commotion was about. We told them about the engagement and it was overwhelming to see how happy Alice, Kate and Samantha were when they realised I was going to be their sister for real. They were all smiling and laughing; so excited for Jake and me.

"Have you told your parents yet Sophie?" asked Greg.

"Yeah we were out there today. Jake actually asked for my parents' permission before proposing to me," I added.

"And what did they say?"

"Well they seemed pretty supportive. Jake told them about his plans to go away to military college this year, so he can make a decent living and look after us. They were pleased to know that we won't be getting married for at least a couple of years though; after he graduates."

Greg turned his attention to Jake. "You haven't even applied yet, how do you know you'll get in?"

"I'm applying next week… and I *will* get in!" The conviction in Jake's voice made it impossible to doubt him.

"Well I hope so," replied Greg.

He had no reason to doubt Jake's abilities or determination. Greg knew his son, as did I, so he understood that if Jake said he was going to do something, then he had the self-confidence and perseverance to make it happen.

Telling Greg and the girls about our engagement was a really wonderful moment. *One down, one to go,* I thought to myself.

I have to say I was more nervous about breaking the news to Greg than Mary, but since it went down well with him I was feeling quite relaxed. I had a good relationship with Jake's mother and I was fairly certain she was going to take the news well. I was actually looking forward to telling her about our engagement.

As soon as Mary arrived home from work Jake and I went out to meet her in the kitchen.

"Hello you two," she said as soon as she seen us.

"Hi Mum."

"Hi Mary. How was work?"

"Not bad Sophie; busy though. What've you two been up to?"

"Actually, we've been fairly busy today as well," smiled Jake.

"Really… doing what?" she replied; a hint of suspicion in her voice.

"Mum, Sophie and I have some news for you."

Jake's sisters had come out to the living area to watch us break the good news to Mary. She stopped still and looked at Jake; giving him her undivided attention. I took a deep breath and prepared myself for my fiancé's next sentence.

"Today I asked Sophie to marry me and she said yes," Jake announced happily.

Without saying a word, she stared directly into his eyes; her expression impossible to read. It was like she was waiting for it to sink in. I held up my hand to show her the engagement ring, thinking it might break the awkward silence.

Mary grabbed hold of my hand, lifted it up and glared at the ring. "Well congratulations Sophie," she snapped in the most horrendously terse and sarcastic tone before dropping my hand in a way that made her disappointment and anger clearly evident. Her piercing stare immediately returned to Jake.

Oh fuck! This is bad!

I tried to swallow the lump in my throat, which had instantly formed as a result of Mary's reaction and was now choking me to death. There was absolutely no mistaking her expression now… she was fuming.

"What's wrong?" snapped Jake; angered by the way Mary had dropped my hand like a piece of rubbish.

"What do you want me to say?" she hissed back.

The realisation that Mary was upset with us reduced me to tears. I turned my head away from her only to see the looks of confusion on Alice, Kate and Samantha's faces. They knew this wasn't going well, and seeing me in tears was making them upset too.

"Well if you don't know what to say, then don't say anything!" growled Jake in a voice I hadn't heard him use before. He was pissed off… *really* pissed off!

"I'm just so disappointed in you!" she said sharply.

"What the hell are you disappointed about! Sophie and I are in love Mum. I thought you would've understood that after everything we've been through!"

I need to get out of here. I could feel myself trembling.

"You're only teenagers Jake!"

"So what!" he thundered; absolutely ropeable. "There's no perfect age to get married. And yeah, we might be teenagers but we have more life experience than some people do in their twenties. Age has absolutely nothing to do with being in love!"

Mary didn't reply. She just stood there shaking her head; frowning. It actually looked like she felt betrayed. I couldn't understand it.

It was such a tense and horrible experience. I was so embarrassed and just wanted Jake to get me the hell out of there; to save me from this nightmare which was painfully unfolding.

He looked at me. The tears which rolled down my cheeks only served to infuriate him even more, to the point where I thought he was really going to lose it.

Jake slowly turned his head and focused his attention back to his mother. Mustering every ounce of control not to explode in a barrage of emotion, he spoke. "Thanks a lot… *Mum*," he said; emphasising her title. His ice cold tone and even colder expression clearly accentuated the disgust he had towards her.

Jake and Mary had always had such a good relationship and it was hard to see him speaking to her that way, but he was angry; angry for treating him and the girl he loved so poorly.

He held his hand out to me. I grabbed it without hesitation.

"Let's go," he said calmly.

As he turned and led me towards the front door, he looked at his three sisters who were now fighting back the tears as well. Alice, Kate and Samantha were all hurting; it broke my heart.

"I'm sorry girls. Don't be upset. Everything will be ok," Jake said, apologising for what they'd just seen. I wanted to give them all a cuddle and tell them everything was going to be alright, but I couldn't wait a second longer to get out of the house; away from Mary.

I grabbed my bag and keys on the way to the front door, then Jake and I left. I passed Jake the car keys; there was no way I could drive in my current state.

As we drove to my house I didn't say too much, instead listened as Jake attempted to dissect what the hell just happened.

"Just because Mum and Dad's marriage is falling apart doesn't give her the right to treat you like that. I'm so fuckin angry with her!" He paused for a moment and took a few deep breaths before continuing. "The part which pisses me off the most is she doesn't trust that you and I can make this kind of decision ourselves. She knows how serious our relationship is and how strong we are together, yet she still doubts us."

"It's alright Baby, calm down."

He looked at me briefly then back to the road. "I'm sorry, but she had no right to make you feel like that Soph; no right!"

"Maybe she was just a little bit shocked and confused." I tried to defend Mary, even though she'd hurt me deeply.

"Well maybe she was, but it doesn't make it ok. You've never done *anything* to deserve that. She owes you a fucking apology!"

It was hard to hear him speaking with such anger in his voice, and I wanted him to stop. "It's alright Jake."

"No it's not. I still can't believe how she reacted. She upset you Soph and that's bullshit!"

Jake was always so protective of me, and it was now blatantly obvious the thing which angered him the most was that Mary had hurt me. Seeing tears rolling down my cheeks was not helping him to curb his infuriation either, so I figured the faster I could get control of myself, the faster he would be able to calm himself down.

I took a few deep breaths and wiped my eyes. "I'm ok Jake. I'll be fine," I said softly. I placed my hand on his arm. "Just take a few breaths and relax. I know you're upset with your mum, and I know you're angry, but I'm ok... really." Even though I was still hurting, I did my best to appear strong; to show him I was alright.

I could see that Jake's breathing had begun to ease; he was calming down.

"Sorry I got so worked up, I should've had more control," he said; disappointed in himself. "I guess I don't like seeing someone upset you."

"I know… you're just worried about me. I'll be ok, I promise. I think Mary just needs some time."

"Well as far as I'm concerned, she can have all the time she needs. I sure as hell don't want to see her anytime soon," he said sternly.

We arrived back at my place; my brother Shaun wasn't home from work yet. Jake and I had only just walked in the door when the phone rang.

"Hello, Sophie Speaking."

"Sophie it's Sharon. I was wondering if you could come in this afternoon?"

Sharon was my boss. She wanted me to come in to cover another girl who couldn't do the late night shopping shift, which was starting in about an hour's time.

"I would come in, but Jake proposed to me today and we were hoping to celebrate tonight," I explained; leaving out the details about feeling like shit after Mary's reaction. I was in no state to deal with customers and I didn't want to leave Jake either.

"Well we need you Sophie; there's nobody else. You're just going to have to come in," Sharon replied firmly.

"Ok. I'll be in soon," I replied reluctantly.

"Good. See you at five." She hung up the phone without so much as a 'congratulations', or even a 'goodbye'. It was obvious she didn't give a damn about my engagement, or me for that matter.

As soon as I hung up the phone I started crying… *again.* I was an emotional wreck, and going to work was the last thing I felt like doing. All I wanted to do was curl up with Jake.

"Sharon told me I have to go into work, but I can't do it Jake… not tonight," I sobbed.

"Hey, calm down Baby." He put his arms around me comfortingly. "Once you've had a shower and something to eat you might be feeling better."

"It's a four-hour shift Jake, plus lock-up. I can't do it. I want to stay here with you."

"Well if your too upset then call her back and tell her that you aren't up to it today. I'm sure she'll understand. Or I can call her if you like?"

I thought about it for a few minutes before deciding to give my boss a call back. I gave her the entire story of what went down with Jake's mum, and explained how emotional and upset I was. I told her how I genuinely didn't think I'd be able to deal with customers that night, then politely asked if it would be ok if I didn't come in. I knew I would be letting her down but I had to ask. Besides, I'd never said 'no' to being called in since I started working there over a year ago.

"Sophie it's not good enough. I need you to come in and cover the shift, there's nobody else!" Her voice was sharp and direct.

"I can't Sharon… I'm sorry," I pleaded.

"Look if you can't come in tonight, then don't bother coming back at all!"

Did she just threaten me? I realised my boss didn't give a shit about how I was feeling, and had resorted to giving me an ultimatum in an effort to force me to come in.

I went quiet for a few seconds, and in that time my emotions did a one-eighty; sadness was quickly replaced with anger. The emotional roller coaster I'd ridden the entire day had finally taken its toll; I'd had enough.

"Fine. Then I quit!" I said calmly before hanging up. It was a pure 'heat of the moment' decision which put an abrupt end to the problem.

Jake looked at me with raised eyebrows; a surprised expression on his face. "What the fuck just happened!" he exclaimed; astonished by how fast things went south.

"Sharon basically said that if I didn't come in tonight then she'd fire me, so I quit."

"Baby are you sure that's such a good idea?" A look of concern quickly replaced the surprised expression. "I know you don't feel up to it but maybe you should just try and get through this shift?"

I shook my head. "No Jake, I'm not going." I'd made up my mind and wasn't about to change it.

"But you don't want to lose your job for the sake of one day. We can celebrate tomorrow night."

"I was going to quit soon anyway."

"Why? What are you going to do for money?"

"Well I've got a bit of money saved up to get me through until you get accepted into college. I will get a new job when I move to Canberra with you."

I knew Jake wasn't impressed with my spontaneous decision to quit my job, considering he was always so organised and calculated in the choices he made. But the fact was, I didn't even want to *think* about work. I was becoming more frustrated as each second passed. The thing which pissed me off the most, was that Jake's plan to transform this day for me from one of pain and sadness, had somehow managed to unravel in the space of an hour. His proposal was so beautiful and sweet; a complete surprise which could never be tainted, but Mary's reaction and the drama with work had really knocked me. I hated that both these issues had taken the shine off what was supposed to be a perfect day.

I know quitting my job wasn't the right thing to do, and I was certain my parents were going to have something to say about it. I actually expected Jake to give me a bit of a talking to with regards to the consequences of quitting so abruptly, but he must have sensed I was at my limit of emotional turmoil for one day.

Instead of a lecture, Jake opened his arms to me. "Come here Baby."

I moved over and he wrapped his strong arms around me firmly. I put my head on his chest and closed my eyes.

"No more tears for today. Take a few deep breaths and relax. Everything will be ok, I promise." Jake's words were exactly what I needed to hear.

He must be sick of telling me everything's going to be ok, I thought; taking comfort in his embrace for the hundredth time. The thing is I believed him whole heartedly, because with Jake everything was *always* ok.

As instructed, I took a few deep breaths in an attempt to calm myself. "I'm sorry," I whispered.

"What are *you* sorry for?" He sounded confused as to why I felt the need to apologise.

"I don't know why, but I feel like it's my fault the day has turned out so bad."

"Babe… none of this is your fault. And this day isn't bad. You're forgetting one important thing… you said *yes* remember. We're engaged and there's nothing anybody can say or do to change that. Today is one of the best days of my life, so there's no need for you to apologise at all."

I hugged him as tight as I could. "You're right… we're engaged!" I opened my eyes and looked up at him.

As soon as I saw his beautiful blue eyes staring back at me, I instantly felt better.

"Kiss me Baby," he whispered.

I obliged immediately; kissing him with all the love and passion I could muster.

"I love you Jake. And I promise I will love you forever."

Jake didn't want me to come over to his place until Mary had 'sorted her shit out', as he so eloquently put it. It was well over a week until she spoke even one word to him.

Eventually, Mary opened up about why she reacted so poorly when we announced our engagement. As Jake and I suspected, the main reason for her harsh reaction was based on the reality that unfortunately her own marriage was failing. She and Greg had married fairly young, so when she learned Jake and I were planning on doing the same, she immediately thought it was a case of history repeating itself. Mary didn't mean to take it out on us, it's just that she didn't want the same thing to happen to our relationship. As it turned out, Mary and Greg separated within the next two months.

Jake had obviously explained how hurtful her reaction had been and how upset it made me, because the next time I saw her she apologised sincerely for how she handled the situation. I forgave her immediately, which was testament to the relationship Mary and I had built prior to my engagement to her son. Never has an ill word been spoken between us since, and with all honesty, Mary and I have a friendship seldom found between mother and daughter in-law; I cherish it to this day.

As planned, Jake visited the local Defence Force Recruiting Office in Sunbury the following week where he submitted his initial application to the Royal Military College.

He had picked up full time work at a local factory, manufacturing gas heaters and high pressure washers, and was putting in some solid hours each week while he waited for news about his application.

Within a couple of weeks Jake received confirmation that his application was accepted. The next step in the process was to travel to Melbourne to sit a number of aptitude tests, and undergo a variety of medical examinations and psychology interviews. Although the recruiting officer said there wasn't much you could do to prepare for the entrance exams, as always, Jake left nothing to chance. Academically, he felt his mathematical abilities were an area of weakness, so he enlisted the expertise of a private tutor for a number of weeks to ensure his math skills were up to speed prior to being tested in Melbourne. In terms of his physical preparation, Jake had already ramped up his time in the gym since completing high school. He had also started sprint training after finishing up in martial arts. His health and physical fitness was at its peak, which for Jake meant another box the assessors could tick come testing day.

Jake returned from testing in Melbourne, confident that he'd done enough. Now we had to wait for notification from Defence Recruiting who would let us know if Jake had successfully made it through to the final round of testing.

It was about a week or so later when Jake received a call to let him know he would be required to return to Melbourne once again.

The final round of the selection process would involve a full day of interviews and decision making exercises. In addition, he would be required to perform in a number of leadership and team work scenarios in competition with the other applicants.

Jake had decided to go to the city on the Friday night, the day before testing, so he would be relaxed and well rested come Saturday morning for the final phase of selection; one of the most important days of his life! I made sure he knew how proud of him I was before he left.

"Jake, no matter what happens tomorrow, I want you to know I'm so proud of you for everything you've done so far. I know you're not just doing all this for yourself, but for me too… for *us*! Whether you get in or not, just remember how much I love you. And if it doesn't work out, we'll come up with another plan for the future."

"Thanks so much Baby. That means a lot to me."

"I know how much pressure you're putting on yourself Jake. Try and stay relaxed and just do your best. I will be thinking of you from the moment you leave until you get back. My fingers and toes will be crossed the whole time. Good luck Baby. Just be yourself and you will do fine. I love you."

"Thanks Soph, I love you too. I'm feeling pretty confident. I've asked around at my army reserve unit for any info on what I should expect, and I've been told a few little things which could come in handy. I feel ready Babe; so hopefully I won't need any luck," he grinned.

Jake never ceased to amaze me. He couldn't have been more prepared if he tried, and if he was at all nervous he sure wasn't showing it. In contrast, I was that nervous I could barely think straight. When I tried to imagine the interviews and assessments he was going to go through it made me anxious, to the point where I actually felt physically ill. I don't know how Jake managed to stay so composed. Maybe he was nervous on the inside, but it sure didn't look like it! His calm exterior went a long way towards settling my own nerves.

The thought of Jake not being accepted was too much to bear, especially after all the work and commitment he'd put in. But the truth was, even though I was nervous; even scared for him, there was never a time when I actually thought he wasn't going to get in… not one. I had complete faith in him.

As expected, Jake returned home with positive news. He was again 'quietly confident' that he'd done enough. I asked him about the kinds of questions he had to answer during the interviews, and what the group activities were like. He didn't go into great detail, but from what he told me they tested his ability to communicate, think under pressure and make calculated decisions. I think it was pretty safe to assume the entire day would have been quite stressful. I knew Jake would have tried his absolute best, I just prayed his best was enough. So again we played the waiting game to see what direction our lives were about to take.

It must have been close to a month and we still hadn't heard anything. I could tell Jake was starting to get a little anxious, even though he was staying positive. Eventually he got a call from Defence Recruiting; Jake was at my house at the time and the recruiting officer had tracked him down to deliver the news.

While Jake was on the phone, I watched his face intently for any indication as to whether he'd been successful. It wasn't long before his lips curled into a *dead giveaway* smile.

Oh my god... he's in!

I raced over to be by his side. As soon as he hung up the phone I threw my arms around him.

"Holy shit! I actually did it! I did it Baby!" Jake beamed happily.

I laughed and jumped up, wrapping my legs around his waist as well. "Oh Jake, I'm so proud of you," I said before kissing him on the lips. "You must be so happy?" I laughed as he spun me around in the middle of the lounge room.

"I am. I'm so happy… and a little bit scared at the same time. Now I actually have to get through it!"

"Ha… of course you will Jake. Everything you say you're going to do, you end up doing. College will be no different."

I was in awe of him. I already knew I'd never met anyone like Jake before and I always had faith in everything he said, but now, with his latest accomplishment, those same feelings had multiplied exponentially.

"Looks like we're moving to Canberra in June Baby. You excited?"

"Hell yeah! I can't even begin to tell you how excited I am. I'm over the moon."

"I'll have to live on base for at least the first six months. Are you sure you want to move with me straight away?"

"Of course I am. I want to be as close to you as I can, so even if you only have a few spare hours I will be able to see you. I couldn't stand being here in Sunbury with you four hours away. It would absolutely kill me to go back to a long distance relationship; especially now we're engaged. There's no question… I'm definitely coming with you in June."

"OK then. Sounds like you've made up your mind," he chuckled; alluding to how emotive I'd become whilst presenting my reasons for going with him.

There was absolutely no chance of me staying in Sunbury and letting Jake go without me, even if he had to live on base for the next six months. I was going with him; end of story.

Jake called his parents, then I called mine to give them the news that he had been accepted, and that we'd be moving to Canberra in June. Both our families were happy for us.

The next few weeks flew by. Jake and I made a couple of trips to Canberra to have a look at a few rental properties and I submitted a number of job applications in the area. It was my intention to begin a hair dressing apprenticeship at the same time Jake started military college.

Even though I'd been living away from the farm since I was seventeen, moving interstate to a new city was still quite unnerving, especially when Jake wouldn't actually be living with me.

We had saved some money to get me by until Jake began receiving fortnightly pay from the army, but even so I couldn't afford to live in Canberra. I ended up finding a suitable apartment in a small town called Queanbeyan; a ten-minute drive from the city centre. I nicknamed the tiny unit the 'Fifty Cent House' because the building was shaped like a fifty cent piece. I have to say it was a very *unusual* looking place; a least four or five stories high with four apartments on each floor. The upside though, was that it was located across the road from a beautiful park with a stream running through it, and was also within walking distance to the main street and shopping precinct which was convenient.

We'd already inspected at least five other places and this was by far the best of a pretty rough bunch in our price range. I remember standing in the small apartment with Jake. The real estate agent had stepped out to let us decide if we wanted to lease the property.

"Sophie, I don't want you to feel like you *have* to do this. I'll understand if you want to stay in Sunbury at your brother's place. As soon as I start training, I'm going to ask how long I have to live in the barracks before I'm allowed to move off base. Maybe it would be better if you waited a while… till I find out at least."

"No Jake. I want to be close to you."

"I know that but I don't want you to feel unsafe or alone."

"I'll be ok. Once I get a full time job I'll make some friends at work, and this place does feel pretty safe."

"Sophie." He held me by the hands and looked directly into my eyes. "Are you one hundred percent sure about this?"

I returned his serious stare. "You're always telling me everything will be ok; well now it's time for me to say it to you. Trust me Jake, everything is going to be just fine. I'm moving with you and I'm not changing my mind."

"Ok. I'm not trying to change your mind Baby, it's just a big decision."

"And I've decided! I feel comfortable in this apartment and I'll get a job here in Queanbeyan. This is the place."

It felt good to be the one making the plans for a change. I was glad Jake was the kind of man who listened to my opinion and trusted my judgement.

"Well at least you'll be close to me. The college is only a ten-minute drive so if you really need me I'll be able to get here pretty fast. You're sure this apartment is ok?"

"Definitely. Besides, you're always worried about being there in case I need you, but this time it's different… I want to be close in case *you* need *me*!"

He smiled. "What are you talking about… I *always* need you."

His reply melted my heart. I hugged and kissed him with deep affection.

That afternoon I signed a six-month lease and paid the bond on the apartment in the 'Fifty Cent House'. I was happy, excited, worried and scared all at the same time. But through all the emotions I knew it was the right thing to do.

The following week Jake and I returned with my parents and all my belongings. We'd managed to fit my bed, a fridge and all my other gear and furniture onto a trailer which Dad towed all the way from Sunbury to Queanbeyan.

It didn't take us long to unpack, and within an hour of arriving I'd officially moved in. I could tell my parents were a bit worried about me living on my own in a new town, but they did take some comfort in the knowledge that Mum's brother and his wife were reasonably close by. Mike and Janet lived about forty-five-minutes away in a country town just outside of Canberra.

Jake was due to catch a bus home to Sunbury the following day; Mum and Dad had decided to stay with me for a few more days to help me settle in. He had to pack all his gear then drive to Melbourne where he would attend a ceremony and be officially sworn in as an appointed officer of the Australian Army. After the ceremony he would be flown back to Canberra where he would begin his officer training at the Royal Military College – Duntroon; RMC for short.

That night we went out for dinner with Mum and Dad to a local club which was a short walk from my apartment. After dinner, my parents decided to stay at the club for a while to play the poker machines so Jake and I decided to leave them to it. It was our last night together and we wanted to make the most of having the place to ourselves.

"Jake and I might skip the pokies. We'll meet you at home," I said.

"Ok. We'll be at least an hour; probably see you guys a little after nine," replied Dad as he checked his watch.

My parents weren't silly. They knew Jake and I wouldn't be able to give each other a proper farewell considering they were staying in the lounge room of my one-bedroom apartment. Their decision to give us some time alone was thoughtful and appreciated.

I clung to Jake like glue as we slowly strolled home in the cold night air. I wanted to be as close to him as I could until I had to put him on the bus the following day.

I already knew the answer but I asked again anyway. "So once you start at RMC when will you be able to come and visit me?" I guess I thought that talking about when I'd see him again would bring me some comfort; it didn't.

"Well the first eight to nine weeks of the course is initial training, kind of like the boot camp I did when I joined the reserves. I'm almost certain I won't be able to leave the base during that entire phase though. I can't say exactly, but I'm pretty sure after that first part of the course we're given a couple of days off; I should be able to see you then."

I didn't respond. The thought of not seeing him for the next two months or more caused me physical pain. It was a pain which resonated through my entire body, with my heart the unmistakable epicentre.

"Don't be upset Baby." He could feel my body tensing up as I tried to control my emotions. "I know it sounds like a long time, but I think if you keep busy it should go pretty fast."

"Well hopefully it doesn't take me long to find a job, then I'll be able to focus on work while you're gone."

"I'm sure you'll find something, but in the meantime if you need cash don't hesitate to use my card. My whole wage will go into that account so it should be enough for you. All my accommodation and meals are automatically taken straight out of my pay so I won't need any money for a couple of months. It's all yours."

I looked up at him. He knew how I felt about using his money.

"I'm serious… what's mine is yours Baby. I don't want you to worry about money at all. Use the card to get whatever you need. If you're feeling down, spoil yourself. It's only money. What's important is that you're comfortable and happy."

"Ok. I'll only use it if I have to though. Thanks so much."

Even though I didn't want to use his money, it was very comforting to know if it did take me a little longer to find a job I wouldn't have to stress about paying rent or buying food. The day Jake proposed, he told my parents he was going to take care of me… he meant it.

"Sophie you've moved all this way for me, it's really the least I can do. Anyway, once where married everything that's mine will be yours so we might as well start now."

We arrived at the apartment. As we walked up the stairs to my front door I had a mixture of emotions running through me. I was feeling excited about making love with Jake one last time before he had to leave the following day, but at the same time I couldn't help but feel a deep sense of sadness. The reality was it would be months until we were together again.

As soon as we walked into the apartment Jake closed the door behind us, scooped me off my feet and carried me into my bedroom in his arms. He placed me gently on the bed and lay down on top of me.

As he stared into my eyes I looked back at him; spellbound, totally captivated by the love and affection I felt. It was during beautiful moments like these, looking into my lover's eyes, that I would find myself completely astonished. I still couldn't believe how infatuated I was with him. Never in my wildest dreams did I ever imagine I would fall for somebody so hard. I would do anything for this man. Anything he needed from me… he could have, anything he wanted me to do… I would do without hesitation, and any desire he spoke of… I would be all too eager to satisfy. It's an incredible feeling, when you find true satisfaction and happiness through the act of making your lover happy. Whenever I made Jake smile I would be overwhelmed with my own feelings of joy and gratification, and the best part was I completely trusted that he felt exactly the same way about me.

"Jake Freeman?"

"Yes," he chuckled; amused at the way I addressed him.

"I'm going to make love to you now."

"Really?"

"Uh huh. And I'm going to take my time with you because I want you to remember every feeling, every sensation. I don't want you to forget me while you're away."

He raised his eyebrows. "Forget you! I couldn't forget you if I tried. I guarantee all I'll be thinking about is you Baby. Since the day we met, you're all I've ever thought about; it's automatic for me now."

"Good to hear. Now no more talking," I whispered as I pushed him off me and onto his back.

I straddled him, sitting on his groin with my knees either side of his hips. Jake laid his head on the pillow and I gently ran my fingertips over his eyelids; forcing him to close them. I leant forward and let my hair fall onto his face, then moved my head from side to side so my soft locks gently caressed his cheeks and neck. He inhaled deeply; savouring the smell of my hair. I flicked my hair to one side then slowly and ever so lightly placed kisses all over his face; starting in the middle of his forehead, down to the tip of his nose, across each cheek then on his lips. I extended my tongue, licking back and forth across his lips before darting it inside his mouth. Jake immediately grabbed hold of my tongue between his teeth, briefly holding me in position before letting me go. I loved when he would do little things like that; subtly reminding me of his dominance, even though I was the one in control. It drove me wild when he would let me take him over.

I reached down and unzipped his jacket then slowly unbuttoned his shirt; revealing his bare chest. I ran my hands over the sculptured contours of his torso. The look and feel of his hard body worked its magic as usual, making me wetter with each tender caress of his well-formed chest and abdominal muscles. Jake sat up so I could completely remove his jacket and shirt then lay back down again.

As I'd done to his face, I tickled his bare torso with my hair before covering his chest with kisses. I paid particular attention to his nipples; licking, sucking and biting each one in turn before slowly making my way south. I placed deliberate butterfly kisses all the way down his stomach to the edge of his jeans; I felt his body move underneath me as he let out a quiet moan. He was enjoying every tantalizing second. Slowly, I unzipped his jeans; his white boxers doing a poor job of concealing his straining erection.

"What have we got here?" I said cheekily; stroking *him* through his underwear before squeezing it firmly. The feeling of his warm shaft immediately caused my pelvic floor muscles to contract.

I freed *Jake* from his underwear and quickly grasped hold of him with both hands. As I admired his beautiful instrument of pleasure, I found myself at a crossroad; a greedy, lustful crossroad. I wanted so badly to feel him slide into me; to fuck me until he emptied his hot love deep inside, but I also craved his throbbing shaft in my mouth so I could lick and suck him; giving him no choice but to deliver his eruption all over my tongue and down the back of my throat.

What's a girl to do?

Instinct took over and I hastily engulfed his meaty serving, taking as much of his length in my mouth as I could. He moaned as I moved my head back and forth; sucking him in long vacuumed strokes. Jake's hips rose off the bed and his hands hastily found the back of my head as he gently made love to my mouth. He was obviously enjoying himself because it wasn't long before he upped his pace; transitioning into a deliberate, yet careful rhythm which was more akin to fucking than making love.

Having him slide in and out of my mouth that way was such a turn on for me. There was no doubt if he blew his load right then I would've immediately followed suit, even though my patient *kitten* was yet to make an appearance; despite aching for attention.

I was enjoying every thrust of my fiancé's cock, and took great pleasure in rolling my tongue around the head of his shaft with each entry. The sensation of his strong hands on the back of my head, locking me in position, reminded me that I was never really in control of this man. Just as I began to taste the unique flavour of his - pre-cum, I felt the familiar throb which usually gave me a few seconds warning before he climaxed. As I prepared for him to release in my mouth, my favourite part, he pulled my head back; removing *himself* from between my lips.

"Don't stop!" I begged; frowning with disappointment. "I wanted to taste you."

"I know you did, but that wouldn't be fair now would it?" he smiled; glaring at me with blazing eyes.

I shook my head. "I guess not," I replied softly; still grasping his erection firmly with one hand.

"Then sit on my hard cock and ride me!" he ordered.

I didn't need to be asked twice. After giving *him* one final lick from the base to the tip, I hastily jumped off the bed and ripped off my pants and knickers. Jakes eyes never left me as he slid his own pants and underwear off completely. I straddled him again, letting my wetness rest against his dick. The warmth against my lips felt incredible and I couldn't wait a second longer to feel him inside me.

I raised myself off him, reached down and grabbed his hard muscle with my hand then slowly lowered myself onto it. There was no need to take his length bit by bit, I was so wet that his entire shaft impaled me in one smooth action. I closed my eyes and a drawn out moan escaped as the welcome feeling of fullness invaded my body. I put both hands on his chest and started to ride him; exactly as Jake had ordered moments earlier.

Promptly finding a perfect rhythm, he grabbed my hips and drove his cock into me with vigour as I bounced up and down on top of him; riding him like a galloping horse. It was the most heavenly feeling and I could only keep my eyes open for a few seconds at a time; the intense pleasure forcing them shut. I savoured every glorious sensation as my lover filled me, occasionally going so deep that his *tip* would rub against my cervix, causing me to emit an involuntary squeal; a high pitch sound which only served to drive him even wilder.

I didn't even bother trying to hold on; I let myself go. My hips thrust back and forth violently and I let out an uncontrollable scream as I climaxed; coating Jake's cock in a cascade of slippery come.

"Oh my god you're beautiful Baby," his voice snapping me back from the brink of pleasure induced unconsciousness.

I opened my eyes and waited for them to focus. I looked down to see him staring up at me; admiring me. Realising I still had my top on, I lifted it over my head and removed my bra; Jakes hands immediately finding my bare breasts. I leant forward so he could lick my nipples, and as soon as his started to suck and tease them with is mouth I felt another orgasm rapidly building.

"That's it. Oh… that feels nice. That's it Baby," I panted; unnecessary coaching all I could mutter.

Realising I was *close,* he sucked hard on my nipple and drove himself into me with force; rapidly delivering me to another mind altering orgasm which ripped through my body like wildfire, causing me to twitch and jolt uncontrollably.

I paused for a moment to catch my breath; collapsing forward onto his chest.

"I want to taste you," he whispered. "Sit on my face." A usual request of his which was always a huge turn on for me. I loved the feeling of Jake's tongue inside me after I'd climaxed. Coating his shaft with my essence was fantastic, but seeing my come all over his lips and face drove me completely insane.

During sex, I was particularly fond of switching between intercourse and having him go down on me. Transitioning from being penetrated to receiving oral was a fantastic change of sensation which would always induce a couple of rapid orgasms. This time was no different.

As soon as I straddled his face and lowered my completely saturated snatch onto his mouth, Jake drove his tongue inside me; lapping at my juices like he was dying of thirst. Now it was *me* who was holding *his* head as I fucked his face, deliberately rubbing my swollen clit against his top lip as his tongue plunged into me. I thrust my hips back and forth and within a few seconds was vigorously grinding my groin against his mouth and face. He often joked that one day I'd fuck his face so hard I'd end up breaking his nose! He had assured me though; it was an injury he'd be more than happy to endure so I wasn't about to slow down now. I squealed as I let go and I could hear Jake's muffled moans as I drowned him in a torrent of slippery sex. If I'd let him, he would have stayed down there forever.

As wonderful as it was to have multiples, they'd rendered me hyper sensitive to Jakes tongue. He was relentless, exploring my tunnel and circling my clit feverishly; immediately pushing me to yet another head spinning orgasm. I quivered as he softly licked and nibbled my delicate lips, generously letting me recover my senses so I could 'return to earth'.

Usually I would stay for another, satisfying Jakes thirst for my nectar, but I couldn't take it anymore. I was no longer confused by my earlier cross road dilemma. I needed Jake inside me… now; to leave a piece of himself behind so I could hold onto him for as long as I could.

As I made an attempt to climb off his face, he grabbed hold of my thighs with vice like hands and pulled me back down onto his mouth; diving his tongue deep. He was obviously hungry for another sweet serve and I was only too happy to oblige. After all, it was going to be a while until he tasted me again.

"Greedy boy!" I teased; resuming a hip grinding rhythm which was guaranteed to take me over the edge in no time at all.

"Mmm," he moaned as he savoured the taste of me. I looked down to see his eyes staring up at mine; mouth and nose obscured by my pubic bone and the trimmed light brown hair covering it. It was a vision I've definitely become quite fond of.

"That's it Baby," I breathed as he focused his attention on my clit; flicking it rapidly with his tongue. "Oh fuck Jake… that's it! Yes! Yes!" My pelvis uncontrollably twitched and jolted as I came for the third time in my lover's mouth and over his face. I felt greedy for receiving so much pleasure, but at the same time I wanted even more.

I looked behind me and saw his cock pointing to the ceiling; thick veins protruding up and down the length. It looked so lonely, patiently waiting for my attention. Well *his* time had come… so to speak.

I climbed off Jakes face and stood on the bed above him with one foot either side of his hips; his swollen rod directly below me. His eyes were like saucers as he looked at me towering above him; long, messy hair all over my face and a look in my eye as though I wanted to devour him like a sex crazed amazon.

Still on my feet, I slowly descended towards him. The lower I squatted, the wider my *lips* parted. Jake's eyes were now firmly fixed on my glistening entrance; paused only millimetres above his cock. I knew it was a sight which would drive him wild.

"Fuck Soph… that looks amazing!"

"I know," I replied with a smile as I lowered myself onto him; every inch of his shaft slowly disappearing inside me.

As I began to squat up and down, providing a visual display he wasn't going to forget any time soon, I watched his expression with deep satisfaction. He couldn't take his eyes off the display in front of him; dividing his attention between the sight of my pussy engulfing his thick bone, and my breasts as they bounced in unison with our sexual rhythm.

Knowing how much my lover was enjoying it, I upped the tempo; riding him as though it was my last fuck; a move which significantly reduced Jake's ability to hold back his imminent release.

"I'm not going to last long," he confessed; his hands now under my ass cheeks taking some of my weight, for which I was very appreciative. This wasn't a position you could hold for hours and my thighs were already getting one hell of a workout!

"I know… you're so hard! I'm ready when you are Baby," I gasped; fighting to hold myself on the precipice of my final orgasm until Jake was ready to let go.

I'd barely finished my sentence when I felt him swell. His rigid shaft felt like a shuttle pointing to the heavens; mere seconds away from lift off.

I closed my eyes and rode my stallion hard. "Come in me Jake… come in me!" I begged in between pleasurable moans as he penetrated me with ferocity.

Jake thrust his hips off the bed and growled loudly as he climaxed. The feeling of his lava-hot come shooting deep inside me was exactly what I'd been waiting for and I let go; simultaneously exploding with him. I threw my head back as my final orgasm consumed me; my 'big one' so intense that I couldn't help but scream like a wild banshee. A combination of intense pleasure and emotion flowed through me, one wave after another. It was glorious and felt like it was never going to end.

Throughout all my sexual experiences with Jake, I'd definitely felt some intense orgasms. But with all the emotion surrounding the inevitable goodbye the following day, this one reduced me to tears.

I still had my head tipped back as my orgasm slowly subsided. Tears had already started to stream down my cheeks. As I looked forward and collapsed on Jake's chest I tried desperately to get control of myself. I didn't want him to know I was upset but it was a futile attempt, considering my audible sobs were unmistakable.

Jake wrapped his arms around me. "Baby… are you ok?"

I gathered myself before answering. "I'm ok. I'm just overwhelmed that's all."

He kissed me on the forehead.

"I feel so good when I'm with you Jake. Words can't describe how happy you make me. I don't know how I'm going to say goodbye tomorrow."

"I don't want to leave you either, but I keep telling myself it's going to be worth it in the end. You've just got to remember it's not forever, and I won't be too far away."

He was right. I needed to keep focused on our future, the future I'd dreamt about; the one we'd planned together.

With Jake still inside me, I looked into his eyes. "I don't want to let you go," I smiled; clenching my pelvic floor muscles and holding *him* firmly in place.

"Believe me, I wish we could… but we can't stay like this forever," he chuckled as he rolled to the side; tipping me off him.

We both burst out laughing at the feeling of him sliding out of me; one I would never get used to.

"I don't know how I'm going to go a couple of months without you Baby. It's going to kill me!" Jake said as I lay beside him. His eyes travelling up and down my naked body; freshly fucked and totally relaxed.

"Well all *this* will be waiting for you Lover," I teased; running my fingers across my breasts and down between my thighs.

"You're incredible Sophie… so sexy and beautiful."

"And don't you forget it," I giggled.

"Impossible!"

Jake and I had a quick shower before my parents returned from the club. I had to open the windows to freshen the place up as the distinct smell of sex filled the air in my tiny apartment. It was then that I recalled how loud I'd been moments earlier in the throes of pleasure.

Well the neighbours definitely know this unit isn't vacant anymore! I cringed at the thought of people listening to me having sex and vowed to do my best not to bump into any of my new neighbours for at least a few weeks.

Jake and I crawled into bed half an hour or so after Mum and Dad got home. I don't think we slept all night as both of us savoured every precious second we had together. We didn't talk much, just the odd whisper; careful not to keep my parents up. Mostly we just lay there gazing into each other's eyes; lost in our own perfect world. It was beautiful, but at the same time I felt a constant flow of sadness surging through me. My heart ached at the thought of what I had to do when the sun came up.

Jake talked with my parents as we drove him to the bus stop; located in the heart of Canberra. I barely said a word the entire trip. As we sat in the back seat he rested his arm around my shoulders and I snuggled into him like a baby monkey clings to its mother. I wanted to melt into him.

We arrived at the terminal with half an hour to spare. Jake went and brought his ticket then Mum and Dad said their goodbyes and wished him the best of luck at RMC. He'd earned the love and respect of my parents, and I could see in their eyes that they were both proud of him.

Mum gave him a kiss and a hug. "Take care Jake and good luck."

"Thanks Lynn, it means a lot."

Dad shook Jake's hand. "Look after yourself won't you?"

"I will David, I will. And I want to thank you both for helping us move all of Sophie's things up here. I really appreciate all your help. Thank you."

"It's our pleasure," replied Mum. "Sophie will always be our daughter and you can always ask us for help… anytime," she added; looking in my direction.

"That's right, we're only a few hours away so if either of you need us just pick up the phone," Dad reiterated.

"Thanks Lynn, thanks David. I appreciate it," said Jake sincerely.

I knew I should have probably said 'thanks' as well, but I could barely speak.

My parents decided to go and have a coffee in a nearby café, so we could farewell each other in private. They said a final goodbye to Jake then left us alone.

We were sitting on a bench outside, close to where all the buses pull in.

"I'm glad your parents are staying with you for a few more days. It makes it just that little bit easier to say goodbye. I wouldn't be able to leave you knowing you were going back to your unit on your own."

"Yeah they said they're going to stay until you're back in Canberra later in the week. I hope you have a safe flight from Melbourne back here on Wednesday."

"To tell you the truth I'm actually a little bit nervous about flying. Remember I've never been on a plane before!"

"Oh that's right I forgot! Well I'm sure you'll enjoy it; especially the take-off."

"It will definitely be an experience. I'll give you a call this afternoon when my bus gets back to Sunbury to let you know I'm home."

"Ok that'd be good." I paused for a moment. The realisation we were about to begin another extended stint apart wasn't easy to accept, especially since he was only going to be living ten or so minutes away.

"I don't want you to go Jake. I want you here with me. I can't stand not being able to see you and touch you. It kills me."

"I know… it hurts me too Baby. I'm going to miss you like crazy. I'll call you whenever I can, but just remember the first couple of months will be fairly intense so I'm not sure how often I'll get to a phone. But when I get the chance I'll definitely be calling as often as I can. I will also suss out when you can come and visit me too. I've heard that some Sundays everyone is allowed an hour to go to church, so maybe you'll be able to come in then. We might be allowed to stay outside the Chapel and catch up. I know an hour is nothing but it would help both of us get through each week."

"Oh I hope so, that'd be so good. I wouldn't care if it was only for five minutes, I'll take whatever I can get!"

"Well just don't get your hopes up Baby. If the last boot camp I did was anything to go by, I'll barely have a minute to myself for weeks."

"I love you Jake. Whatever happens at RMC, just remember I love you and I'm so proud of everything you've done so far. I know you'll do great and I want you to know how much I appreciate you doing all this for us."

"Thanks Soph. It means everything to hear you say that. And you're right, I am doing this for us, just like you have moved all the way to Canberra for us. Thank you so much for moving Baby, it makes me feel stronger knowing your so close by. Promise me though, if things aren't working out and you don't feel comfortable or safe, or you miss your family too much, you can move home. I will completely understand if you decide to move back to Sunbury. I don't want you to stay here on your own if you're not happy."

"I won't be going anywhere without you Jake. I'll be fine. Once I get a job and settle into a routine everything will work out. I don't want you to worry about me too much; just focus on getting through this first few months."

"Ok I will. But you know me, I can't help but worry about you. I promised I'd take care of you forever, so I can't help but worry when I'm not with you. I can't switch it off."

A bus pulled into the terminal and Jake looked down at his ticket to check his coach number.

"That's my bus now," he said solemnly; intensifying the pain in my heart.

Quite a few people had gathered outside the terminal ready to board, a clear signal that it would soon be time for Jake to leave. We stood up and wrapped our arms around each other. I kissed him passionately on the lips and could feel the sting of tears in my eyes as our lips locked together in our final goodbye. All I could feel was sadness and pain deep inside my chest. A heavy, cold feeling of emptiness I would never get used to.

As we kissed I could feel tears rolling down my cheeks but I didn't care, I never wanted our mouths to part. I wanted time to just stop, never to restart again so I could stay with my *angel* forever.

"Canberra to Sunbury now boarding… Canberra to Sunbury," a voice sounded over the speaker.

Oh my god I have to let him go. My stomach twisted itself into a knot at the sound of the announcement.

I savoured every last second of our farewell kiss. I buried my head under his chin and squeezed him as hard as I could.

"Don't stand here and watch the bus drive away Baby. Just go straight to your parents at the café."

I nodded. I knew if I tried to answer him my tears would turn into uncontrollable sobs; just as they had last night.

Jake put his hands on my cheeks and lifted my head up so he could look directly into my eyes. "Sophie Taylor, I love you more than you'll ever know. I always have, and I always will."

The sight of two tears slowly trickling from the corner of his eyes and down his cheeks completely shattered my heart to pieces.

"I love you too," I breathed quietly. I was trying so hard to hold myself together.

Jake kissed me on the lips again and pulled me to his chest one last time. I closed my eyes.

"I know this will be hard but when I let you go, just turn and walk. Don't stand there and watch me drive away… just turn and walk."

I couldn't breathe, I felt like I was going to faint. *Just turn and walk Sophie!* I thought, desperately trying to find some courage.

"Bye Baby," Jake whispered as his arms let me go.

I lifted my head and looked into his beautiful eyes one last time, then turned and took two or three steps in the opposite direction; walking away without looking back just as he said.

My broken heart literally felt like it stopped beating altogether, when suddenly I felt Jakes hand on my wrist. He spun me back towards him and planted one final kiss on my lips; one last precious moment of pure passion.

As our lips parted I found my voice; I would have no other chance. "Jake I love you… I love you so much… I'm yours forever… I love you," I said feverishly. "Goodbye Baby," I cried.

"Bye Sweetie." He let go of me, walked to the bus and put his bag in the luggage compartment underneath.

As he made his way to the door at the front of the bus he turned and waved goodbye; a vision that scarred itself into my memory. I waved back until Jake was on the bus, then turned and walked away in the direction of the café.

I'd been alone for less than a minute and already I missed him. It was such a painful farewell and I felt as though I'd just said goodbye to a piece of my body. Jake was more than just my lover or my fiancé; he was a part of me… and now he was gone.

CHAPTER TWENTY-TWO

A CHANGE OF PLANS

As much as I had my heart set on starting a hairdressing apprenticeship in my new town, it wasn't meant to be. I put in job applications at every salon in Queanbeyan and even a few in Canberra, but nobody would take me on. I'm pretty sure it was because I was up front about my fiancé going to RMC, which meant I'd more than likely be moving in the next eighteen months. Right from the start my potential employers knew I wouldn't be staying with them for the entire duration of my apprenticeship. I suppose I could have lied and said I'd moved here indefinitely just to get the job, but that wasn't my style. So after nearly two weeks without a job, I'd resigned to the fact hairdressing wasn't going to happen; at least not for now.

Since I had a lot of experience in retail, particularly fashion, I decided to go to the main shopping centre in Queanbeyan and ask the store managers if there were any available positions. I made sure I was well dressed and had my hair and make-up looking sharp. I knew first impressions were everything so I was determined to make a good one. I desperately needed a job, and not just for the money but for my sanity too. I couldn't handle spending another week without having anything to do.

That morning I left my apartment, unemployed and worried. By lunchtime I had managed to secure three job interviews, and within the next two days I had a full time job as a sales assistant at a major clothing outlet; as luck would have it after only the first interview.

I was so happy and felt like a giant weight had been lifted off me. I was relieved to be able to start making some money and to have something to take my mind off the pain of being away from Jake.

I hadn't heard from him since the night before he went to Melbourne to be appointed, which was over two weeks ago. I thought about him constantly and prayed he was coping with the demands of the course, even though I was confident he'd be doing ok. I guess I always thought of Jake as doing everything well, so I assumed RMC would be no different. I still wanted to hear from him though, to let me know he was alright. Plus, I wanted to tell him all about my new job. I was certain it would help him concentrate if he knew I'd found work and was keeping myself busy.

It was about 8:30pm when the phone rang.

"Hey Baby! How are you?"

"Oh Jake… I've missed you so much!"

It was such a relief to finally hear from him. My heart fluttered at the sound of his voice.

"I miss you too Soph, more than you could imagine."

"Well as much as you miss me, times it by a million and you still wouldn't be close to how much I miss you. It's driving me crazy not having you here with me." I wasn't joking either. I actually *was* going a little crazy without him.

"I know what you mean Babe. When I think about you I swear I can actually feel my heart aching. It's hard not being able to see you, especially when I know you're only minutes away."

"I could always jump in the car and come and pay you a sneaky visit," I teased.

"Please… don't even suggest it. If you arrived here I would be in your car in a flash so you could take me away with you."

I closed my eyes and briefly imagined going through with it. *Sounds like a good idea to me!*

"By the way, how is the apartment? Have you met your neighbours?"

"It's not too bad. I haven't met any neighbours yet." I was still keeping a low profile after screaming the roof off the last night Jake and I were here together. "The people next door to me are pretty noisy though. They play loud music well into the night which keeps me up till all hours."

"Inconsiderate bastards!"

"Yeah they are."

"Maybe you should give the real estate a buzz and let them know."

"I thought about it, but I've only just moved in and don't want to cause any trouble. I'll put up with it a while longer. How's the course going?" I asked; quickly changing the subject. I didn't want to spend my first call from Jake talking about the neighbours.

"It's madness. We don't have a spare second. It's very similar to the boot camp I did before I went into the reserves, but there is definitely a lot more pressure here. A few people have already started to show signs of giving up. I guess it's not for everyone. I'm sorry I haven't been able to call you; the instructors don't want us to call home too often. They say it's to get us used to being away from family."

Get used to being away! I didn't like the sound of that at all, but I didn't say anything to Jake; he had enough to worry about.

"Hey guess what?" I exclaimed; changing the topic again.

"What… have you got a job?" he replied excitedly.

"Sure have… full time in a clothing store. It's in the shopping complex over the bridge from my place so I'll be able to walk to work."

"Oh sweet! Congratulations Soph. I'm so happy for you. You must be so relieved and excited?"

"Yeah I am. I was a bit disappointed I didn't get a hair dressing apprenticeship but now I'm just glad to be working. I start in a couple of days' time."

"Well good luck Baby… not that you'll need it. I'm so proud of you."

"I'm proud of you too Jake. I hope the training isn't too hard?"

"The fitness stuff is great but all the theory is fairly tough."

"Just keep trying your best."

"I will… thanks. I'll have to love you and leave you Baby. I'm not sure when I can call again but hopefully it will be soon.

"It's ok, call me when you can. Just stay focused on your course; I'll be fine."

As much as I was missing him, I put on a brave front to keep him positive and to stop him from worrying about me anymore than he already was.

"I'll do some asking around and find out when you'll be able to come and visit me. Hopefully next time I call you I should have some more details."

"I hope so. I love you Jake and I never stop thinking about you."

"I love you too Baby. Be careful when you're walking to work, and don't walk home in the dark. If you know you're finishing late then make sure you drive."

"I will… promise. Dream about me ok?"

"I dream about you every night Sweetie. I love you and take care."

"Bye Jake. I miss you."

"Bye Soph."

As soon as he hung up I felt upset; on the verge of crying. *Breathe Sophie, Breathe.* I followed my own advice and took a few deep breaths. I managed to calm myself down; enough to avoid a pouring of tears anyway. I figured I was going to have to get used to Jake being away, and breaking down every time he called wasn't going to help me at all. I was actually proud of myself for being able to control my emotions, and couldn't help but feel a little more confident about coping on my own.

Starting full time work at the clothing store was a blessing. In addition to making some much needed cash, it went a long way towards diverting my mind away from constantly thinking about Jake and how much I missed him. The interaction with the other staff and customers made living on my own a lot easier as well. Some days, after talking pretty much all day, I was actually glad to get home to an empty house; the peace and quiet a welcome change at the end of a busy day. That's not to say I wouldn't have given anything to walk in the door and see Jake standing in my apartment; arms wide open.

I instantly made friends with a couple of girls who worked at the shop. It was great to be able to talk with them about Jake and what we were going through, as well as hear their stories of love and family. With each passing day I felt more comfortable living in my new town. It was definitely starting to feel like home.

Eventually I met one of my neighbours; a single man in his late forties. I think his name was Bill and he seemed nice enough. Unfortunately, the people who lived directly beside me, and I mean *directly* as in on the other side of my lounge room wall, were absolute fuck wits! I'm pretty sure it was a couple with one, maybe two children. I never heard a peep out of them during daylight hours, apart from the odd cry of a small child, but as soon as the sun went down they'd start drinking and without a doubt taking drugs; then the relentless noise would begin. Whether it was them swearing and abusing each other, yelling at the child (or children), or cranking up their music until all hours of the morning; the inconsiderate noise of these people defied belief. It was absolutely relentless. Sometimes their fighting would even spill out of their apartment and into the stairwell right outside my door. It was a nightmare.

I remember one particular night. It was at least 2:30am, probably closer to 3. I was sitting on the couch in the lounge room, wide awake and furious thanks to the combination of music, yelling and screaming coming from the neighbours from hell. I've never been so frustrated and angry in my entire life. It was at least the third or fourth night of madness in a row, and I had to work the next day. The sheer desperation for sleep caused me to go a little crazy, and I found myself staring at the brick wall which divided my apartment from theirs; my patients at boiling point. I know the thoughts I was having were out of character for me but I couldn't help it. I was staring and concentrating so hard on that wall, more specifically the people on the other side. I wanted them to just die… to shut the fuck up and die so I could get some sleep!

Nights like these would drive me insane, and I would've called the real estate to complain except something told me it wouldn't have been a smart move to get on the wrong side of them, especially considering I was living on my own. So I resorted to sleeping with earplugs and double checking they were nowhere in sight every time I left the apartment, so I never bumped into them.

At one point I had a chat about them with Bill. He lived on the other side of the inconsiderate dickheads and was fed up with their shit as well. He told me he was taking steps to have them kicked out of the building and asked if I wanted to sign a petition to have them removed. As much as I wanted them gone, I was concerned about pissing them off so I declined. Turns out it was the right move because when the trouble makers found out Bill had complained about them, they abused him, urinated on his door and trashed his car. *Fucking losers!* I was glad I wasn't involved.

So thanks to the assholes next door, I quickly developed a hatred for my apartment in the 'Fifty Cent House'. I'd signed a six-month lease so I knew moving would be an expensive option. I figured my best bet was to avoid the neighbours at all costs, keep to myself and spend as much time at work as possible.

Isn't it funny how things work out?

Because I couldn't stand being at the apartment, I asked the boss to give me every extra shift at the store to keep me out of the house, and since I was working so much I was able to sell more stock than any other staff member. This led the Regional Manager to take notice of me and how 'dedicated' I was to my job. I didn't think I needed to tell her the reason why, instead opting to soak up the praise which was offered. It wasn't long before the store manager, my boss, moved on. Due to my performance and 'dedication', I was offered the store managers position which I gratefully accepted. So I guess in hindsight, I should probably be grateful to the noisy pricks next door. Good things really can come out of bad situations after all.

I couldn't believe how lucky I was. I'd only been working at the store for a little over a month and I'd landed the manager's job. Of course it was a lot more responsibility but the beauty of it was, apart from earning more money, I could set my own hours. My staff must have thought I was the best boss in the world, because I'd constantly do every late night and weekend shift. Pretty much all the shifts that my staff hated… I did; anything to keep me out of my apartment.

Working all the time was wearing me out and the battle for sleep didn't help the situation. Getting through a twelve hour shift on only two hours' sleep was a prick, but I was grateful for having something to keep my mind off missing my *lover* which meant the weeks ticked by just that little bit faster.

It was close to a fortnight since I'd heard from Jake, and apart from the fact I needed to hear the sound of his voice as much as I needed air to breathe, I also was busting to tell him about my promotion at work. I knew he'd be proud of me and that my success at work would go a long way towards confirming that I was coping well on my own.

Jake must have sensed how desperately I needed to talk to him, because when I got home from work that night my phone rang just as I walked in the door. I put my bag down and seen 'unknown' appear on the caller ID. Jake had to ring me from RMC on a pay phone so I guessed it would be him.

"Hello gorgeous boy!" I answered excitedly.

"Hello gorgeous girl!" Jake chuckled. "How did you know it was me?"

"I could sense it Baby. How are you?"

"Slowly getting there. The instructors are still running us off our feet every day. Quite a few people have already pulled the pin, but I'm doing ok."

"That's good to hear. I've been praying you were doing well."

"Hey, I've got some great news Soph."

"Me too," I replied eagerly.

"Really! You first Baby."

"Well to cut a long story short, the people who live next to me are complete fucking assholes and I can't stand being home because they keep me up all night with their music and yelling."

Jake cut me off. "Wait, I thought you had good news for me?" he said; understandably puzzled by my rant.

"Yeah I do. I'm getting to it."

"Ok…"

"So because I hate the neighbours, I've been working pretty much every day; picking up extra shifts and staying back if the boss needed me too, just so I don't have to be here. Anyway my boss ended up leaving and I was offered the store managers position. So now I'm running the shop!"

"Are you shitting me!" Jake replied excitedly.

"No I'm serious… I'm the manager now!"

"Sophie you are an absolute legend!" he yelled into the phone, making me laugh out loud. "I'm so happy for you… and proud!"

"And I get a pretty good pay packet now too! I think I make more than you now," I teased.

"Well at least I know where I need to go for a loan. I wish I was there to give you a kiss and a cuddle Baby. I'm just blown away."

"I wish you were here too."

"Your parents must be wrapped Soph?"

"Yeah, they're really happy for me."

"Well so am I Babe… so am I."

"So…" I prompted. "What's your news?"

"Oh yeah. You know how I said we might get a chance to go to the chapel on Sunday's?"

"Yeah!" My ears pricked up and eyes widened.

"Well it starts this weekend, and I've asked one of my instructors if it'd be ok if you came and visited me for an hour, instead of me going into the chapel for the service. He said it would be fine as long as we stayed in the chapel car park and didn't go anywhere."

I screamed with excitement.

"So if you're not busy this Sunday night at 5:00pm, I'd love you to come and see me?"

"Are you kidding? Of course I'll be there!"

"Great. I can't wait to see you… and hold you… and kiss you. I miss you like crazy!"

"I can't wait either."

"Awesome. Well I'd better get going; there's a bit of a line up for the phones. I won't get a chance to call you before Sunday so I'll see you in a couple of days ok?"

"You will Jake… I'll definitely be there. 5:00pm Sunday at the chapel."

"That's it. When you drive into the base just stay on the main road. You'll see signs directing you where to go."

"Ok. I love you."

"I love you too, and awesome news about your job Soph."

"Thanks. I'll see you in a couple of days."

"Can't wait. See you soon."

"Bye Jake."

He hung up the phone; I could never hang up on him first.

Sunday couldn't arrive fast enough. From the moment I found out when I was going to see Jake again it seemed like time slowed down to a snail's pace. After a long and painfully slow week, Sunday afternoon finally rolled around. It was time to go and see my lover.

I spent ages getting ready because I wanted to be looking my absolute best for him. In a way I felt like I was making a first impression all over again. I didn't know exactly what to expect, I mean we only had an hour together. Just in case though, I decided to wear a skirt which would give Jake 'easy access' if the opportunity presented itself. I knew there was a slim chance of anything sexual happening but I was so horny I didn't want to let an opportunity slip by because of a poor choice of clothing. It had been close to a month since I'd seen Jake, but due to the constant distraction of my dick head neighbours, I'd only masturbated a few times since he'd left. I was on edge and in desperate need of a release at the hands of my fiancé. Truth be told, just the thought of being in a car with Jake aroused me. I had a severe craving for him and was doing my best to avoid getting my hopes up.

As I drove into the base my belly was alive with butterflies. There are a lot of shit things about being away from your lover, but there is one positive… just one. The incredible anticipation and the nervous, excited feelings that run through your body when you prepare to be reunited. My butterflies always reminded me of such feelings.

I drove slowly and marvelled at the beauty of the college. The crisp white buildings and perfectly sculptured gardens were breath taking, and the entire place had an aura of discipline and excellence. As I drove past the enormous parade ground which was surrounded by immaculate three-story barrack blocks, I could hardly believe a place like that existed.

I followed the 'Chapel' signs, eventually arriving in the car park Jake had spoken of. I pulled into a space and noticed maybe four or five other cars with women sitting in the front seat; obviously waiting for their partners as I was.

It was about ten to five, so I had a minute to quickly check my appearance in the mirror and spray another hit of perfume on my neck. I got out of the car and leant against the bonnet; waiting for him to arrive.

Within a couple of minutes, I saw a group of maybe thirty or so soldiers marching towards the chapel. My heart started to thump as soon as I saw them; knowing *my* man was among the group.

As they drew closer I spotted him. *Thump! Thump! Thump!* I was so excited I honestly thought I was going to have to sit down.

"Alamein Company… Halt!" barked the soldier in command. "Fall Out!"

The soldiers turned sharply, took three steps in unison then broke away from their neat formation. Instantly Jake turned and started running towards me; removing his hat so it didn't blow off his head. I was going to run towards him too but I was so nervous I wasn't entirely confident my legs would work properly, so instead took a few steps away from the car and opened my arms; ready to embrace him.

As soon as Jake reached me he wrapped his arms around my waist and lifted me off the ground. I looked down at him, into his beautiful eyes, before placing my hands on his cheeks and planting a passionate kiss on his lips. It felt so good to be in his arms again, and even better to feel his mouth on mine after so many weeks apart. After savouring the taste of each other, Jake put me down.

I wrapped my arms around his neck and hugged him tightly. "It feels so good to hold you again. I've missed you like you wouldn't believe."

"I've missed you too Baby." Jake nuzzled into my neck and inhaled deeply. "Oh my god… you smell amazing!"

"And you *feel* amazing," I replied; running my hands over his back and down his arms. "How long can you stay with me?"

"Only an hour unfortunately, then I have to go back. Let's get in the car so we have a little privacy," he suggested; looking around at the other couples who were doing the same.

I got back in the driver's seat and Jake climbed in the passenger side. Once we were in the car we started kissing again. I would've been happy not to talk for the entire hour; kissing and holding each other was absolutely magic. Every time our lips and tongues moved against one and other, I was overcome with similar feelings to the night of Kylie's Debutante Ball, back when Jake and I shared our first kiss outside in the cool night air. The love and energy flowed between us like a raging river… as always.

Jake stopped kissing me so he could talk. "By the way congratulations Soph… store manager already! You must be pretty happy with yourself?"

"Yeah I am actually. It was a real surprise. I guess spending so much time at the shop must have worked in my favour."

"I reckon you're probably right, but don't forget the fact that you're great at your job too! They wouldn't have given you the position if you weren't"

"Thanks Babe," I smiled modestly.

We talked for a short while about a few different things; like his training and my annoying neighbours. We never let go of each other's hands the whole time, and we'd regularly pause mid-conversation to steal another passionate kiss.

"Now… I need to ask you something," Jake spoke as though he had been waiting for the right moment to bring it up since we got in the car.

"It sounds serious. Should I be worried?"

I guess it's just human nature but I couldn't help but feel anxious. For some reason I was prepared for bad news.

"I guess it's pretty serious. The thing is, since I've been here I have been asking a lot of questions; trying to find out exactly when I will be able to move off base and live with you."

"Ok."

"And basically, as the situation stands, it looks like I'm not going to be allowed to move out at all."

My heart sank instantly, but before I could get upset Jake quickly continued.

"The thing is, only married members or those in de-facto relationships are allowed to live off base."

My eyes widened as I waited anxiously for his next sentence.

"So with that in mind, I was wondering if you'd consider getting married earlier. I know we told our parents that we planned on having a long engagement, but if we bring our wedding forward it means we can live together while I'm here at RMC. I don't want you to feel pressured Babe, but the way I see it the whole point of getting married is to be together, which *is* what we want after all. I hate not being with you, and the thought of living on base for the next eighteen months is unbearable."

For a brief moment I was somewhat stunned into silence as I attempted to process everything I'd just heard.

"Soph?" Jake prompted me for a response.

"So when were you thinking of having our wedding?" I was trying to keep calm but inside I felt like screaming with joy at the top of my lungs.

"Well I get close to four weeks off over Christmas and New Year's, so I was thinking maybe early January; the sixth to be exact."

By now I was unable to hold back my happiness; an ear-to-ear grin stretched across my face. Without realising I was doing it, I'd let go of Jake and was clapping my hands together like an excited child.

"I gather by your reaction… it's a yes!" he chuckled.

"Oh it's a yes alright! Oh my god Jake… of course it's a yes!"

We hugged and kissed again.

"January! I can't believe we're getting married in January!" I repeated aloud. As I sat there looking deep into Jake's eyes, all of a sudden the realisation I had about four months to organise our wedding hit me like a ton of bricks. "Holy shit! We're getting married in January!"

Jake started laughing. "Looks like you've got a bit of planning to do Baby. I'd love to help but I'm a little busy."

"Yeah that'd be right… leave me with all the dirty work," I joked.

"I know four months or so isn't a very long time to plan a wedding, so to make things easy you have my permission to organise whatever you like. You can run ideas by me if you want, but if you need to make decisions and you can't get hold of me, know that I'll trust your judgement completely. All you have to remember Baby, is if *you're* happy… *I'll* be happy."

"Thanks. I'm sure Mum will help me out, especially since I will be organising it from here. You just keep focused on training and I will take care of the wedding."

"Are you sure about this Soph? I really don't want you to feel pressured."

"Pressured? Becoming your wife has been a dream of mine since we first met. I've never been more certain of anything else in my life. You're not pressuring me at all; I want this."

"It's such a relief to hear you say that. I wonder what our parents will think? I mean I basically *promised* your mum and dad it would be a long engagement."

"I'm sure they'll understand. Besides, by the time we actually get married we'll have been engaged for almost a year anyway. How long did they want us to wait?"

"Two!" Jake smiled.

I couldn't help but laugh. *My poor parents!*

"So we're just going to have to hang in there till the end of the year. Are you going to be ok to live by yourself until then?"

"Yeah I'll be fine, but once we're married we're not living in the fifty-cent house!"

"We won't have to. Once we're married, the army will give us rent assistance so we'll be able to find a place a little bit nicer. Leave the housing part to me and you focus on the wedding plans."

"Sounds good," I replied; excited at the prospect of only having to spend a few more months in my apartment.

"There is a little bit of bad news though. This week we'll be heading out to another military base for the next phase of our training. It's about a twenty-minute drive from here and it's where we'll be doing all our field exercises and live firing."

"How long will you be out there?"

"It's at least six weeks I think; maybe longer. Pretty much till the end of boot camp. But when we finish out there we will get the weekend off, so I'll be able to come and stay with you for a couple of nights."

"So will you be able to call me?"

"That's the thing. I'm not sure if there are any public phones out there, but a few of the guys have mobiles. Hopefully I will be able to borrow one of theirs every now and then to make a quick call to you."

"It's ok, I'll just keep myself busy with work and wedding plans. I'll be fine."

Again I forced a positive response, even though I was already finding it hard not hearing from him on a regular basis. There was no point in giving Jake any sign that I might be struggling on my own. It would only serve to distract him.

The hour had slipped away in the blink of an eye. A lump formed in my throat at the thought of saying goodbye again. I think the vast range of emotions I'd experienced in the last sixty minutes was the reason for the sick feeling which had rapidly developed in my stomach… and I wasn't the only one.

Jake looked at his watch then back to me; the sadness in his eyes clearly visible. "Fuck this is hard!" he said; catching me off guard. "I feel like I need to apologise for putting you through this shit." He dropped his head down as if he was ashamed of something.

"No Jake. Stop." I knew he was feeling bad about leaving me again, and the thought of him taking it out on himself hurt me far greater than any goodbye.

"I'm supposed to be looking after you, protecting you, but how can I do that when I can't even be with you?" He continued to look down. "I feel like I'm letting you down… like I'm failing you."

I took a deep breath and held back the tears which pricked the corners of my eyes. It was absolutely heart wrenching to see the man I loved and adored, who is usually so confident and strong, and always has everything under control, with his head down and shoulders slumped because he honestly believed he was failing me.

I immediately knew this was serious because Jakes body language literally changed as though someone flicked an emotional switch. He went from happy and smiling while we talked about the wedding, to sad… almost depressed, within the space of a few minutes; all because he thought he wasn't looking after me like he promised he would.

Be strong Sophie. Be strong for him! I had to help him and I only had a few minutes to do it. The thought of leaving him in this state was like a spear through my heart.

"Jake… look at me Baby," I said softly; lifting his head with my hand under his chin.

He wasn't crying but his blue eyes spoke a thousand words. He really *did* think he was letting me down. It was then I realised, he could obviously see through the strong and positive exterior I was trying so hard to exhibit. He knew I was struggling without him, and what killed him the most… was there was absolutely nothing he could do about it.

Say something! Help him! Tell him the truth!

"I'm not going to lie Jake. I'm finding it hard too. But now that I know we'll be together soon, I'm going to be fine. I'll get through the next few months… I promise."

He didn't respond.

"You always say that you trust me right?"

"Of course."

"Well I'm asking you to trust me now, when I tell you I'm going to be ok. I have my work, I've made a couple of friends; and even though my apartment isn't the best, I still feel safe. Please, please, don't ever feel like you've let me down. It breaks my heart to hear you say that."

His eyes softened and an appreciative smile gradually appeared on his face.

You're on the right track Soph. Keep going!

"Jake, I know why you're here at RMC. I know you're here for me… for us. I'm so grateful for everything you've already done for me so far, and for what you are trying to achieve for me in the future. I love you." I wrapped my arms around him and squeezed tightly. "I'm alright… believe me."

"You really mean it? You'll be ok?" he said quietly; nuzzling against my neck.

I put my hands on his cheeks and looked directly into his eyes; our noses almost touching. "Yes Jake. I mean it."

"Sorry for getting upset. I just worry about you Baby… constantly."

"I know you do and it's ok. I'm glad you worry about me because it shows how much you love me."

"I do love you Soph. Always have."

"Always will," I butted in; finishing his sentence.

I looked out the window and seen the soldiers getting into formation for the march back to the barracks. "Looks like you've got to go Sweetie."

Jake sighed loudly. "Yeah I'd better let you go. Give me one more kiss."

"Gladly," I grinned as I latched onto him one more time; my mouth greedily drinking in the taste of my lover.

Our lips separated and Jake hugged me tightly. "I love you Soph and I will call you when I can."

"Ok Babe. I'll let you know what ideas I can come up with for our *wedding*," I emphasised. "And I love you too… with all my heart."

He let go of me and climbed out of the car. I watched as he lined up with the rest of the soldiers. I noticed he was the last one to take his position, and the soldier in command looked like he was waiting for Jake. The formation marched off immediately.

Shit, I hope he's not in trouble! I thought to myself.

I waited in the car and watched as the group marched away in perfect step. My eyes were glued to Jake who was at the back. Once they were out of sight I started the engine and began the lonely drive home.

Naturally I was sad to say goodbye and leave Jake behind. My heart ached painfully as usual and the thought of not knowing when I would hear from him again was horrible, but aside from this, I couldn't help but feel excited at the prospect of getting married so soon. I was thankful Jake had told me of his plans, because it did make it slightly easier to recover from leaving him… *slightly*. Don't get me wrong though, I could still feel a lump in my throat after saying goodbye, and it took a few hours for my heart to fully recover from seeing Jake so upset with himself, but I was managing to hold things together; no tears at least.

So for the next few weeks I was in full throttle wedding planner mode. As much as I wanted to run ideas past Jake before making decisions, there just wasn't time; and waiting for him to call before making bookings wasn't possible.

As it turned out I pretty much planned the entire wedding on my own from my little apartment in Queanbeyan. I organised the church and reception centre in Sunbury, the dinner menu, cars, photographer, cake and all the other minor arrangements. I did make one trip home to Sunbury to organise my wedding dress and the bridesmaid dresses, and to finalise a few of the other bookings but apart from that it was all done over the phone.

Naturally I felt like Jake was missing out on a lot of the excitement and it was a shame we couldn't have planned more together, but the reality was his focus had to be on his training, and I knew that. I have to admit though, I couldn't help but feel a little selfish making all the decisions and I prayed Jake was serious when he said, 'If you're happy, I'll be happy'. I guess I'd find out soon enough.

By the time I heard from Jake again, almost everything was organised. He was so appreciative of all the effort I'd put in, and when I gave him a run-down of the wedding plans he was excited and happy with all the choices I'd made. Even if he wasn't, not once did he give me any indication that he would've liked something done differently. It was such a relief to have everything organised, now all we had to do was hang in there until the sixth of January.

Over the next month I only received three or four phone calls from Jake, and since he'd borrow his friends phone to ring me, our longest call would've only been around three or four minutes. It was so hard not seeing him, but not being able to talk to him either made it all the more frustrating. I remember telling him that as soon as he got some time off, the first thing we were going to do was buy him a phone. So the next time he had to go away at least he wouldn't have to borrow a phone and rush his calls to me. I lost count of the number of times I cursed myself for not getting a phone organised before he left.

I cherished every second I got to speak with Jake while he was away, but there was one particular call which left me brimming with excitement, and actually turned out to be quite the adventure.

"Hey Baby it's Jake."

"Hi Honey! How's everything going? I've missed you!" I beamed ecstatically before giving him a chance to reply.

"I miss you too Babe. Listen I can't talk now, but I need to know if you have some time off tomorrow?"

"I'm working but I can get someone to cover for me. Why?"

"Just be at the RMC Rugby field tomorrow at 10:00am. The college has a team playing one of the civilian universities so they want all the RMC cadets there to support the team…"

"I get to see you!" I squealed; cutting him off.

"We've been told by the instructors that there's some aviation training happening out here on the range tomorrow. They said we'll be picked up by helicopter, flown back to RMC and then landing on the rugby field before the game starts."

"Are you serious?"

"Yeah. We all thought it was bullshit too but apparently they take their sport pretty seriously at the college. Anyway I gotta go. Just be there at ten and we can spend some time together."

"I'll be there. I love you."

"Love you too Soph. See you soon."

"Bye Jake." I said as the dial tone sounded.

I was so excited. I'd expected it to be weeks before seeing his face again, so to find out I was actually going to spend some time with him tomorrow was incredible. I couldn't believe it.

It was almost ten the following day. I was just about to drive in the gates of RMC when the phone rang. Normally I would've ignored it, given I was on my way to see Jake, but something inside me told me to answer it so I pulled the car over and took the call.

"Hello."

"Soph it's me. Where are you?" The tone of Jake's voice instantly alerted me that something was wrong.

"I'm just outside the RMC entrance."

"Fuck!"

"Why? What's wrong?"

"We're not coming!" he snapped angrily.

"You're kidding!" My heart sank instantly. Never in my life had I ever experienced such painful and abrupt disappointment.

"I think they fucked with us deliberately. Everyone is so pissed off, especially the ones who were planning to catch up with their partners."

"When did you find out?"

"Only a few minutes ago. We were all standing out in the open field, waiting for the arrival of the choppers. We were told to be ready to go at 9:30am. Everyone was so excited. Anyway, twenty minutes later and still no choppers. We were all starting to get worried when one of the instructors took a call and yelled out that it's been cancelled. Everyone's so angry and upset. I want to fuck'n kill someone!"

"Calm down Baby… it's alright." I said softly. I could tell Jake was worked up and I didn't want him to do anything stupid; not that I was worried about him actually *killing* somebody.

"No… it's bullshit! I bet this is one of their stupid fucking ideas to see how we cope with this kind of shit! The thing is, now they're screwing the partners around as well… and their children. I mean imagine how the kids feel who were told they were going to see their fathers today… they'd be devastated! Fuck these assholes!"

He was absolutely livid.

"Just relax. I'm ok. It's only a few more weeks till you finish isn't it?"

His rant continued. "Fair enough that they screw us around, but you didn't sign up for this shit! It's not fair on you to get your hopes up then let you down… to lie to you!"

I tried to calm him again. "Jake… I'm alright. I understand."

He went silent.

"Jake… Jake are you there Baby?"

"Fuck this!" he growled. "Sophie…" He lowered his voice. "…I need you to listen to me carefully."

Oh shit… what's he thinking?

"Sure Baby… I'm listening." I couldn't hide the concern in my voice, brought on by the fact that I knew he was about to do something crazy.

"As you drive back towards Queanbeyan, I want you to take the left hand turn just before the airport."

"Why? What are you planning?"

"Just listen to me. The last left before the airport, then drive maybe five kilometres or so; could be more. Look for a right turn. There should be a sign saying 'Majura Training Area' but I can't be certain. Anyway, if there isn't I'll wave you down from the side of the road."

"No Jake. I don't want you getting into trouble."

"Don't worry about me. Since we're not going to the game now we have some free time. They told us to clean our gear and go over our theory work, but fuck that! I'm not letting you down Sophie! I'll pretend I'm going for a run or something then sneak out of the camp."

"Jake no don't do it!" I pleaded with him. "I don't have to see you! I'm ok!"

"Well I need to see *you*!" he answered directly. "Remember the directions?"

I didn't reply. There was no way I wanted him to go through with it, but by the sounds of things he desperately needed to see me.

"Sophie! Do you remember which way to go?" he prompted.

"Yes," I sighed reluctantly. There was no talking him out of it.

"Good, then go now. I'll meet you there."

He hung up before I could reply.

"Fuck! Fuck! Fuck! Fuck! This is fucking crazy!" I said out loud.

I threw my phone on the passenger seat and headed for the airport. My heart was usually racing before I saw Jake but this was different altogether; I was scared. My mind spun out of control at the possible consequences he would face if he got caught sneaking out of the camp. I hoped he wasn't the only one with this stupid, risky and utterly crazy plan, and that he had a few other guys with him.

For a brief moment I considered not going. At least then he wouldn't spend too long away from the camp, then once he realised I wasn't coming he'd have a better chance of getting back undetected. But I knew Jake, he simply wouldn't go back until he seen me. He'd wait on the side of that road until I showed up, and the thought of letting him down after all he was risking made me numb with fear. I had no choice… I had to go.

I turned left just before the airport. At about the two kilometre mark I started scanning for the right hand turn towards the training area. I kept my eyes open for a sign, an intersection and most of all… for Jake. I knew he would be in his green military uniform and not easily seen against the tree line, so I drove as slow as I dared; considering it was an eighty zone.

I felt like I'd been driving for well over five kilometres since the turn off and I started to worry that maybe I'd driven too far, when all of a sudden I spotted the right hand turn. There was a small sign which read 'Military Training Area' on the corner. I made the turn and as I looked up the road I could see a lone figure in the distance; running towards me.

Oh my god! Adrenaline raced through me as I drove towards him; his run transitioning into a sprint once he saw my car. My heart pounded as we rapidly closed the distance between us; me driving towards him… him running to me. As soon as I got close enough to see his face tears sprung from my eyes.

"Jake!" I screamed out; totally overwhelmed.

I pulled over and he ran right up to my door. I dived out of the car and into his arms before kissing him as if it was our last.

"Oh my god Jake… you're fucking crazy!" I cried; kissing him again.

He wrapped his arms around me so tight I almost couldn't breathe. "I'm sorry Baby but I couldn't let you down again." He looked deep into my eyes and wiped my tears away with his thumb.

"You're absolutely mad!" I exclaimed.

"Maybe just a little," he grinned.

"Are you on your own?" I looked back up the road to see if there was anyone behind him; anyone other cadets with the same crazy idea to sneak out of the camp.

"Yeah. I told some of the others I was sneaking out but they didn't want to risk it."

"Shit Jake! Couldn't you get into trouble?"

"What are they going to do… stop me from seeing you? They're already doing that! I don't care anyway, I just had to see you Baby. Now kiss me again," he commanded; our lips locking together immediately.

"I don't want to stay very long. The longer you're here with me the more chance you have of getting into trouble."

"If you drive me back up this road to range control, I'll have about twenty-minutes or so with you. Let's go now so we're not out here on the side of the road. If one of the instructor's drives passed I'm fucked! There's a car park for civilians up at range control. We can park there. It's a few hundred meters outside the camp, so I won't have far to go to sneak back in."

We climbed in the car and drove up the road from the direction Jake came. We must have driven nearly two kilometres before reaching the range control building.

"Geez you had to run a long way?" I couldn't believe how fast he'd made it down to the main road since calling me.

"No shit… I'm buggered!" he laughed.

We pulled into the car park at the top of a hill. A large boom gate and a control station marked the entrance to the camp.

"Won't the people in there see us?"

"They're civilian security contractors. They waved at me on the way out. As long as I've got my ID we're fine. Relax Baby… it's ok," smiled Jake reassuringly.

Our discussion for the next quarter of an hour or so was primarily about the wedding plans I'd made. Never once did we break physical contact, and in between sentences we'd take the opportunity to steal a kiss. His lips felt so good on mine; I'd forgotten how amazing I felt when I was with him. For that short time, I was whole again.

Our time was up in what seemed like the blink of an eye. I would've given anything to have him stay with me for another ten minutes.

Jake looked at his watch then back to me. "I don't want to get out of this car," he said sombrely. "I can't leave you again."

I wrapped my arms around his neck. "You have to Baby," I said assuredly; hoping a confident reply would give him strength. "I'm so glad I got to see you."

"Me too."

"Thank you so much Jake," I said sincerely. "I know you couldn't stay with me for long, but I loved *every* second. I hope you don't get into trouble."

"Well if I do, so be it. I had to see you today and I'm glad I took the risk," he grinned.

We kissed passionately.

"Can you try and let me know if you got back without getting busted? Otherwise I'll be worried sick!"

"Sure. I'll try borrowing a phone and sending you a quick text once I'm back."

"Great. Give me one more kiss before you go," I demanded greedily.

We locked lips, and with my hand on the back of his head I pulled his mouth against mine; savouring every sensation.

"I'll see you in a few weeks," he smiled; kissing me on either cheek then once more on the lips.

"I can't wait. I love you Jake."

"And I love you too," he smiled affectionately; tenderly stroking my cheek with the back of his hand. "Always have."

"Always will," I whispered, for fear that Jake would be able to hear the sorrowful emotion in my voice.

He climbed out of the car, closed the door behind him and walked towards the boom gate. After flashing his I.D. card towards the control station window, the gate lifted. Before entering, Jake turned around and gave me a huge smile, waved goodbye and mouthed the words 'I love you.' I smiled back, blew him a kiss and watched as he started running back towards the camp; disappearing over the rise.

Please don't get into trouble. I remember being so worried for him that I actually felt a little nauseous. The thought of him getting punished for my sake was distressing, and I prayed he'd be able to sneak back into the camp without being detected.

I was almost home when my phone alerted me of an incoming message. I pulled over at the first opportunity and grabbed it out of my handbag. There was a text from an unknown number which read, 'All good :-) I love you Soph xxx'.

I couldn't help but laugh out loud with overwhelming relief. My man, my wild and crazy man was alright. Finally, I could breathe again.

Jake eventually finished the boot camp phase of his training. It seemed to last forever, but finally he was allowed some time off which meant he was able to stay with me for a couple of nights. To say I was excited was literally the understatement of the year!

It had been almost three months since Jake and I had slept together, and the anticipation of having sex with him had me at boiling point. As I drove from my apartment to the military base to pick him up, my mind was bombarded with images of us together; our bodies naked, exploring each other like it was our first time again. I tried desperately to focus on driving but my body had other ideas, and had already begun its preparations to be 'reunited' with my lover.

Initially I didn't realise I was doing it, but as I squeezed my thighs together the slippery feeling between my legs soon became impossible to ignore. I was so wet that I looked down to check the state of my arousal couldn't be seen seeping through my jeans! *The road Sophie! Concentrate on the road!*

I arrived at the base, drove through the entrance and followed the directions to the pick-up point which Jake had given me over the phone. I spotted him standing on the side of the road; waiting patiently for me.

Oh my god! There he is! Bees, grasshoppers and a host of other energetic insects joined the butterflies which were madly buzzing, flying and jumping around in my belly. I'd never been so excited before in my entire life and my cheeks ached from the huge smile on my face.

I pulled over to the curb where he was standing. The passenger side window was down. Jake leant over, grabbed hold of the door and put his head in through the window.

"How nice of you to stop. I was wondering if I could trouble you for a lift?" he said in a horrendously bad foreign accent which made me giggle out loud.

"I don't know. Depends on where you're going?" I replied; playing along with his little game.

"Well I was actually trying to get to a place called Queanbeyan. You wouldn't be heading that way would you?"

"As a matter of fact I am. I don't usually pick up strangers though!"

"Well what if I told you I was a really nice guy?"

"How nice?" I asked seductively; unable to keep a straight face.

"Well why don't you take me for a ride...." His voice deepened. "...Give me a chance to show you."

I raised an eyebrow. "You promise you're not a serial killer?"

He put his hand on his heart. "Promise."

"Well in that case... hop on in!" I beamed in an overly excited voice.

Jake laughed loudly as he opened the door and climbed into the car. "Shit, you're an easy target Soph!"

"What can I say... I'm a sucker for a man in uniform. Now shut up and kiss me Stranger."

Jake leant over from the passenger seat. We embraced and began kissing feverishly.

"Get me outta here Baby."

I could tell he was well and truly in need of some space between him and the Army.

"My pleasure. To Queanbeyan is it?" I asked with a giggle.

"Well to be honest, now that I'm in the car why don't you just head out to some abandoned back road?"

"I knew you'd turn out to be a serial killer."

"Yet you still let me in the car!" he chuckled.

We both started laughing again. I had been with Jake for less than three minutes and he'd already made me laugh more than I had in the past week.

I felt so relieved to have my man with me again, but as we drove home it didn't take long for me to realise something wasn't quite right with him. We were talking and catching up but he wasn't entirely himself; I could sense he was holding something back. On the outside he still appeared fine but I knew my *baby* and something was definitely on his mind.

I squeezed his hand. "You ok Babe?" I asked sympathetically.

"To be honest, I feel a little strange." He opened up immediately; obviously realising he couldn't hide whatever was troubling him from me.

"Why? What do you mean?"

"I don't know. For some reason I just feel… emotional. But I know I should be happy," his voice crackled slightly.

I let go of his hand, reached up and gently tickled the back of his neck. "Hey, that's ok Baby. The last few months have been tough. It's ok to feel emotional."

Jake nodded then turned to look out the passenger window.

I thought I'd give him a minute to relax; occasionally taking my eyes off the road to look at him. He continued to stare blankly out the window. I felt horrible, and was about to say something comforting when I heard him sniffle. He was crying.

"Hey it's ok Honey. You're with me now. Don't be upset," I said; consoling him as best I could, considering I was still driving.

He continued to stare out the window; doing his best to hide his tears from me.

"I'll pull over for a minute," I suggested; decelerating slightly.

"No! Don't pull over!" he said firmly. "Just keep going. I'll get myself together."

"Are you sure? I can stop Jake."

"No just take me home. I don't want to make a big thing out of this. I'll be ok."

As I continued to drive there was an awkward silence between us that I didn't know how to break; a new and unwelcome situation. I was worried about him but at the same time I didn't want to make matters worse by forcing him to talk. I stopped tickling the back of his neck and put both my hands on the steering wheel. The longer the silence went, the more upset I became until I couldn't stop the tears from forming in my eyes as well.

I wasn't upset with him for not talking; far from it. I was sad because he was obviously hurting and I didn't know what to say or do to comfort him. Jake had always known exactly what to say to make me feel better, and now when he finally needed *my* help, I was literally speechless.

He looked over and noticed the tears on my cheeks. "Fuck… I'm sorry Baby. I didn't mean to upset you." He grabbed my hand and kissed it. "God, I'm so embarrassed and angry with myself for ruining everything. I'm sorry I've upset you."

"You haven't ruined anything Jake. I'm just worried about you."

He reached over and wiped the tears off my cheeks. "We're almost home. We can talk more when we're there."

"Sure," I sniffed.

Jake held my hand for the rest of the trip.

We arrived at my apartment and I went directly to the bathroom to tidy myself up. When I came out Jake had already taken his uniform off and was in some jeans and a t-shirt.

"I had to get out of that uniform," he said; relief resonating in his voice. "Please forgive me Soph. I'm really sorry for upsetting you."

"I'm fine… really. It just hurts me to see you so upset. Can you talk to me about it?"

He nodded.

I grabbed hold of his hand and led him into the bedroom. "Lie down with me Baby. Tell me what's going on."

Jake lied down on his back and I climbed onto the bed with him. I draped one leg over both of his and rested my chin on his chest so I could look into his eyes. I wanted to be as close to him as I could. As he spoke, I run my hands through his hair.

"To be honest Soph, I really don't know why I was upset. I think the last few months have just been harder than I thought. I mean while I was training I didn't really have time to think, I was just so flat out all the time. This afternoon when I got in the car with you I felt like I could finally just breathe."

"You mean you could be yourself?" I prompted.

"*Exactly*! In a place like that it kind of feels like you lose your identity to some degree; always doing everything as a group; following orders and having every minute of your day planned out for you. After a while you start to feel like a robot. So when I realised I was actually allowed to leave with you, that I was able to relax and be myself again, I suppose it just made me emotional."

"I understand. It makes sense."

"To tell you the truth, I'm actually really embarrassed."

"Oh Baby you don't have to feel embarrassed or apologise, or anything like that. It's obviously been a hard few months for you and it's no wonder that it eventually wore you down."

I could tell he was still disappointed in himself for getting upset, but he forced a smile nonetheless.

"Trust me Jake, it's perfectly fine. I just hope you feel better now?"

"I do. Thanks Baby… for understanding. I love you so much."

He lifted me up so I was now on top of him and we kissed passionately.

"How about we just start a fresh?" he suggested; looking much more relaxed and more like the Jake I knew.

"There's no need to start over, everything has been fine the way it is."

I meant what I said, and was actually relieved that he opened up to me. It gave me a chance to help *him* through a tough situation for a change, or at least feel like I helped.

I gave Jake a full update on the wedding plans. It was fantastic to see him alive with all the excitement and anticipation I'd been feeling while planning the event. Over and over, he said how he couldn't wait for our wedding day; I knew exactly how he felt. I wanted to become 'Mrs. Sophie Freeman' more than anything, and even more so now since Jake would be allowed to come and live with me after the wedding.

For a short while I was caught up in the excitement of all the wedding talk, but it wasn't long before I realised one very important fact. *Jake is here... with me... in my bed!* The moment I'd dreamt about for months had finally arrived.

He must have read my mind because the conversation stopped, and the vibe in the room changed instantly. The way we looked into each other's eyes completely negated the need for speech. As we stared at one and other, lost in the deep intensity of the moment and totally oblivious to the outside world, powerful feelings of lust and desire washed over me like a wave. I swear I could literally feel *Jake* inside me already.

Of course our mood and body language screamed sexual energy, but it was an energy mixed with something else; something hard to define. I think what I felt was a level of desire so strong, so achingly potent, that it was more like some kind of craving or hunger… it was pure *starvation.* I didn't simply want to fuck Jake, I wanted to tear him apart; to devour him.

In that instant I understood the sexual beast which lived inside my lover, the one that scared me every time it surfaced; melting the line between euphoria and fear. I understood his beast because mine was now wide awake… and hungry like a wolf!

I put my hand on his forehead and pushed his head back so his chin pointed to the ceiling. With his neck exposed, I latched onto the side of his throat and clamped my teeth onto his skin.

"Fuck that's nice!" Jake moaned loudly; his noise fuelling my instincts further.

While I licked, sucked and gnawed his neck I reached down and slid my hand into his jeans; wasting no time grasping his member. I squeezed it firmly, with enough pressure to feel his pulse forcing more and more blood into his shaft. It was a sensation which immediately caused my pelvic floor muscles to clench… hard!

Oh I need that! I need that in me now!

I climbed off him and unzipped his jeans before hastily pulling them off along with his underwear; throwing them on the floor. Then I helped him out of his shirt. It'd been so long since I'd seen my man's naked body, and I almost came at the sensation of my hands running over his sculptured form.

I stood on the bed above him and undressed as quickly as I could. I'm sure it wasn't very graceful but there was no time to be sexy. I needed to fuck; hard, fast and without delay. I was aware that Jakes vacation from my snatch would've no doubt taken its toll on his stamina, so I was prepared for a 'down to business-no frills-hard core-fucking!' Just what the doctor ordered!

I stood naked above him with one leg either side of his hips. His eyes were fixated on my most intimate place; the wetness clearly visible as it seeped from my slightly parted lips. I knew the sight of me was driving him wild so I slowly ran my hand across my stomach and down between my legs; deliberately sliding two fingers between my lips and gradually spreading my pussy, giving Jake a show which almost caused his eyes to pop out of their sockets.

As much as I wanted to squat down, slowly sinking onto his cock, I needed Jake to take control of me; to use my body as he pleased.

"How do you want me Baby?" My question causing him to divert his eyes from my groin to my face.

"Get on your knees!" he commanded sternly; eyes blazing.

I swallowed with trepidation, as if I was about to jump from a cliff into the ocean far below. There's no other way to say it, I knew I was definitely about to be pounded.

Jake rolled over and off the bed, standing up with his legs resting against the edge of the mattress. I turned around and knelt down on the bed, assuming the classic 'doggy style' position with my backside pointing directly at him. I closed my eyes and prepared for Jake to take me, when without warning I felt his warm thick tongue run from my clit, slowly and deliberately up to my ass… *right up!*

Now kneeling on the floor behind me, Jake spread my cheeks with both hands to give him *all* the access he needed. I moaned loudly as he continued his pleasurable assault; giving both my pussy and ass equal attention. The feeling of him sliding his tongue inside me was almost hypnotic, and the added excitement of not knowing which hole he was going to explore had me on the brink in no time. It was as hot as it was dirty, and I absolutely loved it!

I couldn't help but push my hips back to meet his probing tongue. He knew I was seconds from climaxing.

"That's it Jake! That's it! Yes!" I panted.

And just like that… he stopped.

"Argh!" I cried out in frustration. "You tease!" I said, looking over my shoulder at him.

"You *really* want me now don't you?" he tormented; grinning proudly.

I was quick to figure out he wanted me on the absolute brink, ready to climax so as soon as he entered me I would let go.

"Yes! I want you!" I snarled aggressively; arching my back and thrusting my hips back and forwards as if I was already being fucked.

Jake stood up and grabbed me by the waist. I closed my eyes as he pulled on my hips; the tip of his cock lightly touching my pussy lips.

"Ready?" he warned.

I nodded.

As he pulled me backwards, I felt his hardness force my lips apart then slowly sink into me. The feeling I'd longed for finally arrived.

"Ahh," I sighed, before grimacing as he fed me another inch. "Fuck you're hard!" I winced as his rod stretched me open. It had been a while since I'd had anything bigger than a finger or two.

"I know I'm not going to last long," he said as he began to slide in and out of my dripping tunnel.

"Then fuck me! Fuck me hard!"

My direction was obeyed immediately; Jake gripping hold of me firmly and driving into me again and again. I was so turned on thanks to his earlier exploration with that heavenly tongue, I was ready to give in after only ten or so thrusts.

"I'm ready Jake… I'm ready!" I squealed, as he buried himself into me; my butt cheeks meeting his hips with a distinctive skin on skin *slap!*

Either his cock had grown or my pussy had reverted to 'virgin like' tightness over the last few months, because it seriously felt like Jake was going to split me in two. I gripped handfuls of bed sheet to brace myself, trying desperately to hold myself together.

Usually I moaned and squealed in synchronisation with my lover's rhythm, but I fell silent as he began to grunt loudly with the imminent approach of his own orgasm; his animalistic growling perfectly matched to his actions. Jake rarely made a sound when we'd have sex, preferring to listen to me and my erotic crescendo, but when he did let it out it would drive me wild.

The harder he got the louder he became. The feeling of him fucking me combined with his mind blowing sound track was a sensory overload for me. I gasped one final breath as Jake's *muscle* swelled inside me to what felt like double its width, then he groaned loudly as his orgasm detonated. Instinctively, he reduced his rhythm to a final five or six deliberately slow, deep thrusts; perfectly timed with each injection that fired into my pussy, which was now overflowing as a result of my own fierce orgasm that tore through my body like a category five tornado. Without realising it, I was still holding my breath so I could listen to my lover as he came. This caused the pressure to grow with intensity to the point where I felt like my head was about to explode.

Once my orgasm subsided, my arms gave way and I collapsed onto my chest. I was panting breathlessly like a runner crossing the finish line after a marathon; completely exhausted. Jake was still holding my hips and revelling in the sensation of having his cock firmly enveloped by my insides; slowly sliding back and forth, stirring the delicious cocktail of sex inside me. As he gradually withdrew completely I felt our infusion trickle from my used and abused lips, all the way down my inner thighs. It was as hot as hell.

I rolled onto my side and looked up at him. He was standing beside the bed in the same position as when I backed up to him moments earlier. His eyes were closed and he was drawing deep breaths. I studied him, the man who just fucked me the way animals do; his muscles visibly pumped, thick veins running from his shoulders down the entire length of his arms, his stomach ripped as if he'd been carved out of stone. Jake was always a vision, but never more so than the few minutes after he'd pleasured me, ravaged me, possessed me like a supernatural entity claiming my soul.

He opened his eyes. "I might have to hitchhike more often," he smiled.

I laughed before I could think of anything witty to say.

As much as being away from Jake absolutely sucked, there was always one positive I couldn't ignore… the sex when we were finally reunited.

I've heard of people describing how amazing 'make-up sex' is after an argument with their partner. Well I have to say, sleeping with Jake after being apart for so long was like 'make-up sex' on steroids! It had all the passion, primal instinct, energy and aggression but without the disagreement to begin with; pure bliss. Words simply fail to do such an out of this world experience justice.

That weekend was absolutely perfect. We went shopping, out for dinner, sat in the park and talked about the future, and of course enjoyed a few passionate sessions in the bedroom. Oh, and we brought him a phone too! It was one of those times when you're utterly caught up in the moment and wouldn't want to be anywhere else in the world.

I have to say there was one moment which lifted my spirits so high I was absolutely certain I could make it through until the end of the year. It was when Jake told me he'd be allowed off base every Saturday and Sunday afternoon from now on, with a 10:00pm curfew, until the Christmas holiday period arrived. I was ecstatic. Knowing I could see Jake and spend time with him every weekend, apart from a two week block which would see him deployed to the field, was such a relief. It gave me all the strength I needed.

I *was* worried about how I'd cope on my own for the next few months until our wedding, but now I was filled with confidence, even excited. I already had a plan too, immerse myself in work during the week, then let Jake immerse himself *in* me on the weekends. A perfect strategy to get through to the end of the year.

CHAPTER TWENTY-THREE

A DREAM COMES TRUE

Text message sent to Jake: 06 January 2001 01:12am
r u awake?
Received: 06 January 2001 1:12am

Reply sent to Sophie: 06 January 2001 1:13am
Can't sleep Baby?
We're not supposed to talk till tomorrow.
Received: 06 January 2001 1:13am

Text message sent to Jake: 06 January 2001 01:14am
Not a wink!
I know we're not supposed to but I'm so excited that I can't get to sleep!
Received: 06 January 2001 1:14am

It was the night before our wedding. Jake was staying over at a friend's house along with his Dad and four groomsmen; Chris, Richard, Dan and Aaron. I was staying with Jake's sisters at their place since they were my bridesmaids. My brother's girlfriend, Jane, was my maid of honour.

I was lying in bed staring at the ceiling, my mind was spinning. The realisation I'd be walking down the aisle in a matter of hours had rendered sleep all but impossible.

Reply sent to Sophie: 06 January 2001 1:17am
Well technically tomorrow is already here since it's after midnight, so I guess we're in the clear!

I can't sleep either. Tomorrow is going to be crazy so try and get some sleep lover.
Received: 06 January 2001 1:17am

Text message sent to Jake: 06 January 2001 01:19am
I'm trying to but how do I stop thinking about a dream that's about to come true?
Received: 06 January 2001 1:19am

Reply sent to Sophie: 06 January 2001 1:21am
:-)
It's a dream come true for me too Soph.
Are you sure you want to be Mrs. Freeman?
Sophie Taylor is such a beautiful name. :-)
Received: 06 January 2001 1:21am

Text message sent to Jake: 06 January 2001 01:23am
YES! YES! YES!
I've never been so sure of anything in my entire life!
Is this really happening? Are we really getting married tomorrow?
Received: 06 January 2001 1:23am

Reply sent to Sophie: 06 January 2001 1:24am
No Baby…
We're getting married today!!!!!! :-)
Received: 06 January 2001 1:24am

My heart raced.

I'm getting married today! I'm actually getting married today! My cheeks ached from the huge grin on my face; the same one which had been there for the past week.

Text message sent to Sophie: 06 January 2001 01:26am
Now get some sleep.
You've got a big day tomorrow.
And a pretty busy night too!

;-)
Received: 06 January 2001 1:26am

I closed my eyes after reading his text. My groin tingled pleasantly at the thought of sleeping with Jake on our wedding night. Sleeping with… my *husband!*

Reply sent to Jake: 06 January 2001 1:27am
How am I supposed to sleep now!!!
Received: 06 January 2001 1:27am

Text message sent to Sophie: 06 January 2001 01:27am
:-)
Goodnight. xxx
Received: 06 January 2001 1:27am

Reply sent to Jake: 06 January 2001 1:29am
Very funny!
I love you Jake.
Always have.
xxx
Received: 06 January 2001 1:29am

Text message sent to Sophie: 06 January 2001 01:29am
Always will.
x
Received: 06 January 2001 1:29am

Warmth flooded through my body. I put my phone down and closed my eyes. Eventually I drifted off to sleep; for the last time as Sophie Taylor.

A soon as I woke up and realised it was *the* day, I was greeted by a belly full of my fluttering companions. My butterflies stayed with me the entire morning; a constant reminder of the nerves, excitement, and suspense which flooded through me as I prepared to be married.

From the moment we were all awake the energy in the house was electric. Everyone was absolutely buzzing. Seeing how excited Jake's sisters were as they got ready for their big brother's wedding was something I'll never forget. I'd given serious consideration to asking some of my friends from school to be bridesmaids, but I was so glad I'd eventually decided on asking Alice, Kate and Samantha. I wanted them to know the sisterhood they'd provided me for the last five years was appreciated, so I felt it was important for each of them to have a formal appointment on our wedding day. Jake's three sisters would soon be *my* sisters too, and having them as my bridesmaids would be the perfect start to our official beginning as in-laws.

Even though the ceremony didn't start until 3:00pm, giving us plenty of time to get ready, time whipped by like someone had their finger on the fast forward button. In what felt like minutes not hours, we'd returned from having our hair done at the hairdressers, finished our make-up and were ready to put on our dresses.

Mum was with me the entire morning to help us all get ready. Standing in front of a huge mirror in Kate and Samantha's room, I watched as she laced up the corset of my wedding dress. The girls were all helping each other into their bridesmaid's dresses; full length in blood red. They were stunning and the exact colour of the roses in my bouquet.

I looked in the mirror and noticed a change in my mother's expression. "Are you ok Mum?"

"I'm ok Soph," she sniffled. "You just look so beautiful. I can't believe you're getting married today," she said softly.

"Neither can I!" I giggled.

"Are you sure about this Sophie? I mean are you *absolutely* sure this is what you want?"

The girls quietened down and looked in our direction; waiting on baited breath for my response.

"Don't you remember what I said to you right after I met Jake for the first time? You know… when you picked me up from the lake?"

"Yes I remember," she smiled. "You said you were going to marry him!"

"That's right. Well today's the day!" I beamed joyfully.

"I just want you to be absolutely sure. I love you Honey."

"I love you too. Trust me Mum… I'm sure this is what I want," I reassured her convincingly.

The joy and excitement was so overwhelming that I started laughing. I was so happy, and not just because I was getting married but because I was so sure it was what I wanted. Jake was all I ever wanted. Mum and the girls started laughing as well. They all knew there was absolutely no doubt I wanted to marry Jake; definitely no sign of cold feet that's for sure.

Once my corset was laced up, my bridesmaids helped me with my shoes and jewellery then put the finishing touches on my make-up. We all checked each other over to make sure nothing had been missed, then stood in front of the mirror for one last look at ourselves. Jane and my sisters-to-be were beautiful. They all looked so grown up, especially Samantha who was still only twelve years old. I think she was just as nervous and excited as I was. I'm pretty sure it was only the first or second time she'd ever worn heels, and the thought of having to walk down the aisle in front of a crowd filled her with trepidation.

Mum and the girls walked out to the family room where Dad was patiently waiting. In my final moment alone I looked at my reflection one last time. As I gazed into the eyes of the bride staring back at me, I took a deep breath and exhaled slowly. *This is it. I'm getting married today. Jake is finally going to be my husband!* The thought made me giggle and I quickly turned from the mirror; feeling stupid for smiling at myself.

I walked out to the family room and stood in front of Dad.

"You look amazing Sophie," he said, gently kissing me on the cheek; taking care not to mess my make-up.

"Thanks Dad. I'm so excited. I can't believe it's finally time."

He looked at his watch. "It *is* time! We'd better get in the cars and head to the gardens."

Dad and I were travelling together, with Mum and the bridesmaids going in the other two cars. My two brothers and one of Jake's friends were the drivers. Our first stop was the botanic gardens for some pre-wedding photos.

I must say getting in and out of the back seat of the bridal car in my wedding dress was no easy feat, and it was a good thing I had my trusty bridesmaids on hand to help me. The last thing I wanted to do was accidently damage my dress or get it dirty before I even got to the church.

Once we arrived at the gardens we met up with my four-year-old niece, Zoe, who was my flower girl. Leah and my brother had recently separated but I was still appreciative that Leah took the time to bring Zoe in to town to be part of my wedding. One of my Dad's friends from Crystal Creek had let us borrow their five-year-old son to be the page boy. They too met us at the gardens.

We spent about half an hour with the photographer, who took a heap of pictures of me with the bridesmaids, with my parents, as well as with the page boy and flower girl. We also got a heap of individual shots and some fantastic group photos; the gardens serving as the perfect backdrop. Before long, Dad announced it was a quarter to three and time to go.

My heart was absolutely pounding as we got back in the car; next stop Saint Michaels Church. It was a boiling hot summer's day and the temperature combined with my nerves and excitement had me sweating. As soon as I was in the car Shaun blasted the air conditioning, which went a long way towards cooling me down but did nothing for my racing heart and excited nerves.

My father and I sat in the back seat while my brother drove us to the church. He grasped hold of my hand, looked into my eyes and asked me a similar question as Mum had earlier that morning.

"Are you sure you want to do this? Are you one hundred percent sure?"

"Dad… I'm a *thousand* percent sure! I've never wanted anything so much."

"I just want you to be certain."

"I know; you're only looking out for me. Well trust me this is what I want. I have no doubts Dad."

I answered him confidently and with conviction in the hope of putting his mind at ease. I noticed his eyes were getting glassy; he was starting to well up. There was one thing which was guaranteed to reduce me to tears faster than anything, and that was seeing a grown man cry. Watching tears form in my father's eyes tore at my heart strings instantly, and I was crying before I even had a chance to try and hold myself together. I guess the realisation hit him that in less than an hour he was going to walk his little girl down the aisle and give her away; effectively handing responsibility over to another man. I'm sure he was happy for me but at the same time I can understand he must have been feeling somewhat bitter sweet, and it eventually got the best of him.

"Don't cry Soph," Dad said, his voice crackling as he offered me a handkerchief.

"Well *you* stop it," I giggled, finding the lighter side of the situation. I carefully dabbed at my tears, trying desperately not to smudge my make-up.

"Why don't you both stop crying you big babies!" teased Shaun from the driver's seat; looking at us both in the rear view mirror and laughing.

It was just what I needed. Shaun's comment snapped us both out of the emotional vice we were in. Thankfully I was able to stop crying and compose myself.

Once I tidied myself up Dad grabbed hold of my hand again and didn't let go until we reached the church.

"Just remember I'll always be your father, and I'm here if ever you need me."

"Thanks Dad. I love you," I smiled.

As we arrived and drove in through the huge iron gates at the entrance to Saint Michaels Church, I was bursting with anticipation.

"We're early aren't we?" I noticed there were still guests making their way into the church prompting me to ask Dad the time.

He looked at his watch. "It's a bit before three. Usually the bride is fashionably late, so I guess we are a bit early."

I was thankful for the dark tinted windows which prevented any of the guests from seeing me in the car.

"You two wait in the car. I'll go in and make sure everyone is seated then I'll come out and get you," suggested Shaun.

"Good idea son. Leave the air-con running," replied Dad.

"See I told you I really want to marry Jake!" I laughed. "How many brides arrive *early* for their wedding?"

Dad smiled. "I believe you Soph." He squeezed my hand. "Jake's a good man and I know he's going to take the best care of you. I'm sure the two of you will be very happy together."

"Thanks Dad that means a lot. Just remember, I might be marrying Jake today but I'll be your daughter forever."

He leant over and kissed me on the cheek. "I love you Sophie."

"Love you too." I looked out the window and noticed Shaun on his way back to the car. "Now let's get this show on the road!"

Shaun opened the car door. "They're all inside. Are you ready?"

"Ready." I replied confidently.

Shaun gestured to the bridesmaids, who were parked behind us, to come and help me out of the car. Within a few minutes we were all lined up in front of the large wooden church doors, ready to take our turn walking down the aisle.

Mum gave me a kiss and a cuddle. "You look beautiful. Good luck ok."

"Thanks Mum."

"I love you so much Sophie." Her raspy voice and the redness in her eyes was a giveaway she was emotional.

"I love you too Mum, and thanks for everything," I said as she lifted my veil from behind my head and draped it over my face; ensuring it was properly positioned.

"My pleasure Honey. I'll see you inside," she replied, wiping a stray tear as it rolled down her cheek.

"I'll see you in a minute," I smiled warmly; raising my eyebrows in an excited expression which made her giggle as she disappeared inside the church.

Shaun was at the door and waited for Mum to take her seat before signalling for the music to start. Jane, Alice, Kate and Samantha all gave me a quick hug and wished me good luck one last time before lining up in order again; ready to enter the church before me.

With the first beat of the music Shaun opened the church doors. The intro to *'From This Moment On'* by Shania Twain filled the air. As the lyrics started, my entire body was flooded with a single emotion... love.

Her voice sounded angelic as it echoed through the church, and her words were such a heartfelt truth for me. '*Through weakness and strength, happiness and sorrow, for better for worse, I will love you...'*

I didn't just hear them, I felt them, and I knew Jake would be standing at the altar listening and feeling them too; waiting patiently for me to stand beside him.

The lyrics are so symbolic of the struggles Jake and I endured, particularly at the hands of my *monster*, and the strength and power of love we shared which guided us through those hardships. As we faced the coming years together the words became even more poignant. Still to this day, whenever I hear the song I'm filled with such appreciation for the relationship I have with Jake, as well as certainty that together we'll be able to carry each other clear of any obstacles which arise in our future.

I was standing back from the door, unable to see inside. I watched as Samantha entered the church and I pictured her steadily making her way down the aisle. I knew she'd be crying from the moment she saw her beloved brother standing at the end of the aisle, and I was certain Jake would be reduced to tears at the sight of his baby sister looking so grown up. Kate, Alice and Jane all followed each other one at a time, patiently waiting until the bridesmaid before them was halfway down the aisle before starting their own nervous walk. Then it was my turn.

I moved closer to the entrance and looked inside the church. The pews were full of people all facing my direction; smiling and waiting eagerly for me to make my entrance. I looked to the far end of the aisle and although I couldn't see him clearly, the sight of Jake standing in front of the alter, waiting for me with the priest to his right and his four groomsman to his left, was like a scene from a movie. It was magical.

It was time, time for a dream I'd waited so long for to come true. Arm in arm with my father and led by my gorgeous little flower girl and handsome page boy, I made my way through the large wooden doors of the church and stepped onto the red carpet of the aisle.

The next chapter in my life was about to begin and although my heart still pounded in my chest, I felt no fear, trepidation or nervous anxiety, only a sense of calm and safety. I knew within the next few moments I would be by my *hero's* side, and I was about to make a promise to stay there for the rest of my life.

As I walked down the aisle my gaze was fixed on Jake, and although he was still too far away for me to see his facial expression, I knew his eyes would be on me too; seeing his *bride* for the first time.

As I slowly made my way towards him, step by careful step, the more detail I was able to see. He was dressed in a ceremonial military uniform called 'Blues', which were such a dark shade of blue they looked black, even when compared to the groomsman's black suits. His pants had a deep red stripe down the side of each leg which ran all the way to his high shine boots; so polished they actually looked mirrored. His jacket was perfectly fitted and adorned with polished gold buttons down the centre, on each breast pocket and each epaulette; an ornamental shoulder piece which displayed three gold letters; 'RMC'. I also noticed two gold emblems affixed to both sides of his collar. Each piece of gold sparkled under the lights of the church. His uniform was finished with a white-as-snow belt, clasped at the front with polished brass buckles, and complemented with crisp white cotton gloves. He held a matching cap under his arm; dark blue with a red stripe and polished brim.

Since meeting Jake, the sight of him had taken my breath away on more occasions than I could count, but never like this! I hadn't seen him in this particular uniform before. Prior to our wedding, he assured me that I'd like the uniform he'd be wearing but said I wasn't allowed to see him in it until he was standing at the altar. Turns out he was right, only I didn't just *like* it… I was utterly blown away!

Jake looked like no man I'd ever seen before. The vision of him was even more astonishing than anything I could have possibly dreamt. If I didn't have more than a hundred sets of eyes on me, I would've literally pinched myself to make sure the man waiting for me was actually real.

Standing both sides of the aisle, I was surrounded by family and friends who were all feeling the emotions of love and happiness which filled the church, but I was immersed in a sensation of my own; one I'd experienced many times before. It was like Jake and I were the only two people in the room. I had tunnel vision for my lover, and every other sound in the church was silenced, all except the words of my favourite song.

By the time I reached the altar, tears were rolling down my cheeks; Jake's too. Seeing him display his emotions so openly in front of such an audience caused my heart to melt. I had no choice but to bite my lip softly under my veil in a desperate attempt to prevent audible sobs from escaping. Thankfully it worked.

As my father and I carefully made our way up the steps of the altar, Jake removed his gloves and extended his hand out to me. We couldn't have timed it any better if we tried, and just as I grasped hold of his hand the final words of the song echoed softly through the church. '*I will love you, as long as I live… from this moment on.*'

I looked into Jake's eyes. As if by pure telepathy, we both took a deep breath just as the priest began the ceremony.

"Dearly beloved, we are gathered here together in the sight of God, to join this man and this woman in holy matrimony."

I exhaled slowly. Finally… we were getting married.

When Jake and I discussed the format for the ceremony we came to the decision to have a fairly traditional one, given we were getting married in a Catholic church. That said, we modified it slightly. Considering the wedding was in the middle of summer, we thought a somewhat shorter version would be appreciated by the guests. It turned out to be the right move because the mercury hit forty-three degrees Celsius that afternoon; it was absolutely boiling.

As much as I hate to say it the uncomfortably hot interior of the church detracted somewhat from the ceremony, even though there were fans spinning in a futile attempt to cool the place down. Jake even had sweat running down the side of his face and was passed a handkerchief from one of his groomsman to wipe his brow and face; much to the amusement of the audience.

Through tearful eyes, Dad announced to the priest that he was giving me away. He hugged me firmly, kissed my cheek through my veil, then shook Jake's hand before leaving me at the altar with my husband-to-be.

There we stood, hand in hand in front of the priest. He covered a few points about what it means to be married and how important it was for both of us to be there for each other, through good times as well as bad.

Now I don't mean to sound like a 'know it all', but Jake and I pretty much had that covered within the first year of our relationship. The priest's comments were appreciated none the less. If anything, they reaffirmed to both of us that no matter how bumpy the road may get we'd never leave each other's side.

Before long we got to the juicy part of the ceremony. I can't help but smile every time I think about it. Here's why.

The night before the wedding I had a copy of the ceremony sent over to Jake, who was actually having an impromptu buck's night at one of the groomsman's houses. Mind you he'd already had a buck's party a week earlier, so this particular event became known as 'Bucks Night two'. I didn't mind, but secretly prayed he wouldn't rock up the next day with his eyebrows shaved off or something just as horrifying. I did however expect him to read through the ceremony booklet, so at the very least he would know what to say when the priest asked us three very important questions immediately prior to us saying our vows.

It turns out he was too busy having a good time and 'accidently' forgot to read the booklet. So Jake's responses to the priest's questions were based on the few wedding ceremonies he'd seen on various TV shows. Subsequently, he gave the only response he remembered from those particular scenes. Bear in mind we had to answer each question in unison; at least Jake got that right!

The priest asked the first question. "Jake Mathew Freeman and Sophie Lee Taylor, ***have*** you both come here freely and without reservation, to give yourselves to each other in marriage?"

My response, "I have."

Jake's response, "I ***do***."

A few members of the crowd chuckled quietly. I looked at him with a confused expression. Jake raised his eyebrows at me and smiled innocently.

Then the second question was asked. "***Will*** you honour each other as man and wife for the rest of your lives?"

My response, "I will."

Jake's, "I ***do***."

This time majority of the crowd was amused by Jake's second incorrect response. I immediately realised my beloved had *not* in fact read the copy of the ceremony which I sent over the night before. I raised my eyebrows back at him in utter disbelief. Once again he smiled innocently; knowing full well he was busted.

Ok Jake, one more chance. Think about it now!

As the priest asked the third question Jake grinned confidently; knowing this must be the 'I do' question. I felt relieved that he'd finally worked it out.

"***Will*** you accept children lovingly from God, and bring them up according to the law of Christ and his Church?"

My response, "I will."

And Jake's, in a nice loud confident voice with accompanying smile, "I ***do***."

Three from three, nice work Jake!

The entire crowd laughed out loud. I couldn't help but giggle and shake my head, even the priest laughed. "We'll get to that part in a minute," he said to Jake, who was now visibly embarrassed but smiling nonetheless.

The priest paused for a moment so we could compose ourselves before continuing. "Since it is your intention to enter into marriage, join your right hands and declare your consent before God and his Church."

We faced one and other and stared deeply into each other's eyes.

Jake repeated after the priest, "I, Jake Mathew Freeman, take you, Sophie Lee Taylor, to be my wife. I promise to be true to you in good times and in bad, in sickness and in health. I will love you and honour you, all the days of my life.

Then it was my turn. "I, Sophie Lee Taylor, take you, Jake Mathew Freeman, to be my husband. I promise to be true to you in good times and in bad, in sickness and in health. I will love you and honour you, all the days of my life." I'd waited so long to say those words and it felt even more amazing than I'd imagined.

The priest then asked the best man for the rings. Chris checked each of his pockets twice, pretending to have forgotten them. After getting a good laugh from the crowd he handed the rings over.

The priest blessed the rings then continued. "Jake Mathew Freeman, do you take Sophie Lee Taylor to be your wife?"

"I do," Jake replied confidently, smiling proudly at the fact he actually got an answer right!

Everyone in the crowd held back their laughter, though a few giggles escaped.

Jake took my wedding ring from the priest and slid it onto my left hand. I was breathing heavily and my heart pounded as I watched him gently push the gold band onto my finger.

"Sophie Lee Taylor, do you take Jake Mathew Freeman to be your husband?"

"I do," I answered; my voice shaking. I'd given up worrying about the tears which trickled freely down my cheeks.

I placed Jakes wedding ring on his left hand. *Finally... he's all mine!*

"By the power vested in me, I now pronounce you man and wife. You may kiss the bride."

Jake carefully lifted my veil, gently placed his hands on my cheeks then kissed me passionately, giving me a sneaky bit of tongue just for good measure.

Kissing my *husband* for the first time was the realisation of a dream. It was such a surreal and wonderful moment in my life; totally unforgettable.

All our family and friends clapped and cheered as I looked out to the crowd; arm in arm with my husband. The room was filled with smiling faces and a good number of teary eyes. We were married and everyone was happy for us.

As we walked outside to the ringing of the huge church bells, we were mobbed by family and friends, all eager to offer their congratulations and in the process smother us with hugs and kisses. Cameras flashed continuously as everyone was eager to get a shot with Jake and me. It was hectic to say the least but it felt wonderful to be surrounded by such positive energy from all those we loved and cared about so dearly.

The rest of the afternoon was spent with the photographer, bridesmaids and groomsman at a beautiful parkland situated next to a river. We were probably there for a little over an hour and had an absolute ball posing for different shots together. I think the best part was that both my brothers were there, as drivers, and of course Jake's sisters were there as bridesmaids, so we were able to get some fantastic family photos which ordinarily wouldn't have been possible if we hadn't involved our siblings like we did.

I cherish all my wedding photos, and god forbid if ever we have a house fire, I pray I will at least have a few seconds to rescue my photo albums.

The reception was without question the best party I've ever been to; no bias whatsoever! The room looked beautiful, the meal was delicious and the DJ did a fantastic job as MC. I have no doubt every guest in attendance had as much fun as Jake and me.

Amongst all the celebrations, dancing, smiling and laughter, there was one standout moment. A moment in time which wasn't captured by either photograph or film, and will forever remain only in the memories of those who were there. It was Jake's speech.

My father, the best man and the maid of honour had all made their speeches and toasts. Each was heartfelt and touching and I greatly appreciated all that was said. Then it was Jake's turn.

To be honest, I can't remember the beginning of his speech all that well. I'm fairly certain he thanked everyone for their generous wedding gifts, as well as the guests who had travelled long distances to share our special day with us. He thanked his groomsman for their years of friendship; and he made a special mention to his sisters and how much he loved them. Alice, Kate and Samantha all broke down as he spoke to them which reduced most of the guests to tears. Then it came time to say a few words to me.

"Sophie Freeman, you already know everything I want to say to you, because I tell you I love you every day. So I have decided to say something a little different."

He asked me to stand up then led me from my seat at the head table to a single chair in front of the entire room. He kissed me on the lips then gestured for me to sit, before kneeling down in front of me. With microphone in hand, he began to sing.

I was a complete mess from the first line, with tears streaming from my eyes with every word. Jake doesn't profess to have a great singing voice, but I swear hearing him sing the words to *'Grow Old with You'* by Adam Sandler and Tim Herlihy, utterly took my breath away. I don't know how many times he practiced but it sounded brilliant.

I didn't take my eyes of him for the entire song and once he'd finished the whole reception erupted with cheers and whistles. There wasn't a dry eye in the room; I even caught one of my brothers trying to wipe a stray tear from the corner of his eye without anybody noticing.

While the clapping and cheering continued I stood up, wrapped my arms around Jake and kissed him deeply. Having him sing to me on my wedding day had completely taken me by surprise, and in the best possible way. The entire day had literally played out like the most amazing dream, but never in my wildest did I think Jake would serenade me with such a beautiful song in front of all our family and friends.

"I love you Jake. You'll never know how much I love you!"

He smiled, and wiping a tear from my cheek with his thumb replied, "Yeah I do… *half* as much as I love you."

I understand my story so far has been filled with an number of our erotic escapades, and you'd be forgiven for expecting that our wedding night would be listed as one of the best. But as I've said a number of times this is a true story, and the reality was, like on most wedding nights, the bride was absolutely exhausted. I actually researched it and discovered that on average, over fifty percent of newlyweds don't have sex on their wedding night. I couldn't believe it.

Extreme levels of excitement and a severe lack of sleep, an intense beauty regime of body, hair and make-up, and hours spent in a stunning yet slightly uncomfortable corset; there were countless conversations with friends and family, and some energetic dancing thrown in for good measure. By the time Jake and I reached the honeymoon suite I was running on empty. Now that said, don't for one minute think Jake and I didn't consummate our marriage. Missing an opportunity to make love was never our style.

After opening the hotel door, Jake picked me up in his arms and carried me inside.

"So traditional," I smiled.

He laid me down on the bed then turned the spa bath taps on. While the hot tub filled, Jake took off my shoes, unlaced my dress and helped me take over a hundred bobby pins out of my hair. My scalp ached as my hair was released from its style and allowed to fall to my shoulders. After stripping me naked, he helped me into the warm water and bubbles. It felt so soothing against my skin and caused my whole body to feel relaxed and heavy.

I watched with anticipation, and lust, as he slowly removed his uniform one piece at a time; neatly folding each item in turn. There was no doubt Jake was deliberately drawing out the process, knowing full well the anticipation of seeing him gradually reveal his naked body was driving me wild. I thought he looked amazing in his uniform, but I have to say watching him take it off took my visual pleasure to a whole new level. Once undressed, he stood at the edge of the spa allowing me the opportunity to survey his naked form before joining me in the water; my eyes struggling to look anywhere else other than his semi-erect member.

I turned around and lay against Jake with my back to his chest; closing my eyes while he ran his soapy hands all over my body. We soaked in the bubbling water for maybe twenty minutes or so and talked briefly about the highlights of the day. The pressure of the jets against my aching body combined with his firm hands caressing my most *delicate* areas felt heavenly.

Jake climbed out first and quickly dried himself, then grabbed a fresh towel and extended his hand to help me out of the water. I carefully stepped out of the spa and he gently dried the beading drops from my skin.

"Lie down Lover. I know you're tired, but I promise you'll sleep like a baby after I make love to you."

I smiled and climbed onto the soft white sheets of the kings sized bed. I lay on my back and immediately opened my legs wide; repaying him with a visual gift similar to the one he'd given me moments earlier. He bit his lip at the sight before him.

That night we made love, for the first time as husband and wife. It was gentle, passionate and just as the rest of the day had been... simply unforgettable.

Oh, and Jake was absolutely right... I slept like a baby.

CHAPTER TWENTY-FOUR

DISMISSED

Due to Jake's commitments at RMC there just wasn't time for us to go on a traditional honeymoon; not that we felt like we needed one considering we were moving into a new apartment once we returned to Canberra the following week. It would be the first time Jake and I would be living under the same roof, and although we were enjoying our time at home with family and friends, we couldn't wait to get the keys to our new place and move in together.

Although we didn't go on an extended honeymoon, we did spend the two nights following our wedding in a beautiful resort in Sunbury. When Jake booked, he mentioned to the receptionist that our stay would commence the day after our wedding, so when we arrived it appeared that hotel management had graciously booked us into the honeymoon suite… or so we thought.

We were in the middle of an energetic session of hot sex in the shower. With my back pressed against the tiled wall, my right leg was comfortably propped up on one of the conveniently placed stainless steel rails; Jake gripped another one firmly so he could brace himself as he thrust into me.

We were in the throes of pleasure when he commented on how thoughtful the hotel was for putting rails in the honeymoon suite shower. "I love these rails. We need them at our place!"

It was at that moment when the penny suddenly dropped. I looked over at the toilet and noticed a similar rail positioned beside the bowl. *This isn't a honeymoon suite at all!*

Now don't get me wrong, there's absolutely nothing amusing about people having to live with a disability, but the rather amusing thing was that neither Jake nor I picked up on the fact we'd actually been booked into a room for the disabled. Based on the 'features', we assumed it *was* the honeymoon suite! It was in the best location in the hotel; close to the pool, spa, restaurant, bar and reception, and the room was absolutely huge inside. It had the biggest bathroom and shower we'd ever seen and to top it off there were polished stainless steel rails strategically located in the bathroom, which Jake and I assumed were for kinky newlyweds who wanted to 'get it on' in the shower. It wasn't until we were actually making good use of these rails that we put two and two together.

"Jake?" I said breathlessly. I'd closed my eyes again and was revelling in the euphoric feeling of being fucked under the cascading water.

"Yeah Baby," he puffed as he continued his passionate rhythm; his hard muscle sliding in and out of me like a piston.

"I think this is a room for the disabled," I panted in between thrusts.

He stopped suddenly. I opened my eyes to see him looking at the hand rails beside the toilet.

He looked back at me. "You're right. These hand rails aren't here for fucking! There to help people in wheel chairs!"

We both started laughing at the totally inappropriate way we were currently using them.

"Oh well, there pretty handy when you want to fuck in the shower too!" I added.

"Hell yeah they are!" Jake exclaimed; easing himself out of me. "Now turn around, bend over and grab that rail," he ordered.

I couldn't help but giggle as I complied with his direction; turning my back to him.

"Now put your feet apart and hold on tight Baby."

I knew exactly what I was in for, and as I spread my feet apart and grasped the rail firmly with both hands I became even more aroused.

Jake reached up and angled the shower head so the water streamed over my back. He knew how much I loved the combination of sex and water. Grabbing hold of my hips, he fed his length into me and began fucking me from behind… hard!

"How's that hand rail holding up?"

"Good… *real* good," I stammered; my voice interrupted by the energetic ramming I was receiving.

The hand rail was ideal. I was gripping hold of it and pushing my hips back to meet each powerful thrust. In all seriousness and with absolutely no disrespect to disabled people, I think all showers should be fitted with them. At the very least people who like having sex in the bathroom should definitely have them installed; in the interest of 'safety' of course!

"Oh fuck!" I moaned; wincing as his shaft throbbed inside me. "I'm ready… I'm going to come!" I squealed.

The sensual sounds of running water and erotic pleasure echoed throughout the bathroom as Jake and I let go; powerful orgasms ripping through us both simultaneously. Glorious feelings of love and connection washed over me as I revelled in the sensation of climaxing at exactly the same time as my husband.

As he slowly withdrew from me I attempted to stand up straight. I was slightly unstable on my weary legs which prompted Jake to hold me steady while I turned around to face him. As soon as we made eye contact we couldn't help but laugh at the idea of christening a disabled shower.

"We shouldn't laugh… it's not funny," I said; feeling guilty for abusing the facilities which were clearly not intended for use by horny newlyweds!

"You're right… it's not," Jake smirked; causing me to giggle again.

I pressed my body against his, and as we kissed Jake proceeded to wash me in what can only be described as 'after play'. I was hyper sensitive to his touch. Having his hands gently smooth the slippery body wash over my skin was magnificent; so relaxing I could barely stand.

Still to this day I absolutely love showers, *especially* with Jake.

Now since I'm on the topic, after watching a variety of documentaries and reading various books about sex, I'm led to believe that simultaneous orgasms shared between lovers is considered to be the 'Holy Grail' of sexual connection and pleasure. Apparently, there's quite a large percentage of couples who rarely experience orgasms at exactly the same time, even those who share a healthy sex life.

I don't know if it's because Jake and I were each other's 'firsts', which allowed us to teach and learn through experimentation and communication together, or whether it's because we place such a high priority on the amount of pleasure each other feels during sex, but I rarely have my final orgasm out of sync with Jake's.

I'll always have a decent number of small orgasms throughout the entire sexual encounter, 'Little Ones' I call them, but at least nine times out of ten I'll have my final 'Big One' at exactly the same time as Jake. Either I will hold off for him, or he'll wait until I'm ready to come before releasing too. I honestly thought this was a normal thing for couples to experience but according to what I've seen and read over the years, it's not the case.

Now before you think I'm blowing my own trumpet, I haven't brought this up to boast and big note myself or anything like that. I raised the issue to highlight just how sexually compatible Jake and I are. Our ability to climax together just seemed to come naturally for us. Even as teenagers we would release in unison majority of the time. Anyway, I'm only going off what the 'sexperts' say. They definitely have one thing right though; simultaneous orgasms with your lover feel absolutely incredible!

Sex is the closest physical connection a couple can have, and for me, sharing a simultaneous orgasm with Jake elevates the entire experience to an even higher level of euphoria. When he and I climax together it's as though the unity between us occurs not just physically but on a mental level as well. I become so close to him, so in sync that I almost feel as though I actually become part of him, and him of me. It's like every feeling, sensation and thought travels between us telepathically; a truly magical and surreal experience.

After saying goodbye to family and friends, and thanking them for all their love and help in making our wedding such a magnificent occasion, Jake and I left Sunbury. We headed back to Canberra and moved straight into our new apartment which we organised prior to coming home for the Christmas break.

The apartment was in Queanbeyan which was nice and close to my work, however Jake would have to ride his motorbike to and from RMC each day. He really didn't mind though since he'd bought himself a brand new Kawasaki sports bike prior to Christmas. He'd always loved motorbikes, and with both of us working full time we were finally in a financial position where he could afford to buy one.

We'd already moved all of my furniture from the 'Fifty Cent House' into the new apartment prior to going home, but we hadn't officially moved in until arriving as *Mr. and Mrs. Freeman.*

We pulled up in the driveway with a car full of wedding gifts, a couple of boxes containing some of Jake's things he'd brought back from Sunbury and a few other bits and pieces.

Before getting out of the car he turned to me. "This is it Baby. *Finally*, we're moving in together!"

"I know. I'm so excited and happy. I've waited so long to be able to live with you."

"Me too, but it's been worth the wait. We're married now so we'll be living together for the rest of our lives," he grinned.

"Damn right we will," I smiled as I leant over and kissed him tenderly. "I love you Jake."

"I love you too Baby. Now let's get all this stuff inside and start unpacking."

In all honesty I would struggle to think of a time when I've ever been disappointed with Jake; he's always been so thoughtful and caring. But the day we moved into our new place was one such occasion where I was, let's just say, less than impressed.

He played what he thought was a harmless prank on me, which ended up affecting how I felt in that apartment for the next twelve months; basically the entire time we lived there. I understand he was only trying to be funny and at the time didn't really grasp the seriousness of what he did, but it was a situation where an innocent joke turned out to have a rather horrible and long lasting consequence.

The prank itself was really quite simple. Jake and I love horror movies and we used to watch them together all the time, we still do. Especially ones about ghosts, spirits and other creepy subjects. We'd watched plenty of flicks about haunted houses and people moving into places that were once the scene of a grisly crime. So knowing this, my beloved husband decided to give me a bit of a scare for real!

As we unloaded the car, Jake paid close attention to the box which contained the landline phone. He waited until I grabbed that particular one and took it inside. The box was open with the phone sitting on top so Jake knew I would plug it in straight away. He also knew the new phone number for the apartment, so as I walked inside he keyed in the number on his mobile phone. Then he covertly spied through the lounge room window and waited for just the right moment to press 'Call'.

I took the phone out of the box, prompting Jake to immediately call the apartment number. He knew the instant I plugged the phone into the wall it would be ringing. His plan worked perfectly and it gave me quite a fright. I remember thinking what a coincidence it was for someone to be trying to call at the exact moment that I connected the phone.

"Hello," I answered.

In the most blood curdling voice imaginable came the reply. "Your apartment is haunted. If you want to live… get out now!"

I swear my heart stopped beating and I felt the blood drain from my face. The voice was so dark, so terrifying; like nothing I'd ever heard before.

I slammed the phone down and ran out to Jake. He was walking towards the front door with a box in his arms; a clever alibi which convinced me to the point of certainty that it couldn't have been him on the phone. I was absolutely terrified.

"What's wrong Soph?" he asked sincerely.

"We have to go Jake! We can't stay here! We have to go now!" I replied, my frightened voice beginning to crackle as I grew more and more upset.

"What are you talking about? What's happened?" he asked; displaying a look of genuine concern.

"As soon as I plugged the phone in it was ringing, and when I answered it this really creepy voice told me that our apartment is haunted, and if we want to live we have to get out now! We have to go Jake. I'm not staying here!" My eyes stung as I began to tear up.

Now, this was the point where Jake should've put a stop to the prank and come clean after realising how terrified I was, but I think seeing how perfectly it had worked prompted him to keep me going a little longer. To make matters even worse, as if adding fuel to the fire, he concocted a bullshit story which elevated my fear to a whole new level. This took the joke from something which could have been laughed off after a simple explanation, to an experience that came back to haunt me on countless occasions thereafter. And this was the main reason I was so disappointed in him.

"I wasn't going to say anything Soph, but when the real estate agent showed us through last year I got a really horrible vibe as soon as I walked into this place. I felt like *something* was already in there with us."

"Why the fuck didn't you say something!" I scowled.

"Well I knew how much you loved the place, and I thought I was just being stupid."

"We're going Jake! I'm not staying here!"

"Ok, ok. Calm down Soph. Let me put this box back in the car and you go inside and start packing."

"You're kidding me right! I'm not going back in there! Let's just get in the car and get the fuck out of here!" My tone was dead serious. Every haunted house movie I'd ever seen flashed through my mind resulting in a very real feeling of panic and fear.

It was then that I noticed Jake smirking. My dramatic out-burst and suggestion to leave all our stuff and high tail it out of there was obviously too much for him to keep a straight face.

"What's so bloody funny?" I asked angrily. I still hadn't twigged that he was playing a prank on me.

"Calm down Soph. We don't have to go."

"Why. What are you talking about?"

"I called you with my mobile from outside. The scary voice was me," he confessed; taking his phone out of his pocket and holding it up to prove it was him. He wore a proud smile on his face knowing he well and truly had me going.

I didn't say anything for a second. I just stood there waiting for my brain to process the whole event.

"Soph?" Jake prompted for a response. His smile was quickly replaced with a concerned expression once he'd realised he'd gone too far.

"Why would you do that to me? Why would you scare me like that?" My voice echoed with disappointment.

"I'm sorry Baby. It was just a spare of the moment thought. I really didn't think you'd believe me."

"Well I did! That voice you used scared the fucking shit out of me!" I hissed; still in shock.

"Come hear Baby." Seeing that I was quite shaken up, he walked over and gave me a hug. "I'm sorry Soph. I really didn't think it would work like that."

"It's all those scary movies Jake. And I believed you when you said you felt something in the apartment when we first looked at it. You know I believe *everything* you say."

"I really am sorry. I apologise for scaring you. I should've known it was a stupid prank to play on you. I just didn't think." His apology was sincere and I could tell he was disappointed in himself for upsetting me. Even now, if that prank is ever bought up he still says how much he regrets it.

I forgave him immediately, after all it was only a joke and I knew he didn't mean to hurt me. But as it turned out, the fear I'd just experienced from Jake's prank re-surfaced every time he had to go away on field exercises as part of his RMC training.

For the entire time we lived there, whenever I was alone at night in that apartment I was scared. I know there wasn't a ghost in the house but I think because the first emotion I really felt in the place was complete terror, I never felt relaxed and comfortable being there on my own. It wasn't long before the ramifications of the harmless prank began to surface.

We'd only been in the apartment for a week when Jake came home and told me he would be deploying to the field within the next few days. He was due to complete a starvation and sleep deprivation exercise that was scheduled to last for at least a week. It wasn't unexpected because he told me there was a fairly good chance this particular exercise would be sprung on them immediately after the Christmas break, while everybody was still in holiday mode. Even though I knew it was coming, I still didn't want him to go. So two days later, Jake and I said our goodbyes before he left for work and his subsequent deployment on what was renowned as being one of the toughest exercises of the entire course.

"Bye Jake. Make sure you look after yourself." I said as we stood embracing in the driveway of the apartment; Jake's motorbike idling beside us.

"I will Baby. Don't be surprised if you have trouble recognising me when I get back. No doubt I'll be looking pretty tired and worn out."

"And hungry," I added with a smile.

"Yeah I'll be hungry all right."

"Just be careful ok. I love you."

"I will. I love you too Baby. Are you going to be ok on your own for a few days?"

"Yeah I'll be fine." I lied.

I was already dreading my first night alone in the apartment. The ironic thing was that it was so much nicer and far safer than the 'Fifty Cent House' ever was, and I lived there on my own for six months! Plus, the new place didn't have those crazy neighbours on the other side of the wall that used to keep me up all night with their arguing and loud music, yet I was still worried about being at home alone for a week.

"Don't worry about me. Just get through this week and I'll see you when you get home," I said reassuringly.

"Ok Baby, I love you and I miss you already."

"I miss you too."

Our goodbye kiss was as passionate as always, and we squeezed each other tightly before letting go. I took a step back and I watched as Jake climbed on his bike and rode away. I stood in the driveway listening until the sound of the engine disappeared into the distance; emptiness once again flooded into my heart.

I worked at the store all day, arrived home sometime after six and made myself dinner. It was the first time I'd sat down for a meal without Jake for over a month. I missed not being able to talk with him about our day and not being able to curl up with him on the couch to watch a movie before going to bed, like we'd done most nights since moving in together.

That night I still watched a movie, even though I didn't find it as enjoyable on my own, then had a long shower before climbing into bed; my cold, lonely bed. As soon as I flicked off the bedside lamp, fear began to invade my mind. I lay awake in the darkness like a young child who just woke up from a terrible nightmare. I closed my eyes and tried to block out all the frightening thoughts that were manifesting in my head. I knew I was being silly, and I was no stranger to spending nights alone in an apartment by myself but it didn't matter. The harder I tried to convince myself that I was safe and that nothing was in the house with me, the more nervous and frightened I became.

Eventually I realised there was no way I was getting to sleep lying in the dark, alone in bed and frightened. I got up, pulled the covers off my mattress and went out to the lounge room. I switched on the TV and made myself comfy on the couch. The light and noise from the television gave me the illusion that I wasn't on my own, and eventually I was able to drift off to sleep.

This was the beginning of a routine I carried out almost every night Jake was away on exercise. No matter how many times I talked myself into sleeping alone in bed, I just couldn't do it and would eventually find myself curled up on the couch with the TV on to keep me company.

I remember one particularly bad night when Jake was away. I went to bed and was doing some reading in an attempt to drift off to sleep without having to go out to the couch. I heard an unusual noise out in the lounge room and a shot of adrenaline raced through my body in a millisecond; I absolutely panicked. I reckon I held my breath for about two minutes, waiting to hear the noise again with my eyes firmly fixed on the door. I was certain somebody was in the house.

After I don't know how long, I built up the courage to go and investigate. There was nothing on hand that even resembled a weapon so I cautiously ventured out of my room unarmed. Slowly I made my way down the hall towards the lounge room and kitchen area; towards the location of the noise.

I remember being so scared. My heart was thumping loudly, so loud I swear I could hear the sound of my own pulse. As I neared the end of the hallway and peered into the lounge room I got the fright of my life.

I looked over towards the far side of the room and gasped when I saw what I thought was a man standing next to the entertainment unit, bending over as if he was trying to lift the TV.

I bolted as fast as I could back to my room, closed the door carefully behind me and dived into my bed; utterly petrified. I was breathing heavily and my eyes were stinging; pure fear causing me to weep. I was convinced that my mind wasn't playing tricks on me, and was one hundred percent certain there was somebody in my house!

I quickly thought of my options. One of which was to run from my room, go through the internal door that gave access to the garage then run next door. My other option was to call the police from my mobile phone which I had with me.

It was going to be a fair run through the house, into the garage then over to the neighbours and would require me to leave the *perceived* safety of my room. On the other hand, calling the police would mean waiting in the house with the intruder for god knows how long before they arrived.

I sat still for a moment and listened patiently. The house was silent. I started to second guess what I'd seen in the lounge room.

Was there somebody there or did it just look like it? No there was definitely someone there! It's so quiet, maybe he's gone? It could have been a shadow from the light coming in the window? No! I'm sure I saw him turn and look directly at me! How would he have got in, all the windows are locked and the doors are dead bolted?

As each thought played over in my head I started to feel more certain I'd actually imagined the scary figure I had seen.

I decided not to call the police, and after what felt like ages, somehow managed to build up the courage to investigate.

There's nobody there Sophie. It's all in your head! No one else is in the house. Damn Jake and his fucking stupid prank. It's made me paranoid!

I slowly opened my bed room door, pausing every couple of seconds to listen. I stepped into the hall, and with my eyes fixed on the open door at the end; I gradually made my way towards the lounge room. Every couple of steps I would stop and listen, ready to bolt back to my room at the first sound; the first indication that I wasn't alone.

When I reached the entrance to the lounge room I slowly peered around the corner, towards the TV cabinet. Again, I got a start when I looked into the room, it really did look like someone was crouched down near the television; as if they were about to pick it up. But instead of running, I squinted and had a decent look.

I wanted to be sure it wasn't a man before turning the lounge room light on. If it was somebody, then I definitely didn't want to alert them of my presence by flicking on a light. I stared for a moment, focusing as best I could in the dim light, and when I was convinced it wasn't moving I took a deep breath and flicked the switch. There was nothing there. I turned the light off again and the crouching figure reappeared instantly, then disappeared again when I switched it back on. The figure was actually the side of one of the couches, the light coming in through the lounge room window casting a shadow which clearly resembled somebody crouching down by the TV.

I exhaled as relief washed over me and I was so glad I decided not to call the police. *How embarrassing to have them come over for the sake of a few shadows!*

It turned out that after the entire ordeal was over, I actually felt safer in my bedroom and eventually fell asleep in my own bed; well that night anyway.

After finishing his week of hell without food and sleep I expected Jake to ride home that night, so I was surprised when he called me.

"The CO decided to keep all the cadets who completed the exercise on base for the night. It's for our own safety. He doesn't want anybody driving or going out on the town after such a fatiguing week."

"So you're not coming home until tomorrow then?" I questioned; clearly disappointed.

"Unfortunately not, but you can come and visit me if you like."

Even though Jake lived with me, he was still required to maintain a room at the college so he could store all his uniforms and military equipment on base.

"Great! I'll be there as soon as I finish work."

"Awesome. Also, if it's not too much trouble, do you think you could pick me up some food on the way?"

"Sure. What do you want?"

"Um… a big mac, chicken burger, milkshake, fries and a box of chicken nuggets please."

"Anything else?" I asked sarcastically; amused at the size of his order.

He when silent for a moment. "Actually… grab us a caramel sundae too."

I burst out laughing. “Geez! Where are you going to put all that?”

“In my mouth! I’ve been starved for a week remember? I don’t think you realise how hungry I am.”

Mmm, Jake’s mouth. I couldn’t help but fantasise about what else I could put in his mouth! My groin ached at the possibilities.

“I know what *I’d* like to put in that mouth of yours!” I whispered. I was at work and didn’t want anyone to hear me talking dirty.

“In that case, cancel the sundae… so I’ve got room left for dessert,” he laughed. “See you soon Baby.”

“I’ll get one of the girls to close up so I can finish work earlier. I’ll see you around five thirtyish”

“I can’t wait.”

“Can’t wait to see me, or eat your Macca’s?” I joked.

“I can’t wait to eat *you* and my Macca’s.”

I giggled and felt my cheeks blush red from his cheeky reply.

“Love you Soph. I’ll see you soon.”

“Love you too Baby. Bye”

After my shift finished I went to ‘McDonalds’, collected my starved lovers order then drove to the college. As I arrived at Jake’s accommodation block, a huge white three story building lined with rows and rows of windows, I spotted him standing out the front. I found a park and he rushed over, opened my door and helped me out of the car before wrapping me in his arms and showering me in kisses. As much as I hated Jake going away, I absolutely loved the feeling of hugging and kissing him for the first time on his return.

“Holy shit! What did they do to you? Look how skinny you are!” I said; taking a step back to survey the damage that a week of next to no food, barely any sleep and continuous physical activity had taken on my husband.

His face was gaunt and pale, his eyes dark and his body looked half his normal size. I couldn’t believe how much weight he’d lost in only a week. Considering Jake didn’t have an ounce of fat on him when he left, it was clear most of the weight he’d lost was muscle.

“I know I look like shit. I’m sorry,” he replied, looking down at the ground; noticeably embarrassed.

"Oh no Jake… I'm sorry… I didn't…"

Jake cut me off. "No it's ok. It shouldn't take me long to get back into shape. I just need to eat some decent food and hit the weights again. I reckon two or three weeks and I'll be back to normal."

"Well speaking of food, here's your order. I hope nobody else planned on having Macca's tonight because you almost cleaned the whole place out," I laughed as I produced the mountain of food Jake ordered.

"Yum. It smells so good. Let's go up to my room and I'll give you a run down on the past week, which will explain why I look like shit."

"You don't look that bad Jake," I said as sincere as I could in an attempt to undo my last comment on his appearance.

He looked at me and raised an eyebrow. It was clear he didn't believe me. "I look like death but I'm sure a belly full of Macca's will bring me back to life," he grinned; holding up the bags of food.

It was the first time I'd been up to Jake's room and I was a little nervous. We walked through two glass doors at the entrance of the building which opened up into a large foyer. The place was spotless. Jake had told me about the weekly inspections they would have which demanded the highest standards of cleanliness, so every square inch of the place was immaculate.

"Up those stairs," directed Jake.

I followed him up to the second floor and down the hallway. There must have been about twenty or so doors lining either side of the hall; most were open. There were cadets walking in and out of each other's rooms and down the hall, some carrying packs, boots, and clothes; others with rifles.

"Their cleaning all their gear from the exercise," said Jake after noticing that my attention was captured by the cadets carrying rifles.

"And you're allowed to just walk around with them?" I asked curiously; surprised they weren't in a safe or something.

"Yeah we have them with us almost all the time. It's good practice."

"Oh. I thought they be locked away."

"Nope, we keep them in our room," he smiled. "It's ok Baby… you're safe."

"Of course I am. I'm with you," I said calmly, grabbing his arm and squeezing him.

Music emanated from a few of the rooms as well as heaps of talking and laughing. There really was quite a lot of activity and a happy vibe in the place, no doubt because many of them had just completed a torturous exercise.

A number of cadets said 'Hi' to Jake and I as we passed them in the hall. Jake introduced me to a few who were in the same class as him; offering them some fries after hearing comments about how good the food smelt.

"Don't worry, they'll be eating well in the mess tonight," he said; assuring me not to feel bad that they too didn't have a mountain of fast food to get through. Jake always commented on how good the food was at RMC so I believed him.

About halfway down the hall Jake stopped. "And this is my room." He unlocked the door with a key which was hanging from his dog tag chain around his neck and we walked inside.

"We're supposed to leave the door open when we have someone in our room, but it's too bloody noisy out there. Besides, we're married anyway," said Jake; closing the door behind him.

As soon as I entered his room the first thing I noticed was the absolutely stunning view from his bedroom window. From the third floor, Jake overlooked a few of the other buildings as well as the RMC parade ground, and in the distance the view stretched out across Canberra towards my town of Queanbeyan. It was incredible.

"Wow… nice view Baby!" I beamed.

"Yeah it's pretty cool hey. Sometimes I sit there and look out the window while I'm polishing my boots. It looks really nice at night."

"It sure does… it's beautiful!"

His room was small. There was a single bed with the covers perfectly made, as well as a desk and chair, above which was a bookshelf displaying a few neatly stacked military manuals. On the wall beside the door was his rifle; locked in a heavy steel security device. I also noticed two doors, which I assumed was a built in wardrobe. I gestured to Jake if it was ok to take a peek. He nodded so I opened it up. All his boots and shoes were neatly laced and lined up on the bottom shelf. His uniforms were all pressed and hung in order and his foldable items were perfectly organised on a number of shelves. On the top shelf were Jake's polished brass uniform accoutrements, neatly displayed on a green towel.

The order and presentation of his room was impressive to say the least. I had imagined how neat and tidy Jake's room would be, but this was on a whole new level!

"Everything is so particular isn't it?" I said; admiring the organisation.

"That's the standard. If it's anything other than what you see here, then we're given extra drill practice as punishment. You could go into anyone's room in this whole building and they'd all be as neat as that," he added in a very 'matter of fact' tone.

"Wow! It's so neat. It's almost like you have obsessive compulsive disorder," I teased.

"I suppose you sort of have to… to keep the instructors off your back."

"You won't get in trouble will you?" I asked as I closed his wardrobe doors; genuinely concerned. I think the level of organisation revealed just how strict this place was, and I was anxious about breaking any rules.

"What… for having you in here with me?"

"Yeah."

"I highly doubt it. All the staff would've gone home after the exercise by now. They've been with us all week so they wouldn't be hanging around the barracks this late. And we're just having *dinner*, it's not like we are up to no good!" he joked.

"Not yet anyway," I added swiftly.

Jake raised an eyebrow; his lips curling into a suggestive grin.

"As long as you're sure that you won't get into trouble," I reiterated.

"It's fine Baby, relax. Besides, they're the ones who wouldn't let me go home, so how else was I supposed to see you, and kiss you, and…"

"Eat Jake!" I commanded, breaking his train of thought. "Tell me about your week."

He handed me the cheeseburger I'd ordered for myself. "Sit on my bed Babe."

Jake sat down at his desk. As he started to work his way through the mountain of food in front of him he gave me some brief details on the exercise.

"In every twenty-four-hour period we slept for an average of about two hours; usually that wasn't in one block either. And since we were doing all types of physical challenges and activities all hours of the day, the fatigue aspect of the exercise was the worst. You just get so tired that your mind starts playing tricks on you. You see things that aren't there and you forget where you are, and what you're supposed to be doing. I lost count of how any times I caught myself hallucinating from utter exhaustion."

"What's the point of it though?"

"Well everybody takes turns at being in command, so they want to see how well each cadet copes in leadership scenarios when they're exhausted, hungry and stressed. They also want to see how well you follow orders and work as a team, especially when you're tired and faced with situations where working together is the only way to successfully complete the task or mission."

"Sounds hard. How'd you go?"

"Ok I think. We haven't been debriefed yet, so I'll find out tomorrow before they let us go."

"What about the food. How much did you get to eat?"

Jake finished his mouthful before answering. He was making short work of all the food I'd brought for him.

He really is starving!

"Well over the whole week I ate half a cups-canteen of cold baked beans, which is about three mouthfuls for me, and one tin of cold 'beef kai si ming', about the same size as a small tin of spaghetti you'd get at the supermarket. Usually it tastes like shit, but since I was starving it was absolutely delicious. I licked the tin spotless."

With a mouth full of cheeseburger, I laughed at the thought of Jake licking the tin dry.

"And that was it! Pretty much what I'd call a morning tea snack was all I had for the entire week! I was bloody starving! That's why I'm so fucking skinny and all my muscles have disappeared!" he snapped; a hint of anger in his voice.

"It's alright Jake. You'll get it all back soon."

"Yeah I know, I just hate feeling so skinny and weak."

"Awe Baby… you still look gorgeous to me." I tried to reassure him that he didn't look so terrible.

"Yeah if you're into skinny assed corpses," he joked as he looked at his tired reflection in the mirror on the wall beside his desk. "I was manning the gun late one afternoon. I was so hungry and tired when all of a sudden, I saw this huge goanna walking past the camp; fifteen or so meters in front of me. He was enormous, and I was watching him walking slowly through the grass, wondering how good he'd taste if I cooked him. All of a sudden, I swear his big juicy legs turned into what looked like four fried chicken drumsticks! I was rubbing my eyes and trying to focus, but that's what his legs looked like… chicken drumsticks! I wanted to eat him so bad."

I laughed out loud; almost choking on a piece of burger bun.

"I'm serious. I thought I was losing my fucking mind!"

"Oh my god Jake, you poor thing," I sympathised; still giggling.

We finished eating and I helped Jake polish off the last of his milk shake.

"Feel better now?"

"Hell yeah," he smiled; leaning back in his chair and rubbing his belly. "Sooo much better."

He climbed on the bed and we laid down beside each other. As soon as his head hit the pillow he let out a huge yawn. He was exhausted.

"Shit I think I've put myself into a food coma. I can barely keep my eyes open," he yawned again. "I wish I could come home with you."

"I know; I want to snuggle up with you too. I miss crawling into bed with you every night."

"Well I promise I'll be home with you tomorrow night."

"Probably a good thing you're not coming home with me now," I hinted.

"Why's that?"

"Well you'll need to be well rested to get through what I've got planned for you!" I reached between his legs and rubbed his groin as I spoke.

"Mmm… I like the sound of that!"

"Apparently!" I giggled, feeling *him* grow beneath my hand.

He was getting harder by the second which prompted me to gently rub his shaft on the outside of his tracksuit pants. I couldn't help myself.

"Don't start something you can't finish!" he warned.

"Who said I can't finish? Is your door locked?"

"No."

I quickly climbed off the bed and turned the lock.

"You know you're going to get me in trouble Soph?"

"You're already in trouble," I replied as I climbed back on the bed.

I wasted no time pulling his pants down and releasing his rock hard erection. It was hot to touch and throbbed as thick veins pumped blood up and down his length. It was clear that Jake was eager for a release after more than a week without me.

"Holy fuck! You're so hard!" I said quietly; wrapping both hands around him.

"Well what do you expect? I haven't had sex for a week!"

"What makes you think you're getting sex now! We're not allowed to sleep together in your room," I teased; slowly massaging his cock. It was making him even harder and driving me completely wild.

"No… we're not." He was visibly disappointed.

I had no intention of sleeping with Jake in his room that night. First of all because I wanted him to fuck me hard and vigorously which was exactly how I needed it, and we definitely didn't have enough privacy for that variety. Secondly, I *really* didn't want him to get into trouble for the sake of some 'quiet sex'. I'd rather wait until tomorrow when we were home, where Jake wouldn't have to hold back and I could scream the roof off.

"That's a shame Baby," I said sarcastically as I continued to stroke him. By now he was so hard there was already pre-come trickling from the eye of his cock; my eyes almost popped out of my head at the sight.

I can assure you he wasn't the only one in the room who was on the brink. I was so moist I could've mistaken my utterly ridiculous state of arousal for accidently wetting myself. I know that's overly descriptive, but I was literally soaking!

Jake closed his eyes; laying back to enjoy the massage.

"Is there a rule against blowjobs?" I whispered.

He opened his eyes and looked at me. "No. I'm pretty sure blowjobs are perfectly acceptable," he chuckled.

"Liar," I grinned.

I flicked my hair to one side, leant forward and with my eyes firmly fixed on Jake's, wrapped my lips around his cock. Slowly I engulfed his length, from the tip all the way down his shaft; taking as much as I could.

"Fuuuck!" he moaned quietly. "You're spoiling me."

I nodded in response, unable to answer as my mouth was full of his thick, straining muscle. I reached up and put my hand on his chest, forcing him to lay back and relax. I wanted him to really enjoy this.

With slow, firm suction and the occasional full shaft lick, I gave Jake a blow job he'd never forget. I figured he would be so horny after not seeing me for an entire week that it would be a fairly brief performance. *Well worth the risk.* Besides, I wanted a nice long fuck the following night, so taking the edge off my man now meant I'd get exactly what I ordered in bed tomorrow.

Within minutes I felt him throb; an unmistakable warning of his approaching orgasm. He grabbed the back of my head and gave a few gentle thrusts with his hips; slowly fucking my mouth. I heard him gasp then hold his breath as he began to deliver his hot serving which I was only too eager to receive. I moaned with satisfaction at the feeling of him shooting into the back of my throat, over and over again; a glorious sensation which almost made *me* come too. I waited until his cock stopped pulsing, ensuring he'd finished injecting his creamy syrup before greedily drinking down every last delicious drop.

It never ceases to amaze me that some girls don't actually like swallowing. For me, I absolutely love it. Not just the sensation of siphoning his hard member and the alluring taste of his come, but also the sense of domination and control that I feel over him when I bring Jake to orgasm using my mouth. Watching his eyes blaze as I devour his offering makes me feel so powerful. It really is for *my* pleasure as much as his, and has always been such an empowering act for me which never fails to give me a great deal of satisfaction.

I licked Jake's slippery cock like an ice-cream; gently milking it from base to tip with my hand to ensure not a single drop remained. He twitched and quivered as I polished his hypersensitive dick; cleaning the residue of come and saliva with my tongue. I smiled each time he flinched at my touch.

"A bit sensitive are we?" I grinned before licking him again.

"Yes!" he replied, flinching again suddenly before putting his hands on my shoulders in an attempt to keep me at bay.

"You're a bad girl," he breathed; pure satisfaction resonating in his voice.

"Don't you mean *good* girl!" I replied; licking my lips suggestively.

"Bad… but unbelievably good at what you do!"

"Lots of practice," I laughed. "I bet you're tired now Baby?"

He nodded; barely able to keep his eyes open, let alone speak.

"So what time can I come and get you tomorrow?"

"You don't have to. I've got my bike here so I'll ride home after they debrief us; sometime mid-morning I hope." Jake yawned as he finished his sentence.

"Ok. Well I'll head off Baby and let you get a good night's sleep. I've got the next few days off work so we can spend the entire weekend together. I'll see you when you get home."

"Can't you stay a little longer?" he begged.

"You're exhausted Jake. You'll be asleep in the next five minutes. Look at the bright side, you only have to wait until tomorrow to see me again."

"Thank god," he smiled. "Well if you're going, let me walk you out."

"No you stay there, I'll find my way out."

He didn't listen; climbing out of bed and fixing himself up. "You're not walking out on your own."

Jake unlocked his door and opened it slowly, taking a quick look in either direction down the hall. "Coast is clear."

He extended his hand out to me and I grasped it tightly; following as he led the way. We passed a couple of cadets in the hall who smiled as Jake acknowledged them, no doubt aware he and I had been up to no good. I couldn't help but blush at their 'I-know-what-you've-been-doing' glances.

"Don't worry Soph, I'm not the only one who's had a visitor in their room," said Jake reassuringly.

Once we reached my car he let go of my hand and wrapped me in his arms; kissing me tenderly on the lips. "Thanks for coming Babe."

"I was going to say exactly the same thing," I grinned, causing him to chuckle and blush slightly.

"You've got a dirty mind Soph. I like the way you think."

"And I like the way you taste!" I exclaimed.

Jake started laughing. "You poor thing. How are you going to sleep tonight?"

He could sense I was itching for sexual attention, and was right on the money. After servicing him up in his room, I was using every ounce of self-control not to beg him to throw me in the back seat of the car and fuck me senseless.

"Honestly, I have no idea. I might need to *look after* myself before I go to bed."

"Well I promise I'll repay the favour tomorrow. As soon as I get home I'm going to bury my face between your legs!"

He wasn't helping the situation.

"Stop it Jake. I'm going."

He smirked knowing how on edge I was, and I couldn't stop myself from grinding my pelvis against him through pure sexual frustration.

"You're killing me!" I groaned.

"I'm sorry Baby. Tomorrow… my tongue…your pussy… I promise."

"Jake!"

He laughed again before pulling me to his chest and kissing the top of my head; signalling he was done with tormenting me. "I'm sorry Baby."

I squeezed him firmly before looking up into his eyes. "Goodnight. Get some sleep and I'll see you in the morning. I Love you."

"Love you too, and thanks so much for the food."

"No problems. Thanks for dessert," I winked; kissing him once more as he helped me into the car.

"You've got it bad," he said sympathetically.

"Oh you have no idea! Tomorrow can't get here fast enough! See you soon Lover."

"Bye Soph." Jake closed the door.

I clenched my thighs together the whole way home; the thought of Jake's promise firmly in the front of my mind. I wasn't joking when I said 'Tomorrow can't get here fast enough'. I didn't just *want* his face between my legs… I *needed* him there. The tension was so intense it had manifested into genuine pain!

As expected, getting to sleep that night proved difficult. Eventually I managed to drift off, though not before giving into my desires and lending myself a *helping hand.*

For the rest of the year Jake and I cherished every moment we had together. His commitments at RMC were relentless and he was always getting home late or going in early for one reason or another. I understood it was an intense course and required one hundred percent focus and dedication if he was to have any chance at all of passing, but it was still a tough way to spend our first year of marriage.

Most of the other cadets on the course were single and lived on base. I'm sure not having the distraction of a wife or husband, or kids for that matter, would've made the training and unwavering commitment to the army a little more bearable.

Jake would tell me every time another cadet in his course would either withdraw themselves from training or be 'back classed' for not meeting the required standard. 'Back classed' was the term used when a cadet would be put back six months from where he or she was in their training; effectively adding half a year to the duration of the course. I distinctly remember Jake being afraid of it happening to him.

"If I get back classed, I honestly don't know if I could stay. Not because I'm a quitter, but because I'm already giving this course one hundred percent effort, so what would I be able to do better the *second* time around."

He never had to worry about it.

Over the next twelve months Jake went on at least five field exercises, maybe more, and some were over two weeks long. I dreaded every time he had to go away, mostly because I had to spend lonely nights at home on my own, just me and my over active imagination. While Jake was away I'd put in more hours at work so my weekends would be free when he returned, allowing us to spend every spare minute we had together. I lost count of how many times Jake took me out for dinner, to the movies, shopping and on different dates and adventures. He definitely made sure our time together was well spent and took every opportunity to spoil me rotten. So much so, that when I look at photos of me taken throughout that year, I'm always shocked by how much weight I'd put on. Jake's generosity in taking me out for dinner so regularly definitely took its toll on my figure. It was all worth it though and I wouldn't have changed a thing. Mind you, pounding the treadmill to get my figure back was torture.

One thing which did get me through some of the harder parts of that year was definitely my friendship with Tanya. She was Josh's girlfriend; one of Jake's classmates from RMC.

Whenever Jake was away on exercise, Josh usually was too. If her university course allowed, Tanya would often come over and spend a few days with me. She didn't stay over every time Jake was away but I always appreciated her visits and welcomed her company, especially at night when being on my own was the hardest. Just having someone there to talk to, watch movies and have dinner with was invaluable, and the fact Tanya and I both knew how each other was feeling caused the bond between us to form quickly. We stayed friends long after the boys finished at RMC.

After eighteen months of dedicated military training, which was as much mental as it was physical, Jake had reached the end. Unmeasurable levels of commitment, stress, anxiety and the continued pursuit of his goal, had seen Jake fulfil a promise he made to me almost three years earlier. Words cannot even begin to describe how proud I was of my husband, and how elated I was for him and what he achieved.

Completing officer training at the Royal Military College wasn't for the faint hearted. Proof can be seen in the harsh reality that almost half the cadets who started the course with Jake's intake didn't reach graduation.

All his family had travelled to Canberra to take part in the celebrations. Jake's mother and father, his three sisters and his grandparents all made the trip. My mum and dad also came to watch the parade and the presentation ceremony. We would all be going to the formal dinner that evening as well.

There were three events scheduled throughout the day, the first being the graduation parade which started at 9:00am. It was such a grand display of discipline and training that I wouldn't have thought possible unless I'd seen it with my own eyes. I remember it like it was yesterday.

To gather some perspective on how impressive the RMC graduation parade was, one only has to look at the amount of time spent rehearsing. When Jake completed boot camp, back when he joined the army reserves, the march out parade was so good it still gives me shivers when I think about it. It was brilliant to watch, and Jake said they'd only practiced it for a couple of hours each week then a few hours each day as the parade grew closer. Well imagine how good the RMC parade was, given they would complete a full rehearsal *every* week, apart from when they were out field, for a year and a half! Then in the final week before the parade took place, they were rehearsing *all* day; hours upon hours of practising every drill movement and step. The result was a spectacle which can only be described with one word… perfection.

Their uniforms looked amazing. They were all dressed in polished black shoes, black pants with a red stripe down each leg and crisp white jackets with gold embellishments. Matching black and red caps completed the uniform, and each cadet carried their rifle which hung off their right shoulder from a white sling. They all looked so bright, so white, that it was hard to look at them without squinting; the glare of the sun reflecting off their uniforms as they marched.

As hard as we all looked, we couldn't spot a single crease in a uniform, nor did we see a hand or foot out of place for the entire parade. Some of the movements the formation completed were breathtaking and no doubt difficult to perform. I swear it looked like an army of robots programmed to march in unison, not actual people full of excitement and nerves; at the mercy of human error. Honestly, it was as if human error didn't exist on that parade ground.

As the cadets marched with their chests up and heads held high, full of pride and accomplishment, there was no doubt every single person in attendance that day was completely immersed in similar feelings. It was impossible not to feel the energy in the air. An uplifting sense of pride washed over the crowd of family and friends as they watched their loved ones. Every spectator was in awe as the formation completed their final lap of the parade ground. Eighteen months of dedication and perseverance to finally be able to count themselves among the graduating class. An equally powerful sense of patriotism for our country could be felt as we watched the future leaders of the Australian Army give their final salute, before marching off the RMC parade ground for the last time.

As incredible as the whole parade was, I don't have to think too hard to pick my favourite moment of all. Watching as the cadets marched off the parade ground and onto a side road in the distance, still in clear view of the crowd, they halted and turned sharply to face the Battalion Sergeant Major; the highest ranking cadet. He said a few quiet words to them all, then gave the order which I'm sure *every* person longed to hear.

At the top of his lungs, causing the hairs on my arms to stand on end, he commanded, "Graduating Class of 2001… for the last time… dismissed!"

The formation turned sharply, took three steps in unison then with an enormous roar of cheers and whistles, threw their hats high into the air. Everyone in the crowd joined in their happiness; cheering and clapping from the distance. They were finished, and I can only imagine the feelings of accomplishment and relief which flooded through them in those moments.

Jake's family, my parents and I were all buzzing. As we waited for him to make his way over to us, we talked about the incredible demonstration we'd just witnessed. As impressive as we thought the parade was going to be, no amount of expectation could have prepared us for how wonderful it *actually* was.

Jake eventually arrived and was showered in hugs, kisses cuddles and handshakes. I have no doubt everyone was proud of him, especially Greg and Mary, but I had lived with Jake and watched him every step of the way. I knew the struggles he'd overcome and the pressures he had to deal with each day, and I was also there when he doubted himself and lost faith in his ability to get through to the end. As I wrapped my arms around him, the feelings I had in my heart went far beyond that of being proud… I was *honoured.* And at the risk of sounding self-centred, now that it was finally over, to be by his side through it all made me feel as though I too had graduated with him.

As I held him tightly Jake whispered in my ear. "Thank you Baby. Thank you for everything you've gone through and done for me. I would never have made it here if it wasn't for you."

Tears pricked my eyes. After all Jake had endured and accomplished, after all he had done for me, he was the one giving *me* thanks. It meant everything to hear him say those words. To know he understood, and even more importantly appreciated how hard it was for me too, was a wonderful feeling. It confirmed to me yet again that Jake and I were a team. Once more we'd proven that, together, absolutely nothing can beat us!

The presentation ceremony took place in the gymnasium and consisted of each cadet being called up to the stage, one at a time, and being presented with their graduation certificate. A number of cadets were also presented with various awards for outstanding performance in certain areas of training. Although Jake wasn't one of the people to receive an award, I couldn't have cared. In my eyes getting to the end of the course and graduating was an outstanding performance in itself. When he was called to the stage to receive his graduation certificate from the Commandant, I clapped so hard that my hands hurt.

After the presentation ceremony there was a break in the formalities. We all headed home and chilled out for a few hours before getting ready for the final event of the day; the graduation dinner.

Jake's mum was staying at a hotel with her parents. Our house was overflowing with Greg, the girls and my parents all squeezing into our two-bedroom apartment. We had some lunch then Jake went to the hotel to see Mary and his grandparents; the rest of us had an afternoon nap before getting ready for the graduation dinner. Before long we'd all showered, changed into our formal evening wear and were all on our way to the Canberra Civic Centre in a taxi.

I was wearing a black strapless gown which went all the way to the floor; deliberately matching Jake's uniform perfectly. Although I'd put on a few kilos, thanks to our dining out habits, I was grateful for the added volume in the bust area. Quite frankly… my boobs looked amazing in that dress! I know Jake stared at them all night, and to be honest I even caught myself glancing down to admire my ample cleavage on more than one occasion.

Jake was dressed in a black formal dining uniform, with red lapels and a single red stripe down the side of each leg; again with gold accoutrements. He really did look delicious in every uniform he owned.

All eleven of us sat on the one table. The food was delicious and the conversation was good, even though it was a little awkward having Mary and Greg on the same table given they had separated the year before. Nonetheless, I give credit to both of them for putting their differences aside for the night; for my husband's sake.

After dessert the dance floor came to life to the sound of a full brass band and accompanying singers. We all had an absolute blast dancing, laughing and celebrating, with a few wines thrown in for good measure. The fun continued right up until midnight when the time finally arrived for each graduate to be presented with their new rank; Lieutenant. It was actually time for Mary and I to get serious as well, since it was tradition for the partner and mother to pin the rank on each shoulder of the graduating cadets, just as the clock struck midnight. Earlier, Jake had given Mary and I two gold diamond-shaped insignia each, 'pips' as they're known, and we held onto them like precious jewels.

All the graduates gathered on the dance floor with their partner and mother either side of them. The rest of the guests formed a circle around the edge of the dance floor, close by their loved ones, so they could watch as the newest officers in the Australian Army were promoted from cadet to Lieutenant.

As we waited patiently for the countdown to midnight, Mary and I took the opportunity to say a few words to Jake; words directly from our hearts.

Mary went first. “I’m so proud of you Jake, of everything you’ve achieved so far. I’m proud of you for finishing RMC, for becoming the man you are, and I’m so proud of the relationship you have with Sophie. I love both of you more than you could imagine, and seeing how much you love and care for each other makes me so happy.”

Both Jake and I were tearing up as Mary spoke sincerely. There was a hint of sadness in her voice as she talked about Jake and I; no doubt as a result of her fairly recent separation from Greg.

Mary looked at me. “Sophie I’m proud of you too, and thank you for being there for Jake over the last eighteen months. You are the best daughter-in-law a mother could ever ask for. Thank you.” She gave the two of us a hug.

“I love you Mum,” he said as he embraced her tightly.

“Thanks Mary. That means a lot to me,” I added; kissing her on the cheek.

The MC’s voice sounded. “Less than a minute till midnight!” The excitement in the room grew as he made the announcement.

I looked at Jake. “You already know how proud I am of you Baby. Thank you for everything. You are my life and I will *always* love you.” My words were brief but they encapsulated everything I felt in my heart. There was nothing else I needed to say.

“I love you too Soph. I know there’s no way I would have made it here without you.” He smiled warmly before wrapping his arms around me and kissing me tenderly.

Ten... Nine... Eight...

Everyone on the outside of the dance floor joined in the countdown to midnight.

Seven... Six... Five...

The smile on Jake's face spoke a thousand words. He looked towards the ceiling as if thanking God for allowing him to finally reach this moment.

Four... Three... Two...

With our hands resting on Jake's shoulders as we stood either side of him. Mary and I looked at each other; smiling excitedly.

One!

The crowd clapped and cheered as the band roared to life with a celebratory piece.

Mary and I unbuttoned Jake's epaulettes and pinned on the four gold insignia; all three of us unable to stop tears rolling down our cheeks. I sniffed and looked around at the other people on the dance floor. I can assure you we weren't the only ones struggling to control the emotion. It was a beautiful moment for everyone; a special event that only a few will ever get to experience.

With Mary and me on each arm and wearing his rank with pride, Jake made his way over to the rest of his family who hugged and congratulated him on finally becoming an officer… Lieutenant Jake Freeman.

His time at the Royal Military College was over, which meant time to move and begin the next chapter of our lives. As luck would have it, there was a junior officer's position at the military base in Sunbury which Jake applied for and was successful in securing. I was so excited to be moving home and took comfort in knowing we would be there for at least two years, at which time Jake would be due for his next posting. I knew a career in the military would mean lots of moving for us as well as time away from our family and friends, so I vowed to make the next two years at home count.

I couldn't help but feel like moving home was fate, considering Jake was almost sent to Townsville which was over two thousand kilometres away. It was like the universe was telling me something, or giving me an opportunity that I didn't expect.

Moving home... surrounded by family... maybe it's time we start our own.

CHAPTER TWENTY-FIVE

TWO YEARS AND TWO DAYS

Fuck! An agonising pain, unlike anything I've ever experienced before, suddenly develops around my stomach and lower back. I sit up, turn on the bedside lamp and look across at my husband lying beside me; he's still sound asleep.

I shake him with my free hand; the other clutching my midsection. "Jake… Jake wake up!"

He rolls over and opens his eyes to see me sitting up in bed, slightly hunched over and holding my enormous belly.

"I think it's time!" I wince as the wave of pain intensifies. It's almost like a belt is being pulled unbearably tight around my waist.

"Holy shit!" Jake exclaims as he throws the covers back and sits up beside me. He immediately puts his arm around my shoulders and a hand on my tummy in a futile attempt to sooth my contraction.

It was close to 2:00am on the 29th of November. The moment Jake and I had waited the past nine months for was upon us. Our family was about to grow by one.

Now I'm not about to give you a detailed play by play of my entire labour experience. Quite frankly, there have been billions of babies born throughout time, and I'm under no illusion the birth of my child was more special than any other. As far as I'm concerned the birth of *every* child is one of life's great miracles. The most amazing thing is even though women all over the world go into labour every minute of the day, no two births are ever exactly the same.

Some women begin to feel contractions or their water breaks to signal the beginning of labour, prompting them to head off to the safety and sterility of a hospital. Then after a few short hours, sometimes less, they emerge from the delivery suite with a healthy new baby; easy as that. No complications or unexpected situations to deal with; both mother and baby meet each other for the first time, healthy and happy. In stark contrast however, there are the unfortunate situations where childbirth is *far* from easy. Anguish can be described as pain, agony, suffering, misery, despair, heartache, grief and sorrow, and as horrible as it is to accept, unfortunately 'anguish' is a fitting word to describe the labour experience of some mothers and fathers. Just the *fear* of something going wrong during the birth of your child is hard enough to deal with. I can't even begin to imagine what it takes to get through a time when those fears actually become reality.

I've highlighted the best and, as compassionately as I could, the worst case scenarios of child birth, because for me… well I slotted somewhere in the middle.

When Jake and I arrived at the Sunbury maternity ward; anticipation, excitement and fear of the unknown coursed through my veins. With my arm over Jake's shoulder and his around my waist in an effort to help me walk, I took one last breath of fresh air before making my way through the sliding glass doors. As I entered the ward the sterile smell of antiseptic filled my nostrils, instantly inducing a sickening collection of flashbacks from my time at the Royal Children's Hospital and the life or death battle I fought against my *monster* four years ago.

"I hate the smell of hospitals," I groaned; immediately feeling nauseas.

"I know Baby, but this is where we need to be," replied Jake sympathetically.

He was right, it was *exactly* where I needed to be and as frightened as I may have been, I was still thankful to be in the safety of a hospital; in the care of its doctors and nurses.

After a few strange fingers, a couple of nauseating doses of laughing gas and a shot of pethidine to take the edge off; a failed epidural followed by a successful one, thirty-one hours of contractions not to mention a complete loss of dignity, I was ready… ready to actually *give* birth. I was utterly exhausted and hadn't even started pushing yet!

With Jake holding my left hand firmly and Mum holding my right, an obstetrician between my legs and a couple of midwives assisting, I prepared for my next contraction which would be the cue to give my first real push.

"Here it comes," I winced.

"Ok Sophie, now I want you to push. Bear down and push as hard as you can," prompted the doctor without making eye contact; her undivided attention focused between my legs on a sight I can only imagine.

As I attempted to push I was greeted with a rather unusual sensation. The second epidural, the one which actually worked, had effectively numbed all feeling from the waist down so I wasn't sure if I was actually pushing or not.

"That's it… that's the girl… keep pushing," encouraged the doctor; confirming I was in fact bearing down.

As my contraction subsided I was instructed to stop pushing and relax until the next one began, at which point I would push again. This process was repeated more times than I could count; for well over an hour anyway.

In between contractions Jake would talk to me, telling me how brave I was and how well I was doing. I wish I could have remembered exactly what he was saying but the combination of drugs and exhaustion rendered memories of the ordeal somewhat hazy. I do recall a few things he said though, and 'The heads out!' is one that springs to mind.

I opened my eyes to see Jake, who still had hold of my hand, down the end of the bed with the doctor getting his first look at our baby.

He glanced up at me, eyes like saucers, "Oh my god Sophie it's amazing! Have a look!"

I shook my head. "I don't want to see it." I was a little freaked out at the thought of seeing a head protruding from between my legs.

"That's ok you don't have to look," said one of the midwives; sensing I was getting a little anxious, maybe even scared.

I don't know what made me do it but instead of looking I reached down and gently touched my baby's head with my fingertips. Maybe I thought it would settle my nerves… it didn't.

"Whoa!" I shrieked, as I felt its wet sticky head. I was stunned at such an unexpected sensation. A person was actually coming out of me! It definitely wasn't the best idea because after touching my baby's head I was even more freaked out.

Up until that point, being in labour was dominated by feelings of pain, discomfort and exhaustion but not anymore. After touching my baby for the first time, *all* my focus was now directed towards the new person Jake and I had created; the new life I was about to deliver into the world. Our baby was well and truly on its way. Actually… it was already here!

"Ok we just need to get one of the shoulders out," the doctor said to Jake, who was still watching the whole process like some kind of medical intern. He was in awe of the entire experience. Again I was told to push when I felt the next contraction.

The next contraction arrived, and even though I couldn't feel it, I must have been pushing because the doctor and midwives kept reassuring me I was doing everything right. "That's it Sophie. That's it… almost there," urged the doctor.

"Keep going Baby, keep pushing! It's almost out. Push, push, push!" I squeezed Jake's hand as he encouraged me through it. Mum, who was still on the other side of the bed, held my hand and *her* breath in anticipation.

I was running out of air and my head felt like it was going to explode when the doctor said sternly, "Don't stop now! Keep pushing Sophie… this is it!"

"Good girl Soph you can do it. You're almost done." Jake's final words before becoming a father.

At nine minutes past midnight and after thirty-two hours of labour, I took a quick gasp of air and mustered every last bit of energy I could. I clenched my teeth, pushed with all I had, and with a final squeal… gave birth to a brand new person.

As soon as the doctor had a good grasp of my baby she put it directly on the bare skin of my chest. It all happened so fast and was such an overwhelming feeling that I immediately burst into tears. I was a mother, and in that split second realised every minute I spent in labour and every ounce of pain and exhaustion was such a small price to pay for the most amazing gift I could ever have hoped for.

I looked over at Jake; he was a mess. With tears streaming down his cheeks he leant over and kissed me on the lips. "I love you Soph. You're absolutely amazing. Thank you Baby… thank you so much," he sobbed. "I'm so proud of you."

He kissed me again then kissed our baby on the forehead. I smiled at him and wiped the tears off his cheeks with my thumb.

"So what is it?" beamed Mum from the other side of the bed as she too wiped away the tears.

Jake and I, the doctor and the midwives all started laughing. It had been close to a minute and we still hadn't checked the sex of our new born! I carefully rolled our baby to its side which was still completely covered in amniotic fluid, a little bit of blood and a white waxy substance which I later found out was called vernix.

"We've got a little boy Jake. We have a son," I whispered; the elation of holding my baby boy prompting a new overflowing of tears. "He's so beautiful. I love him so much," I wept.

"He *is* beautiful… just like his mother, and he's ours. I can't believe we have a little boy," Jake said; his voice course with emotion.

Mum kissed me on the forehead. "Congratulations Sophie, you did such an incredible job Love," she said before moving around to Jake's side of the bed to give him a kiss and a cuddle too.

As Mum turned her attention to her newest grandchild, Jake put his hand on her shoulder. "Thanks for being in here with us Lynn. I really appreciated everything you did for Sophie."

"It was my pleasure. I wouldn't have missed it for the world. Thank you for letting me share it with you both."

I was so glad for asking Mum to be in the birthing suite with us. As well as relying on her love and support when I needed it the most, being there for the birth also gave her and Jake the perfect opportunity to bond as mother and son in-law. Having her in the delivery room was one of the best decisions I've ever made.

One of the midwives passed Jake a pair of surgical scissors and he cut through the umbilical cord. I could see the joy and happiness in his eyes as he gazed at his family with complete and utter devotion for his wife and son. He was already a loving husband and I knew he was going to be a gentle and caring father as well.

I was given an injection of oxytocin to bring on a final contraction so I could deliver the placenta. As I listened to the doctor's directions, I didn't take my eyes of my baby the entire time. I was so mesmerized by our little boy that I can barely remember delivering the placenta at all.

As one of the midwives wiped my baby down with a towel, the doctor congratulated us. Jake thanked her for all the help and guidance she'd provided.

"It was my pleasure. You have a beautiful family," she said before leaving me in the care of the two midwives.

Jake smiled at me. "The most beautiful family in the world," he said softly as he stroked our son's cheek and kissed me gently on the forehead.

As the midwives cleaned me up, Mum left the room to go and tell Dad the news.

"So have you two already decided on a name?" asked one of the nurses.

Although we had a short-list of names, we thought we'd wait until we met our baby before making the final decision.

I turned to Jake. “What do you think of Nathan?” It was one of the names on our list.

He paused for a moment; looking down our son. “Nathan is perfect. Nathan John,” he smiled.

“Oh I love it Jake. Nathan John Freeman!” I said proudly.

“What a beautiful name,” commented one of the nurses; the other agreeing.

Dad arrived moments later to meet his new grandson. He gave me a kiss and cuddle, shook Jake’s hand and congratulated us both.

“Sophie, he’s beautiful. I’m so happy for you both,” he said quietly. Nathan still hadn’t cried yet so we were all talking softly.

I once heard someone say that you never think you could love anyone as much as your own children… until you have grandchildren. Well after seeing how my mother and father looked at baby Nathan, how completely besotted they were with him, I understood why. Nathan was a part of the next generation, a continuation of my parent’s lineage, and they adored him from the moment he arrived.

As I said earlier, I’ve struggled to remember many of the events which took place that night, a combination of medicine and fatigue have rendered specific details unclear. There was one moment however which I can still see vividly; clear as the light of day. It was the phone call Jake made to his father.

I watched as Jake dialled his father’s number into his mobile. As soon as Greg answered, Jake burst into tears; so overwhelmed with emotion he could barely speak. I couldn’t hear exactly what Greg was saying on the other end of the phone, but I gathered he must have been asking for details about the progress of my labour. Jake was beside himself and couldn’t answer. In fact, he only said three things for the entire call before hanging up. “Boy… Nathan John… Love you too.”

I’d never seen him so emotional, and have no doubt that Greg understood exactly how Jake was feeling. Mum, Dad and I all smiled at one another as Jake tried to compose himself after the call to his father; we could tell he was a little embarrassed.

"You ok Baby?" I asked, extending my hand out too him.

Jake nodded as he took a deep breath, before exhaling forcefully to calm himself. "I'm ok. I'm just so happy. I can't believe we have a baby. It's the greatest feeling in the world!" he smiled as he grasped my hand and squeezed it gently.

I couldn't have agreed more. My son had only just been born and I already loved the feeling of being a mother.

Earlier I referred to all babies as little miracles. Well the birth of our son was no exception and sometime after Nathan was born, Mum told me some information which revealed just how much of a miracle he was.

Years earlier when I began chemotherapy treatment for Hodgkin's disease, my parents questioned Professor Ericson as to whether I'd be able to have children later in life after taking such an aggressive drug as an adolescent. He told them it wasn't a priority at that stage, and there simply wasn't time to extract some of my eggs to be frozen and stored. He further explained that because my illness was stage IV and I was deteriorating by the day, his main concern was ensuring I had the best chance of survival. In short, the chance of me being able to conceive children later in life was dramatically affected from having chemo at such a young age. So giving birth to Nathan was actually a greater miracle than I first thought.

Our family had grown to three and as soon as I returned home from hospital with Nathan, our lives took on a totally new direction and meaning. It was as if we finally understood the whole point of living. It was such a primal and animalistic feeling to give birth, and both Jake and I agreed that we felt such an enormous sense of responsibility; like our *entire* purpose for being on this earth was to love, protect and teach our son. Having a child was an awakening. I finally knew my purpose and was in no doubt as to what really mattered in my life… my two boys.

From the first moment Nathan entered our world, Jake and I became devoted parents and vowed we'd do our best to raise him to be loving, compassionate and honest above all else.

My love for Jake had always grown stronger with every major event which had occurred in my life. He'd been my saviour, my protector and my angel on so many occasions I was starting to lose count. I have to say though, deifying the odds and giving me a child was by far the most amazing thing he'd done for me.

I've often thought about the emphasis Jake put on staying fit and healthy throughout his life. Always eating well and exercising, never experimenting with drugs and rarely drinking, even though he was in the army from the age of seventeen… and they *love* a drink! I'm absolutely convinced it was fate that I ended up with somebody who represented the absolute pinnacle of health, given mine was so tainted. I believe with all my heart that if Jake were any other man, I would still be without a child to this day. Yes, it *was* fate that he and I met. No question… Jake was my *hero*.

I loved being a mum and was thankful to be able to cut my work at the clothing store back to a few hours each weekend; I'd received a transfer when Jake and I moved from Canberra and was employed by the same company. Only working a couple of hours a week was great as it gave Jake a chance to spend one on one time with Nathan.

Undoubtedly one of the best things about motherhood was watching Nathan achieve all of life's little milestones. It was so exciting and rewarding all at once; I cherished every second I spent with my son.

Nathan was one-year-old when we moved to Townsville; well over two thousand kilometres from Sunbury. Jake had received a two year posting to the Queensland town. Since we'd been home for two years already we were eager to move and spend some time in a new place; just the three of us.

Although it was usually quite hot, Townsville was a relaxed place to live. It was nice living so close to the ocean, and to escape the heat of the tropics we would often spend the weekends at the beach.

Jake liked his new unit and was enjoying the changes that came with working in a different role. He was the 2IC of a workshop and although he rarely talked about work to me, preferring to switch off when he would get home, he did tell me that his favourite part about the job was running the daily physical training for the soldiers under his command. He loved the idea of getting paid to keep fit.

We had been 'up north' for close to three months, when I woke up one day with and unusual feeling of discomfort in both my boobs. They were tender to touch which instantly sparked 'alarm bells'; prompting me to get a pregnancy test from the local pharmacy.

That afternoon when Jake got home from work I met him at the door.

"Hey Baby," he said as he kissed me on the lips; his routine greeting after arriving home.

"How was your day Honey?"

"Not bad… the usual," he replied, bending to pick up Nathan who'd rushed in from outside as soon as he heard his father's voice; a daily ritual.

"How are you going little man?" he said; kissing Nathan on the forehead.

"Tell Dad you've been playing with Simba and the hose out on the veranda," I prompted. Simba was our two-year-old Labrador.

"Dog!" replied Nathan, pointing towards the back veranda. He had the cutest little voice and was slowly picking up a few one syllable words.

He and 'dog' were inseparable and would spend hours out the back playing with the hose. Simba, with her thick black fur, struggled with the heat and loved playing with the water as much as Nathan did. I have a stack of photos of the two of them playing together; best friends forever.

I couldn't hide the elated smile on my face.

"What's with the cheesy grin Soph?" Jake prompted.

I didn't answer and couldn't stop myself from giggling. I casually placed my hand on my tummy, knowing full well he'd immediately guess the news.

Jake laughed as he turned his attention back to Nathan; lifting him high into the air. "So Nathan, looks like you're going to be a big brother," he said happily.

He kissed Nathan again on the cheek before putting him down, then wrapped his arms around me and squeezed tightly.

"Oh my god Soph, I'm so happy," he whispered as he buried his face into the side of my neck. "I can't believe it's happened so fast."

Jake released his grasp on me then placed both hands on my cheeks and kissed me passionately.

"I know; we've only been trying for a few months!" I was also surprised by how fast I'd fallen pregnant.

"When did you find out?"

"When I woke up this morning my boobs were sore so I decided to do a pregnancy test. I could hardly wait for you to get home to tell you. I'm so excited."

"Me too Baby. I wonder what we'll have?"

"As long as it's healthy I don't mind."

"You're right, but I'd love to see you with a little girl Soph. Guess we'll just have to wait and see."

As much as I enjoyed living in Townsville, from the moment I called home to tell my family and friends the good news, I began to feel homesick. A feeling which continued to grow stronger as my belly grew larger.

By the time our second child was due to be born, Jake would still have over a year left of his Townsville posting. The more I thought about it, the more I didn't want to live so far away from my family with a new born baby and a two-year-old. It wasn't as though I wouldn't be able to cope, but being pregnant and not being able to share the entire experience with loved ones made me realise that living away meant *we* were also missing out on important events and milestones in their lives. For example, Jake missed my brother's wedding, though I flew home with Nathan to be there, and we also missed Alice's engagement to her boyfriend Travis as well as a host of birthday parties and other family events.

The isolation was starting to get to me and I didn't know if there was a solution.

My pregnancy with Nathan was smooth sailing from start to finish, but this time around I was dealt a number of bouts of morning sickness. I understood it was perfectly normal but every time I'd be down on my knees with my head over the toilet, I couldn't help but think about what the professor had said to my parents so many years before. That having chemo so young significantly reduced the chance of me being able to conceive. This thought played over and over in my mind, and every time I would dry reach or vomit I was scared something was going to go wrong. I'd been blessed with the birth of Nathan and I always felt like I was pushing my luck by trying to have a second child. My worst fears came to fruition eight weeks into the pregnancy, when I woke one morning to find a large amount of blood between my legs.

Jake had already gone to work. When I pulled the sheet back I immediately noticed the blood stains on my underwear, legs and the mattress. The sight of the blood caused me to panic and I immediately started crying. I carefully climbed out of bed, made my way to the phone in the kitchen and called Jake's office.

"Good morning… this is Lieutenant Freeman."

"Jake something's wrong!"

"What do you mean? What's happened?" he said anxiously.

"I'm bleeding. There's a lot of blood and I know something's wrong!" Just saying the words made me cry even more.

"Shit! Ok Baby, just try and stay calm." Jake instantly wiped the panic from his own voice in an attempt to keep me as calm as possible. "Are you still bleeding or is the blood dry? I mean does it look like it's stopped?"

"Hang on a minute."

I put the phone on the bench and looked down. The blood on my legs was dry, and when I checked my underwear I noticed there was a little bit of wet blood but most of it was dry as well. I was still scared but was glad there wasn't blood pouring from me.

"It's mostly dry. It's definitely slowed down… maybe stopped but I'm not sure."

"Do you think you need an ambulance or can you wait till I get home? I'm leaving right now so I should be less than ten minutes."

"I'll wait for you."

"Ok I'll be there as fast as I can to take you to hospital. Everything will be alright Honey. Try to stay calm and as relaxed as possible. I'll be there soon, but if it looks like the bleeding starts again call an ambulance straight away."

"Ok I will."

"I'll be there in a minute."

"I'm scared Jake. Hurry."

He hung up the phone without replying.

I went into the bathroom to clean myself up and get dressed to go to hospital. The more I tried to relax the more frightened I became. Ever since my health scare in Canberra, when a lump appeared on my neck which I had biopsied and thankfully turned out to be a benign cyst, I'd come to accept the harsh reality that my *monster* would always be with me; lying dormant and waiting to exploit any decline in my health. I felt like it was always searching for any moment of vulnerability, just the right time to begin its next assault, and this felt like one of those times. My thoughts even went as far as to imagine the possibility that since I defeated it back when I was a teenager, maybe it'd shifted its menace to my unborn baby. The thought sent a cold shiver straight through me.

Still to this day I live in fear of the possibility that I've somehow passed my affliction to my offspring. Jake continues to remind me that our love for each other beat cancer, so how could a child *born* of that same powerful love ever be in danger of the same illness I battled. I pray he's right.

By the time I'd got dressed Jake was home. He burst in the front door and held me in his arms.

"Everything's going to be ok Baby… trust me. Is Nathan up yet?"

"No he's still asleep."

"Go and get in the car and I'll wake him up and change him," he directed calmly before turning towards our son's room. "Nathan… time to get up little man!" he beamed in a cheerful voice so as not to alert our son of our distressed state.

"Ok Sophie this might feel a little cold," warned the obstetrician as she squirted gel onto my belly. "Now just relax and I'm going to check that your baby's ok."

Jake stood beside the bed holding one of my hands with both of his. I looked into his worried eyes and he forced a smile. "I love you," he mouthed silently.

Tears pricked my eyes as I turned my head towards Nathan, who was sitting quietly in a chair; his tiny little legs dangling off the edge of the seat gently kicking back and forth. He looked so adorable; calmly watching us in the dim lighting of the ultrasound room. He was always so peaceful and happy, and I prayed he had no idea of how scared his father and I were.

The doctor gently slid the ultrasound receiver across my belly, stopping every so often to click a few buttons on the keyboard. After a few moments she turned to me. "Ok take a look at the monitor."

Jake and I looked up at the blurry indistinguishable image on the screen.

"Can you see that little flicker just there? That's your baby's heart beating away nicely."

"My baby's ok?"

"Yes your baby looks absolutely fine."

Jake squeezed my hand then leant over and kissed me on the forehead. We both knew exactly what each other was feeling; indescribable relief that our baby was ok.

"The ultrasound hasn't shown any abnormalities to explain the bleeding."

"So what could have caused it?" queried Jake.

"To be honest it's not easy to say. There is the possibility that cervical changes could have resulted in some bleeding. Sometimes intercourse can trigger a bleed like you experienced. Or it's possible you may have actually been pregnant with twins and one of the embryos failed to develop causing you to miscarry."

"Well there is a history of that in my family. Both my mother and grandmother were pregnant with twins. My Mum lost one and my grandmother lost both," I explained.

"Well then it's possible a similar thing has happened to you. To be honest we will never know what caused the bleeding. The important thing is your baby is healthy. I would however recommend you take extra care for the rest of the first trimester. Make sure you get plenty of rest and it's important not to exercise too vigorously. If you do experience any more bleeding, then come back to the hospital immediately."

"We will. Thank you so much," replied Jake. "I'll look after her," he said smiling down at me as he wiped the gel off my tummy with a towel the doctor gave him.

"Thank you," I added sleepily. I was relieved but rather exhausted from the fear and anxiety which had been with me the entire morning.

Jake could sense my exhaustion. "I'll take you home to rest now Baby."

"You've been such a good little boy for Mummy and Daddy!" the doctor said to Nathan who was still patiently waiting on the chair. He flashed her a toothy grin. "He seems like such a placid child," she added.

"He's a dream; always happy and content," I smiled. "You're always a good boy for Mummy aren't you?" I said turning to look at him dotingly.

As soon as we arrived home, Jake tucked me into bed. "I'm taking the rest of the day off. You get some sleep and when you wake up I'll make you something to eat."

"Thanks."

"It's my pleasure Baby."

Jake fluffed my pillow and tucked me in under the sheet.

"I'm sorry Jake."

"Hey, what have you got to be sorry for?"

"I just feel like it's my fault." More specifically I felt like it was all my *monster's* fault.

He gently stroked my face. "Remember I said you never have to apologise to me?"

I nodded.

"Well I was serious. This hasn't been your fault Soph; not at all. These things just happen so don't feel like you need to apologise. I'm just relieved you and the baby are ok."

I smiled at him.

"Now get some sleep. Hopefully you'll feel better after a snooze and some food."

He kissed me on the lips and left the room.

I lay awake for a short while thinking about the events of the morning; about Jake and Nathan by my side in the hospital. I pictured both their faces looking at me, the love and concern in Jake's eyes mirrored by a similar expression in Nathan's. It was then that I realised how much my son was like his father. It wasn't luck that Nathan was such a gentle and calm child; he was exactly like his dad. It was a thought that warmed my heart as I drifted off to sleep.

As directed by the doctor I took things pretty easy for the rest of the pregnancy. Apart from fainting twice in the backyard while hanging out the washing, which I attributed to the relentless heat and humidity of the tropics, I reached the final trimester.

During the year we had a visit from my parents for a couple of weeks. It was perfect timing because Jake deployed to the field during their stay, which meant Nathan and I didn't have to spend two weeks alone. I was so grateful to have my parents with me while Jake was away. A month or so later Greg and Samantha came up for a four-day visit. We also had Alice and her fiancé stay with us for a few days later in the year.

I loved having family come and stay with us, but the reality of spending another year away from them didn't sit well with me, so one night I sat down and discussed the options we had with my husband.

"I don't know if I can spend another year up here Jake. Is there any possibility of getting a posting home at the end of the year?"

"I can ask my commanding officer, but I'm really not that hopeful. I've already spent two years down in Sunbury and requesting another posting back to our home town would be a big ask, considering I haven't finished my scheduled two years here in Townsville. I'll do my best though."

I could hear in his voice that he wasn't confident of getting a posting home, but I appreciated he was going to try anyhow?

Jake wrote a number of requests and had a few meetings with various superiors to discuss a transfer back home. A few weeks passed and he finally received word that a decision had been reached; his request had been denied. He even suggested to his commanding officer that he'd be more than happy to serve additional time as a Lieutenant before being promoted to Captain, as a sort of penalty for requesting the posting, but it didn't have any effect on the army's decision either. The answer was still no.

I remember Jake telling me the bad news. He was gutted and I knew it tore him apart to have to tell me we weren't going home. It was hard to hear and I dreaded the thought of another year in the heat of the tropics; away from our families. I had an enormous belly and the temperature was blistering every day. I was literally uncomfortable all the time and couldn't help but feel saddened, even depressed at the thought of being stuck here for the rest of my pregnancy and the following year.

It was probably the first time in our relationship where Jake felt like he wasn't able to look after me like he wanted to. He knew I was struggling and wanted nothing more than to make me happy; having to say no to me hurt him.

A few days passed. Jake came home from work and as I gave him his usual welcome home kiss, he whispered in my ear. "I have an idea."

"About what?"

I followed Jake into the kitchen and watched as he poured himself a glass of cold water from the fridge. He had ridden his bike home in the heat and was sweating profusely. He skulled it, put his glass in the sink and leant against the kitchen bench.

"Well come on… what's the idea?" I prompted impatiently.

He took a deep breath. "So you really want to go home Baby?"

"Yes! I'm so hot and uncomfortable up here, and I miss everyone at home. I thought it would be nice to live away, just the three of us, but watching Nathan playing outside on his own with Simba every day makes me feel like he's missing out on getting to know his family. I know for a fact they all miss him, and us too!"

"I understand Baby. I don't want you to feel bad for wanting to go home. The military life doesn't suit every family. We weren't going to know if it was for us until we tried it," he said understandingly; moving towards me and putting his hands on my shoulders.

"Do *you* want to go home though?" I asked sincerely. I knew how much Jake was enjoying his job and I needed to know if he wanted to move home or if he was just saying it because I did. I needed the truth.

"To be honest Baby, I don't care where I am as long as I'm with you and Nathan. I want you both to be happy, and if you're not… then neither am I."

It was clear he didn't mind living in Townsville and was only moving because he thought it'd make me happy.

"We don't have to go Jake. I could stay here another year if we had too." I was trying to be reassuring so he didn't feel as though he was letting me down.

"Well I've been doing some thinking…." He paused momentarily. "…and I've decided to discharge from the Army."

"What!" I shrieked loudly. "No Jake! No way! You've worked so hard to get that job… to become and officer."

"Yeah but that's ok."

"No it's not! All that time and effort at RMC, I couldn't possibly let you throw it away just because I'm uncomfortable in the heat and miss my family. No way, you're not getting out!" I was shocked that he'd even suggested it and was adamant I didn't want him to leave the service because of me.

"What have I always said to you? Ever since we started going out when we were kids, what have I always promised?"

"That you'd look after me."

"And?" he prompted.

"That you'd keep me safe."

"What else? What was the most important promise of all?"

"I don't remember," I said softly; lying. I knew exactly where his line of questioning was going.

"Yes you do. What else did I promise you?"

Reluctantly I answered. "That you'd make me happy."

"That's right. So I only want you to answer one question for me Soph… are you happy here?"

I hesitated. With Jake staring intently into my eyes there was no chance I could lie; he'd see straight through me.

"No," I whispered; instantly feeling as though I'd forced him to make such a monumental decision.

"Then to keep the promises I made, I'll do whatever it takes to get you home. Right now the only way I can see that happening is discharging from the army."

If only I'd not said anything. I felt so horrible. Surely I could've put up with another year or so in Townsville. I felt like Jake was throwing his career away because of me. I dropped my head down and looked at the floor. I felt so selfish.

He put his hand under my chin and tilted my head up. "Hey, don't feel bad."

I closed my eyes so I didn't have to look at him. I was ashamed of myself for being so self-centred.

"Open your eyes."

I shook my head.

"Sophie Lee Freeman… open your eyes," he repeated sternly.

I kept them closed.

"Look at me," he whispered gently.

I reluctantly opened my eyes to see him staring directly at me.

"Baby, I'll do *anything* for you. Your happiness is all I've ever cared about," he smiled. "The army is just a job. I can get another one."

"But Jake, all that work, all that time and effort."

"It means nothing to me. Don't you understand… looking after you *is* my job and that's exactly what I'm going to do. When I get to work tomorrow I'm handing in my discharge papers. I'm taking my family home."

My eyes started to sting. All at once I was overjoyed and totally devastated. The thought of going home seemed so amazing, but the price Jake was willing to pay to make it happen was more than I could bear.

"Don't be upset Baby. I have a few ideas on what I want to do once I'm out of the army, and I'm actually really excited about it. Just be happy that we're going home."

He cuddled me and I buried my head under his chin.

"You trust me don't you?"

"Of course I do," I replied; wiping the tears from my cheeks with the back of my hand. "Always."

"Then trust me when I say that everything will work out. I'll make sure of it… I promise."

Jake and his promises. How could I ever doubt him? He'd never let me down.

"Ok. If you think it's the right choice?" I surrendered.

"It is. It's the *only* choice."

For the last year Jake had been working his way through a personal training course by correspondence. He told me of his plans to start his own health and fitness business if he ever left the army. So although I was still struggling to comprehend how he could resign from a job he'd worked so hard to get, I did feel some relief that he had a plan. I just didn't think he would be putting it into practice so soon.

The fear of losing a guaranteed weekly income and starting a business from scratch still scared the hell out of me, but as per usual, Jake's confidence in his ability to achieve anything he put his mind to, masked any fears or concerns he may have had. I distinctly remember him telling me about a quote he'd either read or seen on TV; the exact wording eludes me but I can recall the conversation.

"Soph, all we have to remember is not to chase the money. I'm just going to do what I love and the money will follow." Jake went on to explain the idea in the sense that people who are passionate about their job are usually very good at it, simply because it doesn't feel like work for them, and that when somebody is good at their job the success will follow.

It made sense to me, and knowing how passionate Jake was about health and fitness, I had no doubt he would be able to build a strong business back in Sunbury, even if it did take some time.

As it turns out Jake's discharge papers never made it past his commanding officers desk. He arrived home the next day with the best news.

"Their posting me home at the end of the year!"

At first I couldn't comprehend what he was saying. "What are you talking about Jake?" I was in total disbelief.

"I handed my discharge papers in to the CO and told him about my plans to start a personal training business back in Sunbury. I made it clear I wasn't handing my discharge in as an attempt to force a posting home, and that I understood the reasons why a posting to Sunbury wasn't possible. The boss told me he'd make another call to the career management unit before forwarding my discharge through; to confirm there was absolutely no chance of a posting. Just before the end of the day he gave me a call and asked me to come up to his office. He told me if I was willing to withdraw my discharge papers and commit to another twelve months' service, then I would be posted to a position back in Sunbury at the end of the year. How awesome is that!"

"Are you serious Jake? I can't believe it. I honestly can't believe it." I was so happy and utterly relieved.

"The best part is we'll be able to leave a couple of weeks before you're due, so you can have the baby back home."

"I don't know what to say," I shook my head from side to side in disbelief. "Thank you Jake. Thank you so much." I threw my arms around his neck; squeezing him tightly.

"You don't need to thank me; I didn't do anything."

"Yes you did, you did *everything*! You were prepared to give up everything you'd worked for, for me. Of course I need to thank you."

As much faith as I had in Jake I have to admit I was a little nervous about moving home without a guaranteed income. Jake's idea to start a new business was a good plan, but the fact we would have two children to feed whilst trying to get the business off the ground was a concern. Finding out we were moving home at the end of the year with Jake still employed by the military, alleviated all traces of apprehension. I felt as if a black cloud above my head had opened up and rays of sunshine beamed through, bathing me in light; pure relief. It was the best news ever.

I remember the day we were due to leave Townsville; a five-day journey lay in front of us. I was heavily pregnant and under no illusion I could go into labour any day. To some extent the excitement of going home was overshadowed by trepidation. Delivering my second child in the back seat of a car was definitely not part of my birthing plan!

Jake had mapped out the journey so the furthest we'd be from a hospital at any one time would be four and a half to five hours, and considering my last labour was over thirty-two hours long, we figured a road side birth would be fairly unlikely.

As we drove from Townsville back to Sunbury, every bump we hit on the road caused the pressure in my pelvis area to build, along with my anxiety. Thankfully though we made it home; only just. We arrived on a Wednesday evening, and by 7:00am Friday morning… I was in labour.

Taking into account the duration of my last labour I decided to stay at home as long as I could. The house we had moved into was less than five minutes away from the hospital, so I figured I'd wait as long as possible before heading off to the birthing suite.

Remember earlier in this chapter when I told you every birth was different, well I wish I knew that back then. I'd been getting contractions for close to twelve hours. It was just before 7:00pm when all of a sudden my contractions rolled into one and I had a really strong urge to push. It was time to panic!

Jake's Mum still hadn't arrived at our place so he called her mobile to see how far away she was. Mary was organised to watch Nathan while Jake and I went to the hospital.

"Less than five minutes," he said as he hung up the phone.

In hindsight we should've just taken Nathan with us and met Mary at the hospital, but since she was almost at our place we decided to wait.

"Get in the car Soph and I'll back it out onto the street so as soon as Mum gets here we can go."

"Baby. Baby Mum. Baby!" Nathan repeated in his excited little voice as Jake helped me into the car.

"You jump in the back Nath so I can reverse out," directed Jake as he put our son in the back seat.

We reversed out onto the street. I stayed in the car, holding my belly and praying my baby would stay put just a little while longer, while Jake climbed out and waited with our two-year-old on the footpath; Nathan had his second birthday two days earlier.

As soon as Mary arrived Jake kissed Nathan on the head. "We're going to get the baby now," he smiled and climbed into the driver's seat.

"Good luck you two! Call me if you need anything!" Mary yelled out.

"Thanks Mum. Bye Nathan," Jake replied.

I couldn't respond; using every ounce of concentration not to bear down and push this baby out in the front seat!

I looked at Nathan standing on the footpath beside the car and forced a smile, hoping it would reassure him that 'Mummy' was ok.

Jake planted the foot and sped to the hospital. It was the most uncomfortable five-minute car trip of my life.

I don't know how I managed to get to the front door of the hospital considering the discomfort I was in, but with Jake's help I managed to walk there on my own two feet. He had phoned ahead and a nurse met us at the door; immediately ushering us into the birthing suite.

By this stage it was about 7:15pm. I took my skirt and underwear off and as I climbed up onto the bed my water burst. Liquid gushed from me, down my legs and over the floor.

"Perfect timing!" said Jake; grinning at our impeccably timed arrival.

I frowned at him. It was a little too close for my liking.

This time around I didn't have an obstetrician present, instead assisted by two midwives and my mother, who met us at the hospital.

As the nurse gave me an examination she looked up and delivered a frightening revelation. "Ok Sophie you're ready to give birth now. Unfortunately, we're too far along for any pain medicine. Do you understand?"

Considering I had *every* type of pain relief available for the birth of our son, the thought of pushing a baby out of my vagina with absolutely *no* medicinal relief was unimaginable. But the fact was, I was already in so much pain and discomfort that I just wanted to push this baby out as soon as possible; so it would all be over.

By 7:57pm my wish was granted. I gave birth to a beautiful baby girl; we didn't forget to check the sex this time.

The midwife put her directly on my chest, and just as Nathan had done when he was born, our daughter lay there silently; blinking slowly trying desperately to focus in the bright lights of the delivery room.

I have to say, as daunting as giving birth without pain meds was, and as much as it hurt like fucking hell; a naked flame being held against my vagina springs to mind, I actually think I was able to concentrate more and push a lot harder. It must have been the case because our daughter came out so fast that she emerged with what could only be described as friction burns on her soft little face.

As I expected, Jake was emotional and as he leant over and kissed me on the lips I could feel the cool wet tears drip from his cheeks onto mine.

"We've got a little girl," he whispered. "You're amazing Soph. I love you so much."

"I love you too. Look at her Jake… she's so beautiful," I cried.

The midwife passed Jake the surgical scissors and he cut the umbilical cord. "Congratulations to you both," she said.

Mum leant over and gave me a kiss on the forehead. "You got your little girl Soph," she smiled; recalling a conversation I had with her about how great it would be to have a girl this time around. "A pigeon pair," she added happily.

Jake carefully put his hand on the back of his daughter's head. "Still keen on the name Georgia? I really like it."

"Yes, Georgia. I love it, and I think it suits her." It was my favourite girl's name.

"Georgia Lynn?" he asked; looking up at Mum to see her reaction after hearing the suggestion.

"Really! You're going to name her after me?" she replied; delighted.

"Yes, if that's ok with you Mum?"

She was already emotional, eyes red and glassy as tears of joy lingered, but after finding out we were going to name our daughter after her she really let go. "Of course it's ok. I'd be honoured to have her named after me," she wept.

It was so nice to see how much it meant to her and I knew we'd made the right choice.

"It's settled then. Georgia Lynn Freeman! Perfect!" Jake smiled as he looked down at his baby girl with complete adoration.

I delivered the placenta then the midwives cleaned Georgia and I up before leaving the four of us alone for a while. Mum stayed for about twenty minutes before heading back to the farm. Dad was on shift work so Mum was going to bring him in the following day to meet his new granddaughter.

"Good night Soph. Try and get some rest won't you?"

"I will Mum. I'm exhausted."

"She's beautiful Jake. You should be very proud of your family."

"Oh I am. I honestly couldn't be any prouder if I tried. There's no doubt I'm the luckiest man on earth," he beamed; the honesty in his undeniable.

Mum smiled at his response.

She kissed Jake and I then placed her hand on Georgia's head. "Goodnight Georgia Lynn. Sleep tight," she said before leaving us alone with our baby.

As I cuddled Georgia against my chest, Jake sat beside the bed playing with her tiny fingers. I looked at his face as he marvelled at one of the youngest people on earth; his little girl. I immediately recognised the way he looked at his daughter, because I'd seen the same expression many times over the last seven years. His eyes were full of unconditional love and protection. I could feel the energy, the primordial instinct which radiated from him. There was absolutely no doubt he would give his life to protect his family. I already knew Jake was my *hero,* and as I gazed at my baby girl, I wondered if Georgia knew that the man looking down at her was her *hero* too.

I wish I could say everybody was as happy with the arrival of Georgia as Jake and I were. The following day Jake brought Nathan in to meet his sister, and although he had a fairly limited vocabulary as a two-year-old, we got a pretty clear understanding that Nathan was a little concerned that his days as the only child had come to an end.

"This is Georgia… your baby sister," Jake said as he held her; carefully lowering her down to Nathan's level.

"Baby!" Nathan replied excitedly.

"That's right."

"You're her big brother. Are you going to look after her?" I asked. I was still lying in bed.

"Yes."

"Isn't she little? Touch her soft hands," Jake urged, holding up her tiny arm so Nathan could touch her.

"Little finger," he said as he gently touched the tips of her finger nails.

We didn't say anything for a moment, giving Nathan a chance to take it all in, when all of a sudden he come out with a classic 'one liner'.

He looked up at me and with a seriously concerned expression he said, "Baby live here!"

Jake and I chuckled quietly to ourselves.

"Georgia wants to come and live with us, is that ok?" Jake asked.

"Orgia wants live here," he replied persuasively; his pronunciation making it even more humorous.

"She wants to come home and live with her big brother," I added trying to give him a chance to make the decision that it was ok for her to come and live with us. "She can stay in her own room," I added; sweetening the deal for him.

"Not in Nathan's room?" he clarified, still looking concerned. He often referred to himself in the third person.

"No she'll stay in her own room Buddy. Will that be ok?" prompted Jake.

Nathan looked down at his sister, no doubt contemplating the changes that would come as a result of the new arrival in our home.

"Come home nother day?" he replied as persuasively as he could.

Jake and I both smiled. He had resigned to the fact that his little sister was coming home but wanted a couple more days as number one; it was so cute.

"Yeah in a couple of days. Mummy and Georgia will come home soon," I explained.

Nathan nodded and smiled. "You bring baby?"

"That's right," I replied. "I'll bring Georgia home with me."

"Not in Nathan's room," he clarified a final time. We couldn't help but laugh.

"She wants to stay in her own room," I smiled.

I stayed in hospital for another night. Jake later told me when he and Nathan arrived home after visiting us, all he could talk about for the rest of the day was 'Baby Orgia'. By the time I brought her home Nathan couldn't wait for his baby sister to arrive. I guess even he couldn't resist falling in love with her.

Jake and I always planned to have two children, preferably one of each but it didn't matter as long as they were healthy. We'd hoped to have them about two years apart, and as it turned out Georgia was born exactly two years and two days after Nathan; close enough I guess.

Our family of four was complete, and every day I thank God I was able to give birth to my little miracles. I cherish every day I have with them and I'm absolutely astonished at how true the old saying actually is… 'They grow up so fast.'

They sure do.

CHAPTER TWENTY-SIX

CRUSH

Earlier in my story you may have been a little thrown by the events in Chapter Seven, but my reasons for including 'The Beginning of Pleasure' are about to make perfect sense.

As I've said before, there's no hidden agenda or persuasive objective to my story. It's just about me and some of the experiences I've lived through so far. That said, I wouldn't be surprised if there are people out there who have actually found themselves in a similar situation to the one I'm about to describe. If my story gives even one person the strength to not only accept but embrace who they are, and helps them find the courage to live and love from the heart, then I'd be honoured to have had such a positive influence on their life.

I have no idea how I came to be the way I am, and it doesn't matter how much I think about it, I still can't find a clear cut answer to explain my feelings. Maybe I was just born this way, or perhaps it was my experience with Belinda back in grade six. If I'm really honest though, I can't ignore how I felt watching '*Baby*' and '*Penny*' dancing together when I first saw '*Dirty Dancing*', and I must have only been about seven or eight back then. Perhaps it was the *monster* inside me, trying once more to ruin my life in any way possible.

The reality is the cause for my feelings may never be known. The debate still continues as to whether people feel the way I do as a result of physiological or psychological factors, or in fact a complex combination of both.

I can only speak for myself, but considering how long I'd successfully suppressed the feelings, the time at which they resurfaced shifts the blame directly towards my *monster.* Why else would I start to feel the way I did at a time when my life was as perfect as I could ever have imagined. My husband and I were madly in love, we had two amazing children who were healthy and beautiful, and we were back home in Sunbury; surrounded by family and friends. Life was good, so it makes sense that if my *monster* really wanted to hurt me and devastate everything I loved, it would pick a time to expose my true sexuality which would cause the most damage.

As hard as I tried, there was no way I could hide it any longer. I was bi-sexual, and I can't say I wasn't frightened of what that meant for my husband, my children and me.

For some months beforehand I thought about the best way to break the news to Jake; playing out each conversation in my head. The reality was though, it didn't really matter how I approached the subject because in the end I would just have to come out and tell him I was sexually attracted to women. How he chose to react was entirely out of my control.

Jake had always been open and honest with me; I knew *everything* about him. The thing which scared me about coming out to him, was he believed that he already knew everything about me too.

Will he still trust me when he finds out I've kept such a big secret from him for so long? Naturally I thought about the worst case scenario, which would be Jake leaving me for betraying his trust; a thought which made me sick to my stomach. If that were to happen I'd almost certainly have to come out to the rest of my family and friends, and I didn't want to do that.

There's no way I could come out to my parents! The only person I felt like I needed to tell was Jake because *my* sexuality really had nothing to do with anyone else.

I also imagined what would happen if Jake was ok with it. *What would that mean for us considering we're in a strictly monogamous relationship?*

In all the years I'd been with Jake I hadn't seen him so much as look at another woman. He was a devoted husband whose faithfulness could never be questioned.

Will coming out to him mean I can act on my feelings? I couldn't possibly ask him to let me do something like that... could I? The thoughts which spun around in my head, be they positive or negative, always ended up with me delaying the discussion with him. Whether it was just too hard or too scary, I continued to live in a lie.

The single most important factor which brought me comfort was that I knew the kind of man Jake was. As much as I thought about how bad revealing my true sexuality could turn out, I couldn't ignore the history we shared. Jake was always thoughtful, compassionate and devoted towards me, and more recently to our children, and there was simply no doubt he loved me unconditionally. At the time I was scared and nervous, but in hindsight I should've had more faith in my husband; that he would accept me and continue to love me just as he always had.

Ironically, after all the thought and deliberation I'd put into bringing the issue up with Jake, it turned out *he* was the one who began the conversation with me. I guess he knew me better than I knew myself.

I was looking forward to a barbecue at Brett and Jenny's place. Brett was Jake's boss and he'd invited us along with a few other colleagues over for dinner, to welcome a new officer to their team.

By the time we arrived, there were already three other guests inside who also worked with Jake; a female and two males. I felt a little strange because although Jake and I were the youngest adults there, we were also the only ones with children so I couldn't help but feel like we were the 'oldies' at the party. It didn't bother me though as I'd felt older than I was since the age of sixteen. The amount of living I'd packed into the past seven years made me feel like I had the life experience of someone in their thirties; even older.

After the introductions, we all sat around the dinner table talking about a range of different topics while we waited for the final guests to arrive. Everyone was friendly and polite which made me feel quite comfortable. I did however find myself mainly talking with Jen, who was the only other person there that wasn't in the military. As it turned out she was trying to fall pregnant, so understandably had heaps of questions about Nathan and six month old Georgia.

After maybe half an hour the doorbell rang; Brett left the room to answer it. He returned to the dining area with two other guests; a couple.

Holy shit! My eyes almost popped out of their sockets. I had to make a conscious effort to hold my mouth closed to prevent my jaw from dropping to the floor and my tongue from rolling out of my head and across the tiles like a cartoon character.

"Everyone… this is Simon and his girlfriend Kristen," introduced Brett.

Kristen. I'll never forget the first time I saw her; she took my breath away. She was absolutely stunning, with long curly blonde hair that draped over her shoulders and extended all the way down to the middle of her back. Her olive skin glowed and her make-up was flawless, especially her red lipstick which was painted on two of the fullest and most delicious lips I'd ever seen. Her seductive brown eyes were almost hypnotic and her figure was full and voluptuous. Kristen oozed sex appeal, and she had so many gorgeous features that I didn't know where to look. I must confess though, her size 'D' breasts which caused the buttons of her white shirt to strain grabbed their fair share of my attention.

The longer I stared at her, the hotter I became so I deliberately looked away in a desperate attempt to prevent myself from blushing. I turned my focus towards Jake, who was looking straight at me. His expression was hard to read which was very unusual. Normally I could tell exactly what he was thinking with a simple glance, but for some reason I was at a loss. His impassive expression instantly made me feel guilty, and I couldn't help but feel like I'd just been busted in the middle of a full throttle perve. *Whoops!*

I know this sounds completely superficial, heartless and shallow because I'd only just met Simon and he could've been the nicest guy on the planet, but as I looked at him standing beside Kristen the most awful thought crossed my mind. *How the hell did he get her?* I was ashamed of myself for even thinking it. He wasn't unattractive, had a nice smile and seemed friendly and polite, but I think because I just couldn't get over how incredible Kristen was, it kind of made Simon pale in comparison. I know that's a horrible thing to say but she really was *that* impressive!

Everyone took turns introducing themselves to Simon and Kristen, although I wasn't eager for a face to face; given how nervous I felt just *looking* at the blond bombshell!

"Simon." Jake stood up to welcome him with a handshake. "I'd like you to meet my wife, Sophie."

I also stood up from my seat.

"Hi Jake. Pleased to meet you Sophie," replied Simon; nodding in my direction.

"Hi."

"This is Kristen." He stepped to the side allowing her to move closer to us.

"Hello," she smiled.

"Hi Kristen." Jake put his hand in the small of my back and gently ushered me forward. "This is Sophie."

Moments earlier I'd tried desperately to stop myself blushing but now with Kristen standing directly in front of me, so close I could smell her soft perfume, I could feel the redness flooding back into my cheeks. I prayed the others wouldn't notice.

"Hi Sophie. I love your hair," Kristen smiled; her brown eyes looking directly into mine.

I'd worn my hair out and coincidently it was a very similar style to hers, only I was a brunette.

Talk Sophie!

It took me about one second too long before replying; not long enough for anyone to notice my tongue-tied state.

"I like yours too," I replied; smiling shyly… nervously.

She extended her hand out to me and for a split second I stood there staring at it; the soft skin of her fingers and bright red nails mesmerising me. I blinked, snapping myself out of my brief trance before grasping her hand lightly. Our eyes locked, and instead of shaking my hand she just squeezed it firmly, slightly longer than expected before gradually letting it go.

What was that! I wasn't mistaken, we'd definitely just had a 'moment'.

Returning to my seat and quickly picking up my glass of white, I steadied my nerves with a larger-than-usual sip. *Geez Sophie, get a hold of yourself.*

It seemed like fate. I mean what were the chances of me spending the past few months contemplating how I was going to tell Jake about my feelings towards women, then as if it was meant to be, finding myself face to face with someone who instantly roused every sexual desire I'd ever felt about females. To top it off… she just flirted with me!

Realistically, I probably had a fairly good chance of suppressing my bi-sexuality indefinitely by staying one hundred percent focused on the love and devotion I had for Jake; or so I thought. From the moment I met Kristen, that pipedream went up in smoke! As I sat across the table from her, the thoughts which raced through my mind left me with the abundantly clear realisation that I wouldn't be able to hide from the truth any more. It wasn't like I was about to race off in pursuit of the affection of Kristen, or *any* woman for that matter. What I realised though, was the thought of not telling Jake about my sexuality and subsequently never having the chance to experience what it feels like to be with a woman would be an extremely hard pill to swallow.

Not long after Simon and Kristen arrived, Brett finished cooking the barbeque and we all sat down to eat. I had already given Georgia a bottle and she was now fast asleep in her pram. Nathan was happy enough to sit outside on the back step with a sausage in bread. The dining table looked out to the back yard so Jake and I could keep an eye on him from inside. This gave me the opportunity to sit down and enjoy my meal with some adult conversation; not that I can remember any of it!

To be honest I probably didn't say too much, preferring to eat and listen to the others while at the same time stealing as many discrete glances at Kristen as I could. It turns out I wasn't mistaken about the 'moment' we'd shared earlier, because I caught her sneaking the occasional peek in my direction as well.

As the dinner progressed, so did my confidence in the mutual eye contact Kristen and I were sharing. I couldn't say for sure if she was 'into' girls, or whether she just liked the attention she was getting from me and decided to have some fun, but there was no doubt by the end of the meal she had escalated her occasional glimpses to full blown 'eye fucking!'

Even though her glances were brief, her signals were strong. It reached the point where every time she looked at me, her seductive stare would be accompanied with a suggestive grin; discreet and barely recognisable to anyone else at the table, but *I* didn't miss it.

I would occasionally look at Jake and smile, guilt no doubt written all over my face, or answer the occasional question which was directed at me, but I was really struggling to concentrate on anything but the flirtatious blonde across from me. She was obviously enjoying herself too. There were a few times where she would ask me an innocent question about the children, or where I grew up for example, then proceed to undress me with her eyes while I attempted to answer it; brief muddled responses all I could muster. Then she'd grin with satisfaction at my flustered body language. Kristen knew the effect she was having on me. I was certain if *she* noticed, then Jake would definitely be on to me by now. *Well the car ride home is going to be interesting!*

I couldn't stop looking at her eyes and mouth. It was such a weird, foreign feeling to be so turned on by somebody other than my husband. Since meeting Jake I'd never looked at another person sexually before. I mean sure there were times when I'd steal a quick glance at an attractive person down the street or while I was shopping, but I had never continuously looked at someone over and over again; flirting with them… fantasising about them.

The confusion and feelings of indiscretion, combined with the fact that my underwear was now completely saturated, was becoming too much to handle. Kristen must have seen me wriggle uncomfortably in my chair and realised the *effect* she was having because I looked up to see her staring directly at me; subtly biting her bottom lip before breaking eye contact.

Fuck! I had to get away from her for a moment. I needed to get some sort of control of myself.

I leaned over to Jake. "I'm just going to check on Nathan and go to the bathroom," I said softly.

"Sure Soph. Want me to pour you some more wine while you're gone?" he smiled politely. Only I was able to read between the lines of his seemingly innocent question. He could tell I was in somewhat of a fluster and offering me some more wine was his way of letting me know he was on to me.

"Yes please," I replied graciously before standing up from the table.

"You remember where the bathroom is? Down the hall to the left," directed Jenny.

"Sure, thanks Jenny."

I decided to go to the bathroom first then head outside to check on Nathan and get some fresh air. After going to the toilet I found myself standing in front of the bathroom mirror; checking my make-up and talking to myself!

"What are you doing Sophie?" I said quietly; turning my head from side to side to assess my make-up. "What the hell are you going to say to Jake when you get home? You've got some explaining to do!"

I reached into my bag and pulled out some lip gloss. "He knows… surely he knows now."

I checked my teeth were clean then applied some gloss; rubbing my lips together to smooth it out evenly before looking directly in the eyes of my reflection. "Just control yourself. Be cool and act natural," I whispered calmly.

By this stage I'd probably had three glasses of wine. I'm a bit of a lightweight when it comes to alcohol which explains the conversation I had with myself in the bathroom; something which was fairly out of character for me.

I took a deep breath and shook my head at my reflection. "You're hopeless!"

I switched off the bathroom light and headed back to the dining area. When I retuned everyone 'military' was immersed in an in-depth conversation about work. Jenny was in the kitchen and I noticed Kristen was not in her seat. I looked outside to see her crouched down beside Nathan. She was talking to him while he sat on his small plastic bike, which we brought with us so he could ride around the backyard.

She's gone out there deliberately! She wants to talk with me alone!

My heart raced as I picked up my glass, almost knocking it over. As I walked behind Jake who was still seated at the table, I ran my hand across his shoulders; smiling at him affectionately as I made my way to the glass sliding door.

He smiled back. "I'll come out in a minute Soph." I could tell he was still listening with one ear to the conversation he was in.

"No rush… sounds important," I replied in a cheeky tone.

He smiled at me for poking fun at him, talking 'Army' with his colleagues.

"Need a hand in there?" I yelled out to Jenny who was filling the dishwasher.

"No, all good. Kristen's out the back with Nathan. I'll quickly stack this and come out in a minute. You head out."

Even though Jenny said she was fine with the dishes, I know I'm a terrible guest for not helping her out. In my defence, the 'Bombshell' was outside with only my two-and-a-half-year-old to keep her company; I couldn't get out there fast enough.

As I slid the glass door open, Kristen looked up and flashed me a warm and utterly gorgeous smile.

"Too much Army talk for me in there," she confessed. "Your son is absolutely adorable."

He's not the only one!

"Yeah he's my handsome little man," I smiled; crouching down and kissing him on the head.

Realising we were talking about him, Nathan tore off on a hot lap of the backyard, displaying his skill on his favourite plastic motorbike; always the showman.

As I talked with Kristen I learnt she was actually a hair dresser, which prompted me to tell her about my plans to do a hairdressing apprenticeship when Jake and I moved to Canberra. We also talked about living in Sunbury, since her and Simon had only just moved to the area, and we discussed various issues with regards to our partners serving in the military.

She had a lovely personality and we conversed easily. Spending those few moments one-on-one only increased the attraction I had towards her, and even though our conversation was general, our body language was *suggestive* to say the least. A few times she placed her hand gently on my arm as she spoke, and more than once our eyes met and lingered to the point of being awkward; eventually both of us turning away bashfully. The same signals she was putting out at the dinner table were escalating by the minute. Her flirtatious looks and gestures were unmistakable.

Jake was always affectionate towards me and I never once felt like I lacked his attention. Since being with him, not a day had passed when I didn't feel like I was his number one priority. But to have the attention of a woman, especially one so beautiful and friendly was a totally new and to a large extent forbidden feeling, which is no doubt why it felt so incredible.

There's no question I felt guilty for how I was behaving towards Kristen that night. I mean for all Jake had done for me over the years; his unwavering love and devotion, always keeping me happy and safe, his care and compassion when I was ill… giving me my children! He'd always been so good to me and I loved him with all my heart. I was utterly content in my marriage and absolutely adored the children we'd brought into this world together. I wanted for nothing.

All of these truths raced through my mind as I stood outside flirting with Kristen; my husband only meters away. The worst part of all was that I couldn't stop myself even though I knew it was such an unfaithful act. If the shoe was on the other foot and it was Jake outside flirting with another woman, I would've been mortified; hurt beyond belief. Yet here *I* was.

Jenny came out to join us a short while later. The three of us sat down at the outdoor table and talked about family and children. Jenny was very interested in Nathan and Georgia; mentioning that Brett and her had been trying for their first for quite some time now. She was concerned that if they didn't fall pregnant in the next few months they might have to consider making an appointment with a fertility specialist. I could tell by the way Jenny looked at Nathan that she was desperate for a child of her own. I prayed their luck would change.

Eventually the mosquitos started to bite. I called out to Nathan and the four of us headed back inside, where of course the topic of conversation was still the military.

"Ok enough talk about work," commanded Jenny.

"Sure. Sorry honey," replied Brett compliantly.

Brett might have been the boss at work but he sure as hell didn't command the ship at home. It made me smile because it was somewhat similar in our household.

For the next hour or so the conversation flowed, along with the alcohol, and everyone looked like they were settling in for a big one. My son however had other ideas and started getting restless. By now

Georgia had woken up and was due for a bottle so I gave Jake the signal that maybe it was time to head home for the night.

"Well thanks for your hospitality Brett and Jenny, but it's time for us to get the rug-rats home to bed so you lot can kick on," announced Jake.

I glanced over at Kristen who subtly dropped her bottom lip and shot me a sad-puppy-dog-eyes look, no doubt because I was leaving. I returned an equally subtle smile.

"Sure guys. Thanks so much for coming over," replied Brett.

"Yeah thanks for coming. It's great to see the children," added Jenny; looking affectionately at Nathan who was waiting patiently beside Georgia's pram. "You're such a good little boy," she smiled.

"He sure is," I replied; looking at him with pride. I honestly can't tell you how passive and well behaved Nathan was. I was blessed to have such a calm little boy.

Jake went out the back and collected Nathan's bike and I made sure I had all Georgia's bottles, bits and pieces.

"We'll walk you out," Jenny said as she looked over at Brett; prompting him to get up and see us out.

"No need boss… stay there. You look pretty comfy in front of your beer," Jake chuckled.

"I'll walk them out with you Jenny," offered Kristen; promptly standing up from her seat.

"You don't have to do that," I replied politely; hoping she'd ignore me and come out anyway.

"Well I have to say a proper goodbye to the best bike rider I know!" she beamed; crouching down in front of Nathan and gently poking his belly with her finger.

He giggled playfully as she tickled him. I could tell he liked her. *Poor little bugger. He's a sucker for those brown eyes too*! I smiled to myself.

We said goodbye to the others and followed Jenny out the front; Kristen followed close behind.

As Jake put the kids in the car and folded up the pram so it would fit in the boot, Jenny leaned in and gave me a hug. "Thanks so much for coming over. You're always welcome Sophie and if you ever need help with the kids don't hesitate to give me a call. Brett and I would be more than happy to help out."

"Thanks Jenny I'll keep that in mind, and thank you for a lovely night."

I could tell she would love to babysit them. Her maternal instinct was well and truly running on high and I sincerely hoped she wouldn't have to wait much longer before falling pregnant and becoming a mother herself.

As soon as Jenny stepped back, Kristen seized the opportunity to give me a hug as well. She wrapped her arms around me and pulled me tight against her chest; deliberately pressing her soft breasts against me.

"So nice to meet you," she said before kissing me on the cheek and letting me go. She was careful to ensure her friendly kiss goodbye didn't linger so as not to look too out of the ordinary in front of Jenny, but I certainly didn't miss the hidden affection in her embrace.

"It was nice to meet you too. We'll have to catch up again sometime," I suggested.

"We will." Her eyes were suggestive and dark under the light of the streetlamp.

"Thanks Jenny. Don't let Brett drink too much will you?" Jake called out as he walked around to the driver's side door.

"I'll try my best," she smiled.

"Bye Kristen, nice to meet you. I'll get your number off Simon next week and pass it on to Soph so she can give you a buzz," he suggested.

"Sure that'd be great," she replied before turning her attention back to me; melting me a final time with *those* eyes.

Jake's offer made me feel slightly more relaxed about the conversation we were about to have on the way home, although I was still nervous about him noticing my flirtatious behaviour towards Kristen.

I climbed in the car, wound down the window and said a final goodbye to the girls as Jake started the engine and pulled out from the curb. They both waved then Jenny turned to walk back inside; Kristen loitered for a little longer and watched as we drove away.

Sending signals right to the end of the night. The thought not only made me smile… it gave me butterflies.

It was only a short drive home, but Georgia must have been hungry because she cried the whole time. Nathan was exhausted and drifted off to sleep within minutes; oblivious to his sisters cries.

"So Brett and Jenny have been trying to fall pregnant," I announced; attempting to change the topic before it even began.

"Really? Brett hadn't mentioned it at work. They've been married for a few years though so I guess there ready to start a family."

"Did you see how she looked at the kids? She absolutely adored them. I don't know how many times I caught her staring at Georgia, and her eyes lit up when she held her. I really hope she falls pregnant soon."

"Me too. It'd be nice to have another couple to hang out with who had kids. I felt like we were the old farts at the party," confessed Jake.

I laughed. "Yeah I know what you mean. The funny thing is we were actually the youngest there!"

"And here we are, driving home before eleven while they all party on." He paused for a moment. "Look at the bright side though."

"What's that?"

"Well, while they all sit around drinking, laughing and having fun until all hours of the morning, you and I will be tucked into bed nice and early; getting some much needed rest after a busy day," he emphasised.

I burst out laughing at his sarcasm.

"That's exactly what an old fart would say! Geez Jake you *are* a grandpa!"

He looked over at me with a smirk on his face.

"What are you grinning about?" I asked.

"I was thinking, just because we'll be going to bed early, doesn't mean we will be getting to *sleep* early." He glanced at me quickly; his eyes traveling from my lips to my lap then back to the road.

I could hear the lust for me in his voice, see it in his eyes and feel it in my groin. I reached over and placed my hand on his leg before squeezing his thigh firmly.

I have to admit being ravished by Jake was exactly what I needed. The back and forth flirting with Kristen had left me turned on and desperate to release the built up sexual tension. I craved the feeling of Jake's tongue between my legs, closely followed by something harder… much harder. I clenched my thighs together at the possibility.

We arrived home and Jake took care of Nathan; brushing his teeth and helping him into his pyjamas before tucking him in bed. I fed and changed Georgia, who thankfully drifted off in my arms. She didn't wake even when I put her down in her cot in the nursery.

"Thank you," I whispered as I kissed her on the forehead in appreciation for how easy she was to put to bed. She wasn't usually so compliant.

Jake and I brushed our teeth then made our way to the bedroom. I closed the door behind me then wrapped my arms around his neck; kissing him feverishly and pressing my pelvis against him. I could feel his erection through our clothes and couldn't wait a second longer for him to throw me on the bed and have his way with me. I was as horny as hell and eager to get down to business. I pushed him onto his back and climbed on top; straddling him.

"Whoa somebodies in a hurry! Got an itch baby?" he joked, as I hastily undid his buttons. "What's the rush?"

"No rush Baby… I'm just horny. I want to fuck!" I snapped; opening his shirt to reveal his naked chest.

I kissed him on the lips then ran my tongue over his chin and down his throat to his chest. I was working myself into a frenzy and could feel the slick wetness between my legs. My pussy yearned for attention.

"I didn't think you'd be so turned on by a dinner party?" he grinned.

I looked up at him; still softly kissing his chest. I didn't answer, instead worked my way south and unbuttoned his pants. I was now at boiling point; the aching between my legs almost painful. I unzipped his fly, pulled his briefs down and freed his straining erection before greedily wrapping my lips around him; engulfing his cock in one swift action.

Jake laid his head back on the pillow and moaned with pleasure as I licked and sucked him feverishly.

"We need to be invited to dinner more often," he breathed; lifting his head slightly to make eye contact with me.

What's he doing? I thought; choosing to ignore yet another unusual comment.

I gave him a final lick from the base of his shaft all the way to the tip, then stood up on the bed directly above him. I raised my knee high skirt up and slowly slid my panties down; his eyes watching my every move intently. I knelt down above him and just as I was about to slide his length deep inside my gushing tunnel, finally soothing the ache inside me, he made one final comment which I couldn't ignore.

"Or maybe it was someone *at* dinner who got you all worked up?"

I paused mid descent; raising my eyebrows at yet another oddly-timed comment about dinner. Jake was staring directly at me.

Oh shit! I edged forward and sat on his stomach with my knees either side of his waist. I knew exactly where this was going so I took a second to compose myself before answering.

"What are you on about Jake?"

"I thought you might like to tell me," he responded calmly.

Fuck! There's no getting out of this. In an instant my sexual cravings evaporated and even though I tried my best to hide it, I was overcome with panic.

As I said earlier, I'd played out this conversation in my head many times before, but I have to say I never imagined *this* particular scenario. I couldn't understand why Jake waited until we were just about to make love before bringing it up. He'd had a number of opportunities to raise the issue since leaving the party; at the very least told me we needed to talk before we started foreplay! Even better, he could have brought it up tomorrow… when I wasn't so horny!

At the time I thought maybe it was his way of punishing me for flirting with Kristen, which would've made sense. I can't say I didn't deserve it. To be honest though, apart from being understandably panicked, I was actually relieved that Jake seemed so relaxed, considering how serious the situation was. He would've been forgiven for being upset and angry, but thankfully he wasn't; it only would have made it harder for me to open up.

I know I should've just come clean but I played dumb for as long as I could. "I'm confused. What do you want me to say?"

He raised both eyebrows and shot me a 'don't-even-try-it' expression.

Playing dumb didn't last very long. I climbed off and lay on the bed beside him.

"I'm sorry," I whispered; not knowing what else to say.

"Don't be sorry… just tell me what the hell's going on. Have you met Kristen before?" There was a hint of impatience in his voice.

"No… never!" I replied quickly; dispelling any notion of an affair. The thought of Jake ever thinking I would go behind his back was unsettling. "I've never met her before, I swear."

"Sure didn't look like it. I don't think anyone else noticed, but I did. You two couldn't take your eyes off each other all night." He looked at the ceiling; taking a deep breath as if preparing himself for bad news. "Are you sure you don't know her? You can tell me." His voice was calm and reassuring.

I placed my hand on his cheek and gently turned his head to face me. "Baby, I've never seen Kristen before in my life… I promise. Please tell me you believe me."

The reality of having my devotion come under question made me sick to the stomach. I stared into my husband's eyes and waited desperately for a response.

He could tell I was scared so was quick to put me out of my misery. “I believe you,” he said softly.

I closed my eyes and exhaled; relieved.

“Just tell me then. Tell me what’s going on with you.”

I looked down; breaking eye contact.

“Sophie… talk to me Baby.”

“I’m scared. I don’t know how to say it.”

He didn’t respond, instead he put his hand on my arm and stroked it gently. We lay there in silence for what felt like an eternity; Jake patiently waiting and me not knowing how to begin.

“You don’t have anything to worry about Soph. You *never* have to be scared about talking to me.”

I snuggled into him; pressing my head against his chest and closing my eyes. Jake wrapped his arms around me.

He could tell I was struggling. “We don’t have to talk about it if it’s upsetting you.”

“No I want to tell you… I *have* to,” I whispered. “It’s just not easy.”

“What about this… I’ll ask you questions and you just answer yes or no? Would that make it easier?” he suggested calmly.

I nodded; focusing on the small circles I was tracing on his chest with my finger.

“Ok. First question. Were you attracted to Kristen?”

My finger stopped tracing as a shot of adrenaline flooded through me. *Oh fuck... this is it!* I’d spent so much time imagining this moment and now it was here; happening whether I wanted it to or not!

With a nerve-shaken voice, I answered. “Yes.”

“And were you flirting with her?”

I nodded subtly. “Yes.”

“Ok then…” he replied; drawing out the words as if deciphering my response. It’s not every day you hear your spouse tell you they were flirting with somebody else. I don’t know how he was still so calm.

“Have you been attracted to other women before?”

I answered with trepidation. "Yes."

"So have you *always* been attracted to them?"

"Not always… I mean… not for a while… it's kind of hard to explain," I fumbled.

"Then explain it to me."

"I don't know how… I want to though!" I added hastily in an attempt to assure him that I wasn't deliberately holding back.

Knowing I still wasn't ready to open up, Jake reverted to asking the questions. "So you think about women then?"

"Yes."

"Sexually?"

I nodded.

"Often?"

"Kind of… I suppose." I had to be honest and the truth was that I'd been thinking about them more and more. "Yes… often," I clarified.

"Sophie…" He paused, taking a second to consider the gravity of the question he was about to ask. "… are you gay?"

I took a deep breath before responding. I was under no illusion that my answer had the potential to change everything between us. There was no doubt having this conversation with my husband had left me somewhat shocked, but at the same time I was relieved everything would finally be out in the open.

Just tell him! If there was anyone I trusted with my secret it was Jake. I felt safe telling him the truth. *Here goes!*

"I don't know if gay is the right word because I'm still madly in love with you Jake; I always have been. And I'm *definitely* still attracted to you."

I lifted my head up to look into his eyes. He smiled back; instantly giving me the confidence to continue, though not before taking another deep breath.

"I think I'm… bi-sexual." I held my breath and waited for his reaction.

A few seconds passed then he nodded slowly; with understanding.

I continued hastily, feeling the need to explain myself further. "There's no doubt I want to be with you, I mean I love sleeping with you more than anything! But at the same time I have these feelings towards women… strong feelings."

"When did they start? These… *feelings,*" he questioned.

"Promise me you won't get upset?" I pleaded.

"Soph… of course not." He looked confused, almost disappointed that I'd even think he would be upset.

"Well, remember I said that you were my first… you know, the first person I ever did anything sexual with?"

"Yeah…" he replied; drawing out the word again as if preparing himself for yet another one of his wife's admissions.

"That wasn't exactly true."

"Really?"

"When I was younger, I mean *really* young, like in year six, I used to stay at my friend Belinda's house. And we… we sort of… experimented together."

Jake raised both eyebrows; clearly surprised.

"It happened a few times, maybe five or six, and I think my experience with her has a lot to do with how I feel now."

"So were there others at high school?"

"No way. I suppressed it as soon as I got to high school. I had a couple of boyfriends and then I met you. So since then I haven't really felt feelings like that. I mean I've always looked at beautiful women on T.V. or when I was down the street, but I've never considered acting on those feelings since being with you."

"Until recently?" he prompted.

I nodded. "Yeah."

I didn't say anything else. I wanted to assess my husband's reaction before going any further. I'd just dropped an absolute bomb and he seemed to be handling it pretty well; *really* well actually.

As Jake lay there, looking directly at me, he gently caressed my forehead with his thumb before running his fingers through my hair. I closed my eyes at the sensation.

This is going well.

"Before you tell me anything else, can I say something?"

"Of course," I replied quickly. "Anything!"

"I just wanted to say I know it must've been hard for you to talk about these feelings with me, but I'm glad you did. I want you to know that I understand and I'm here for you."

"You're not angry with me?"

"No… of course not. I'm proud of you Sophie. It took a lot of courage to tell me those things. I'm not angry or upset with you… not at all. I just feel for you, that you've had to keep this a secret for so long."

"Oh Jake." I nuzzled my head against his chest and squeezed him tightly. Pure relief enveloped me like a warm blanket. *He's ok. I've told him and he's ok!*

Tears welled in the corners of my eyes. I'd never talked about this to anyone before; I'd always been so scared. Having my husband tell me he understands then reassure me with his love and support that everything was going to be ok, left me completely elated.

"You have no idea what it means to hear you say that!" I wept.

"I'm your husband Baby. I always will be… remember?"

"I'm so lucky," I whispered as I moved in and kissed him softly.

After kissing me back, he pulled away and looked directly into my eyes; his lips curling into a cheeky grin.

"What?" I prompted; drying my eyes with the sheet.

"So was it just me, or did anyone else think Kristen was fucking hot!" he blurted out unexpectedly; chuckling at his own joke.

I burst out laughing; my tears brought to an abrupt halt as his comment immediately changed the vibe.

"Are you serious?" I laughed. "You're teasing me."

"What?" he replied innocently; still smirking. "Tell me all about it."

I felt myself blushing. "It feels weird talking to you about someone else."

"Well who else are you going to talk about it with?"

"True, but it still feels weird. I feel guilty for looking at Kristen."

"And *flirting* with her."

I blushed even more. "I'm sorry."

"Baby you don't have to be sorry, and you don't have to be shy either. I want you to tell me how you felt."

"I want to but…"

"Then tell me."

I inhaled. "Well I…" I hesitated again.

"Would it help if I told you it's actually quite a turn on for me?"

"What do you mean?"

"Sophie… I'm a red blooded male. I can assure you there aren't too many guys who wouldn't be turned on by the idea of two beautiful women together."

I raised an eyebrow.

"I bet it's the number one fantasy of most men," he added.

"Is it *yours*?" I interrogated.

"Maybe," he smiled. "So don't be embarrassed, I really want to know. Tell me what happened between you two."

"Ok, but let me get a drink first," I stalled; knowing it would give me a minute to gather my thoughts.

"Sure, whatever you need."

I climbed out of bed. Jake's eyes travelled up and down my naked body as I wrapped my silk robe around me before going to the kitchen for some water.

Well that went much better than expected, I thought as the chilled water cooled my lips, mouth and throat. I didn't realise how dry my mouth was. I guess nerves will do that.

I made my way back to our bedroom and crawled up onto the bed. Rather than undressing I thought I would leave my robe on while I discussed Kristen, and what had transpired between us at the dinner party. I sat up and crossed my legs in front of me, Jake rolled over onto one side and propped himself up on one elbow; resting his head on his hand. He didn't say anything, instead he just looked at me with anticipation.

"Are you sure you're ok with this?" I clarified.

"One hundred percent. Trust me… I'm sure," the tone of his voice suggested he was anxious to hear what I had to say.

He's really into this! "Well there isn't much to say because not a lot happened. I suppose when Kristen walked into the room I immediately felt some kind of attraction towards her."

"I don't blame you, she's gorgeous," he agreed.

"I know. She kind of took me by surprise. Anyway I couldn't stop looking at her, and I guess she noticed me checking her out because she started looking at me as well."

"How'd that make you feel; I mean… getting attention from her?"

Jake the counsellor. "Well," I paused; searching for words as I recollected the feelings which she evoked so rapidly. "Good… it made me feel good. Kind of like when you give me attention and look at me that way."

He smiled.

"The more she looked at me the more I wanted her to. She's just so beautiful. And her eyes… they're so seductive."

"So you could probably say she's your *type*?"

"Well if I have a type in women, then yes, she's definitely my type."

It felt strange talking so candidly with my husband about my feelings for another woman, but with each sentence I grew more confident in discussing it with him.

"So what did you talk about when you were outside together?"

"That's the thing, we were just talking about general stuff like kids and hairdressing, just normal chit chat, but the vibe between us was so strong. I think she's definitely into girls too."

"Really?"

"Well if she's not then I'd say she's definitely curious."

"I wonder if Simon picked up on what was going on? I was watching him but I couldn't tell if he noticed the looks you and Kristen were giving each other."

"That's probably a good thing, considering you have to work with him."

"Yeah, could make for interesting lunch time conversation though," he joked.

"You're not going to say anything to him are you?"

"Shit no Soph! Your secret's safe with me. I'm not going to tell anyone. How you feel about women is your secret to share not mine."

"Thanks Baby."

Jake continued. "So about Kristen… I mean hypothetically speaking."

"Yeah," I replied suspiciously. I had a fair idea what his question was going to be.

"If she was single… would you sleep with her?"

He watched me intently; eyes wide as he waited for my response. I could tell he was turned on.

"Well before I answer that, I want you to know I'd never cheat on you. Not with anyone, not ever! I'm not that kind of person. I probably would never be with someone who was in a relationship either. It wouldn't feel right."

"I know you wouldn't go behind my back Baby. I'm talking hypothetically."

"Good. Well hypothetically, I'd have to say yes."

Jake grinned and his eyes intensified. I could tell his mind was going a thousand miles an hour; almost as fast as mine!

"I loved her body. She had such a beautiful full figure. I couldn't stop looking at her boobs; they were huge!" I exclaimed.

"So you're into boobs then?"

"To be honest, I'm into more than just boobs," I said; lowering my voice.

He shifted his position, as if to make himself more comfortable. "Tell me more," he demanded.

"I'm not going into details. I'm too embarrassed," I blushed coyly.

"Don't be, I like hearing you talk about this. I want to know what you like… and what you want."

"I think you've heard enough for tonight," I teased. "For now, all I'm going to say is that I like *every* part of a woman."

"Is it wrong that I'm really fuckin horny right now?" Jake whispered as he threw the sheet back to reveal his rigid cock;

standing to attention with thick veins protruding along the entire length. He grabbed it with his hand. "I'm so hard that it actually hurts!"

I was already wet, all this talk about Kristen had kept me nice and moist, but seeing Jake holding his manhood and practically begging for sex ensured every single pleasure receptor in my groin was on high alert.

"Awe poor Baby," I replied sympathetically. "You want me to take that pain away for you?"

He nodded.

I stood up and slowly slid my robe off; letting it fall to the floor.

"Baby… you are the most beautiful woman I've ever seen." Jake spoke with such feeling and sincerity.

I looked down at the stretch marks on my tummy, courtesy of my two pregnancies, and covered them with my hands. I was still so self-conscious about the look of my stomach after having kids.

Jake climbed out of bed and knelt down on the floor in front of me.

"What are you doing?" I asked.

He grabbed hold of my wrists and pulled my hands away from my belly; exposing my perceived 'problem area'. Then he looked up at me with truthful and loving eyes. "I want you to listen carefully. Listen to every word I'm going to say."

"Ok."

"Baby… I know your self-conscious about your tummy."

I nodded.

"But I want you to know it's the part of you I love the most."

"Why? It's all stretched and saggy."

"You might see stretch marks and saggy skin, but I don't. All I see is the place where my babies came from, and if these stretch marks weren't here…" He placed two soft kisses on my belly. "…Then I wouldn't have two beautiful children. That's why every time I look at your tummy I fall in love with these marks more and more." He kissed my stomach again before looking up at me.

I could hear the honesty in his voice. I believed him and he really did make me feel beautiful.

After letting go of my wrists he grabbed hold of my hips then continued to place soft kisses all over my tummy. I put my hands on his head and closed my eyes at the relaxing sensation of his 'butterfly kisses' on my stomach.

"I love you Jake. Thank you for everything," I breathed; my eyes still closed blissfully.

He kept kissing my belly.

"Thank you for understanding everything I've told you tonight. It feels amazing to be able to talk about it with you," I said appreciatively as I continued to run my fingers through his hair

He stopped kissing my stomach and looked up at me. "You can tell me anything, anytime. I'm your husband."

I leant forward and kissed him on the forehead.

"This might be a bit weird, but I would like to try something with you?"

"Sure, what'd you have in mind?" I replied as I glanced down at his straining rod; finding it hard to imagine anything other than him fucking me with it.

"Lie down on the bed," he directed calmly.

He let go of my hips and I crawled up onto the bed.

"Now lie on your back and spread your legs… wide!"

I complied without hesitation. Jake moved over so he was now kneeling beside the bed, in between my legs with full access to my pussy; glistening with anticipation. He grabbed my ankles and pulled me closer to him, then draped each of my legs over his shoulders so his head was between my thighs.

"Relax your legs on my shoulders. Lay your head back and close your eyes."

I laid back, took a deep breath and closed my eyes as I exhaled.

"Now I'm going to lick your pussy," he said directly.

My pelvic floor muscles contracted instantly as he detailed his intentions; the breath from his words wisped lightly against my *lips* causing me to clench.

"And while I pleasure you… I want you to do something for me."

"Anything," I replied softly.

"I want you to imagine Kristen's mouth." He lightly kissed the inside of my thighs, gently biting the sensitive skin. "Imagine her soft lips between your legs… and on your…"

He placed a soft kiss directly on my pussy which sent a bolt of pleasure straight through me. It'd been just over an hour since I'd seen Kristen, so visualising her gorgeous face between my legs was as easy as it was arousing.

"I want you to feel her warm tongue licking and teasing your clit."

Jake reached up and spread my lips with his thumbs; exposing my swollen and exceedingly sensitive *button* to do with as he pleased. Then with one deliberately slow lick using the full length of his tongue, he delivered me to the brink almost instantaneously. The warmth and perfect texture of his tongue forced me to climax splendidly; my hips twitching uncontrollably as I came.

I raised my head off the bed and looked at him down between my legs. Jake took his mouth off me and shot a cheeky smile my way; a shiny coating of *me* all over his chin.

"That was fast!" he grinned; clearly amused by how horny I must have been to let go so quick.

"Oh fuck Baby… it feels amazing!" I panted; slightly breathless.

"Can you see her… feel her?"

"Yes."

"More?"

"Yes," I begged.

"Then close your eyes again."

I laid back, shut my eyes and resumed my fantasy of having Kristen between my legs; her seductive eyes looking up as she pleasured me with that gorgeous mouth.

"I want you to feel her tongue," he whispered before delicately licking me from my ass right up to my clit.

I wriggled against the mattress.

"I want you to feel it between your lips." He licked me again, only this time firmer; his tongue worming its way between my lips before dipping inside me.

"Oh fuck!" I could feel another orgasm building.

"Feel her tongue sliding deep inside you." He pushed the full length of his tongue into me; curling it up and probing in and out. The tip of his tongue rubbed against my g-spot with precise accuracy causing me to moan with appreciation.

I don't mean to kill the mood, but at this point it's worth mentioning that when Jake was born he was actually tongue tied. It's the result of having a short frenulum; the thin string of tissue connected to the tongue and bottom of the mouth. It wasn't until he was twelve that his parents discovered he couldn't actually poke his tongue out, not more than a centimetre or so.

It was times like these I was filled with gratitude towards his parents for booking Jake in to have it operated on. The frenectomy involved cutting the frenulum which released the tongue and allowed for more range of movement… a lot more!

Now I don't know if the surgeon cut too much or what, and frankly I don't care, because Jake can poke his tongue out so far now that he can literally lick his own nose. Which makes *me* one lucky woman!

The feeling of Jake's tongue inside me combined with the fantasy of Kristen's mouth on my pussy was utterly mind blowing. I grabbed hold of his head and pulled him closer so his mouth was hard against me; his top lip pressing firmly against my clit as he speared me with his long, thick tongue. I wanted him as deep as possible.

"Fuck me! Fuck me with your tongue!" I moaned as the pleasure inside me grew with each thrust. "That's it! That's it Baby! Yes… yes!"

I let go of his head so I could grab a pillow and hold it over my face. Seconds later I exploded. My screams of ecstasy were barely muffled by the pillow as my body writhed about with each surge of orgasmic pleasure. As my orgasm subsided, Jake stayed between my legs; revelling in my wet, silky release.

"Oh fuck… that was so intense!" I exclaimed as I struggled to catch my breath.

As Jake climbed onto the bed beside me I couldn't help but laugh at the thorough 'glazing' I'd given him.

"Damn you taste good," he said; licking his lips.

"Don't be greedy! Come here!" I commanded.

I rolled onto my side and kissed him feverishly. The taste and smell of *me* on his lips and in his mouth immediately stoked my fire.

"You really like the taste of yourself don't you?"

"God yeah… I love it." I confessed. "I guess it makes sense considering I'm bi."

"Guess so," he smiled; kissing me again.

I reached down and wrapped my fingers around his rigid member. "Still painful Baby?"

"Uh huh," he nodded. "I love going down on you like that… and knowing you were thinking about Kristen was such a turn on."

"That makes two of us then," I agreed. "Well we can't have you in pain now can we? I think it's time for you to fuck me with that hard dick of yours," I whispered seductively; positioning myself on all fours.

"I apologise in advance Baby. I'm so horny right now."

"I'm already more than satisfied; this is *all* for you Jake. Just fuck me as hard as you like… and don't hold back."

He didn't need to be asked a second time, and with one swift manoeuvre he was behind me with his hands on my hips, slowly feeding his hot cock into my velvet tunnel. As my pussy wrapped around him, engulfing every inch, I was quickly reminded that as arousing as the fantasy of being with a woman was, there was no question I would always need the addictive feeling of *fullness* that only my man's shaft could provide.

Jake started slow, no doubt in an attempt to prolong his orgasm. He would push his entire length inside me, all the way in until it touched my cervix, then he would pause momentarily to let me revel in the feeling. After a few seconds he would slowly withdraw completely, allowing my lips to close together briefly before forcing them apart again with his throbbing muscle. I moaned every time he repeated the pleasurable operation, and with each re-entry I swear he felt thicker and harder.

"I love it," I breathed in between each meticulous thrust as he hit just the right spot every time.

"I'm going to keep this speed until I come Baby."

"Fuck yeah… it's perfect!" I groaned; my eyes rolling back in my head.

The slow, deliberate fucking allowed me to feel every single part of him sliding in and out, over and over again. I could literally feel the pronounced rim of his cock making its way from the start of my opening, all the way into me, then the same on the way out. The swollen head of his shaft providing an exquisite internal massage.

With each invasion of my body I could feel him edging closer to climax. "Oh Jake! I can feel it… you're close."

"You ready Baby?"

I nodded before biting down on a pillow as I prepared for his delivery.

Jake gradually inserted one final time, driving his cock in as far as I could take. Then he completely stopped moving; resting his engorged tip against the end of my tunnel. The lack of thrusting enabled me to feel every part of his orgasm. The glorious feeling of him expanding inside me was only bested by the sensation of him letting go of his ejaculation. As *he* throbbed and pulsated, I felt every jet of hot come spray furiously from his member. I let go instantly, attempting to muffle my scream again as my 'big one' tore through my body. As if out of my control, my hips instinctively pushed back against him as our fluids infused inside me in a hot mess of love, lust and passion.

I fell from all fours onto my stomach and Jake collapsed onto my back; pinning me under his weight.

"I thought my head was going to explode," he puffed.

"It did," I replied with a breathless giggle. "Trust me… it did."

He laughed then rolled off me and onto his back.

As he lay beside me I marvelled at his perfectly sculptured torso expanding with each breath and I couldn't help but smile to myself at the knowledge that he was all mine. My eyes travelled south, down to his semi-erect instrument of pleasure; polished and shiny after receiving a generous coating from yours truly. In awe I watched as a final bead of come gradually trickled from the eye of his cock; a sight I would never tire of. *Fuck that looks hot!*

"See something you like?" questioned Jake after noticing my line of sight.

"Very much so!" I grinned as I hastily repositioned and took his length in my mouth; the taste of both of us still fresh on his skin. "Mmm," I moaned as I licked and sucked him greedily while staring seductively into his eyes.

"You just can't get enough can you?" he laughed as he wriggled beneath me. He grabbed my head and pulled me off *him*; my vacuum like mouth making a distinct 'pop' as I let go.

We both burst out laughing and I hugged him firmly.

"Never enough." I said as I rested my head against his chest; my favourite place. "If we're going to have sex like that we'll have to talk about my attraction to girls more often!" I beamed with satisfaction. "You seem to like it too?"

"I told you I think it's hot Soph… really hot! I don't know why you never brought it up with me sooner."

"I suppose I was just scared about how you'd take it. I didn't know what you'd think or how you were going to react."

"And how about now?" he smiled, referring to the amazing sex we'd just had.

"Well now that I know it turns you on, I'm feeling a lot more comfortable about coming out to you."

"Good. I hope you feel better Baby. Telling me about it can only bring us even closer together."

"I think so too," I agreed; kissing him with all the passion I had left.

"No more secrets?"

I shook my head. "No more… I promise."

Over the next year or so Jake and I caught up with Kristen and Simon on a number of occasions. We would go around to their place for dinner and a few drinks every so often, and we'd hang out with them at various military dinners and functions. The four of us ended up being really good friends.

Kristen and I continued to flirt with each other, and eventually Simon figured out that there was some sort of connection between me and his girlfriend. It turns out Jake was right about 'two girls' being the fantasy of most men, because once Simon found out he seemed rather keen to see Kristen and I take the next step.

They had only been together for a short period of time and to be honest the more we got to know them the rockier their relationship appeared. This, combined with the fact I had completely no interest in 'putting on a show' for the viewing pleasure of another man, meant that Kristen and I hooking up was never really on the table. Putting on a show for my husband however… well that was a different matter entirely.

As much as we enjoyed hanging out with them, they really loved a drink, which for Jake and I was always a bit of an issue. Quite often we would end up drinking when we really could have gone without, but we did just to keep the party going. Anyway, there was one such occasion where we all had a fair amount of alcohol and a simple game of truth of dare ended up with Kristen and me kissing.

It was the strangest thing because all the flirting, suggestive comments, seductive looks and deliberate body contact over the past few months had me convinced that Kristen was *definitely* into girls. During one particular conversation she actually said she was, but when we were dared to kiss she seemed somewhat reluctant. It wasn't like she had to be pressured into it, but when we did kiss there was simply nothing there. No desire or sensuality; no passion. I'd wanted to kiss her since the moment we'd met and I could have sworn she felt the same about me. But when it finally happened, I couldn't help feeling as though she was only kissing me because she was dared to do it, not because she wanted to. I definitely felt like she'd been caught out, and honestly I don't think Kristen was into girls at all. What she liked was the *attention* I gave her; it had nothing to do with me being a woman.

At the time, thanks to the excessive amount of scotch flowing through my veins, I didn't let it get to me, which turned out to be a good thing because a few dares later I ended up getting a quick squeeze of her amazing boobs. They were so soft and beautiful; I could've played with them for hours. I remember thinking how much I wanted to burry myself in them! Seeing and touching her naked breasts only added fuel to my bisexual fire. It was blazing!

There was no question I developed a crush on Kristen and we still flirted with each other from time to time, but the reality was I felt kind of betrayed, even lied to. I'd told her I was bisexual and definitely attracted to her, and she had deliberately reciprocated. To put it bluntly though, she led me on and it hurt. To her credit Kristen did apologise when she realised how it had affected me, and we were able to remain close friends.

At the end of the year Simon was posted away and the two of them eventually broke up, confirming the suspicions Jake and I had with regards to the fragility of their relationship. We never saw either of them again but a few years later I did get a call from Kristen. It was so nice to hear from her, and to be honest my heart did flutter a little when I heard her voice again. Visions of her seductive eyes and gorgeous lips, not to mention those deliciously soft breasts invaded my mind as she spoke. I guess once you have a crush on someone there's always going to be a special place for them in your heart, or at the very least… between your thighs.

Although I was frightened at the prospect of coming out to Jake about my sexuality, I should have known he would respond with complete understanding and support. Jake's love for me was unconditional, as mine was for him, so the fact that his feelings for me remained unchanged should have come as no surprise, despite harbouring a secret since the beginning of our relationship.

It was definitely a relief to have everything out in the open and I welcomed the feelings of freedom that came with divulging such a personal secret; but the reality was this new found freedom exposed previously uncharted territory in our relationship, sparking a host of questions that needed to be answered.

Now that I was free to discuss my bi-sexuality with Jake, my feelings towards women seemed to grow stronger every day. It was like I developed a craving for them; to experience what was once restricted to pure fantasy. I knew my curiosities and desires were never going to subside until I was given the opportunity to act on them, and even though I knew doing so would ultimately effect the sacredness of my marriage, I still wanted to cross that line.

I was a wife to a devoted husband, a mother to two beautiful children, and I was bi-sexual. A new chapter in my life had begun though never in my wildest dreams could I have anticipated where it would take me. Even now I have a hard time believing the lengths I would go to in the pursuit of satisfying my thirst for sexual discovery.

At that stage of my life my health was quite good and served as no cause for concern, so I hadn't given much thought to the possibility that my *monster* still existed inside me. Although it hadn't surfaced for a number of years, it was lying dormant; waiting for the perfect opportunity to attack me again… and attack it did.

Never could I have predicted that for the next decade I would be plagued by illness and injury. Subjected to a barrage of medical examinations, needles, scalpels and some of the strongest medicines known to man. It reached a point where I almost lost count of the amount of times my *monster's* savage attacks landed me beneath the surgeon's blade.

Through it all, through a seemingly endless highlight reel of torment and suffering, I would still feel blessed. Blessed because every time I was dragged into the darkness, down to the depths of despair by my relentless *monster*, the strong hands of my saviour were there to carry me to safety. There's no doubt, I would endure and indeed survive because of the unwavering devotion and protection of my *hero*…

and our *lover*.

Due for release in 2017

My Monster, My Hero, My Secret

www.ingramcontent.com/pod-product-compliance
Lightning Source LLC
LaVergne TN
LVHW020646110826
845149LV00012B/1924

9780995361713